AUTOMATED DEFECT PREVENTION

BICENTENNIAL
1807
⊛WILEY
2007
BICENTENNIAL

THE WILEY BICENTENNIAL—KNOWLEDGE FOR GENERATIONS

*E*ach generation has its unique needs and aspirations. When Charles Wiley first opened his small printing shop in lower Manhattan in 1807, it was a generation of boundless potential searching for an identity. And we were there, helping to define a new American literary tradition. Over half a century later, in the midst of the Second Industrial Revolution, it was a generation focused on building the future. Once again, we were there, supplying the critical scientific, technical, and engineering knowledge that helped frame the world. Throughout the 20th Century, and into the new millennium, nations began to reach out beyond their own borders and a new international community was born. Wiley was there, expanding its operations around the world to enable a global exchange of ideas, opinions, and know-how.

For 200 years, Wiley has been an integral part of each generation's journey, enabling the flow of information and understanding necessary to meet their needs and fulfill their aspirations. Today, bold new technologies are changing the way we live and learn. Wiley will be there, providing you the must-have knowledge you need to imagine new worlds, new possibilities, and new opportunities.

Generations come and go, but you can always count on Wiley to provide you the knowledge you need, when and where you need it!

WILLIAM J. PESCE
PRESIDENT AND CHIEF EXECUTIVE OFFICER

PETER BOOTH WILEY
CHAIRMAN OF THE BOARD

AUTOMATED DEFECT PREVENTION

Best Practices in Software Management

DOROTA HUIZINGA

ADAM KOLAWA

WILEY-INTERSCIENCE
A John Wiley & Sons, Inc., Publication

Published by John Wiley & Sons, Inc., Hoboken, New Jersey.
Published simultaneously in Canada.

For general information on our other products and services or for technical support, please contact our Customer Care Department within the United States at (800) 762-2974, outside the United States at (317) 572-3993 or fax (317) 572-4002.

Wiley also publishes its books in a variety of electronic formats. Some content that appears in print may not be available in electronic formats. For more information about Wiley products, visit our web site at www.wiley.com.

Wiley Bicentennial Logo: Richard J. Pacifico

Library of Congress Cataloging-in-Publication Data:

Huizinga, Dorota.
    Automated defect prevention : best practices in software management / by Dorota Huizinga, Adam Kolawa.
        p. cm.
    Includes index.
    ISBN 978-0-470-04212-0
    1. Software failures—Prevention—Data processing.   2. Software maintenance—Data processing.   3. Debugging in computer science—Automatic control.   4. Computer programs—Testing—Data processing.   5. Computer programs—Correctness.   I. Kolawa, Adam.   II. Title.
    QA76.76.F34.H85 2007
    005—dc22

                                                                    2007002342

To Ed
—Dorota

To Elizabeth
—Adam

CONTENTS

PREFACE

The rules for processing data are themselves data and can be treated like data.
—John Von Neumann

In this book, we describe an approach to software management based on establishing an *infrastructure* that *serves as the foundation* for the project. This infrastructure defines people roles, necessary technology, and interactions between people and technology. This infrastructure automates repetitive tasks, organizes project activities, tracks project status, and seamlessly collects project data to provide measures necessary for decision making. Most of all, this infrastructure sustains and facilitates the improvement of human-defined processes. This infrastructure forms a *software production line.*

There is a paradigm shift in the software industry. It is being driven by business demands to create larger and more complex software products in less time. How is the paradigm shift changing the way software is produced? Let us look at some of its effects.

Changes in software development processes—consider the agile manifesto versus the waterfall process model as paradigm shift versus status quo. The status quo is a heavy, top-down approach, which works fine as long as all project requirements are perfectly captured and understood up front. "If not, good luck."

This top-down approach proudly proclaims that it fully understands the project from the start and plans accordingly. The new, bottom-up approach humbly admits at the beginning that it does not fully understand the project. As software projects continue to grow in size and complexity, the bottom-up approach often becomes more effective. This is the first part of the paradigm shift.

Here is the second part: *a growing realization that we humans are incapable of fully applying and maintaining our own best practices.* The projects are simply becoming too big and too complex. We must turn back to the founding principle of computing. In the words of its great founder, John Von Neumann, "The rules for processing data are themselves data and can be treated like data." This is what automation seeks to do—use code to evaluate code.

The paradigm shift, then, may be characterized by two words: *infrastructure* and *automation*.

So what does all of this have to do with the developer? No longer will she be given a coding task or two that she, and perhaps a few team members, will work on to the exclusion of the rest of the project. With more code segments and more complex code segments, the likelihood grows that the segments will not work together at project's end, resulting in frantic work sessions, cost overruns, and project collapse.

Consider a large, complex software project. Everyone knows that the root causes of errors should be analyzed and communicated to other members of the team, but no single team member is willing to do it. Should good ideas be recorded for future use? Certainly, but no single team member is going to do it for the team, because no one has the time to do it, right? "The team as a whole benefits but I am penalized for falling behind—I don't think so."

What about consistent use of best coding practices by the team? Would not that improve the work for the entire team? "Sure, but I, a developer on subteam 3, am not going to stick my nose into other peoples' code and make sure they are following my best practices. And I'm not going to take the time to learn and apply their best practices because I am much too busy for that."

The answer is *infrastructure*. The answer is for the software team to do its work in an environment that has a shared repository not only for their code but also for good ideas and a shared repository for best practices and a shared repository for any other group of work elements considered important. Everyone uses the repositories and everyone is required to use the repositories. Perhaps it is just one repository used in many different ways. Notice that *infrastructure* consists of two equally important parts: the technology and willingness of team members to use it.

"Very good," I say to myself as a developer. "This might even work if we could double the size of our software team, because that's what it's going to take in order to run this infrastructure. It is going to take a lot of person-hours to learn how to use and maintain these repositories and that person is not going to be me. What about best practices and coding standards—who is going to check hundreds of thousands of lines of code for these? We do have to do some coding; we can't spend all our time on monitoring and testing and generating reports."

The answer is *automation*. The infrastructure will sustain processes that automatically verify and test best practices and generate reports based on results of these tests.

"Do I like the fact that my work is now subject to multiple standards and processes, some of which I don't understand? Not entirely, but I'll tell you one thing: when the Mars Lander lands properly or the assembly line works the first time out or the web store handles inventory and billing correctly for 1,000 products instead of the original 100, I'm going to like it a lot more.

And so will you."

FEATURES AND ORGANIZATION

We call our infrastructure and automation-based approach, together with the set of best practices described in the book, *automated defect prevention* (ADP). The set of best practices facilitates iterative development and it is defined for each ADP phase: initial planning and requirements, extended planning and design, construction and testing, and deployment.

The overall goal of this book is to provide practical advice on how to implement ADP in a modern software development process. This is not a theoretical book on how to build imaginary software in an ivory tower. Rather, it is a hands-on guide to solving real-world software project problems. We recognize that most readers will not have the luxury of starting a new software process from scratch, so throughout the book, we pay special attention to phasing in ADP to existing projects and processes, and applying it to large complex code bases without overwhelming the team.

The focus throughout is on evolution, not revolution. We do not expect the readers to abandon current processes and workflows in search of a silver-bullet solution that will solve all current problems. There is no such perfect development environment or development process that will be a panacea for all software development groups and projects. Consequently, rather than offer step-by-step implementation details for a one-size-fits-all solution, we describe the key practices that have helped many different teams improve their processes.

In defining the technology infrastructure, ADP describes necessary features rather than specific tools. We have selected only a basic subset of features that are essential for building an effective infrastructure. Many existing commercial and noncommercial tools support these as well as more advanced features. Organizations that have an infrastructure in place should identify features that already exist and use ADP to identify those features that are needed to improve their infrastructure.

In addition, we acknowledge that our methodology is a work in progress, as there is much room for improvement. We believe that the concepts are both practical and stimulating, and they provide guidance rather than dictate a rigid, static approach.

In Chapter 1, we begin the book by describing ADP and its goals as a response to the complexities of modern software development. We categorize the goals into those affecting people, product, organization, process, and project (PPOPP). We then give an overview of ADP—its principles, practices, and policies—and we elaborate on the role of defect prevention and automation. The last section briefly describes the evolution of software development process models from waterfall to iterative and agile. The objective is not to convince our readers to adopt a new development process, but rather to propose ideas for making existing processes more effective.

In Chapter 2, we introduce the ADP principles: establishment of the infrastructure, application of general best practices, customization of best practices, measurement and tracking of project status, automation, and incremental implementation of ADP's practices. We explain these principles and validate them with research studies and realistic examples.

In Chapters 3 and 5, we discuss initial and extended planning together with the minimum and expanded infrastructure required for ADP. Supporting infrastructure is essential for ensuring that ADP practices can be properly measured, tracked, and automated, and thus can be implemented and sustained. We identify the four core infrastructure elements that we have found to be critical to making software work: source control system, automated build system, problem tracking system, and automated reporting system. These four integrated elements form the backbone that allows the teams to maintain and improve their software development process. We also define the roles of people, describe basic and extended plan, and elaborate on parametric cost and schedule estimation models.

Chapter 4 addresses the requirements phase. Software defects that originate in the requirements phase and propagate further into the process are often the most costly to remove. Even issues that do not seem to be related to requirements can often be traced back to this phase of the software life cycle—be it a poorly conceived requirement, an incorrectly implemented requirement, or a missing/incomplete requirement. A key point stressed in this chapter is the importance of determining which requirements will be most difficult to implement, prioritizing them, and building a prototype architecture.

In Chapter 6, we discuss architectural and detailed design. The final product of this phase is a blueprint for implementing requirements with the focus on the most critical features. We discuss design policies, patterns, and architectures, which are different ways of achieving these goals. Along the way, we try to point out how design mistakes can be prevented and how they relate to requirements.

Chapter 7 covers construction, with a focus on the many practices that can prevent defects during this extremely error-prone phase. We describe best practices starting from coding standards, through test-driven development for modules and algorithmically complex units, to conducting unit tests prior to checking in the code to the source control system. In addition, basic policies for use of the source control system and automated build system are outlined in this chapter.

Chapter 8 discusses how testing should be used to verify application quality at the various stages of its construction. We describe our recommended practices for testing together with the test progression criteria that help determine when development and testing should progress from level to level: from unit, through integration, system, and acceptance testing. We also depict a defect life cycle in the context of root cause analysis and prevention, and we describe basic policies for use of the problem tracking system and automatic regression testing system.

The first part of Chapter 9 explains how measures introduced throughout the book can be used to identify emerging problems in the software product and/or process, and how these measures should be used to help identify the root cause of the problem in question. The second part of this chapter discusses deployment to the staging system and then to the production system. Deployment of today's complex applications is an inherently difficult process. After discussing preventive strategies for making the deployment process less error-prone, we offer guidance on automating it for different types of projects and environments.

Chapter 10 discusses how ADP supports industry initiatives that modern development teams commonly face. It describes the infrastructure and practices put in place for ADP that can be leveraged to support outsourcing initiatives and to address regulatory compliance requirements such as Sarbanes-Oxley (SOX). It also shows how the ADP practices, paired with its automation and supporting infrastructure, make quality improvement initiatives such as SEI–CMMI® practical and sustainable.

In Chapter 11, the book concludes with two case studies that show how Lehman Brothers and Samsung Corporation were able to apply some of the ADP concepts to improve their software development processes.

We have also included appendixes that expand the views described in the book and provide a list of software tools that facilitate implementation of ADP.

PRACTICE DESCRIPTIONS

For each of the ADP phases, we describe best practices together with policies for use of the corresponding technologies. Practice descriptions have the following sections:

- *Why*—What problems does this practice solve?
- *Who*—Which team member(s) should perform this practice?
- *How*—How should the practice be implemented?
- *Measurement*—What data should be collected and what measures should be used in order to make informed decisions about the process/project, identify emerging problems, and assess process improvement?
- *Tracking*—What results or data should be tracked and archived for analysis?

- *Automation*—What part(s) of the practice, especially its measures and tracking, can be automated, and how?

INTENDED AUDIENCE

In the software industry, those who stand to benefit from this book the most are software project managers, architects, developers, testers, QA professionals, and all others who are responsible for delivering software on time, on budget, with the correct functionality. This book is relevant to their daily activities as part of the team.

In addition, this book is appropriate for senior-level or first-year-graduate courses in computer science, software engineering, or information system programs. A draft of this book was used in CPSC 546, "Software Project Management," a first-year graduate course for Master of Science in Software Engineering majors at the Computer Science Department of California State University—Fullerton.

To use this book effectively, the reader should have prior experience or training in basic software engineering concepts. It should be understood that there is no silver bullet for making software work. Success is a journey of many small steps that need to be taken into account and implemented meticulously.

Additional teaching materials for instructors, including PPT presentations, can be found at ftp://ftp.wiley.com/public/sci_tech_med/automation.

ACKNOWLEDGMENTS

This book would not have been possible without the efforts of many people.

First and foremost, the authors would like to thank Anastasia Deckard, Computer Science research assistant at California State University–Fullerton, for her creativity and attention to detail throughout the entire project, and in particular for designing graphics and substantial contributions to the sections on user interfaces and requirements, as well as valuable comments and critique as a "first reader" of all other parts of the book.

At John Wiley & Sons, our editor, Paul Petralia, Whitney Lesch, and others also provided us with invaluable guidance throughout the entire process.

Dr. Tae Ryu, Professor of Computer Science, used the draft of the manuscript as a textbook in the "Software Project Management" class at California State University–Fullerton, Computer Science Department, served as a reviewer, and provided continuous support and advice throughout this project.

Laurie A. Haack, Senior Principal Software Engineer at Raytheon Network Centric Systems, critiqued and provided significant input to several parts of the book, in particular the section on CMMI.

Dr. Bin Cong, Professor of Computer Science at California State University–Fullerton, and SEI CMMI Lead Appraiser and Trainer, gave us valuable feedback on the original book proposal and Chapter 10.

Gordon Hebert, Software Integration Manager, GMD/CLE Software Project, Northrop Grumman Mission Systems, wrote "Mars Polar Lander (MPL), Loss and Lessons" included in Appendix B, and provided us with several insightful comments and ideas.

Software engineers enrolled in the class of 2007 of the Master of Science in Software Engineering program read the first draft of the manuscript and posted many comments on the discussion board.

The following software engineering professionals directly contributed to the book by providing valuable comments, quotes, examples, or research: Husam Azma, Ravi Bellamkonda, Li Bin, Nathan Blomquist, Mandy Botsko-Wilson, Frances Castillo, Martin Curt, Megan Fazel, Shan Hina, Justin Ho, Lesley Ku, Enrico Lelina, Shu-Ping (Collie) Lu, Joe Marcelino, William Mayville, Atul Menon, Eugene Ngo, Jason Obermeyer, Scott Sanford, and Nick Stamat.

Dr. Catherine Warner, MD, and Ms. Maryanne Horton, provided valuable insights on the professional end-user experience with the modern user interfaces.

Agnieszka Szuta helped with graphic design.

Dorota would like to thank several people for their help with this project:

First and foremost, her husband, Ed Huizinga, for his stimulating advice, sharing his professional expertise of real-world effects of the IT industry on modern business, and for reviewing the sections on SOX. Most of all, she would like to thank him for his unique ability to keep her in a continuous state of "flow."

Her daughter, Nicole, for an independence and attitude beyond her years and great enthusiasm for this and several other of her mom's projects.

Faculty and staff members of the College of Engineering and Computer Science at California State University–Fullerton, in particular, the Dean, Dr. Raman Unnikrishnan, and Patti McCarthy for their encouragement and continuous support throughout the duration of this and several other projects, along with Phyllis Harn and Sandra Boulanger.

Finally, her co-author, Adam Kolawa, for his vision to initiate this interesting idea.

Adam would like to thank all Parasoft employees, who over the past 15 years helped in the development and implementation of the ideas described in this book. Without their creativity, dedication, and hard work this book would not be possible. In particular, he would like to acknowledge Marek Kucharski, Marek Pilch, Wayne Ariola, and Erika Delgado as well as the writers, especially Cynthia Dunlop for her help in writing and editing the book, along with Marvin Gapultos and Tes Kurtz.

Of course, none of those mentioned above are responsible for what might be unsound in the book—that is exclusively our own doing.

PERMISSIONS

The authors would like to thank the following organizations and individuals for granting permissions for reprints of the copyrighted material:

- Institute of Electrical and Electronics Engineers for the use of their definitions, reprinted with permission from IEEE Std. 1058.1-1987, "IEEE Standard for software project management plans," Copyright 1987, by IEEE; and IEEE Std. 610.12-1990, "1990 IEEE Standard glossary of software engineering terminology," Copyright 1990, by IEEE. The IEEE disclaims any responsibility or liability resulting from the placement and use in the described manner.
- Lehman Brothers for the "Lehman Brothers" case study included in Chapter 11.
- Gordon Hebert for "Mars Polar Lander (MPL), Loss and Lessons" included in Appendix B.
- Software engineering and other professionals who provided quotes for the book.

DISCLAIMER

Several people are quoted in this book. These quotes are personal opinions of those quoted and they are not necessarily endorsed either by the authors of the book or by the employers of those quoted.

The list of software tools in Appendix E is not endorsed by the authors of the book. The up-to-date list of tools can be found at **http://solutionbliss.com**.

CHAPTER 1

THE CASE FOR AUTOMATED DEFECT PREVENTION

Why do we never have time to do it right, but always have time to do it over?
—Anonymous

1.1 WHAT IS ADP?

ADP is a paradigm shift and a mindset. It is an approach to software development and management influenced by three distinct yet related factors:

1. The need for new and effective methodologies focusing on improving product quality
2. The fact that in today's complex world of *perpetual change*, sophisticated technology that assists software development must be an intrinsic part of project and process management, not just an add-on feature
3. An understanding of the broad spectrum of human factors affecting modern software development, in particular the psychology of learning

ADP principles and practices are based on research combined with 20 years of experience managing internal software projects, working with thousands of customers, and dealing with software defects on a daily basis. ADP evolved

Automated Defect Prevention: Best Practices in Software Management, by Dorota Huizinga and Adam Kolawa
Copyright © 2007 John Wiley & Sons, Inc.

from the approach called Automated Error Prevention (AEP) [1], used and practiced by Parasoft Corporation. Both adaptable and flexible, ADP can be applied to either existing or new projects, and it can be introduced as an extension to any iterative and incremental software process model. *When used with a new project, ADP provides a best-practice guide to defining a software development process and managing a project.*

Software has become one of the most pervasive components of our lives. Our unprecedented dependence on it ranges from keeping track of our calendars and financial records to controlling electronic devices in our automobiles, pacemakers, and a host of other applications. Yet few other goods are delivered to market with more defects than software products. This is because there are now more opportunities than ever for defects to be injected into software under development. For example, a typical enterprise system nowadays encompasses many complex multitier applications and is often a precarious combination of old and new technologies, such as legacy systems wrapped as web services and integrated with newer components through a service-oriented architecture. At each layer there are possibilities for making mistakes, and a simple defect in one component can ripple throughout the system, causing far-reaching and difficult-to-diagnose problems. Additionally, today's most common method of verifying system quality is through testing at the end of the life cycle. Unfortunately, this "quality through testing" approach is not only resource-intensive, but also largely ineffective. Since most of the time the number of possible states to be tested is prohibitively large [2], testing often leaves many system states untested, waiting only to reveal previously undetected defects at the most unexpected moment.

Thus, ADP takes an alternative approach of *comprehensive defect prevention* by modifying the development process in the entire software life cycle [3] to reduce opportunities for mistakes. In essence, ADP helps development teams prevent software faults by learning from their own mistakes and the mistakes of others. In order to achieve this, ADP describes a blueprint for life cycle defect prevention in its set of principles, practices, and policies.

At the heart of ADP lies its infrastructure, which defines the roles of people, required technology, and interactions of people with technology. This infrastructure facilitates both the implementation and sustainability of ADP processes through automation of repetitive, error-prone tasks and by automatic verification of error-preventive practices. This infrastructure also assists in the seamless collection of project-related data that is used for making informed management decisions. Thus, in ADP, the technology infrastructure, together with policies guiding its use, becomes an *intrinsic* part of project and process management.

However, no management approach can be effective unless it is based on an understanding of human nature, and aims at creating an environment that provides job satisfaction. This is particularly important in software development, an intellectually challenging task in itself, that is complicated by seemingly endless industry change that requires constant learning. ADP's automation of tedious, repetitive, and mundane tasks combined with gradual, step-by-step introduction of new practices is an attempt to stimulate effective learning and perhaps even help achieve a highly increased sense of satisfaction by entering a peak of mental concentration called "flow" [4].

In the next section of this chapter, we will describe the goals that we set forth for ADP. This will be followed by a high-level overview of ADP's principles, practices, and policies. The last section will delineate the relationship between ADP and modern software development.

1.2 WHAT ARE THE GOALS OF ADP?

The development of ADP was triggered by the need for effective methodologies that counter poor software quality, with its resulting high costs and operational inefficiencies. However, the high complexity of modern software development coupled with continuous changes of technology and short time to market pose a set of unique challenges not found in other industries. To address these challenges, we have defined and addressed the goals for each category of the software project management [5] spectrum, concentrating not only on the four *P*s suggested by Pressman [6]—people, product, process, and project—but on the organization as an entirety.

In subsequent sections, we will explain the primary ADP goals for each of the above categories and the motivation for each goal. (See Figure 1.1.)

1.2.1 People: Stimulated and Satisfied

People are the most important resource in an organization, as they are the sole source of creativity and intellectual power. As much as we strive to define processes and methods to be people independent, people will either make or break them.

Satisfied and motivated people are productive and cooperative. They take pride in their work and they are willing to go the extra mile to deliver a quality product. Therefore, software development, which is a people-intensive process by itself, cannot be successful without creative and dedicated people. However, professional satisfaction is not easily achieved, especially in a business where

Figure 1.1 Resources transform into goals by using ADP.

continued learning is as important as performing routine tasks and frustration can easily inhibit imagination. Moreover, achieving a balance between discipline and creativity is difficult because according to the laws of human psychology [4], in their professional lives, people tend to oscillate between two extreme states: routine and repetitive tasks on the verge of boredom, and new, challenging tasks on the verge of anxiety. *Both excessive boredom and excessive anxiety make people ineffective and error-prone.*

Part of the continuum between these two extreme states of mind includes the *competency zone*, which is the zone where people's skills match the demands of the tasks they must perform. At the high end of the competency zone is the state of *flow*. In this state people forgo their inhibitions, learn, and explore their new skills, and through a high degree of concentration, their performance is enhanced enormously, resulting in an increased level of competence. People who achieve this state report a tremendous sense of accomplishment and success.

According to Phillip G. Armour, software development is subject to the laws of flow, because it is a process of continuous learning. "If software development were entirely the application of existing knowledge, it would be a manufacturing activity and we could completely automate it" [7]. Moreover, since most software defects can ultimately be traced back to "human error," any effective defect prevention approach must create a working environment in which the team members can perform most of their tasks within the higher ends of their *competency zone, where the number of boring or overwhelmingly challenging activities are minimized.*

Thus, the goal of ADP is to keep people positively stimulated and yet not overwhelmed, so they can perform in an advanced manner and consequently achieve the maximum level of professional satisfaction.

1.2.2 Product: High Quality

The high quality of a product not only provides customer satisfaction and helps to maintain the company's competitive edge, but also generates a sense of individual and organizational pride among those who contributed to its development.

Software quality is a complex mix of many attributes such as usability, reliability, efficiency, and more. Focusing on just one of these factors in the development process may impede the others and undermine the ultimate measure of software quality, which is customer satisfaction. While the defect rate is one of many factors used to determine software quality, it is so fundamental that unless its status is acceptable, other aspects of quality are not as significant. Unfortunately, many past and recent reports of system failures due to software faults indicate that defects are the norm rather than the exception in software products. They cause financial losses [8,9], everyday inconvenience [10,11], and even cost lives [12,13]. A comprehensive study conducted in 2002 by the NIST (National Institute of Standards and Testing) states that software errors cost the U.S. economy up to a staggering $59.5 billion per year [14].

As previously mentioned, one of the primary contributing factors to poor software quality is its growing complexity. Multitier and multiplatform environments, unmanageable sizes reaching millions of lines of code, creeping requirements, and ever-changing underlying technology open the door for a host of defects.

Unfortunately, not many people in the industry believe that *defect prevention* in software is possible. The common claim is that because each piece of software is different, the lessons learned from working on one project cannot be effectively applied to others. Thus, instead of trying to prevent defects from entering software, the conventional approach is to test defects out of software. First, a product or its part is built, and then an attempt is made to use testing to determine whether it works. Finally, defects exposed in the testing process are gradually removed.

Yet defect prevention is not only possible, but also necessary in software development. However, for defect prevention to be effective, a formalized process for integrating this strategy into the software life cycle is needed. This formalized approach must include both the application of industry best practices known to avert common problems, and the customization of organization-specific practices to meet project needs. Additionally, in order to be sustainable, this formalized approach must be supported by an adaptable infrastructure that automates many repetitive tasks and that carries defect prevention practices from one product release to the next, and from one project to another. Moreover, the role of testing should not be eliminated, but redefined. Although back-end testing has proven to be an ineffective method of building quality into software, testing can and should be used to help measure and verify product quality. ADP defines such a formalized approach to defect prevention with the ultimate goal of achieving high quality of the product.

1.2.3 Organization: Increased Productivity and Operational Efficiency

Companies are constantly rethinking how to maintain their competitive edge by reducing operating and maintenance costs while attempting to deliver increased value. In the software industry, this manifests itself through the following goals shared by many organizations:

- *Cost reduction*: controlling the spiraling software development and labor costs, producing more with the same resources, and reducing the amount of rework due to poor quality
- *On-time product delivery*: ensuring that projects deliver products on time with the requested functionality

The inability to make effective software without incurring unreasonable costs and delivery delays is blamed on operational inefficiency with its resulting low productivity. The fact that this inability often persists in the face of increasing software development team expertise and resources indicates a serious process problem that has little to do with insufficient resource allocation.

Unfortunately, it is often not realized that the operational inefficiency of organizations stems from the fact that in virtually any software development 80% of the resources are dedicated to identifying and fixing defects, which leaves only about 20% of the resources available for tasks that deliver value and improve the business [14].

These defects span a wide spectrum from incorrectly implemented functionality through performance problems and security vulnerabilities, to failures that crash an entire system. They essentially stifle a team's ability to produce working software within a reasonable time and at acceptable costs.

These problems, coupled with the fact that the cost of identifying and removing defects grows exponentially as a function of time in the development cycle [15], lead to the conclusion that defect prevention is crucial to improving productivity and operational effectiveness.

1.2.4 Process: Controlled, Improved, and Sustainable

A process is a series of step-by-step tasks necessary to reach a specified goal. Thus, depending on its goal, a process can be defined at different levels of granularity. A complete software development cycle needs a process, and so does each of its individual phases including requirements gathering, design, and testing. While the ultimate goal is to create a high-quality product in a timely manner, it is necessary to divide and refine each high-level goal into many subgoals for which detailed step-by-step action plans have to be prepared. For example, a software development life cycle process could consist of a requirements specification process, design process, testing process, and deployment process. However, implementation of a well-defined process is only the first step toward software product quality. The fundamental problem lies in whether and how this process can be *controlled, sustained, and improved.*

Quality initiatives, such as CMMI (Capability Maturity Model Integration) [16], which set a framework for process improvement, do not provide sufficiently practical and detailed guidelines to translate their models into actions effectively. Thus, many organizations failed to achieve the desired results from these initiatives because of the difficulty of implementing and maintaining them in realistic cost-effective development environments.

Some of the common objections to these initiatives are:

- They add a substantial overhead, which is very costly.
- They rely too much on manual labor to set up and maintain. Because of the turnover in the workforce, it is hard to sustain such human-dependent processes.
- They are difficult to automate, but without automation, they decay and eventually become ineffective.

Thus, the goal of ADP is to address these concerns by implementing software processes that are controllable and sustainable. This is accomplished by defining a set of practices, explaining how they can be automated, and by monitoring and controlling the status of the practice implementation using the ADP infrastructure.

1.2.5 Project: Managed through Informed Decision Making

A quality product cannot be created without effective project management techniques applied throughout its development. However, while project managers and developers strive to make the software better and friendlier, the economic pressures of the industry coupled with many external factors pose a multitude of challenges.

Among the external factors are recent government regulations, which place an additional burden on software teams responsible for such tasks as maintaining financial information, protecting human resources data, securing the company's product database and Web accesses, and many more. Current legislation that affects software development includes Section 508 of the U.S. Rehabilitation Act [17], the Sarbanes-Oxley Act of 2002 [18], the Health Insurance Portability and Accountability Act (HIPAA) [19], the Gramm-Leach-Bliley Act [20], and the Family Educational Rights and Privacy Act (FERPA) [21]. For example, the Sarbanes-Oxley (SOX) Act requires that public companies implement effective internal controls over their financial reporting, have auditors verify the existence and effectiveness of these internal controls, and have executives certify that financial reports are accurate. Although SOX is financial legislation, it places a tremendous burden on the software teams of public companies because reliable financial reporting is inextricably linked to a well-controlled system environment and reliable, secure software systems.

Additionally, ensuring application security has become one of the greatest challenges in recent years. Although most organizations strive to release software with zero defects, this rarely happens in reality. While in many cases little harm comes from shipping software with a few functionality defects, security weaknesses can result in great damage. Considering that attackers proactively analyze software hoping to expose vulnerabilities that they can exploit, deploying software with even one security flaw could pose a high risk. In fact, potential intruders are usually better at uncovering security defects than testing teams themselves. As a result, a defect rate that might be acceptable for software functionality could prove dangerously high for security flaws in the same application.

Another external factor affecting management of software projects is offshore outsourcing. Because of the large return on investment that outsourcing promises, many companies elect to pursue such management strategies. However, outsourcing comes with many potential risks stemming from cultural and language barriers to legislative differences that make contractual agreements difficult to enforce. The organization's decision makers may find themselves pondering the possible disastrous consequences of the many unknowns in outsourcing: lack of understanding of company's business, geographical distance, and communication difficulties.

In order to ameliorate project uncertainty caused by the above external factors, one of the goals of ADP is to facilitate management decision making through automated collection of data and through tracking and measurements of the trends of the project status indicators. Analysis of these indicators assists in evaluating the level of project quality, status of requirements implementation, and deployment readiness, and helps to reduce the risks and challenges posed by these and other external factors.

1.3   HOW IS ADP IMPLEMENTED?

ADP is implemented by following a set of principles, practices, and policies. The principles are high-level laws that form the basis of ADP methodology, while the policies and practices comprise low-level development and management rules and procedures at varying granularity. We will expand on each of these in subsequent sections.

1.3.1   Principles

Principles are the foundation of the ADP methodology. They are the basic laws that govern structuring and managing software projects. They correspond to ADP's goals at the highest level and they form the basis for the definition of practices and policies, which are directly applicable to software projects. (see Figure 1.2.)

There are six ADP principles, which will be explained in detail in the next chapter. Each of these principles addresses one or more of the ADP goals. For example, the principle on "incremental implementation of ADP's practices and policies" assures that the organizational change that ADP brings is introduced gradually, thereby minimizing people's unease and apprehension. The incremental, group-by-group and practice-by-practice approach to ADP implementation is an attempt to minimize possible anxiety and resentment by not overwhelming people and teams who apply it. Such a gradual introduction

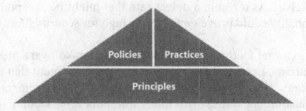

Figure 1.2   Principles, policies, and practices.

of ADP also assures that once the initial practices are mastered and accepted by one group, they can be successfully propagated to the entire organization.

1.3.2 Practices

Practices are *functional* embodiments of the principles. Depending on their level of granularity, best practices can pertain to entire projects, processes, or even individual tasks and people's daily activities. There are two types of best practices: general, which are based on issues common to all development projects, and customized, which are adopted by the organization to meet the needs of its unique projects and improve its processes. While the body of general best practices is already defined and well accepted by the industry, the body of customized best practices is created by the organization.

An example of a general best practice is managing requirements changes. This best practice would define a basic process for recording and tracking updates in software requirements. At a finer level of the granularity, this best practice would describe a specific format for recording such changes, along with the required technology and change approval process.

A customized best practice is project or organization specific. For example, a predefined set of coding standards adopted by the organization and applied by the team to a specific project is a customized best practice. Similarly, a new best practice introduced after identifying a defect in the product under development is a customized best practice used for process improvement.

DEVELOPER'S TESTIMONIAL

Customized Best Practices

At my current job many of our senior developers have worked to put together a document that has our C++ and CORBA best practices. This document helps our junior engineers to learn from the years of experience of the senior engineers. This has helped to reduce mistakes and make code easier to read and understand.

—William Mayville, Software Engineer I

1.3.3 Policies

Policies are *managerial* embodiments of the principles. They mostly pertain to teamwork and define how the team should interact with technology. They are also used to assure that product- and process-related decisions are consistently applied through the entire team, and usually take the form of written documents.

An example is a design policy for the user interface, which should define the elements in the user interface of a product and details such as each element's location, appearance, name, and functionality. Another example is a policy for use of a requirements management system, which should define how individuals and teams use this system in order to most effectively organize and track product requirements.

1.3.4 Defect Prevention Mindset

Successful implementation of ADP practices and policies requires that at least one team member—preferably an architect, lead developer, or anyone else with a deep understanding of the software's requirements and design—assume the responsibility of identifying and removing the root causes of severe defects found. The proper mindset involves realizing that the apparent problems, such as missing requirements, failed builds, unused variables, and performance bottlenecks, are just specific symptoms of a larger, more general problem. These problems can originate anywhere in the development process, from requirements, through design and construction, to testing, and even in beta tests or user feedback. In fact, warning signs often appear downstream from the root cause, and each root cause may generate tens or hundreds of them. If each specific symptom is addressed, but not the more general and abstract root cause, the problem will persist. In the long term, it is much more effective to address the root cause, thereby preventing all related defects, than to try to tackle each one as it arises.

For example, assume that a development team member discovers that the product's automated build is not operating correctly because the wrong library was integrated into the build and old versions of functions are being called instead of the up-to-date versions. After spending significant time and effort investigating this situation, the team determines that, although the correct version of the file was stored in the source control system, an incorrect version was included in the build due to a clock synchronization problem. The build machine's clock was ahead of the source control system's clock. Consequently, the version of the file on the build machine had a more recent timestamp than the file on the source control machine, so the file on the build machine was not updated. The discrepancy in the clocks is just a symptom of the problem. Fixing the time on all of the team's computers might temporarily prevent failed file updates, but it is likely that the clocks will become unsynchronized again. The general, abstracted root cause is that there are conditions under which the most recent files from the source control system will not be transferred to the build system. This could be prevented by configuring the build process to remove all existing files on the build machine and then retrieve all of the most recent versions of the files from the source control system. Acquiring the proper mindset requires realizing that even the most seemingly insignificant symptom may result in a severe problem and point to a root cause that, if fixed, can significantly improve the process and all products affected by this process.

In this book we will give examples of how particular defects can be traced back to root problems, which can then be avoided by developing and implementing preventive action plans.

1.3.5 Automation

Automation is ADP's overarching principle and is essential to making defect prevention a sustainable strategy in software development. When key defect prevention practices are automated, organizations can ensure that these practices are implemented with minimal disruption to existing processes and projects. Moreover, automation is the solution to ensuring that both the general and customized defect prevention practices that the team decides to implement are applied thoroughly, consistently, and accurately.

In many cases, determining how to effectively automate the defect prevention strategies is just as difficult as the root cause analysis required to develop them. One of the other challenging aspects is determining how to integrate new automated practices into the development process unobtrusively so that day-to-day development activities are not disrupted unless a true problem is detected.

1.4 FROM THE WATERFALL TO MODERN SOFTWARE DEVELOPMENT PROCESS MODELS

ADP's best practice approach does not depend on any specific life cycle process model, although it is best suited for iterative and incremental development. This type of development has become prevalent in recent years because of the dynamic nature of the software industry. Due to perpetual technological changes, it is often impossible to entirely define the problem and implement the complete software solution in one cycle. Therefore, an incremental approach is taken, whereby the problem definition and solution construction undergo several iterations. Thus, modern software development has become a dynamic and living process, where modifications and reworking of project artifacts within each phase and the entire cycle are the norm.

The iterative approach, regardless of its flavor, lends itself to the application of ADP. This is because defects identified in each iteration of the life cycle or phase can be prevented from reoccurring in subsequent iterations of the same and future projects.

When defect prevention is built into the process and automated, process improvement becomes an intrinsic part of software development. This results in both a more efficient methodology and higher-quality products.

In the past decade, the software development paradigm has moved away from the traditional *waterfall approach* that features well-defined sequential stages, beginning with communication with customers and requirements specification, progressing through planning, design, construction, and deployment, and then eventually following with the maintenance of the final product. Despite its many supporters, this conventional, staged approach did not provide sufficient flexibility to accommodate the dynamic needs of today's quick-to-market business pressures, where both the technology and the

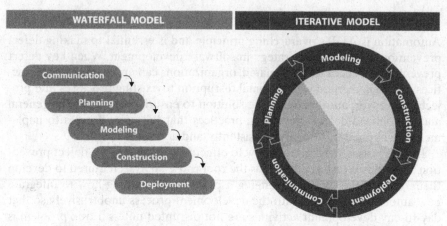

Figure 1.3 The waterfall model versus iterative process model.

customer requirements are subject to unending change. Even though the original waterfall model proposed by Winston Royce [22] suggested "feedback loops," these were so imprecisely specified that the vast majority of the organizations applied this method in a strictly linear manner.

Consequently, this very first, classic life cycle model was replaced by the iterative process approach, whereby the initial version of the system (sometimes also called a core product) is rapidly constructed, focusing on driving requirements coupled with fundamental architecture. The software development process then undergoes a series of iterations and increments, expanding the core product until the desired levels of system functionality, performance, reliability, and other quality attributes are achieved.

Usually five generic phases are identified in the modern life cycle: communication, planning, modeling, construction, and deployment, as shown in Figure 1.3.

The principles of modern software processes focus on architecture, component-based development, automation, risk and change management, modeling, and configurable infrastructure. The architecture-first approach facilitates time and cost estimation, while the iterative life cycle makes risk control possible by gradual increases in system functionality and quality.

Software development process models define phases of software development and the sequence of their execution. They include approaches such as *incremental* [23], *spiral* [24], *object-oriented unified process* [25], *agile and extreme* [26], *and rapid prototyping and application development* [27]. Also, formal methodologies have been proposed for life cycle descriptions [28,29].

At first glance, these models might appear to be quite a departure from the traditional waterfall approach (which has well-defined sequential stages) since they blur the boundaries between development phases, often rely on close interactions with the customer, and require multiple reworking of project artifacts within and between the development phases. Frequently customers are not capable of precisely identifying their needs early in the project, and multiple iterations of requirements definitions are essential to elicit the problem completely. Yet, a closer analysis reveals that each of these models is a natural and logical evolution of the waterfall model. In fact, these models stem from constant progress in improving the software development process. This progress is the result of efforts to improve the existing development processes in ways that would prevent the most common and disruptive problems that were causing project setbacks and product failures. Moreover, each new model still maintains the core element of the original waterfall model: a forward-moving progression through a cycle that involves requirements analysis, specification, design, implementation, testing, and maintenance. The duration, scope, and number of iterations through this cycle may vary from process to process, but its presence is essential—because it represents the natural steps of developing software. Consequently, the ability to execute the waterfall model successfully remains a requirement for success, no matter what process is used.

More discussion about software development process models is included in Appendix A.

1.5 ACRONYMS

CMMI	Capability Maturity Model Integration
FERPA	Family Educational Rights and Privacy Act
HIPAA	Health Insurance Portability and Accountability Act
NIST	National Institute of Standards and Testing
SOX	Sarbanes-Oxley Act of 2002

1.6 GLOSSARY

agile programming process model   A lightweight process model that consists of the following cycle: analysis of the system metaphor, design of the planning game, implementation, and integration.

extreme programming   An "agile" software development methodology characterized by face-to-face collaboration between developers and an on-site customer representative, limited documentation of requirements in the form of "user stories," and rapid and frequent delivery of small increments of useful functionality. [26]

FERPA   A federal law that protects the privacy of student education records. FERPA gives parents certain rights with respect to their children's education records. These rights transfer to the student when he or she reaches the age of 18 or attends a school beyond the high school level. [21]

Gramm-Leach-Bliley Act   The Financial Modernization Act of 1999, which includes provisions to protect consumers' personal financial information held by financial institutions. [20]

HIPAA   An act to amend the Internal Revenue Code of 1986 to improve portability and continuity of health insurance coverage in the group and individual markets, to combat waste, fraud, and abuse in health insurance and health care delivery, to promote the use of medical savings accounts, to improve access to long-term care services and coverage, to simplify the administration of health insurance, and for other purposes. [19]

incremental development   A software development technique in which requirements definition, design, implementation, and testing occur in an overlapping, iterative (rather than sequential) manner, resulting in incremental completion of the overall software product. [23]

prototype   A preliminary type, form, or instance of a system that serves as a model for later stages or for the final, complete version of that system.

Sarbanes-Oxley Act of 2002   An act to protect investors by improving the accuracy and reliability of corporate disclosures made pursuant to the securities laws, and for other purposes. [18]

Section 508   An amendment to the Rehabilitation Act of 1973 that requires that any technology produced by or for federal agencies be accessible to people with disabilities. It covers the full range of electronic and information technologies in the federal sector. [17]

software life cycle   The period of time that begins when a software product is conceived and ends when the software is no longer available for use. The software life cycle typically includes a concept phase, requirements phase, design phase, implementation phase, test phase, installation and checkout phase, operation and maintenance phase, and, sometimes, retirement phase. [3]

software project management   The process of planning, organizing, staffing, monitoring, controlling, and leading a software project. [5]*

spiral model   A model of the software development process in which the constituent activities, typically requirements analysis, preliminary and detailed design, coding, integration, and testing, are performed iteratively until the software is complete. [3]

unified process   Also known as Rational Unified Process, is a software development approach that is iterative, architecture-centric, and use-case driven. [25]

usability   The ease with which a user can learn to operate, prepare inputs for, and interpret outputs of a system or component. [3]*

use case   A use case describes a sequence of actions that are performed by an actor (e.g., a person, a machine, another system) as the actor interacts with the software. An actor is a role that people or devices play as they interact with the software. Use cases help to identify the scope of the project and provide a basis for project planning. [25]

waterfall model   A model of the software development process in which the constituent activities, typically a concept phase, requirements phase, design phase, implementation phase, test phase, and installation and checkout phase, are performed in that order, possibly with overlap but with little or no iteration. [3]*

1.7 REFERENCES

[1] Kolawa, A., *Automated Error Prevention: Delivering Reliable and Secure Software on Time and on Budget*, 2005, http://www.parasoft.com (retrieved: July 7, 2006).

[2] Burnstein, I., *Practical Software Testing: A Process Oriented Approach*. Springer, 2002.

[3] Institute of Electrical and Electronics Engineers, *IEEE Standard 610.12-1990—Glossary of Software Engineering Terminology*, 1990.

[4] Csikszentmihalyi, Mihaly, *Flow: The Psychology of Optimal Experience*. Harper & Row, 1990.

[5] Institute of Electrical and Electronics Engineers, *IEEE Standard 1058.1-1987*, 1987.

[6] Pressman, R.S., *Software Engineering: A Practitioner's Approach*. McGraw-Hill, 2005.

[7] Armour, P. G., "The Learning Edge," *Communications of ACM,* Vol. 49, No. 6, June 2006.

[8] Inquiry Board (Chairman: Prof. J.L. Lions), *ARIANE 5—Flight 501 Failure*, Paris, July 19, 1996, http://www.ima.umn.edu/~arnold/disasters/ariane5rep.html (retrieved: July 7, 2006).

[9] National Aeronautics and Space Administration, *Mars Climate Orbiter Mishap Investigation Board Phase I Report*, 1999, http://mars.jpl.nasa.gov/msp98/news/mco991110.html (retrieved: July 7, 2006).

[10] "Maine's Medical Mistakes," *CIO*, April 15, 2006, http://www.cio.com/archive/041506/maine.html (retrieved: July 7, 2006).

[11] "2005 Toyota Prius Recalls," *AutoBuy.com*, 2005, http://www.autobuyguide.com/2005/12-aut/toyota/prius/recalls/index.html (retrieved: July 7, 2006).

[12] General Accounting Office—Information Management and Technology Division Report, *Patriot Missile Software Problem*, 1992, http://www.fas.org/spp/starwars/gao/im92026.htm (retrieved: on July 7, 2006).

[13] Leveson, N. and Turner, C.S., "An Investigation of the Therac-25 Accidents," *IEEE Computer,* Vol. 26, No. 7, July 1993, pp. 18–41.

[14] National Institute of Standards and Technology, *The Economic Impacts of Inadequate Infrastructure for Software Testing*, Washington D.C., 2002, http://www.nist.gov/director/prog-ofc/report02-3.pdf (retrieved: July 7, 2006).

[15] Boehm, B. and Basili, B., "Software Defect Reduction Top 10 List," *IEEE Computer*, Vol. 34, No. 1, January 2001.

[16] Chrissis, M.B., Konrad, M., and Shrum, S., *CMMI—Guidelines for Process Integration and Product Improvement*, Addison Wesley, February 2005.

[17] Government Services Administration, *Summary of Section 508 Standards,* January 23, 2006, http://www.section508.gov/index.cfm?FuseAction=Content&ID=11 (retrieved: April 3, 2006).

[18] The American Institute of Certified Public Accountants, *Sarbanes-Oxley Act of 2002*, January 23, 2002, http://frwebgate.access.gpo.gov/cgibin/getdoc.cgi?dbname=107_cong_bills&docid=f:h3763enr.txt.pdf (retrieved: June 15, 2006).

[19] United States Department of Health and Human Services, *Public Law 104–191: Health Insurance Portability and Accountability Act of 1996*, August 21, 1996, http://aspe.hhs.gov/admnsimp/pl104191.htm (retrieved: July 25, 2006).

[20] Federal Trade Commission, *Privacy Initiatives: The Gramm-Leach-Bliley Act*, 1999, http://www.ftc.gov/privacy/privacyinitiatives/glbact.html (retrieved: July 25, 2006).

[21] United States Department of Education, *Family Educational Rights and Privacy Act (FERPA)*, February 17, 2005, http://www.ed.gov/policy/gen/guid/fpco/ferpa/index.html (retrieved: July 25, 2006).

[22] Royce, W.W., "Managing the Development of Large Software Systems: Concepts and Techniques," *Proceedings of IEEE WESCON*, Vol. 26, August 1970, pp. 1–9.

[23] Schach, S.R., *Object-Oriented and Classical Software Engineering*. McGraw Hill, 2002.

[24] Boehm, B.W., "A Spiral Model of Software Development and Enhancement," *IEEE Computer,* Vol. 21, No. 5, May 1988, pp. 61–72.

[25] Jacobson, I., Booch, G., and Rumbaugh, J., *The Unified Software Development Process*. Addison-Wesley, 1999.

[26] Beck, K. and Andres, C., *Extreme Programming Explained: Embrace Change*. Addison-Wesley, 2nd ed., 2004.

[27] Martin, J., *Rapid Application Development*. Prentice-Hall, 1991.

[28] Choi, J.S. and Scacchi, W., "E3SD: An Environment Supporting the Structural Correctness of SLC Descriptions," *Proceedings of the IASTED—International Conference on Software Engineering and Applications,* Las Vegas, Nevada, USA, Nov. 6–9, 2000, pp. 80–85.

[29] Choi., J.S. and Scacchi, W., "Formal Analysis of the Structural Correctness of SLC Descriptions," *International Journal of Computers and Applications,* Vol. 25, No. 2, 2003, pp: 91–97.

1.8 EXERCISES

1. What factors have influenced the development of ADP?

2. What are the goals of ADP?

3. Why is understanding of human nature, especially psychology of learning, essential in software development?

4. In what sense does psychology of "flow" apply to software development?

5. Why is it difficult to control modern processes?

6. Give examples of recent software "disasters" not listed in the book and explain their causes.

7. Give examples of recent legislation not listed in the book that might affect the IT industry and explain what kind of effect they might have.

8. What are the primary differences between ADP principles, practices, and policies?

9. Why is modern software iterative and incremental?

10. What are the key lessons to be learned from the past 35 years of software development?

CHAPTER 2

PRINCIPLES OF AUTOMATED DEFECT PREVENTION

> He who has not first laid his foundations may be able with great ability to lay them afterwards, but they will be laid with trouble to the architect and danger to the building.
>
> —Niccolo Machiavelli

2.1 INTRODUCTION

Described in the previous chapter, the goals of ADP and its focus on product quality led us to the definition of its principles. These principles are the fundamental laws that form the basis of the ADP methodology and they are primary guidelines for structuring and managing software projects. They are also a basic reference point for the formulation of ADP's practices and policies, which are directly applicable to software development.

There are six ADP principles:

Principle 1: Establishment of infrastructure that integrates people and technology

Principle 2: Application of general best practices known to avert common problems

Automated Defect Prevention: Best Practices in Software Management, by Dorota Huizinga and Adam Kolawa
Copyright © 2007 John Wiley & Sons, Inc.

Principle 3: Customization of best practices to meet project-specific needs, prevent recurrence of defects and improve the process

Principle 4: Measurement and tracking of project status to facilitate informed management decisions

Principle 5: Automation of repetitive tasks

Principle 6: Incremental implementation of ADP's practices and policies

The first principle stresses the need for the establishment of an infrastructure. People, technology, and the interactions of the people with this technology form such an infrastructure required to support a project. Thus, while all principles are equally important to ADP's successful implementation, without the first principle, the others could not be implemented.

The premise of the second principle is the necessity of applying well-accepted industry best practices, such as those defined for requirements management, design, or coding, in the life cycle. Without understanding and embracing these practices, a company could not operate efficiently.

Next, customization of industry practices is necessary. Customized best practices are organization and project specific. They are created based on action plans after the root cause analysis of defects uncovered during development, to prevent those defects from recurring.

The need for measurements and tracking of project status is crucial to understanding whether the practices are being properly applied, to identifying problem areas requiring corrections, and to making critical decisions regarding project status and release readiness of the product. These factors form the basis for the fourth principle.

The necessity of automation in modern software development hardly needs justification. Not only does automation facilitate implementation of the best practices and collection of project-related data, it also reduces the error-prone human influence on process implementation. All repetitive and mundane tasks should be automated whenever possible in any portion of the software life cycle.

Finally, incremental implementation of ADP is critical to its success. The gradual approach of introducing it group-by-group and practice-by-practice is essential to achieve a desired organizational culture change, as change is unsettling and it always encounters some degree of resistance. Both the complex nature of software projects themselves and the novelty of ADP warrant this systematic approach.

While the establishment of the infrastructure is a starting point and thus a foundation of our methodology, both automation and incremental implementation are the overarching principles that should be applied throughout ADP's life cycle.

In this chapter, we will formally define defect prevention, describe its direct benefits, provide a historical perspective, and explain the ADP principles in detail. Based on these principles we will propose an ADP software process model, which revolves around its people and technology infrastructure. In the last section of this chapter, we will provide examples of applications of ADP's principles to software project management.

2.2 DEFECT PREVENTION: DEFINITION AND BENEFITS

Defect Prevention Defined   We define an *error as a human mistake*, and a *defect as a fault, bug, inaccuracy, or lack of expected functionality in a project artifact*. Project artifacts include, but are not limited to, requirements documents, design models, code, and tests. Our broad definition of defects thus includes problems such as contradicting requirements, design oversights, or coding bugs.

The concepts of *defect root cause analysis and prevention* originated in the manufacturing industry, in the fields of quality control and management, pioneered by W. Edwards Deming [1] and Joseph M. Juran [2]. Its application to software development as a key component of process improvement was introduced by Watts S. Humphrey [3] and gained popularity in the 1990s as part of the quality initiatives such as CMU SEI CMM® (Carnegie Mellon University's Software Engineering Institute Capability and Maturity Model).

Traditionally, *defect prevention* refers to a strategy that identifies *root causes* of defects in a software life cycle and *prevents them from recurring*. It involves collecting defect data in a defect repository, analyzing and identifying the root causes of the most severe defects, and applying a systematic methodology to improve the software development process in order to prevent these defects from recurring. Ilene Burstein identifies two categories of defect analysis techniques: Pareto diagrams and Ishikawa (fishbone) diagrams [4].

A Pareto diagram is a bar graph illustrating the frequency of defect occurrence. After analysis of the Pareto diagram's data, it is recommended to "concentrate on vital few and not trivial many" defects. For example, once a vital defect such as a "dangling pointer" has been detected in a code module, this defect needs to be corrected, and a process should be established to prevent any future dangling pointers in the code. This could be done by automatically verifying with a static analysis tool that all developers adhere to the following practice: "Deallocate the memory pointed by the pointer and set the pointer to null, when memory location is no longer used."

A fishbone diagram is a cause-and-effect graph, an example of which is illustrated in Figure 2.1. Using a cause-and-effect graph such as the fishbone diagram can help identify a spectrum of problems that contributed to a specific defect. These problems could originate in methods, technology, or people. Analysis of the problem root causes should lead to the development of a preventive action plan.

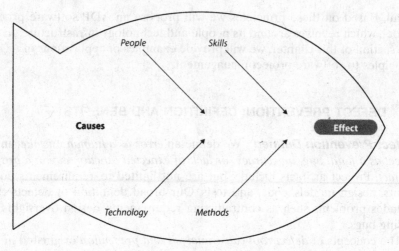

Figure 2.1 A generic cause–effect fishbone diagram.

For example, one of the causes of a module interface defect might be poor communication among development team members. In this case, a means of improved communication should be established. Another cause might be an improperly configured version control system. In this situation, a root cause of the incorrect configuration needs to be determined, and an action taken to prevent it from recurring.

The above approaches focus on improving the process based on the defects encountered during software development of a team or organization.

We have extended this traditional view of defect prevention by defining a comprehensive approach to development and management of software projects by focusing on averting problems through both application of well-accepted industry best practices and customization of these best practices based on root cause analysis of defects uncovered during development.

While many dismiss it as both costly and impractical, benefits of defect prevention have been known for a long time as pointed out by Humphrey [3] and Mays [5]. We outline these benefits in the remaining parts of this section.

Defect Prevention Improves Software Quality and User Satisfaction

Defects can have detrimental effects on software users. Thus, preventing defects has a long-term lasting effect of improved user satisfaction. Moreover, finding the root cause of a defect often allows for fixing a whole class of defects. The system therefore becomes more stable and retains a higher level of quality.

While developers often patch up bugs without identifying their root causes, such an approach usually provides only a short-term solution.

DEVELOPER'S TESTIMONIAL

"What's the problem?"

I had the following experience on my last project. I had periodic server errors that I could not reproduce or find their root cause. I made minor changes to the configurations of the server and I hoped that those changes would magically fix the problem. The client was Autodesk, Inc. (maker of AutoCAD) and this project was very significant to Autodesk. It took about a year to complete the first phase (and millions of dollars). Right before going live, the same defect surfaced again and it was considered a significant showstopper to the whole project. It was embarrassing to report the bug in front of 30+ executives, managers, and colleagues. I had to stay until 4 A.M. to track and fix this defect.

It would have been much easier for me to find the root cause of the problem earlier in the life cycle.

—Husam Azma, Software Analyst

Moreover, unless applied thoroughly and comprehensively throughout the software development life cycle, defect prevention is ineffective.

The following example illustrates a situation where a previously detected, and yet only partially corrected, timing defect caused a failure of a mission-critical system, resulting in lost lives.

The failure of an American Patriot Missile battery during the Gulf War was caused by a previously detected and partially corrected timing defect in its software [6]. The software's system time was counted in tenths of a second and held in an integer, while the seconds used to calculate the position of incoming Scud missiles were real numbers. The defect arose because of a loss of precision when multiplying the integer system time by 1/10 to yield the seconds as real numbers. The longer the software had been running, the greater the integer values for representing time, which caused larger inaccuracies in calculating the position of incoming missiles. The Patriot Missile battery in Dharan, Saudi Arabia, had been running for 100 consecutive hours when it failed to intercept an incoming Iraqi Scud missile. The missile killed 28 and wounded approximately 100 other American soldiers.

Defect Prevention Reduces Development and Maintenance Costs   According to Barry Boehm and Victor Basili [7,8], the cost of removing defects from the software grows dramatically as a function of time in the development. Defect prevention not only reduces the total number of faults, but it also shifts defect discovery to early phases of the development cycle. Also, defects uncovered in one iteration of software development can be prevented from recurring in subsequent iterations. Such an improvement can have a great impact on the efficiency of software development, because removing defects in late phases of the life cycle can be very costly, as illustrated in Figure 2.2.

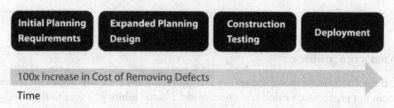

Figure 2.2   Cost of software defect discovery versus time.

Defect Prevention Facilitates Predictability and Improvement of Software Processes   Since the existence of defects is not planned in the software development process, their presence often delays releases and increases the total production costs. While there are a number of techniques for defect estimation, these techniques do not provide guaranteed results. Fewer defects make the process more stable and predictable.

Defects can originate in any of the phases of the development cycle starting with requirements, through design, construction, and maintenance. Thus, identifying a defect's root cause and implementing practices to prevent these defects from recurring facilitates process predictability and improvement.

2.3   HISTORICAL PERSPECTIVE: DEFECT ANALYSIS AND PREVENTION IN THE AUTO INDUSTRY—WHAT HAPPENED TO DEMING?

As mentioned above, the idea of defect analysis and prevention has its roots in concepts based on statistical quality control pioneered by W. Edwards Deming [1] and Joseph M. Juran [2]. To answer the question whether defect prevention can be effectively applied in software development, we will examine Deming's methodology and industries that benefited from it.

Deming versus American Automakers   Manufacturing industries have learned how to control the process of production by utilizing defect prevention techniques as a means of creating high-quality, affordable, and abundant products. The automotive industry is a prime example of this paradigm shift. For the automotive industry, a major advance in product quality was made when the meaning of testing was redefined. In the years prior to the Second World War, automakers in both the United States and Europe would test their products after they came off the assembly line. Defects would be corrected one-by-one.

There were two problems with this approach. First, it delayed completion and delivery of the final product, making production more expensive than it should have been. Second, it was ineffective in identifying all of the defects, allowing many faults to remain in the autos after they had been shipped to market. This led to a short product life and high consumer dissatisfaction.

After the war, this "hunt-and-fix" mentality remained deeply rooted in the U.S. automotive industry. Ironically, it was an American, W. Edwards Deming, who tried to educate the auto industry about error prevention techniques and their application to the assembly line. When his efforts were discounted in the United States, Deming turned to the Japanese, who were quick to recognize and reap the potential profit that Deming's methods offered.

Deming's great insight into the manufacturing process was that quality was essentially locked out of the process if defects were not considered until after the autos were assembled. For instance, finding a rattling piece of metal in a finished automobile would be nearly impossible. This is the same reason why postproduction testing fails in the software industry. Looking for one fatal runtime error in 50,000 lines of code is much more difficult than looking for the same error in only 500 lines.

Deming's Error Prevention—The Concept Deming taught that fixing problems where they occur in the manufacturing process not only eliminates many quality problems in the finished product, but also promotes the ultimate goal of process improvement. He found that by fixing the process itself, it is possible to prevent the same types of errors from reoccurring.

Deming advocated process improvement through a root cause analysis and prevention. The basic procedure for implementing Deming's process quality improvements is as follows:

1. Identify a defect.
2. Find the root cause of the defect.
3. Locate the point in the production line that caused the defect.
4. Implement preventive practices to ensure that similar defects do not reoccur.
5. Monitor the process to verify effectiveness of the preventive practices.

For example, inspectors on an auto assembly line discover that seat bolts are loose. The cause of this defect is that the bolts do not exactly fit the tool used to tighten them. They locate the point in the assembly line where the bolts are being tightened, and apply a corrective action by providing a tool that fits properly. Monitoring the process is accomplished by closely inspecting the seat bolts for tightness and collecting the data about the amount of time saved by using the right tool.

DEFECT PREVENTION VERSUS DETECTION

Defect prevention is a counterpart to defect detection. Defect detection is the process of finding and fixing defects after a product is built; the flawed process that generated those defects is left uncorrected. In the seat bolts example, defect detection would have simply tightened the seat bolts at the end of the assembly line. This action may have ensured that the bolts were installed properly, but it would have left the root of the problem embedded in the manufacturing process. The problem would never go away because the root cause was not corrected.

Implementing Deming's methodology took time, years in some instances, as every step in the manufacturing process had to be analyzed and, in most cases, altered. However, in adopting Deming's defect prevention techniques, Japan, Germany, and other nations saw the quality of their products skyrocket. In turn, the manufacturing process became more efficient, resulting in greater production numbers and reduction of per-unit costs.

The U.S. automotive industry remained skeptical of the Deming approach, despite the unexpected and astonishing quality improvement experienced by the Japanese. Postproduction testing remained the standard approach to quality in the U.S. auto industry well into the 1970s. Only after the 1973 oil crisis, when their customers turned to smaller foreign imports in an effort to save fuel, did the U.S. auto industry take notice. What they saw was an ever-widening gap between the quality of Japanese and European cars and their domestic counterparts. Failure to prevent defects in the production process nearly destroyed the U.S. automotive industry altogether.

2.4 PRINCIPLES OF AUTOMATED DEFECT PREVENTION

The primary reason why the software industry does not embrace defect prevention is that many within the industry itself doubt that effective defect prevention can be applied to software. The rapid evolution of software implies that a stable production process, such as an industrial "production line" model, is not possible in software.

The questions that often arise are: "How can we have repeatability when one product is always different from the next?" and "How can we have a production line when only one thing at a time is produced?" The answer to this quandary requires rethinking what is meant by "production line." Indeed a production line in software development exists, but not one producing multiple copies of the same software. The software production line exists in the transition of raw ideas into usable software products.

*Producing software does not require a traditional rigid production line of machines making machines, but rather **a sophisticated and flexible infrastructure,** capable of both adapting to minor changes within each development cycle, and adjusting to the major overhauls that occur from one release of software to another, or to a new product.*

Thus, ADP defines such an infrastructure as one of its six fundamental principles. The remainder of this section will expand on these six principles.

2.4.1 Principle 1—Establishment of Infrastructure: "Build a Strong Foundation through Integration of People and Technology"

This principle states that people's roles in a software team need to be defined to include active participation in and control of defect prevention in a project.

It also stresses the necessity for technology used both to automate best practices and to track and measure project status data. The details of the infrastructure, which describe how to organize people and technology, are provided in the next chapter. This section gives an overview of this infrastructure. There are three parts of the infrastructure: the people, the configurable technologies, and finally, the integration of the people and the technology.

People—Extending Traditional Roles Building a people infrastructure involves organizing employees in a way that will promote communication, productivity, efficiency, and overall job satisfaction. This includes organizing employees into groups, determining the size and location of groups, and assigning roles to the employees in a group. The roles determine what tasks each member performs and how the members of the group interact with one another. To exemplify our methodology we define defect detection and defect prevention responsibilities, in addition to the traditional roles of project manager, architect, developer, tester, QA (quality assurance) staff, and a system administrator.

Technology—Minimum and More As a minimum, a development group must have a functioning source control system, automated build system, problem tracking system, and an automated reporting system. This technology can be expanded as ADP matures in an organization, as the needs of a project change, or as additional software tools and people are added. In a model situation, each developer, tester, and QA team member has a local installation of supporting technology; the technology configuration is determined by the team architect and standardized across the team.

Gradually, the infrastructure should be expanded to include more technology and support other groups. An automated requirements management system is a good start for a requirements group. A repository of project artifacts including a database of best practices and policies, for team members' easy access, should be created. An automated testing system would facilitate the work of both developers and testers.

Understanding People Roles Experience has taught us that best practices must be directly embedded into the software development groups that will use them. This means that each team member in the development group needs to understand her role—be it developer, architect, or project manager—and that she needs to understand how to adhere to that role. For example, understanding who defines or manages the requirements, where these requirements are stored, and who uses them and when is necessary for the group to successfully adopt requirements best practices. Most importantly, defining group behavior and interactions with technology ensures that the practices adopted remain ingrained and that they do not deteriorate over time.

2.4.2 Principle 2—Application of General Best Practices: "Learn from Others' Mistakes"

Most software development projects share many of the same characteristics and pitfalls, even though each project and organization also encounters its own unique challenges. Consequently, ADP defines *general best practices* to prevent the software defects and human errors common to most development projects. The basic premise of this principle is to integrate industry well-accepted best practices (such as those identified for requirements change management, configuration management, or coding standards) into the life cycle.

The set of general best practices is the product of software industry experts examining the most common errors and then developing rules designed to prevent these common errors. They represent a wealth of knowledge that was created through years of experience of many organizations. By adopting and, where possible, automating these out-of-the-box general practices, an organization can instantly progress from following the few best practices that it introduced over the years to a comprehensive set of standards that have been developed, tested, and perfected by industry experts. When teams are working on any type of project, it is always prudent to follow the practices and standards that industry experts have designed for the relevant application, language, platform, and technologies.

There are multiple levels of granularity for best practices. They could be as abstract as the type of software development process selected for a project, and as detailed as conventions for naming specific variables in the code. At organizational level, they could include a set of templates for project artifacts, a common repository for storing approved best practices, or guidelines for use of a configuration management system. At design level, they could suggest usage of specific design patterns, SOA (service-oriented architecture), or AJAX (Asynchronous JavaScript and XML). At the level of code construction, they could include specific procedures for code reviews, writing unit test cases, or paired programming.

Another example of such an organizational-level practice is an EVM (Earned Value Management system), which tracks and measures project cost and schedule. The purpose of this practice is to help organizations establish a successful process for ensuring that the project is managed according to its plan. The EVM helps in timely identification of the deviations from the plan so early and appropriate corrective actions can be taken to preserve the project's overall cost and schedule. More discussion of this practice is provided in Chapter 9.

An example of a best practice at the code construction level is paired programming. It is common knowledge among developers that when writing challenging code, explaining it to someone and having a second pair of eyes look at it prevents defects: not just typos, but also logical errors that would be very difficult and time-consuming to fix later in the process. However, this explanation was traditionally relegated to team-wide code reviews, which tended to be long, boring, and tedious sessions where all team members would sit in one room poring over lines of code. It turns out that the same effect could be achieved by restricting the code review to two people: partners who watch over one another's shoulder as they write code. Thus, paired programming emerged as one of the best practices to prevent the defects that would have otherwise caused developers much grief.

As another example of such a code construction practice, consider how variables are named. The name of a variable should reflect what information the variable holds and it should not be excessively long or cryptic. This practice helps to ensure that the developer who wrote the code and other developers who work with the code will be able to read it and understand it. By enforcing this general best practice from the beginning of the project, it is ensured that developers in the future will be able to understand and work with the code. To take the variable naming concept a step further, the file names for the source code should also reflect what level or scope of information they contain. This could be achieved by establishing a standard file-naming convention, which will reduce the countless hours spent searching for the right file or component.

This book describes a wide variety of well-known practices. We expect the number of these practices to grow over time as practitioners develop more standards and as the industry introduces new languages and technologies that have most recent categories of defects that will need to be prevented. Teams do not need to implement every practice; rather, they should survey the available practices, and then select the practices that are the most applicable to their projects and goals.

2.4.3   Principle 3—Customization of Best Practices: "Learn from Your Own Mistakes and Improve the Process"

The customized best practices address the project- or organization-specific problems. Some practices are very valuable in one type of development context, but not applicable to others. Customized practices are necessary because many modern development projects have vastly different needs, depending on the nuances of the product. For example, the team working on embedded C software for a pacemaker, the team working on an e-commerce Web application, and the team developing a fast-action software game, will all have very different concerns. Thus, even though the same core general practices apply in most cases, these core practices should be supplemented with the appropriate set of specific practices to create a mix of general and customized practices best suited for the project's unique needs.

Thus, there is a need for a mechanism that provides for *customization of the best practices* in order to prevent project- or organization-specific problems. This mechanism is described by the third principle, which is based on

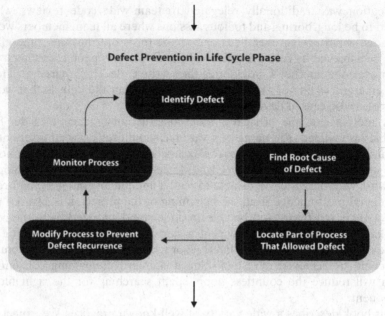

Figure 2.3   Deming's defect prevention applied to a phase in the software development process.

Deming's error prevention concept, as shown in Figure 2.3. Each time a severe defect is discovered, a new customized practice should be defined. Once the new customized practice is defined, it has to become an integral part of the methodology and its application should be, if possible, both automated and seamless. The adherence to the customized practices should be monitored, so consequently, the development methodology would become increasingly defect resistant.

For example, consider the development of software that deals with precise measurements. After adding components to perform conversions between different units, developers discovered that the measurements are not as precise as expected. They find that the precision of the conversion factors is inconsistent: some of the conversion factors have 10 decimal places, but others have as few as two. There was a paper document containing all the conversions factors that should be used, but several of the developers had been looking them up on the Internet to save time. To remedy this situation, the architect made a standardized copy of the conversion table available on the company intranet and specified that all the conversion factors be defined in one table to be included in other files. Their customized best practice would be "Use only standardized conversion factors (available on the intranet), and they must be defined in a single table." To verify and monitor whether this practice is followed, a static analyzer scans the code on a regular basis in order to identify potential violations.

2.4.4   Principle 4—Measurement and Tracking of Project Status: "Understand the Past and Present to Make Decisions about the Future"

To make informed decisions, management must be able to analyze measures reflecting project status information. These measures are quantitative representations of product or process attributes. They could be assigned specific, absolute values, such as the number of defects uncovered, or they could characterize the degree to which a system, or its component, possesses a given attribute. In the latter case, they are referred to as metrics. An example of a metric is a percentage of failed tests. These measures could also denote more general statistical indicators, such as *confidence factors*, derived from many basic measures. Indicators, for example, could provide information such as whether the project progresses according to its schedule and whether the costs are within the planned budget. At a more detailed level, many other project-essential statistics should be available, for example, the number of implemented requirements features, the number of failed tests, coverage of tests, or the number of defects and their severity, and so on. Project indicators help in prompt identification of problems, so they can be remedied in a timely manner. Additionally, when observed over an extended period, those indicators can be used to assess product quality and its deployment readiness.

Consequently, continuous data gathering is critical in our methodology and it is achieved by having a seamless, automated reporting system capable of collecting and storing project data in a repository. Based on the data in this repository, project status measures and metrics can be calculated, tracked, and plotted for management decisions. Thus, in our methodology, software processes are treated as *statistical processes*. It is important that each group review the values of these predefined measures, and then use statistical control limits and target average values to assess the status of the project.

Measurement   Most of the best practices can be measured by at least one related variable. By tracking the history of values for these variables and then statistically analyzing them, it can be determined whether the related practice is being applied correctly and is achieving the desired result.

The key to ensuring that each best practice delivers the expected benefits is to stabilize the measures for each process, determine whether the stable measure is at the expected level, and modify the implementation of that practice until any suboptimal measures stabilize at the desired level.

For the best practices, we answer several questions related to measurements:

• What can be measured?
• How is it measured?
• What does the measure or metric indicate?
• What decisions can be made based on the values of this measure?

Tracking   Tracking refers to the collecting and storing of project data over a given period. The only way to assess progress and keep the project organized is to continuously track project data. For example, the tracking of requirements helps identify their changes and status of their implementation. The number of implemented and tested requirements should gradually increase over time while requirements volatility, which is an indicator of its changes, should approach zero as the project stabilizes.

For the best practices described in this book, we answer several questions related to tracking:

- What data can be tracked?
- How is the data tracked?
- What do we gain from tracking this data?

2.4.5   Principle 5—Automation: "Let the Computer Do It"

We will refer to automation as an activity that can be performed without human intervention.

Today's software systems are large, very complex, and typically consist of many subsystems running on heterogeneous platforms. The trend is for software to continue to become more complex, notwithstanding the advances in modern *integrated development environments* with automatic code generators, and widespread use of off-the-shelf components.

With such complex systems and many different cost-driven constraints, automation becomes a necessity for the delivery of quality software systems. Thus, Walker Royce in his top 10 principles of modern software management [9] lists automation as a critical feature that facilitates or even encourages perpetual change in iterative processes. Although many managers hesitate to invest in auxiliary technology due to the high cost of licenses and training, the long-term benefits of automation largely outweigh these drawbacks.

Automation of Mundane and Repetitive Tasks Improves People's Job Satisfaction and Their Effectiveness   Repetitive, monotonous, and tedious tasks tend to have a negative impact on employee morale. Moreover, as pointed out in the previous chapter, they cause frustration and boredom, which in turn are a source of mistakes.

Automation of repetitive and mundane tasks helps to overcome this ineffectiveness by providing an environment where team members can focus on more challenging and creative tasks by working in the high end of their competency zone [10]. Thus, the role of automation is not to function as a substitute for people, but to improve the working conditions for people. Additionally, since people are excellent at creating new processes, but not very good at maintaining them, automation helps in sustaining existing processes and consequently in embracing change, by providing an environment where people can focus on activities that people do best: being imaginative and innovative.

Moreover, automation forces people to look at even the most seemingly well-known task in a different light. Just as software development can sometimes lead to an improvement in the business process, automation can allow developers to realize that some steps are unnecessary or that there is a better way of accomplishing a task.

DEVELOPER'S TESTIMONIAL

"Oh no, not again!"

Doing tasks that are repetitive and simple is bad for employees' morale. I've seen a task assigned to two co-workers that was quite monotonous. In hearing of the task, I decided to independently see if I could create a program to do the monotonous task they were assigned. Though it took me two weeks to create and test the program, it ran successfully and completed the task in less than 10 seconds. The two co-workers took close to a month to complete the task.

The two co-workers did nothing but complain about the task they were given. They became even more disgruntled when they discovered there was a tool that could have been used instead. *Watching software accomplish a task in seconds that would take a person a month to do is quite refreshing.*

—Software Developer

While not everything can be automated, automation should be implemented as much as possible and when it is practical to do so.

Automation Improves Product Quality A direct correlation between software quality and the "technology index," which is a "measure of the modern tool and method usage," has been recognized for nearly 20 years. The study, which was conducted by McGarry at the NASA Goddard Space Flight Center [11] and then cited many times in works such as Humphrey's classic *Managing the Software Process* [3], shows a linear decrease of fault rate as a function of total technology index, as illustrated in Figure 2.4.

Fault density is one of many measures of software quality, whose main attributes (as defined by the ISO [12]) include functionality, reliability, usability, efficiency, maintainability, portability, and security. Other metrics proposed by IEEE [13] and others take into account requirements compliance, test coverage, and mean time to failure. Software development and project supervision–supporting technologies, such as requirements management systems, facilitate traceability and change control to improve requirements

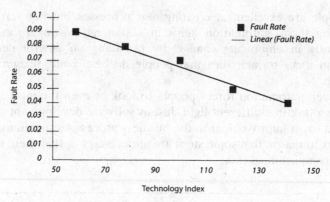

Figure 2.4   Reduction of software fault rate as a function of the technology index.

compliance. Automated test generators provide coverage analysis and statistics, while load testers can uncover performance problems before software is deployed. Modern software systems are so complex that achieving the desired product quality requires the use of these technologies.

Automation Facilitates Human Communication   Automated tasks are well defined and therefore are not subject to natural language misinterpretations. Ambiguities of natural languages often cause interpretation discrepancies, which may have negative consequences—especially in software requirements specifications.

While many of the communication problems cannot be resolved through automation, some can. For example, notification about changes in requirements could be facilitated by sending an automatically generated message to all involved parties as soon as a change is entered into a requirements management system. In addition, notification about feature implementation should be done automatically, so all involved stakeholders could validate it.

Automation Helps to Implement and Verify Best Practices and Organizational Standards   Automation and use of the supporting technology help enforce organizational best practices and standards. Without automation in place, it would be difficult to ensure that the team members are performing all the tasks consistently with the established company best practices. For example, assume that a software project of 1 million lines of code contains several instances of a predefined functionality. The organization implementing the project has decided on the following practice: use a specific automatic code generator for each instance of this functionality. This rule could be verified only by scanning the code using a static analyzer, which finds and evaluates each instance of the functionality for compliance with the predefined practice.

DEVELOPER'S TESTIMONIAL

Best Practices Are Hard to Enforce

From my personal experience in software development, I can vouch for the communication difficulties experienced by a large development team. At my current position, there are various teams that are in charge of different areas of development. There is a development team in charge of coding and implementing the application, an integration team in charge of integrating each subsequent release of functionality from the development team, and the testing team that is in charge of testing each new release from the integration team. All the members within each team have varying levels of expertise while there is even more variation in expertise among individuals from the three different teams. Our various teams attempt to employ the company best practices and standards.

This effort yields varying results as it is difficult to enforce compliance with company standards among so many people with a large range of expertise levels.

—Software Developer

Automation Improves People Productivity In general, the correlation between people's productivity and use of technology is difficult to measure because many factors are involved, and therefore the direct impact is hard to isolate. Actually, one of the disappointing results of the aforementioned study conducted by McGarry at the NASA Goddard Space Flight Center [11] is that it did not demonstrate the productivity advantages of automated tools. However, more recent research that was conducted for selected and well-isolated software processes shows a dramatic improvement in productivity. In particular, this is true for testing tools where a number of case studies have been performed.

For example, James M. Clarke of Lucent Technologies reports that significant savings in effort resulted from automated test generation [14]. Figure 2.5 compares the THCY (technical head count—year) effort required by manual and automated test generation for one of the system features.

Clarke states that the use of the automated tool called TestMaster "provided a test generation productivity improvement of just over ninety percent.

	Manual Generation	TestMaster Generation
Phase One	0.120	0.014
Phase Two	0.050	0.002
Total	0.170	0.016

Figure 2.5 Results of a case study: manual versus automated test generation expressed in people-years.

At this level of test generation productivity improvement, one test engineer using TestMaster can be as productive as ten test engineers using manual test generation."

DEVELOPER'S TESTIMONIAL

Testing and Automation

The task I most want to be automated at my work place is testing. We all hate to test, and to keep us all from going completely bonkers, we try to divide it up among individuals. But, it takes a long time to do it by hand, it's repetitive and boring, and therefore, prone to errors.

An automated activity that I frequently utilize is visual SQL statement building. Although I can write SQL statements by hand, I generally find it less error-prone to build them using visual tools. It keeps me from making mistakes in table names, field names, and syntax.

—Mandy Botsko-Wilson, Technical Consultant

Automation Facilitates Control of the Software Processes by Collecting Measurement Data   Supporting technologies can be used to automatically collect measurement data about project status (e.g., cost performance index or schedule performance index), product quality (e.g., defect rate), stop test criteria (e.g., test coverage criteria), team productivity (SLOC/time period), cost estimation based on historical data, and risk management. This feature directly supports the fourth principle of our methodology: measurement and tracking of project data.

For the best practices described throughout the book, we answer the following questions related to automation:

- What tasks can be automated?
- How is the task automated?
- What is gained by automating the task?

2.4.6   Principle 6: Incremental Implementation of ADP's Practices and Policies

While the ability to embrace change is important to the success of any business, it is a necessary survival skill in the software industry. This is because no other business relies on continuous change through learning, adaptation, and innovation like the software business does.

However, change is unsettling and it can be overwhelming to both the organization and the individuals. Change usually encounters resistance, since people tend to gravitate toward their low-energy state called the "comfort zone." While working in the comfort zone people do not experience a great sense of accomplishment, but they feel settled and secure.

Thus, to minimize the difficulties induced by yet another change ADP should be introduced gradually to an organization: group-by-group and practice-by-practice. A pilot group consisting of talented and motivated people should be selected. The pilot group should be actively working on the code and it should be dedicated to fully implementing the methodology. To gain the momentum needed to drive an organization-wide implementation of ADP, the pilot group must be a well-esteemed team working on an important project. Electing one of the organization's most talented teams as the pilot group yields two main benefits. First, it demonstrates the value placed on the methodology, and consequently helps the organization's most critical projects. Second, it would likely produce a showcase implementation, which provides other groups with real-life evidence that ADP can indeed be implemented in the organization's environment and that it actually delivers the promised benefits.

Once ADP is well-tested and established by the model pilot group, it can be gradually introduced to other teams and ultimately propagated to the entire organization, as shown in Figure 2.6.

Similarly, best practices should be introduced one by one. One reason why implementation of best practices has historically failed is the overwhelming amount of information that is typically delivered to team members. The amount of information could be so overwhelming that many people reject it subconsciously as "noise" and simply ignore it altogether.

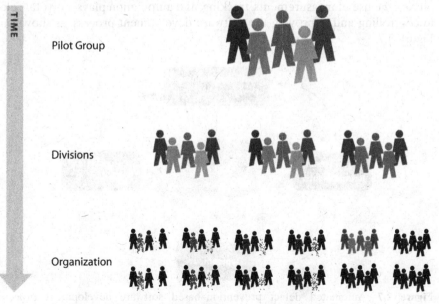

Figure 2.6 Introducing ADP on a group-by-group basis.

The key to overcoming these challenges and successfully implementing a practice is introducing it in phases. This prevents the team from being overpowered by having to learn and follow an unmanageable number of new requirements at once—in addition to performing their regular job tasks. One particularly helpful strategy is to divide each practice into several levels—*critical*, *important*, and *recommended*—then introduce each level incrementally. The team could start following only the most critical practices. Once the team was able to comply with these requirements, it could then proceed to implementing important practices. Once all of these were mastered, the team would phase in the recommended practices. Another useful strategy is to apply new best practices only to activities and project artifacts that started or were created after a predetermined cutoff date. Having a reasonable implementation strategy facilitates practice application and enforcement, and it also maximizes its benefits.

2.5 AUTOMATED DEFECT PREVENTION–BASED SOFTWARE DEVELOPMENT PROCESS MODEL

Based on the above six principles, and best practices described in this book, our methodology defines an ADP-based software development process model consisting of the following phases: initial planning and requirements, expanded planning and design, construction and testing, and deployment. The required infrastructure is created during the initial planning, and is supplemented to meet the needs of the project during the expanded planning. For each of the phases, the use of measurements, tracking, and automation plays a pivotal role in controlling and improving the software development process, as shown in Figure 2.7.

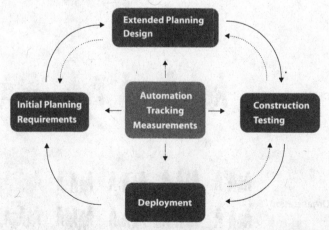

Figure 2.7 Automated defect prevention–based software development process model.

ADP is both iterative and incremental and the phases described do not follow each other sequentially. There are many revisits and refinements of requirements, design, construction, and testing. However, there are core activities that take place during each of the phases.

During the *initial planning and requirements phase*, the product vision and scope document is prepared and the project initial infrastructure, which defines the roles of people and technology and their interactions, is established. Additionally, the defect detection and prevention roles are defined and assigned to the team members. Based on frequent communications with project stakeholders, the key product features are defined and stored in the requirements management system, or another shared repository designed for tracking of requirements.

During the *extended planning and design*, the software development plan is created. The project cost and schedule estimates are prepared, based on the product key requirements and the high-level architectural design. This plan is subject to future updates as the product iterations are completed. At this time, the process for defect prevention is defined and the extended infrastructure necessary to support project specific needs is established. The project key features are continuously refined into more detailed requirements. Based on the features and requirements, the critical design attributes are identified, the product high-level design is prepared, and the detail design policies for the team are defined.

During the *construction and testing phase*, the detailed design is completed by implementing the code. The coding standards for the team are established, together with the policies for the use of source control system, automated build system, and other support technologies. Test-driven development approach is recommended at the service and module level and for algorithmically complex units. Coding standards are applied throughout the development. Defects are analyzed, classified, and new customized best practices are created to prevent those defects from recurring.

The deployment decision is made based on the quality measures collected throughout the product development. During the *deployment phase*, the automated transfer of the application to the target environment takes place. At that time, the additional user testing of the deployed system is conducted, and the monitoring of the released system starts. All new feature requests and the postrelease defect reports are collected and stored in the problem tracking system.

How Automated Is ADP?   Not every activity can be automated. For example, the following four categories do not lend themselves to automation:

- Innovative ideas, such as unique designs or algorithms, have to be created by individuals, and while technology can facilitate in verifying and testing of these new concepts, it cannot replace human creativity.

- People-intensive activities, such as requirements elicitation, cannot be automated because requirements are created based on identifying stakeholders' and project needs. It is important that communication lines are open during these activities and that all stakeholders have a chance to voice their opinions.
- Architectural design does not lend itself to automation. However, recent popularity of architectural patterns opens the door to future automation of some of the design tasks, as automation becomes possible with activities that were previously thought to be unsuitable for automation.
- Peer reviews of code and documentation cannot be automated because they require analytical reasoning and understanding of intended code functionality.

However, in many situations, one can use automation to streamline processes that require human involvement. Automation cannot relieve one from having to manually review code to determine whether it satisfies very subjective, situation-based criteria, but it can automatically identify code that needs to be reviewed. For example, assume there are classes that are designed to perform transactions. The transactions inside these classes always have to be properly rolled back if the transaction encounters problems. However, the team knows from prior experience that transaction rollbacks typically have many problems. There are some general rules that can be applied to make rollbacks less error prone (for example, "Do not throw exceptions unless the class is in the initial state"). This rule is so general that it means different things when applied to different pieces of code, so it is virtually impossible to automatically verify whether the code follows this rule. Consequently, one needs to review all exceptions in transaction-related classes manually. However, if a programmer uses a tool to automatically identify all transaction-related classes that throw exceptions, she is relieved from having to manually search through the entire code base and has more time and energy to dedicate to performing the subjective review that cannot be automated.

Many tasks, however, can be fully automated. This includes requirements change tracking, software configuration management, periodic builds, problem tracking, and many testing activities. Test scripts ought to be automated for repeatability and reliability.

Code generators are gaining popularity, especially for database tasks, such as creating and updating tables, or adding and deleting columns. An example is a generator that looks at the database and creates generic procedures and queries such as Insert, Update, SelectAll, or SelectOne, for each table in the database. The generator also creates the code for the classes that will call the automatically generated procedures. When a change is made to a database table, the code generator should be run and all modifications will be automatically reflected.

Verification of conformance to coding standards can be performed automatically and so can many software maintenance and support activities such as version updates, server or client reboots, or data backups.

Another set of activities that can be automated include collecting and monitoring project status data and generating project status metrics. A variety of metrics pertaining to requirements volatility and implementation over time can be automatically generated.

ADP advocates automation as an essential approach to making defect preventive practices sustainable.

DEVELOPER'S TESTIMONIAL

I have read a few articles on automatic programming (AP). A lot of good articles can be found at the American Association for AI. I think it comes down to a problem of scale; many software engineering problems are complex not because of theoretical difficulties or unique concepts, just size. These problems should be approachable with faster and more efficient (smarter) AP. I think it will require a leap of some kind, if it is possible at all, to move to a system that can generate new and novel programs that are not applications of known principles and concepts.

Fourth-generation programming languages are also a step in this direction. These have been around for a while and usually focus on a specific domain, but are a step in the direction of taking specification to program with less work.

Personally, I think it will not be that long before you will be able to go from specification to application for most common domains without coding. You can get very close with today's tools and component libraries. Unique or original problems will still require programmers, but if these solutions prove useful they will most likely make it into the common domains.

For example, you can create a very complex and unique Web application with many of the modern content management systems with no coding at all. The most you would have to do is choose components and configuration options (the architecture). My site uses Drupal and could have been done without any coding. Of course, I am a geek, so I custom built a few components and tweaked some of the code, but I did not have to.

—Scott Sanford, Software Engineer

2.6 EXAMPLES

2.6.1 Focus on Root Cause Analysis of a Defect

This example shows a Defect Root-Cause Analysis and Prevention Plan for round-off errors [15].

Defect Identification   Our first example of the round-off problem is the Ariane 5 rocket launched on June 4, 1996 (European Space Agency, 1996).

After the 37th second of flight, the inertial reference system attempted to convert a 64-bit floating-point number to a 16-bit number, but instead triggered an overflow error that was interpreted by the guidance system as flight data, causing the rocket to veer off course and be destroyed [16].

Our second example is mentioned in Section 2.2, the Patriot Missile software used during the Gulf War [6]. This software used an integer timing register that was incremented at intervals of 0.1 seconds. However, the integers were converted to decimal numbers by multiplying by the binary approximation of 0.1.

As a result, after 100 hours (3.6×10^6 ticks), an error of

$$\left(\frac{1}{10} - \frac{209715}{2097152}\right)(3600 \cdot 100 \cdot 10) = \frac{5625}{16384} \approx 0.3433 \, \text{second}$$

had accumulated [17]. This discrepancy caused the Patriot system to continuously recycle itself instead of targeting properly, and as a result, an Iraqi Scud missile could not be targeted and was allowed to detonate on American soldiers' barracks.

Figure 2.8 depicts the results of analysis of the round-off errors. First, round-off errors should be avoidable. The main causes of the round-off errors can be broken down into four categories: programmers, skills, test methods, and techniques. Then in each category, more detailed root causes are listed. The causes listed in the diagram are:

- Inexperienced programmers or lack of experts
- Insufficient test methods

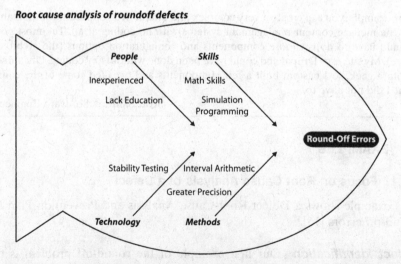

Figure 2.8   Fishbone diagram illustrating possible causes of round-off defects.

- Ineffective development methods
- Low precision

Figure 2.9 depicts a sample preventive action plan for round-off errors.

Preventive Action Plan

Action	Action Description	Automation and Tracking	Measurements
Training	Key programmers must take training courses in related math and simulation programming.	A human resources database can be used to track and update each programmer's skill set so that new responsibilities can be assigned to skilled workers.	1. Number of key programmers trained 2. Number of programmers already having required skills 3. Number of programmers that need to be trained
Changes in coding standards	1. Precision must be at least 64 bit. 2. Data type conversion should be minimized.	Static analyzer can be used to enforce and track new coding standards.	1. Number of precision-related warnings 2. Number of data-type conversion warnings
Consult experts	Consult an expert responsible to perform numerical analysis, provide alternative solutions to problems, create new coding standards and review code.		1. Costs of experts 2. Policies or standards changed per experts-advice
Performing stability testing	Run for extended time to check for stability and accumulative errors.	Load testing can be automated with performance test tools, which should be a part of regression test routine.	1. Code units assigning load tests 2. Defect location found through load tests 3. Number of defects found through load tests
New development methods	1. Use interval arithmetic math technique to check the error. 2. Perform floating-point error analysis. 3. Train developers to these methods.	The learning of new development methods can be tracked with the human resources database to ensure all developers participate and pass the test.	1. Code location using new methods 2. Developers who are proficient in using the new methods

Figure 2.9   Preventive action plan for round-off errors.

2.6.2   Focus on Infrastructure

Consider an example where an organization decided to adopt a number of coding standards as a part of the best practices approach. The development team members will have the appropriate technology installed on their workstations and integrated into their daily development process to monitor implementation of these standards. When a developer creates a new file or checks existing code out of source control and edits it, she must ensure that she has adhered to the practices defined by the team's architect before adding that new or modified code to source control. Practice compliance is automatically checked and if a noncompliant part of code is found, the monitoring raises a red flag. Thus, the developers fix any reported violations so that their code complies with the required practices, and then check their code back into source control.

The testing team performs integration testing on the entire checked-in project baseline (the checked-in work of all project developers) by using workstation versions of the standard team technologies and by manually exercising the application as needed. Preferably, the team tests new and modified functionality as soon as developers add it to source control. To streamline the testing process, the testing technologies are configured to access the same standard team test configurations and files that the developers used and created. The testing team can then extend the developers' tests to perform more complex functional tests (such as system-level tests that check real-life operations that span multiple developers' work) as well as advanced load tests (if applicable). If the testing team uncovers a new severe defect through these or other tests, the team notifies the architect and then works with the architect to diagnose the root cause of this defect. Then they design and implement a defect prevention mechanism to prevent this defect from recurring. This defect prevention mechanism might involve requiring developers to follow a new practice, modifying how developers should perform a current practice, or simply changing the team's standard technology configuration. The testing team also adds to the test suite one or more test cases that verify whether the defect has been comprehensively resolved. At that point, the architect asks the responsible developers to correct the problem. Once the new test cases pass, the defect is deemed corrected.

To verify that the required practices are being implemented correctly and do not decay, the support infrastructure runs as a batch process to test the entire project baseline code at regularly scheduled intervals/ frequencies (usually, at the same intervals/frequencies as the team's automated build). These tests verify whether the appropriate best practices have been implemented. They use the same test parameters and files used by development and testing teams, and automatically generate and execute additional tests as needed.

In addition, the infrastructure should store and help analyze the information from this verification. Team members can access periodic reports and use them to assess the effectiveness of the current practices and determine what additional practices would be helpful to implement. The team can then use this same infrastructure to implement and monitor any process improvements that they decide to adopt.

Similarly, the appropriate infrastructure with well-defined roles of team members needs to be in place for nondevelopment teams, if such exist. For example, if a requirements team uses a requirements management system, this system should be an integral part of our methodology, seamlessly used by both development and nondevelopment groups.

2.6.3   Focus on Customized Best Practice

A company tracks its financial information using an internally built system where a C++ application interacts with a database. At some point, the company employees noticed that some database records seemed to be missing: they complained that some of the records they remembered entering could not be found later when they searched for them. They also noticed that duplicate-records tended to appear around the same time that the other records disappeared.

The IT team was made aware of this problem and started to investigate this situation by talking to the users of the database. The team found out that the staff members occasionally input new data to the database by modifying existing records rather than by creating new records. To diagnose the cause of the missing and duplicate-records problem, the IT team had to analyze the C++ code. After a thorough code inspection, the team realized that when the new data was entered by modifying the existing record, the C++ application created an object for the new record, but the pointer to the data being sent to the database was the same as for the old record. Consequently, when the new data was entered, the old record was overwritten, deleting existing data and causing the missing-record problem. Once the application flushed the new object, the same new data was recorded into two different places in the database: the old and the new record, causing the duplicate-records problem.

The IT team then inspected the code to locate the cause of this problem. The causal analysis identified the C++ class that created the new object for a modified database record but it did not have the explicit *copy constructor*. Thus, the compiler copied the class using a default constructor, and the old data pointer was copied to the new class. Since no new memory was allocated for the entered data, the old data was overwritten with new data, and the newly created object pointed to the same record.

Defining an explicit copy constructor that dynamically allocates memory to the new object provides a solid solution to this problem. However, this is a typical defect detection situation; by fixing only this fault, we have done nothing to prevent similar ones from occurring.

When faced with the above missing and duplicate records problem one should ask the following two questions:

1. Why did the duplicate and missing records occur and how can one quickly and effectively fix this particular problem? This can be understood as an immediate short-term goal.
2. How can one prevent other similar and unpredictable application behaviors? This can be understood as a larger, long-term goal. Asking this question starts the process of defect prevention.

To answer these questions we will use Deming's five steps:

Step 1: Identify the Error. In this case, when new records were created by modifying the existing records, the C++ application created an object for the new record, but the pointer to the data being sent to the database was the same as for the old record. As the input was modified, there was only one old record being overwritten, and then the application flushed both objects, saving the same data twice in two different places in the database. This resulted in the new record being duplicated and the old record being overwritten.

Step 2: Find the Cause of the Error. The class did not define an explicit copy constructor, so the compiler was using the default one. Because the default constructor did not allocate memory for the new data but copied the existing pointer, the same data was used twice.

Step 3: Locate the Point in Production that Created the Error. This part can prove difficult for software development. "Development" is the location of the error. However, is it one particular developer who made this mistake, or is it a common group error that is repeated multiple times? Note that Deming states that the process, not the individuals, should be blamed for errors, and consequently, the process ought to be fixed. Thus, is there a common solution that can be implemented to automatically prevent this problem from reoccurring? Yes, as explained in the next paragraph.

Step 4: Implement Preventive Practices to Ensure that Errors do not Reoccur. In this case, we need to ensure that an *explicit copy constructor* is defined for every class with dynamically allocated memory. One solution to ensure that this practice is applied in future development projects is to enforce automated coding standards. Once the rule is created that mandates that a copy constructor be explicitly defined and is enforced comprehensively through an automated process, any problems similar to the above will be avoided.

Step 5: Monitor the Process. Since the process of enforcing rules is automated, data can be easily collected and it is possible to determine whether the change is effective, or if any further modifications need to be implemented somewhere else in the process.

2.6.4 Focus on Measurements of Project Status

Processes in our methodology are statistical. Data collected through automation and tracking is used for measurements, which help in management decisions. An example of such a metric is the *confidence factor*, which is an aggregate of measures such feature/requirement implementation index, test pass rate, code check-in stability, and others.

Confidence Factor: A Measure of Likelihood That the Software Is Fault Free The confidence factor uses the concepts of stable and capable processes [3]. A *stable process* is predictable; its variation is under control (e.g., when representative variables are plotted on a control chart, they fall between the upper control limit and the lower control limit, which are based on quality controls such as Six Sigma [18]). For a process to be considered *capable*, it must be stable and the average of its plotted variables must fall within the specification limits, which vary for each process. A process that is under control, but does not meet its target levels, would be considered stable but not capable. More discussion of the process capability and stability concepts and the confidence factor will be provided in Chapter 9.

The confidence factor can be used to evaluate software quality and help in making deployment decisions. In order to achieve the long-term stability, the values of confidence factor (also called confidence level) should stay within a small range near the top of the scale. If the values of the confidence level are in this small range, this means that the code is not being broken through feature additions, the test cases are succeeding, and so forth. Consequently, the application can be released.

The corresponding graph illustrates sample confidence factor values over a given period. The process represented in Figure 2.10 is statistically stable, since it remains well within the control limits. However, the average confidence factor is relatively low. Thus, although the process is stable, it is not yet capable.

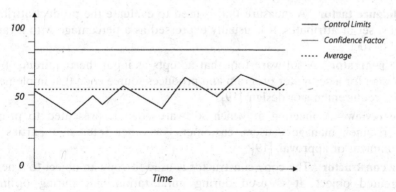

Figure 2.10 A control graph for the confidence factor variable.

To make this process capable, the group must determine what process modifications would raise the values of the confidence factor. The process needs to be modified and continue to be monitored. Once the confidence factor reaches an acceptable level (e.g., an average of 80%), the process is capable.

2.7 ACRONYMS

AI	Artificial intelligence
AP	Automatic programming
AJAX	Asynchronous JavaScript and XML
CMU SEI CMM	Carnegie Mellon University's Software Engineering Institute Capability and Maturity Model
EVM	Earned value management
IEEE	Institute of Electrical and Electronics Engineers
ISO	International Organization for Standardization
NASA	National Aeronautics and Space Administration
SOA	Service-oriented architecture
QA	Quality assurance
SQL	Structured Query Language
THCY	Technical head count—year

2.8 GLOSSARY

Ajax A web development technique for creating interactive Web applications.

architectural design The process of defining a collection of software components and their interfaces to establish the framework for the development of a computer system. [19]*

confidence factor A measure that is used to evaluate the product attribute or a set of attributes. It is usually expressed as a percentage with a range of 0–100.

code generator A software tool that accepts as input the requirements or design for a computer program and produces source code that implements the requirements or design. [19]*

code review A meeting at which software code is presented to project personnel, managers, users, customers, or other interested parties for comment or approval. [19]*

copy constructor The copy constructor is used to copy an object to a newly created object. It is used during initialization, not during ordinary assignment.

dangling pointer   A pointer that points to an invalid memory location.

efficiency   The degree to which a system or component performs its designated functions with minimum consumption of resources. [19]*

fault density   A measure of the number of faults per unit size that can be used to predict remaining faults by comparison with expected fault density in order to determine whether a sufficient amount of testing has been completed, and to establish standard fault densities for comparison and prediction.

fourth-generation languages   A computer language designed to improve the productivity achieved by high-order (third-generation) languages and, often, to make computing power available to nonprogrammers. [19]*

functional testing   Testing that ignores the internal mechanism of a system or component and focuses solely on the outputs generated in response to selected inputs and execution conditions. [19]*

Integrated Development Environments   IDE is a program that facilitates software development by providing an editor, a compiler, a debugger, and possibly other tools that work together.

Ishikawa (fishbone) diagrams   Often called cause-and-effect or fishbone diagrams, are used to display causal relationships by stating a quality characteristic or "effect" at the "head" of the diagram and then listing possible causes along branch arrows. [4]

maintainability   The ease with which a software system or component can be modified to correct faults, improve performance or other attributes, or adapt to a changed environment. [19]*

metric   A quantitative measure of the degree to which a system, component, or process possesses a given attribute. [19]*

overflow error   An error that occurs when the result of an arithmetic operation exceeds the size of the storage location designated to receive it. [19]*

Pareto diagram   A graphical representation of defect categories and frequencies that can be helpful to identify the source of chronic problems/ common causes in a process. The Pareto principle basically states that a "vital few" of the process characteristics cause most of the quality problems, while a "trivial many" of the process characteristics cause only a small portion of the quality problems. [4]

portability   The ease with which a system or component can be transferred from one hardware or software environment to another. [19]*

problem tracking system   A repository that is used for tracking of defects, change requests, and ideas.

service-oriented architecture   A conceptual business architecture where business functionality, or application logic, is made available to SOA users, or consumers, as shared, reusable services on an IT network. Services in an SOA are modules of business or application functionality with exposed interfaces, and invoked by messages. [20]

source control system A system that provides a central place where the team members can store and access their entire source code base. Exmples include SVN, CVS, RCS, Visual SourceSafe, and ClearCase.

test case A set of test inputs, execution conditions, and expected results developed for a particular objective, such as to exercise a particular program path or to verify compliance with a specific requirement. [19]*

* From IEEE Std. 610.12-1990, Copyright 1990, IEEE. All rights reserved.

2.9 REFERENCES

[1] Deming, W.E., *Out of Crisis*, MIT Center for Advance Engineering Study, Cambridge MA, 1986.

[2] Juran, J.M., "Product Quality: A Prescription for the West," *European Organization for Quality Control*, Paris, June 9–12, 1981.

[3] Humphrey,W., *Managing the Software Process*. Addison Wesley, 1990.

[4] Burnstein, I., *Practical Software Testing: A Process Oriented Approach*. Springer, 2002.

[5] Mays, R., "Defect Prevention and Total Quality Management," in *Total Quality Management for Software*, Schulmeyer, G. and McManus, J., eds., Van Nostrand Reinhold, New York, 1992.

[6] General Accounting Office—Information Management and Technology Division Report, *Patriot Missile Software Problem*, 1992, http://www.fas.org/spp/starwars/gao/im92026.htm (retrieved: July 7, 2006).

[7] Boehm, B., *Software Engineering Economics*. Prentice Hall, 1981.

[8] Boehm, B. and Basili, V., "Software Defect Reduction Top 10 List," *IEEE Computer*, Vol. 34, No. 1, January 2001.

[9] Royce, W., *Software Project Management: A Unified Framework*. Addison Wesley, 1998.

[10] Csikszentmihalyi, Mihaly, *Flow: The Psychology of Optimal Experience.* Harper and Row, 1990.

[11] McGarry, F.,Voltz, S., and Valett, J., "Determining Software Productivity Factors in the SEL," *Proceedings of the 11th Annual Software Engineering Workshop*, NASA Goddard Space Flight Center, December 1986.

[12] International Organization for Standardization, *ISO Standard 9126: Information Technology Software Product Evaluation—Quality Characteristics and Guidelines for Their Use*, Geneva, Switzerland, 1991.

[13] Institute of Electrical and Electronics Engineers, *IEEE Standard for Software Quality Metrics Methodology*. New York, 1998.

[14] Clarke, J., *Automated Test Generation (From a Behavior Model)*, November 2000, http:// www.stickyminds.com/se/S2018.asp (retrieved: July 8, 2005).

[15] Li, B., Blackboard Online Discussion Posting, CPSC 542, "Software Validation and Verification," Department of Computer Science, California State University–Fullerton, June 2006.

[16] Inquiry Board (Chairman: Prof. J. L. Lions), *ARIANE 5—Flight 501 Failure*, July 19, 1996, *http://www.ima.umn.edu/~arnold/disasters/ariane5rep.html* (retrieved: July 7, 2006).

[17] Weisstein, Eric W., "Roundoff Error," from *MathWorld*—A Wolfram Web Resource, 2002, http://mathworld.wolfram.com/RoundoffError.html (retrieved: July 8, 2006).

[18] Breyfogle III, F. W., *Implementing Six Sigma: Smarter Solutions Using Statistical Methods*. John Wiley & Sons, 2003.

[19] Institute of Electrical and Electronics Engineers, *IEEE Standard 610.12-1990—Glossary of Software Engineering Terminology*, 1990.

[20] Marks, E.A. and Bell, M., *Service-Oriented Architecture: A Planning and Implementation Guide for Business and Technology*. John Wiley & Sons, 2004.

2.10 EXERCISES

1. What are primary benefits of defect prevention?

2. Why do you think Deming's efforts originally failed in the United States?

3. Why is defect prevention often dismissed by software development organizations?

4. Which of the six principles of software defection prevention would you consider the most critical, or are they all equally important? Why?

5. What are primary benefits of automation?

6. Give examples of general and customized best practices and explain how (if at all) they can be automated. For example, think of a general best practice in requirements definition, and a software tool in the infrastructure that would support this practice. Similarly, think of a best coding practice and how it can be automated. Be as specific as possible.

7. Give real-world examples of software development activities that you believe can and should be automated. What cannot be automated?

8. What data, do you think, should be collected in order to facilitate defect prevention throughout the life cycle? Be as specific as possible.

9. What measurements could be used to support software development–related decisions?

10. Why do you think traditional (manual) defect prevention approaches are rarely used?

CHAPTER 3

INITIAL PLANNING AND INFRASTRUCTURE

One does not plan and then try to make circumstances fit those plans. One tries
to make plans fit the circumstances.

—General George S. Patton, Jr.

3.1 INTRODUCTION

The infrastructure is the foundation of our methodology and the backbone
supporting a project. As we described in the previous chapter, this infrastructure includes both the people and the technology. The roles of the people in
the project must be clearly defined and their use of the supporting technologies well understood. Factors such as the experience, knowledge, and expertise
of the people within the infrastructure must be assessed. Additionally, the
status of the current technologies must be evaluated.

For a new project, it is important that the infrastructure is formed early in
the life cycle, preferably as soon as the vision for the product has been created.
Establishing the infrastructure early in the development cycle supports
comprehensive defect prevention during software development: starting from
requirements elicitation and tracking, through design, construction, coding,
testing, and deployment. For an existing project, it is critical that the methodology is introduced in stages by gradually redefining the existing roles of
people, progressively adding new technology, and introducing best practices

Automated Defect Prevention: Best Practices in Software Management, by Dorota Huizinga
and Adam Kolawa
Copyright © 2007 John Wiley & Sons, Inc.

on a step-by-step basis. *The infrastructure carries defect prevention from one project to another. Thus, it needs to be flexible and adaptable.*

This chapter describes the initial software development plan that includes the definition of general infrastructure necessary to support our methodology: the roles of the team members, the supporting technologies, and the interaction of the team members with the technology.

3.2   INITIAL SOFTWARE DEVELOPMENT PLAN

The components of the initial software development plan include a preliminary description of the product, an assessment of the existing people and technology resources, a definition of the needed infrastructure, and an adaptation of a software process.

3.2.1   Product

A product is the outcome of the software development process, including all the artifacts of the project, such as requirements specification, design, test plans, code, documentation, manuals, and training materials.

For a new project in the initial phase of the development process, the product definition is usually vague or incomplete. However, it is an essential best practice to create a *Vision and Scope* [1] document at this point. Created by the project manager or the architect, this document provides a general view of what the project aims to accomplish in the long term, and what restrictions exist in the short term. Based on this document, an infrastructure can be created to support the initial project's needs.

An existing project has a current version of the product and its supporting technologies. These technologies should be assessed, verified, and then configured for integration with ADP. For existing projects with faulty behavior, our methodology will help to remedy the problems by applying root cause analysis and recommending best practices supported by the necessary infrastructure. For stable projects looking to add product features, our methodology will specify both the infrastructure and those best practices that will verify that previous functionality is not negatively affected and defects are prevented as new features are added.

3.2.2   People

People are both the most important and most challenging resource to manage. Thus, identifying roles and matching people to roles requires prudent decision-making based on a careful examination of project needs and people skills. Each organization has its own structure; thus, many different roles for project participants can be defined. However, for exemplifying our methodology we will use the following five roles: *project manager, architect, developer, test engineer, and system administrator*. Later in this chapter, we will show how these traditional roles should be extended to support ADP. We will also describe how to define project groups to carry out the projects efficiently.

Often, there are other people involved in the project; they can be customers, partners, or business experts qualified to guide the product development. We will refer to all the people who directly or indirectly benefit from the project as project stakeholders. In its initial planning phase the stakeholders should be involved in helping to define the overall product goals and requirements.

3.2.3 Technology

Configurable technology is necessary for organizations to create their products and sustain their processes. In addition to each developer's *integrated development environment* (IDE),[a] our methodology defines the minimum amount of technology needed for the groups to collaborate properly on a project. This minimum technology infrastructure, which will be explained in detail later in this chapter, includes a *source control system*,[b] an *automated build system*,[c] a *problem tracking system*,[d] and *an automated reporting system*.[e] Additionally, this minimum technology infrastructure helps identify the groups and the projects.

3.2.4 Process

A software process is a sequence of tasks defined with the intention of producing a high-quality product on time and within budget. Many organizations do not have formalized software processes. Others follow strict models such as the waterfall or unified process. However, most organizations apply the best practices from many models to fit their needs. The process is dictated by the management, the organizational needs, and the type of project—and it should be documented. The process defines project schedule, milestones, and deliverables—and it has a direct influence on the budget.

---

[a] An integrated development environment (IDE) is a set of integrated tools for software development, which commonly combines a text editor, compiler, linker, debugging tools, profiler, and sometimes version control and dependency maintenance.
[b] A system used to keep track of all source code and revisions in its repository.
[c] A system that builds the application automatically by executing the required build procedure steps at the scheduled time without any human intervention.
[d] A system in which defects, issues, change requests, and programmers' ideas are stored and tracked.
[e] A system that stores information about the project status and generates reports to help in decision-making and processes analysis.

If the organization does not have a software process in place, the introduction of ADP will help *define it through the application of its six principles and the best practices described in this book*. For organizations with existing well-defined software processes, our methodology merely *extends* them in such way that defect prevention becomes an intrinsic element of software development.

3.3   BEST PRACTICES FOR CREATING PEOPLE INFRASTRUCTURE

Forming a people infrastructure requires identifying groups within the organization, ensuring that each group has supporting technologies, training the groups, and then making sure that each group follows a group workflow by applying ADP's best practices. The supporting technology within the infrastructure thus facilitates applying these best practices consistently, thoroughly, and efficiently within the group and the organization.

As described in the previous chapter, the ADP should be introduced into the organization one group at a time. Thus, before practicing our methodology, it is necessary to identify how the organization can be organized into groups that are logical for defect prevention, identify a pilot group to start practicing the methodology, and implement a supporting technology infrastructure for that pilot group. Having these components in place ensures that the pilot group members adopt a workflow that integrates our methodology into the full software life cycle. Once the pilot group is successfully practicing ADP, work can begin on building an infrastructure and training schedule for the second group. This process is repeated until all groups are fully practicing it.

3.3.1   Defining Groups

An important aspect of defining groups is determining the size of the groups. Ideally, groups should be small, composed of five to eight people. However, depending on the project and on the organization size, the groups can be larger, consisting of 10 or even 20 people. Smaller group size, however, facilitates team communication and coordination of tasks. It also helps in fostering positive group culture.

To determine how the organization's software development projects should be organized into logical groups, first an inventory of the existing projects needs to be completed. Specifically, for each of the organization's current development projects, the following must be determined:

- Where does the development take place?
- What are the programming languages used to implement the project's code?

Project	Development Location	Build/Testing Location	Projects with Shared Code?	Source Control System	Language	Testing Environment
Project A	Location 1	Location 1	Yes, C and E	RCS	Java	Windows
Project B	Location 2	Location 2	Yes, D	SVN	C++/Java (GUI)	Windows
Project C	Location 1	Location 1	Yes, A and E	RCS	Java	Windows
Project D	Location 2	Location 1	Yes, B	SVN	C++/Java (GUI)	Windows
Project E	Location 1	Location 1	Yes, A and C	RCS	Java	Windows
Project F	Location 2	Location 1	No	SVN	C++	Win/Sol/Linux

Figure 3.1 Tracking details about groups.[f]

- Where do the builds and testing take place, and how frequently are they performed?
- What are the project's target platforms?
- Does the project share code with any other projects?

These details could be tracked in a table such as the one shown in Figure 3.1.

Taking an inventory of the projects yields the information needed to determine how those projects can be organized into logical groups.

As a rule of thumb, all developers who are working on shared code or closely related code form a logical group. To confirm whether two or more projects form a logical group, one should ask the following question: "If I move a developer from Project A to Project B, will that developer be able to start working the next day?" If the answer to this question is positive, then all the developers who work on these two projects could form one logical group.

Thus, the projects referenced in Figure 3.1 should be divided into the following groups:

- *Group 1*: Projects A, C, and E
- *Group 2*: Project B and D
- *Group 3*: Project F

Projects A, C, and E form a logical group because they all share code, they have the same development, build, and testing location, and they use the same type of source control system [2] [3], language, and testing platform. Projects

[f] RCS [2] and SVN [3] are source control systems.

B and D are developed in two different locations, but they share code as well as the same build/testing location, type of source control system, languages, and testing platform; consequently, they should form one group. Project F has little in common with the other projects, so it forms its own logical group.

3.3.2   Determining a Location for Each Group's Infrastructure

An infrastructure needs to be implemented for each logical group. Generally, the group's infrastructure should be implemented in the same location as the related projects' build/testing location. However, teams that have a wide geographic distribution do not pose a problem. In fact, the infrastructure can actually help bridge the gap across multiple locations, even when the locations are on different continents. This is very useful for organizations that outsource work. In these situations, it is common to have management in one location and the developers in a different location. Another common outsourcing situation is to have all project team members concentrated in one remote location. In either case, it is recommended that the infrastructure be placed in the same location as the developers; system performance is improved by having the infrastructure close to developers, and there is no advantage to having the system close to managers. If the connections are not fast enough, the infrastructure can be mirrored in a remote location.

3.3.3   Defining People Roles

Traditionally, groups are made of architects, who design the product; developers, who write code to implement the architect's design; test engineers, who test the developers' code; system administrators, who configure and maintain technology infrastructure; and project managers, who oversee the entire development process. ADP additionally defines the responsibilities of defect detection and defect prevention for team members. Defect detection responsibilities extend testing roles to include root cause analysis of defects and recording of vital defects in the problem tracking system. Defect prevention responsibilities include the development and implementation of a defect prevention plan based on the root cause analysis performed by the defect detection team.

After observing numerous development groups and researching many software process models, including *agile development*, we have learned that defect prevention works best when the responsibilities of the architects, developers, and testers are extended to include defect detection and prevention tasks. For the purpose of ADP, the people roles are redefined as follows:

Project manager: The project manager is responsible for delivering quality software products on time, with the designed functionality, and within budget. The project manager is responsible for primary business decisions and relies strongly on the expertise of the architect. The project manager assigns tasks and responsibilities to the team members, including the roles of the defect detection and prevention, and promotes ADP practices.

Architect: The architect is responsible for all primary technical decisions of the project, including the definition of its functionality, design of the underlying architecture, and supervision of acceptance testing. The architect also makes a final recommendation concerning software deployment by statistically monitoring variables that represent different aspects of the project status. Responsible for most of the technical decisions, the architect's expertise must be beyond dispute and is the foundation of her leadership.

Additional responsibilities of the architect may include verifying that the application is implemented according to specifications and improving the processes used for building software. In this latter role, the architect becomes the main figure in using ADP methodology, chaperoning and guiding the process throughout the entire software development life cycle. Through feedback loops within the software development life cycle, the architect, in collaboration with the testing team, correlates each vital and severe defect or issue with the particular process, and takes appropriate steps to correct the process. In some organizations, however, the primary defect prevention responsibilities can be delegated to a lead developer, or a QA group, reducing the burden placed on the architect.

Developer: In our methodology, the developer's role is consistent with its traditional definition (i.e., the developer is a programmer who is concerned with one or more facets of the software development). At a minimum, this person is responsible for writing source code based on the design created by the architect and verifying that the code is correct. To follow Deming's philosophy, the same person who creates a product must be responsible for verifying that it is built correctly. The developers, not testers, are therefore responsible for writing test cases that verify that each piece of code operates as expected.

Test engineer: The test engineer is the architect's and lead developer's essential partner in defect prevention. Test engineers and the architect work together to customize the methodology so that it not only prevents common development problems, but also prevents defects unique to the team and project. The test engineer needs to understand how the code is built, then try to break it to expose any hidden defects. Each severe defect found is then used to fuel the process improvement procedure discussed in the previous chapter. Each time the testing team exposes a severe defect, they work with the architect to diagnose the root cause of the defect, and to design and implement a defect prevention mechanism to prevent this defect from recurring. Test engineers also add to the test suite one or more test cases that verify that the defect has been resolved. The goal is to expose as many defects as possible to correct any process weaknesses that have permitted unique defects that have eluded the standard defect prevention best practices.

In some organizations, QA groups hold roles similar to those of test engineers. However, more mature organizations tend to have independent QA

Group	Projects	Managers	Architects	Developers	Testers
Group 1	Project A				
	Project C				
	Project E				
Group 2	Project B				
	Project D				
Group 3	Project F				

Figure 3.2 A table for mapping team members to roles.

groups that conduct audits verifying whether the standards and processes are properly followed. In such cases, QA groups should assume defect detection and prevention roles through collaboration with both the architect and the testing team.

System administrator: The system administrator is responsible for maintaining, upgrading, and verifying that the technology infrastructure supporting the project is functioning correctly. Additionally, the system administrator works with the architect (or the lead developer) to configure the technology infrastructure in order to support defect prevention practices.

Group adoption of these redefined roles is essential for the successful introduction of ADP as well as for nurturing the group culture, which we will discuss later in this chapter.

Depending on the organization and project size, one person can assume multiple roles within a single project, or different roles for different projects. We recommend mapping team members to groups and roles by completing a table such as the one depicted in Figure 3.2.

The key requirement is that the team's architect or lead developer and testing team members are willing and able to extend their traditional roles. Testing team members need to adopt a new approach to uncovering defects. Each time a severe defect is found, they need to consider what other defects might be related to it and how to abstract a general defect prevention mechanism from it. The most talented testing engineers have a sharp intuition about where defects originate, and they can write test cases to check whether the anticipated defects are actually present. They attempt to break the system and understand the root cause of defects. This requires that they are familiar with the overall system architecture as well as have an intimate understanding of that part of the architecture related to that defect. Moreover, to help the team improve the process and monitor attempted process improvements, testing team members must understand the statistics behind measuring, stabilizing, and managing processes, as well as how to identify whether a special case or variation is affecting the process.

The architect needs not only to be able to design the system, but also to ensure that this system is built properly and works properly. She needs to be astute and experienced, and have a keen sense of where problems can occur in the software development life cycle as well as the ability to abstract from technical details to a higher-level understanding of project and process operations.

Both testers and the architect must be able to determine a method by which the team designs, writes, deploys, and monitors the project in a way that will prevent defects from recurring; for each severe defect found they need to adopt the mantra "I will find this defect only once." To do this, they need to be skilled at determining the root cause of a defect, and determining how this single defect can provide insight into improving the team's process.

If an organization that is introducing our methodology does not have the same people roles, defect detection and prevention roles should be assigned to other group members with responsibilities similar to those defined above.

3.3.4 Establishing a Training Program

Once the people roles have been defined, it is important to establish a training program for the pilot group. Since the pilot group is relatively small, initially this program could be informal and could take place during regular group meetings. However, once ADP is expanded to the organization level, training should be comprehensive, ongoing, and consist of the following components:

- Establishing a list of required training dependent on people skills and expertise
- Training activities for learning new ADP practices and policies
- Training activities for learning how to use the technology infrastructure
- Creating and maintaining a training database to track completed and future training
- Establishing training for common practices across the organization
- Updating the training program based on defects found to prevent their recurrence

3.3.5 Cultivating a Positive Group Culture

ADP can be introduced at any phase of the group's software development life cycle, from the start of the planning phase to immediately before release. However, for our methodology to become an enduring part of the project, it must be supported by a strong group culture. Group culture is a development team's way of working together, including their shared habits, traditions, and beliefs. A positive group culture should promote code ownership, group cooperation, peer learning, common working hours, and mutual respect. When managers and leaders focus on developing and supporting a positive group culture, the team is typically more self-regulating, creative, effective, and satisfied.

The most important element of such a group culture is the sense of code ownership. Code is the group's greatest asset because their code is the show-case for all of their hard work. It also serves as a means of communication: developers exchange the majority of their ideas by reading and writing code. Just as mathematicians communicate their ideas most precisely with equations, developers communicate their ideas most precisely with code. Thus, by protecting the quality of their code, developers can preserve their best ideas in the clearest, most concise way possible.

The goal is to build a culture where the developers' attitude toward the code reflects the code's importance. Developers should show that they care about the code because caring about the code is synonymous with caring about the group. It is thus fundamental that everyone feels they have a stake in maintaining a high-quality product. This positive attitude also helps filter the problem developers out of the group. In an environment where group members feel a strong investment in code quality, any developer who does not care about the code will withdraw from the group. Conversely, most group developers will soon become frustrated with someone who constantly introduces problems into the code and they will try to help this developer to improve. If the developer gets better, the group becomes stronger; otherwise, group conflict will generally lead the developer to leave the group.

DEVELOPER'S TESTIMONIAL

Some of the tenets of XP are highly conducive to generating a positive group culture. They include open workspaces, face-to-face communication, pair programming, and a high level of interaction and collaboration. Collaboration and camaraderie are crucial to developing a positive group culture. When workers work together face to face and interact, they feel more a part of the group. This is in stark contrast to the stereotypical "silent coder" who locks himself in a room, works all night, and emerges with the final product. Such a solitary approach often leads to burnout and a poor group culture.

—Joe T. Marcelino, Senior Software Engineer

Another important aspect of group culture is promoting common work hours among group members. For example, it may be most efficient for all group members to have work hours between 9 A.M. and 6 P.M., or a similar schedule. The important point to note is that it could be counterproductive to have developers in the same group work on different schedules, as this would impede verbal communication. Thus, it is necessary to establish core work hours, for example from 10 A.M. to 3 P.M. Some team members could come in early and others later, as long as there is a core time for communication and meetings.

3.4 BEST PRACTICES FOR CREATING TECHNOLOGY INFRASTRUCTURE

Not only is the software that is being developed complex, but so is the software supporting its development. Technologies that assist in software development have become quite sophisticated, often requiring customization and intensive training.

Our methodology defines a flexible technology infrastructure by identifying its minimum requirements, and providing examples of its intermediate and expanded configurations.

In defining the technology infrastructure, ADP describes necessary features rather than specific tools. We have selected only a basic subset of features that are essential for building an effective infrastructure. Many existing commercial and noncommercial tools support these as well as more advanced features. Organizations that have an infrastructure in place should identify features that already exist and use ADP to identify those features that are needed to improve their infrastructure.

Creating an adaptable and sophisticated technology infrastructure is, in and of itself, a production process. Many people in the software industry believe that developers can build their own tools and manage their use. However, in any mature industry, a division of labor is necessary: those who work on production lines do not build the tools used on the production line themselves. Specialization is essential. If development groups have to write code outside of their area of expertise to build in-house tools, an increased number of defects is inevitable.

The key element of the technology infrastructure is an automated reporting system, which we describe in detail in the subsequent sections.

3.4.1 Automated Reporting System

An automated reporting system is a central component of the technology infrastructure. It integrates with and gathers information from other elements of the technology infrastructure. Depending on the composition of the technology infrastructure, the reporting system should seamlessly collect data from the source control system, automated build system, problem tracking system, and other systems as needed. Based on the collected data, the reporting system should calculate project metrics and product status data and generate reports for team members to review. Project metrics may include cost and schedule status indexes such as actual cost versus budgeted cost and actual schedule versus planned schedule. Product metrics may include the number of implemented features, the size of code (SLOC), and the number of passed tests. Process indicators may contain, for example, adherence to coding standards metrics, test pass rates, defect rates, the number of modified files, and the number of functions/procedures added or deleted. Other indicators may be included such as a requirements stability index, or deployment readiness confidence factor. The reporting system's metrics should be configurable and used consistently with the organization and project needs. Reports should be customized to both the needs of the project and the individuals using them.

Additionally, reports such as the Current Activity Log (CAL) can be used to review the team's effort on a daily basis (Figure 3.3). The CAL report shows the team members their highest priority tasks and notifications from the other systems in the infrastructure. This allows team members to view all the most important work activities that have been assigned to their group without having to access each system separately and without having to analyze an overwhelming number of items that are low priority or assigned to another team. The team members should review the CAL report and reprioritize their activities on a daily basis.

Current Activity Log (CAL): Team A

Automated Build Errors

Module	File	Line	Error	Priority
Module D	FileD2	32	illegal...	High
Module H	FileH7	119	identifier not...	Medium
Module B	FileB3	83	nonstandard...	Low

Problem Tracking

Problem ID	Description	Status	Testing	Priority
27	Login...	In Progress	Failed Test	High
13	Database...	In Progress	Not Tested	High
84	Email...	Unresolved	Not Tested	Medium

Requirements & Testing

Req. ID	Description	Status	Testing	Priority
58	Admin...	In Progress	Failed Test	High
39	Sorting...	In Progress	Not Tested	High
29	Exporting...	Unimplemented	Not Tested	Medium

Figure 3.3   The current activity log.

Role of the Reporting System   The automated reporting system is essential to sustaining the ADP processes in place. Because of the continuous feedback provided by the reporting system, potential problems can be identified and corrected early, before they propagate through the product. Additionally, the trend indicators of the project progress can be periodically evaluated, and the application of general and customized best practices can be reassessed. Team members can inspect and evaluate metrics, such as number of tests passed, and whether the style and coding rules are being followed. From the reports, the architect can decide whether the groups are working on the correct requirements needed for the project, and whether the groups are properly refactoring the code. Many implementation defects can be caught early or prevented altogether based on the information provided by these reports.

In addition, reports can be used by the project managers to review project management metrics. Managers, for example, can estimate the team's productivity and consequently the completion time for particular projects. The reports can also provide comprehensive views of the project status, including project cost and schedule index. Figure 3.4 provides an example of such a report.

The bar on the right shows the timeline of the project from the start to the deadline. As the project progresses, the bar fills from left to right. For example, project "Database Checker 1.0" is in its initial phase, so most of the bar is empty. The color of the filled portion of the bar indicates whether the project is on schedule. The project "Painting Tool 2.0" is within its projected schedule, which is indicated by its color (dark gray in Figure 3.4, but

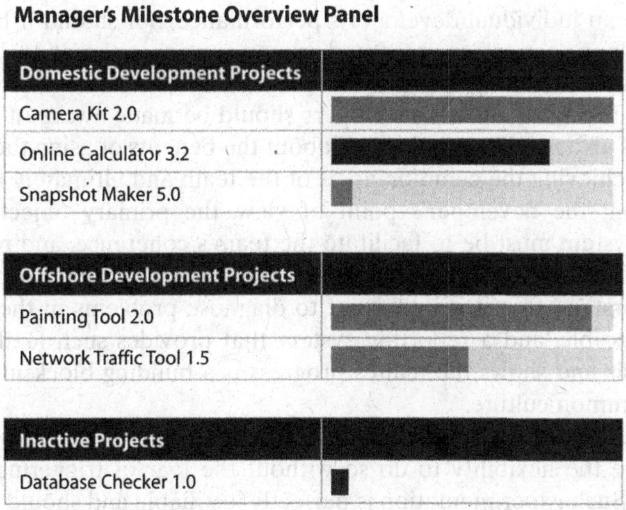

Manager's Milestone Overview Panel

Domestic Development Projects	
Camera Kit 2.0	
Online Calculator 3.2	
Snapshot Maker 5.0	

Offshore Development Projects	
Painting Tool 2.0	
Network Traffic Tool 1.5	

Inactive Projects	
Database Checker 1.0	

Figure 3.4   The Manager's Panel provides a high-level overview of the project status. Dark gray would appear green on-screen to show a project is on schedule. Black would be red on-screen to indicate a project is behind schedule.

green on a screen). However, the project "Online Calculator 3.2" is behind schedule, which is indicated by its color (black in Figure 3.4, but red on a screen). *Actual versus planned project progress* is calculated by evaluating the implementation status of requirements, test results, and other factors that contribute to meeting the desired level of confidence predefined for this project.

For example, if the beta milestone was to have 80% of requirements finished by a given date, and 85% of requirements were implemented by that date, the slider on the screen would be green to indicate the milestone was met. If only 60% of requirements were implemented, the slider would be red to indicate the milestone was not met. Intermediate values would be yellow and all color/milestone parameters would be set in the initial stage.

Throughout this book, we will describe many examples of metrics and reports generated by the reporting system.

3.4.2 Policy for Use of Automated Reporting System

One of the important human factors to consider when using a reporting system is the fact that automatic and seamless collection of data can make developers feel constantly watched, and uncomfortable. Using data from the reporting system in an insensitive manner can cause a stressful working environment, reduce trust in management, and ultimately have the very counterproductive effect of inhibiting the developers' creativity. Developers must *embrace the infrastructure, in particular the reporting system, for the successful implementation of ADP.* Thus, the reporting system should never be used by management to evaluate an individual developer's performance, nor should it be used for any disciplinary action, or construed in any way as a threat to individuals. Making sure that the reporting system is not used to assess performance of individuals is critical and all developers should be made aware of this policy. Developers also need to be educated about the benefits of using the reporting system in achieving the common goals of the team and ultimately the organization. From the developer's point of view, the primary objective of the reporting system must be to facilitate the team's coherence, and provide the team with instantaneous feedback when unexpected problems occur. Developers understand that it is important to diagnose problems in the system as early as possible, and a reporting system that provides such feedback on a regular basis and shows the team's progress is a building block in creating a positive common culture.

If a developer is focused on creating a unique or innovative solution, she should have the flexibility to do so without the fear of triggering excessive error flags. Such experimentation is perfectly justifiable and should be encouraged regardless of the results shown by the reporting system. On the other hand, if a developer mistakenly linked an old file to a newer version of the source code, and consequently caused a regression system failure, the correction needs to be done immediately so that the old and new versions are not inadvertently interchanged. The reporting system can help identify such a problem quickly and facilitate its resolution.

In addition, it is very important that the developers be allowed to run all static analysis scans and tests, and view their own results before they are required to check in their code to the source control system and have their submission used by the reporting system. Such a self-assessment can prevent unnecessary and misleading reporting and also create a positive sense of accomplishment.

Therefore, the following section defines a general policy for use of the reporting system. This policy should be customized to project and organization needs.

The Reporting System Is a Developer and Team Analysis Tool, Not Big Brother The reporting system collects data from many sources and summarizes this data in report format; it therefore has the potential to be the developer's valuable ally; however, if misused, it will be seen as her worst enemy. Therefore, the developer and her team should be given first access to defect reports specifying her (team's) development problems and a reasonable amount of time to fix these problems or explain them to management. These reports should never be used as a management tool for making cursory judgments and subsequently punishing the developers. If misused in this manner, such reports could be frequently misinterpreted by managers and deeply resented by developers. *If used appropriately, developers will want to use the reporting system because it gives them instantaneous feedback and helps them improve the code quality.*

DEVELOPER'S TESTIMONIAL

This is a difficult problem. Even though management may not want to use the reporting system to evaluate their employees, we're all human and the results will probably find their way into how we look at our employees. It's my belief that employees will know this, so the task is to prove that other methods are used in evaluating a person (i.e., there may be an onus on management to prove that they are using other aspects, like project success, to evaluate an employee). Additionally, although statements promising that the reporting system will not be used as a "Big Brother" are necessary, they are not sufficient in themselves. Obvious as it sounds, management members must make sure they don't spot a lack of code check-ins and say, "I noticed you didn't check anything in yesterday, why weren't you working?"

—Eugene Ngo, Software Developer

Use of the Reporting System Should Be Open and Transparent; It Should Not Be Constrained by Group or Role Although some organizations may make different parts of the system visible only to certain groups and roles, we do not recommend this, except in the case of defect reports as discussed above. Limited visibility may lead to a culture of secrecy that will only increase the perception of the system acting as Big Brother. Maximizing system openness and availability for everyone is important for achieving the comprehensive views required to identify trends. Having full visibility within a development group helps the team members see where defects occur, pinpoint the cause of the defects, and determine whether these defects are prevented from happening again.

Reporting System Reports Should Be Reviewed Frequently by All Involved Teams and Individuals Once a reporting system is correctly introduced into the organization, a policy should be implemented for periodically reviewing results from the reporting system; the more frequently the better. While all team members could benefit from reviewing reports, the architect or a lead developer should be responsible for evaluating them on a regular basis. If problems are observed, they should be addressed and resolved immediately.

The results of regression tests and any new failures that were introduced since the last reporting date are of primary importance for the review. From the report, it should be determined whether the regression tests should be modified, how the failures occurred, and how the code should be fixed. Although this review may take an hour or two, it is vital because it creates a consistent process in which defects are being investigated and fixed rather than accumulated.

Similarly, the managers should view the reports in order to assess the project progress status with respect to schedule, milestones, and costs. If delays or budget overruns are observed, their causes can be studied and mitigated early in the cycle.

3.4.3 Minimum Technology Infrastructure

In addition to the reporting system, each group's infrastructure will generally require the following elements at minimum:

- *Integrated Development Environment (IDE)*: IDE is a software development support system with a built-in editor and compiler. A code compiler is needed to compile any code before it is checked into the source control system. The IDE is normally installed on each developer's workstation and should include all technologies available in the shared infrastructure that facilitate coding, such as automated testing and static analysis tools.

- *Source Control System:*[g] The source control system is a database where source code is stored. Its purpose is to provide a central place where the team members can store and access the entire source code base. We use this as a generic term for both version control systems and configuration management systems [4]. The code is organized, versioned, and accessible to all team members. Conflicts due to parallel updates are automatically detected, and rollback as well as merge features are supported.
- *Automated Build System*: An automated build is a process for building an application on a periodic basis by automatically executing the required build steps, including compiling and linking of the code at the scheduled time.
- *Problem Tracking System*: A problem tracking system is a repository for storing and tracking of defects and issues, as well as the developers' ideas for improving the application. Defects are stored so they can be tracked, analyzed, and ultimately prevented from recurring. Once resolved and prevented from recurring, defects are removed from the repository. Developers' ideas are stored so they can be recalled and used for future development. The problem tracking system can also be used for storing requirements, feature requests, and tracking feature and requirement changes, if the project does not use a separate requirements management system.
- *Shared Project Artifact Repository and Other Tools*: A shared project artifact repository should be created to store, organize, and access the documents that are created throughout all the phases. This repository can be a directory created in the source control system, a directory on a server with all the documents with a spreadsheet to summarize their information, or even an entire separate system. Any additional verification technologies or tools that the team is currently using and any tools that the group finds useful can and should be used with the infrastructure. For example, if the team already has a test suite or currently uses a project management program to oversee project progress, the related technologies should be integrated into the infrastructure.

Figure 3.5 shows the minimum infrastructure.

For a project to be successful, a set of general best practices must be implemented to ensure the proper workflow and effective use of the infrastructure. We will now describe how it should be set up, controlled, and supported.

Developing and Compiling Code   As shown in Figure 3.5, the supporting infrastructure and workflow begins at the developer's workstation where

---

[g] A generic term for a version control system or configuration management system.

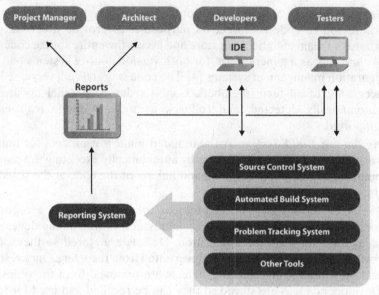

Figure 3.5   The minimum technology infrastructure for ADP.

the code is built. Typically, developers use IDEs when creating their code. Developers should resolve all compilation errors and compile-level warnings before checking in their code to the source control system. Developers also may use the desktop as a mini-testing system to verify the code that has been compiled. Software built on code with compilation problems has little chance of achieving its quality goals.

Like other practices, this practice cannot be implemented all at once. In most situations, it is not practical to suddenly require the development team to clean all the compiler warnings for the entire existing code base. A more reasonable strategy is to require that any new code compile cleanly.

Developers should use the reporting system graphs to verify that their recently added code did not introduce compilation problems into the build. For instance, if they see that warnings are increasing rather than decreasing, they should explore the situation and take corrective measures, such as requesting additional training.

Ultimately, the developers should also be able to use other technologies available in the infrastructure, such as automated testing and static analysis tools. Their code should pass all the required project standards before it is committed to the source control system.

Role of the Source Control System   Once code compiles on the developer's workstation, it is checked into the source code control system. The source control system gives each developer the freedom and safety to write, modify, and refactor code on her workstation. If any code change turns out to be undesirable, the developer can easily undo these changes by reverting to the code in the source control system. While one developer works on changes, the rest of the developers within the group can always access previous working versions of the code.

Having a source code repository is also a prerequisite for the periodically scheduled automated build system. All of the files needed for the build process should be in the source control system so they can be accessed by the scheduled build process.

Role of the Automated Build System   The automated build system is needed in order to create a repeatable and sustainable build process to avoid errors associated with linking of incorrect libraries or using an outdated version of the code. The automatic build contains make files and scripts to communicate with the compiler. Those scripts are used to access the source control system in order to perform compilation and linking of all files in the project. A scheduled task initiates the script that builds the application. If the automatic build system fails to create the application properly, compilation results will display warnings to the appropriate developers.

This entire process should take place at least once a day, preferably at night so the project status can be reassessed in the morning. Additionally, each night, all the source code and other related files should be backed up from the source control system. This redundancy is necessary so the project can be restored in case of unexpected system failures.

Role of the Problem Tracking System   The problem tracking system records and tracks unresolved defects, issues, and developer ideas. Severe defects recorded in the problem tracking system are analyzed to identify their root causes. People who are assigned defect prevention roles (e.g., testers, QA staff, or architects) are responsible for analyzing the defects and developing new customized defect prevention practices. Resolved defects are removed from the problem tracking system.

Additionally, the problem tracking system should be used to track project issues and developers' ideas for product improvements. As described in an example later in this chapter, even if they do not require immediate attention, issues and ideas should be recorded so they can be recalled and revisited later and/or during subsequent product releases.

The problem tracking system can also be used for tracking features and requirements if the team does not have a separate requirements management system. In such situations, it is important to configure it in such way that the reporting system can generate separate views of features and defects or issues.

Role of Shared Project Artifact Repository and Other Tools   Project requirements, design, and its implementation status are subject to perpetual changes. Having a shared document repository provides a common reference point to all stakeholders and assures that everybody involved in the project has the most recent versions of the documents. Also, policies and practices should be stored in the shared repository so developers can easily access and review them.

3.4.4   Intermediate Technology Infrastructure

The minimum infrastructure can be extended by adding more technology such as a requirements management system, a regression-testing system, or any other support tools necessary for the project. When the organization matures in auto-mating its processes, and in using ADP, the need for more technologies will become apparent. However, as in any other ADP practice, these technologies should be introduced gradually and after proper training of the involved team members. A sample intermediate infrastructure is depicted in Figure 3.6.

The elements of the intermediate infrastructure may include:

- *A Requirements Management System*: A system used for recording and tracking product requirements. This system can be a simple, manually-

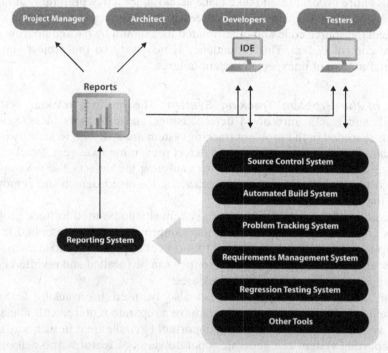

Figure 3.6   A sample intermediate technology infrastructure for ADP.

maintained spreadsheet table that stores the requirements and tracks changes to the requirements, or it can be a sophisticated repository with features such as the automatic tracing of tests to use cases and back to the requirements, requirements change rate, and statistics about the implementation status.

- *A Regression Testing System*: A regression system is the set of core existing tests for the entire code base that is executed on a regular basis (preferably nightly, after each automated build). Its purpose is to help determine whether code modifications caused previously working functionality to fail.

Role of the Requirements Management System   Using a requirements management system helps in tracking requirement changes and notifying developers about such changes. This is an essential defect prevention practice because requirement changes are one of the leading causes of software project delays and cost overruns. Additionally, the system records requirements implementation status that can be traced through the development phases to the corresponding test cases, helping to verify that requirements are implemented correctly.

Role of the Regression Testing System   Regression testing is the process of running all existing test cases and verifying that previous functionality of the code was not negatively affected by recent code modifications [5]. The purpose of regression testing is to detect unexpected faults, especially those faults that occur because a developer did not fully understand the internal code dependencies when modifying or extending code that previously functioned correctly.

3.4.5 Expanded Technology Infrastructure

The intermediate infrastructure can be further expanded by adding more technology such as an automatic code generator, static analyzer, automatic testing system, and other software tools, as deemed necessary for the project. A sample of an expanded infrastructure is depicted in Figure 3.7.

The elements of the expanded infrastructure may include:

- *Automatic Code Generator*: A system that converts design artifacts (such as class diagrams) into implementation artifacts such as object-oriented code classes. In addition, it is possible to create class diagrams such as UML (Unified Modeling Language) graphs from the code.
- *Static Analyzer*: A system that scans the source code to verify the code adheres to a set of predefined rules. Static analyzers include style checkers, which identify excessive error-prone code complexity or scan for required practices in coding.

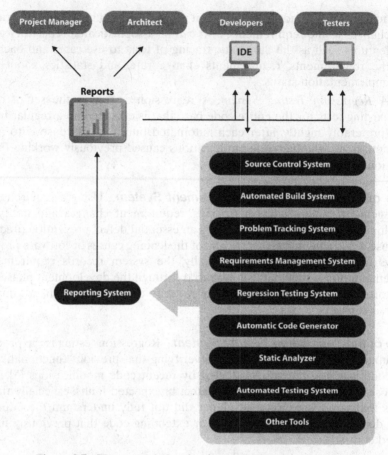

Figure 3.7   The expanded technology infrastructure for ADP.

- *Automated Testing System*: This system includes technologies that support automatic generation and/or execution of tests for unit, integration, functional, performance, and load testing. In addition to reporting on traditional defects such as missing or mismatched parameters, or null pointers, such systems can provide comprehensive information about product quality such as achievable code coverage or average response time.

Role of the Automatic Code Generator   An automatic code generator can be helpful in both defect prevention and reduction of coding time. Use of a code generator reduces human errors by automatically converting high-level artifacts into code.

Role of the Static Analyzer Coding standards are programming rules that reduce the probability of introducing defects into applications, increase code maintainability and can prevent an entire class of defects. Static analyzers scan the code to validate its adherence to such standards.

Role of the Automated Testing System Unit testing involves testing software code at its smallest functional point, which is typically a single class. By testing every unit individually, most of the errors that might be introduced into the code over the course of a project can be detected very early and prevented from propagating to other parts of the project.

In many cases, tests can be generated automatically for units, and then progressively for submodules and modules, as integration testing moves forward. Similarly, performance and load testing can be done automatically to uncover possible response-time problems as early as possible in the development cycle. Automatic generation of tests not only assures thoroughness of the testing process but also prevents injection of possible errors during the manual creation of test harnesses.

The policies for use of the above systems will be described in subsequent chapters.

DEVELOPER'S TESTIMONIAL

I would additionally include technology to collect and track discrepancies and other related actions regarding improving/fixing the project's products and processes. The system we use tracks software, document, and process issues. It is also integrated into our baseline system such that no products can be delivered if there are any open issues in the system. It is important to have a tracking system of this nature to help ensure problems are addressed in a timely manner. It also allows other development teams to see problems across the board that may affect them, rather than keeping them isolated. It is also a useful tool in collecting metrics.

—Frances Castillo, QA Engineer

3.5 INTEGRATING PEOPLE AND TECHNOLOGY

Project-specific technologies will clearly vary between groups working on different projects. For example, if a group is developing a web application, they might need technology that supports Java coding standards analysis, Java unit testing, web coding standards analysis, web functional testing, and web load testing. If a group is developing C++ applications, they might need technology that supports C++ coding standards analysis, C++ unit testing, and C++ runtime error detection.

If the team already has some of these technologies in place, it is important to verify that the components are configured and functioning properly before adding more elements to the infrastructure. For example, if the team already has a source control system, it is critical to assess that it works correctly and that its configuration is appropriate for each group member. If the project is divided into logical components, the source control repository should also be divided into corresponding logical components.

Once the necessary elements are identified, the work of assembling them into an infrastructure can begin. The goal is to assemble a fully integrated system that performs as much work as possible without human intervention.

The reports and the infrastructure should be used as follows:

Project managers: Project managers should periodically evaluate graphs and summaries generated by the reporting system to assess overall managerial project status. The frequency of this evaluation depends on the project type and its development phase. For example, the project manager may choose to review reports once a week at the development cycle and check them on a daily basis when the product approaches its deployment deadline. Through these reports, project managers can verify overall project cost and schedule status and compare them to the planned cost and schedule. This information is necessary to make decisions concerning possible budget overruns, rescheduling key production dates, and moving development milestones.•

Architects: Reporting system graphs and summaries should be periodically evaluated by the architect to assess the technical aspects of the development process, from initial requirements definition, through design, coding, and testing to full application deployment. While the frequency of this periodic review depends on the project type and its development phase, it is expected that the architect conduct her reviews more often than the project manager, who oversees more high-level goals of the project.

Additionally, the architect should be equipped with the configurable technologies needed to verify application of best practices for requirements management, coding standards, and testing. The architect should make decisions about the configuration of these technologies to customize best practice applications to meet the needs of a particular developer, development team, or project.

Developers: The reporting system provides information to a developer regarding her and her group's product implementation status. For example, the reports include the number of features implemented, tests passed or failed, defects detected, and coding standards violated. The developer uses these reports and the supporting technology infrastructure to ensure that the required best practices are comprehensively applied and automatically verified in her code before this code is added to the source control system.

Test engineers: Testing engineers evaluate the reporting system's defect data on a periodic basis. If they learn of a new, severe defect, they notify the architect (or a lead developer) and then they collaborate with the architect to diagnose the root cause of the defect. Next, a preventive action plan is created and implemented. In addition, the testing team adds to the test suite one or more test cases that verify whether the defect has been resolved. Once the new test cases pass, the defect is deemed corrected. Ideally, each tester should be equipped with the technologies needed to perform high-level testing on the integrated application.

3.6 HUMAN FACTORS AND CONCERNS

While we strive to remove the dependence on human factors as much as possible, in the end, humans will make or break the system. Following are the most important concerns to be considered when facing human factors that can negatively affect implementation of ADP:

- *Insufficient Management Support*: The project manager does not sufficiently support ADP and does not require that team members follow the prescribed practices and correct exposed problems.

   This problem would ideally come to the attention of the program manager, or other higher-level supervisor, and be corrected at this level. First, it should be determined whether the project manager understood her role and the benefits of ADP. One of the remedies would be to request weekly (or even daily, depending on the severity of the situation) reports to the supervisor about the status of ADP implementation. In addition, a formal presentation of the project's implementation status should be reported to the company as a whole.

- *Insufficient Architect and/or Testing Team and/or QA Team Support*: The architect, testing team, and/or QA team are not dedicated to ensuring that the process is modified to prevent similar problems each time a severe defect is detected. If the architect, testers, and (when appropriate) QA teams are not committed to defect prevention, the team will not be able to improve the way in which they produce software.

   A plan for addressing this issue would require the project manager's intervention. When it comes to the manager's attention that severe defects were recurring and no process modification was being undertaken, she should request frequent and perhaps one-on-one status reports from the architect, the testers, and, if needed, from the QA team. All involved parties may need to be retrained regarding the project's procedures, including ADP implementation.

- *Lack of Commitment to the Importance of Defect Prevention*: Developers often argue that if a reported problem does not result in a runtime error, then the code does not need to be modified.

   Proper training should be provided to all developers so that they have a strong understanding of the importance of defect prevention. Management needs to educate the team on why defect-prone artifact needs to be taken just as seriously as defect-causing artifact. The developers should be trained on practices, policies, technologies, and all other aspects of ADP. Both the time and cost issues should be brought up during training so that developers understand the benefits of defect prevention and the consequences of not implementing it. Data from the problem tracking system should be used to validate the need for defect prevention. Other technologies, such as static analyzers, could be used to help developers apply and verify ADP's best practices.

- *An Overwhelming Introduction to this New Methodology*: Suddenly requiring the application of many general best practices might cause team members to become overwhelmed, reject the findings as "noise," and simply ignore the results altogether.

  As explained in APD's sixth principle, it is important to introduce practices gradually. One particularly helpful strategy is to divide each practice into several levels of importance, then introduce each level incrementally. Also, as mentioned in Section 2.4.6, another useful strategy is to apply the practice only to projects started after a predetermined cutoff date or, even better, to apply the practice to only the specific parts of the project after the cutoff date. Additionally, ADP practices could be partitioned to pilot subgroups before having the entire group use the entire methodology. The successful participants in a pilot subgroup could then help to introduce ADP practices mastered in their subgroup to other subgroups.

3.7 EXAMPLES

3.7.1 Focus on Developer Ideas

This example illustrates the necessity for storing and tracking requests for new features and developers' ideas. Imagine that a development team is working on a new product. As the product nears release, many good ideas for product improvements are mentioned by beta testers, salespeople, and QA team members. In addition, the developers have some last-minute improvement ideas of their own. However, since the release date is approaching, there is no time to implement these ideas. After version 1.0 of the product is released and the initial chaos dies down, the team is ready to start working on the next version. At the planning meeting, they try to remember all of the improvement ideas that were suggested before the 1.0 release, but they were very busy at the time. They did not record these ideas and they cannot recall many of them.

Because the team did not have a central, easy-to-access place for recording improvement ideas, those ideas have been lost. System requirements were recorded in the requirements management system, and reported defects were recorded in the problem tracking system. However, while some suggestions for product improvements may have been informally recorded by group members outside of the system, most of the new ideas could not be recalled.

This problem can be prevented by using a problem tracking system that not only tracks defects, but also serves as a central, comprehensive idea repository. Thus, customer complaints, documentation change/enhancement requests, or even new feature suggestions should be recorded in the problem tracking system, then carefully labeled and prioritized. When it comes time to plan the next release, team members can easily retrieve a list of all of the potential improvements, and then decide which should be implemented in the next iteration.

3.7.2   Focus on Reports Generated by the Minimum Infrastructure

The information collected from the source control system can be used by the team members to evaluate project status. In a graph similar to the one presented in Figure 3.8, the architect would look for a number of files checked in to the source control system. An excessively large number of check-ins indicates that the developers are probably refactoring the code. A low number of check-ins in early development can indicate developers are having difficulty in implementing a module and consequently may need the architect's help.

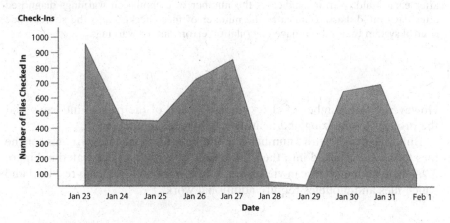

Source Code Statistics

Revisions by Team

Team	Week 4	Week 5	Total
Team A	81	2	83
Team B	10	46	56
Team C	34	5	39
Team D	65	32	97

Figure 3.8   Source code statistics.

Build Results

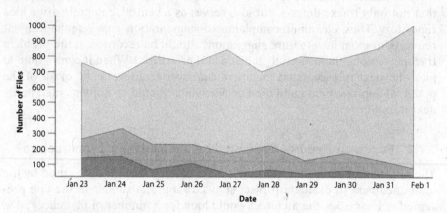

Build Results Detail

Date	Failed	Warnings	Passed
Jan 23	120	250	750
Jan 24	130	320	680
Jan 25	90	220	800
Jan 26	100	250	750

Figure 3.9   Build results. Failed indicates the number of compilation errors diagnosed after each build. Warning indicates the number of compilation warnings diagnosed after each build. Passed indicates the number of files checked into the source code control system that did not have compilation errors and or warnings.

However, a low number of check-ins at the end of the project indicates that the project is stabilizing and nearing deployment readiness.

Build results show the number of compilation errors and warnings for the files that were checked into the source control system, as illustrated in Figure 3.9. The team members can view whether the warnings are being resolved and which files and modules require additional work.

3.8 ACRONYMS

IDE   Integrated development environment
RCS   Revision control system
SLOC   Source lines of code
QA   Quality assurance
UML   Unified Modeling Language

3.9 GLOSSARY

automated build A process for building an application on a periodic basis by automatically executing the required build steps, including compiling and linking of the code at the scheduled time.

automatic code generator A system that converts design artifacts (such as class diagrams) into implementation artifacts such as object-oriented code classes.

automated reported system A system that stores information about the project status and generates reports to help in decision-making and processes analysis.

check-in Placement of a configuration item in the source control system. A check-in occurs when modified local files are copied to the source control system or another shared repository.

configuration management system A broad term for a system that at minimum stores configuration items (units of code, test sets, specifications, test plans, and other documents), facilitates control changes to these items, records and reports change processing and implementation status, and verifies compliance with specified change control process.

fault An anomaly in the software that may cause it to behave incorrectly, and not according to its specification. A fault or a defect is also called a "bug."

Integrated development environment (IDE) An integrated development environment (IDE) is a set of integrated tools for software development, which commonly combines a text editor, compiler, linker, debugging tools, profiler, and sometimes version control and dependency maintenance.

problem tracking system A system in which defects, issues, change requests, and programmers' ideas are stored and tracked.

RCS The revision control system (RCS) manages multiple revisions of files. [2]

regression testing The process of retesting software that has been modified to ensure that no defects have been introduced by the modification, and that the software is still able to meet its specifications. [5]

regression testing system Any tool or combination of tools that can automatically run the core of the existing tests on the entire code base on a regular basis (preferably nightly, as part of the automated build). Its purpose is to help in identifying when code modifications cause previously working functionality to regress, or fail. For example, the regression system may be a script that runs one or more testing or defect prevention technologies in batch mode. [6]

requirement A statement of a customer need or objective, or of a condition or capability that a product must possess to satisfy such a need or objective. A property that a product must have to provide value to a stakeholder. [1]

requirement management system A system that stores and facilitates tracking requirements status, managing changes to requirements and versions of requirements specifications, and tracing individual requirements to other project phases and work products. [1]

requirement stability index A derived measure defined as a complement of requirements change rate. When the requirements change rate approaches zero, the requirements stability index approaches 100%.

Quality Assurance group A group that audits the process and products. The process is audited to ensure that it is properly followed and the product is audited to ensure that it satisfies standards and requirements.

source control system A database where source code is stored. Its purpose is to provide a central place where the team members can store and access the entire source code base. We use this as a generic term for both version control systems and configuration management systems. The code is organized, versioned, and accessible to all team members. Conflicts due to parallel updates are automatically detected, and rollback features are supported. Examples include SVN, CVS, RCS, Visual SourceSafe, and ClearCase.

version control system A system that keeps track of multiple versions of the source code files and other project artifacts. It is common, but inadvisable, to use the terms "configuration management" and "version control" indiscriminately. A company should decide as to which meaning it will attach to "version control" and define the term relative to the meaning of configuration management.

vision and scope document The document that presents the business requirements for a new system. This document covers the statement of the vision of the project, which is what the project will accomplish in the long term. The project scope description defines what parts of the vision will be implemented in the short term. [1]

stakeholders People who benefit in a direct or indirect way from the system that is being developed; they can be customers, partners, team members, and management.

subversion Version control system.

3.10 REFERENCES

[1] Wiegers, K., *Software Requirements*. Microsoft Press, 2nd ed., 2003.

[2] Purdue University, *Official RCS Homepage*, 2006, http://www.cs.purdue.edu/homes/trinkle/RCS/ (retrieved: September 27, 2006).

[3] Tigris.org, *Subversion*, 2006, http://subversion.tigris.org/ (retrieved: September 27, 2006).

[4] Has, A., *Configuration Management Principles and Practice*. Addison Wesley, 2002.

[5] Burnstein, I., *Practical Software Testing: A Process Oriented Approach*. Springer, 2002.

[6] Kolawa, A., "Making Your Regression System Work For You," 2006, http://www.wrox.com/WileyCDA/Section/id-130092.html (retrieved: February 16, 2006).

3.11　EXERCISES

1. Many companies may not have the titles/positions of project manager, architect, developer, test engineer, and QA staff. What other titles/positions at a company could be used to fill each of these roles?

2. For the roles of architect, developer, tester, and QA staff, explain their function in defect detection and prevention. For each of these roles, why do you think it is or it is not important that they are involved in software testing?

3. What do you think facilitates creating a group culture that makes satisfied and productive employees?

4. What other issues than those described in Section 3.6, "Human Factors and Concerns," could negatively affect implementation of ADP? Explain your plan for remedying these issues.

5. What commercial and noncommercial source control systems are available, and what are some of their features?

6. What commercial and noncommercial requirements management systems are available, and what are some of their features?

7. What automated software development tools are available, and what are some of their features?

8. What challenges can you foresee when introducing developers to new software tools? How would you solve these?

9. What is the minimum technology infrastructure necessary to facilitate ADP?

10. What other technology (not described in this chapter) would you add to the minimum technology infrastructure, and why?

CHAPTER 4

REQUIREMENTS SPECIFICATION AND MANAGEMENT

The greatest challenge to any thinker is stating the problem in a way that will allow a solution.

—Bertrand Russell

4.1 INTRODUCTION

The infrastructure described in the previous chapter lays the physical foundation for our methodology. Once this infrastructure is in place, active development of the product can start. This happens by a steady transformation of intellectual creativity and people's ideas into formalized project requirements, which are gradually refined until an acceptable level of clarity is attained.

Specification of these requirements forms the initial stage of the software production process. However, requirements specification and management has long been one of the most challenging aspects of software development. Not only are complete requirements difficult (if not impossible) to define at the beginning of a project, they tend to change and grow along with the project. Since requirements are usually written in a natural language, they are subject to contradiction, ambiguity, lack of clarity, and omissions. Moreover, something as minor as a misinterpreted sentence can spell disaster for a project if it is overlooked until late in the life cycle.

Automated Defect Prevention: Best Practices in Software Management, by Dorota Huizinga and Adam Kolawa
Copyright © 2007 John Wiley & Sons, Inc.

Ensuring that requirements are correctly implemented has become even more difficult over the last several years, where product specification changes are often the norm. Moreover, it is common to have a domestic manager struggle to understand customer requirements and a development team overseas struggle to understand the domestic manager's requirements.

Several attempts have been made to ameliorate some of the communication problems between stakeholders with nontechnical and technical backgrounds. These include the development of notations, languages, and technologies that can be understood and used by both groups, such as the Universal Modeling Language (UML) designed by Ivar Jacobson, Grady Booch, and James Rumbaugh [1], or Framework for Integrated Testing (FIT), proposed by Robert Martin [2]. Despite these recent efforts, requirements specification and management remains one of the most difficult tasks in software development and it is critical to have defect prevention implemented in this phase.

Ilene Burnstein [3] lists the following four categories of requirements-related defects:

- *Functional description defects*: which stem from an incorrect, incomplete, or ambiguous overall product functionality description
- *Feature description defects*: which are caused by a missing, incorrect, incomplete, or ambiguous description of specific functional or quality characteristics of a software element referred to as a feature
- *Feature interaction defects*: which result from an incorrect description of feature interactions with respect to both control and data flow between the features
- *Interface description defects*: which occur due to an incorrect description of how the final product is to interface with users, and external software, and hardware components

With its supporting infrastructure, ADP will guide the product development through the application of best practices to avoid and minimize the impact of the above problems. In addition to the best practices for requirements defect prevention discussed in this chapter, we will describe a general policy for use of the requirements management system. This basic policy should be expanded and customized to project and organization needs in order to provide a common reference point for all team members interacting with technology infrastructure, and to facilitate synchronization of their tasks.

The expected work products for this phase are:

- Requirements documents:
  - Vision and Scope document
  - Software Requirements Specification (SRS) document

- Use cases[a]
- Conceptual test cases
- Customized policy for use of requirements management
- Requirements entered in the requirements management system

4.2   BEST PRACTICES FOR GATHERING AND ORGANIZING REQUIREMENTS

Within the process of iterative development, each phase can also be iterative within itself. Certain best practices within the requirements phase may need to be iterated several times, or the whole requirements phase may need to be reiterated. In addition, the parts of the requirements phase may need to be revisited during later phases of development, leading to iterations of several requirements best practices while in other phases.

These best practices can be applied to both existing and new development projects. Revisions of existing projects are more common than new projects, and are often equally complicated. Although many organizations may take shortcuts during the requirements elicitation process for revisions of existing projects, such adjustments should be avoided because requirements specification and management best practices are just as essential in this context, where extra complexity is added by merging legacy code with new code.

4.2.1   Creating the Product Vision and Scope Document

The Vision and Scope document gives a general view of what the project aims to accomplish in the long term, and what restrictions exist in the short term. The product vision outlines the purpose of the product, major features, and any assumptions or external factors that must be considered. The product scope defines what will be included in the project, and states limitations that define what will not be included [4].

Why   The Vision and Scope document is needed because it serves as a unifying theme across the development stages. The product vision serves to give all involved parties a common long-term purpose for the entire development process. A new project scope document is created for each iteration of development, based on the product vision, and defines what will or will not be included for that iteration. Whenever there is a question about interpreting requirements or including certain requirements, the Vision and Scope document can be consulted for clarification.

---

[a] A use case describes a sequence of actions that are performed by an actor (e.g., a person, a machine, another system) as the actor interacts with the software.

Who   The project manager, in collaboration with the architect and other stakeholders, creates the Vision and Scope document. The project manager is ultimately responsible for all requirements-related tasks starting from requirements elicitation to their final specification. The project manager should be the owner of the requirements documents; however, most of the technical responsibilities usually will be delegated to the project architect. The architect should understand the overall direction and motivation for the project and will need to know the requirements intimately in order to develop an appropriate design. The owner of the Vision and Scope document will need to gather information about the project from those who understand its significance and scope. The owner could also be a senior manager, a subject matter expert, or a member of the marketing department.

How   At the beginning of the project, the product vision should be described in the vision document. This document should cover who will use the software, why it is different from other products, its major features, and what the software aims to accomplish. A product scope document should be created at the beginning of each iteration of development. This document should detail what major features will be included in the current iteration of development and explicitly state any scope limitations.

Measurement   The product vision statement often undergoes many revisions throughout the application's life cycle to accommodate changing needs and/or to correct misunderstandings. However, it is usually not possible to determine whether revisions are needed until later in the application's life cycle: the need for change typically will not surface until after completing at least one iteration of the requirements analysis phase and starting the design phase.

One way to determine when the product vision needs to be updated is to monitor the ratio of change in use cases. Assuming that the best practices recommended later in this chapter are followed, the product vision will be parsed into requirements, and requirements will be further refined into use cases. Thus, a high rate of use case change indicates that the project's initial vision and scope was not well defined (for instance, as a result of misunderstanding customer requirements) or that the product vision changed since the project's inception. In either case, it is very likely that the product vision has changed, and the Vision and Scope document should be revised accordingly.

The product vision may also need updating when the project stakeholders develop additional use cases to assess the validity of the model (this occurs after the initial application model has been developed). If new use cases are developed at this point, the Vision and Scope document may need to be modified to accommodate them.

Proactively reducing the risk of excessive change is preferable to merely reacting to it. The key to reducing the risk of excessive change is to forge a close relationship with the project stakeholders, and then interact with them throughout the project.

Tracking   The quality and completeness of the document should be manually reviewed and approved before it is added to the requirements management system. If the document is edited, both the changes and their authors should be recorded. Whether the document is approved or pending approval, who approved it and when should also be tracked.

Automation   Upon changing the document, all parties that need to review the document for approval should be automatically notified. Once the document is approved, all parties that need to read the new document should be automatically notified.

4.2.2   Gathering and Organizing Requirements

Requirements describe the capabilities or features that need to be implemented in order for the software to achieve its purpose (solve a business problem, satisfy user needs, etc.). Gathering requirements is one of the most challenging tasks in the software development process. This is due to the size and complexity of modern software products, coupled with the difficulties customers may have when trying to define and then communicate requirements.

Requirements should be divided into several subcategories, such as business requirements, user requirements, system requirements, performance requirements, deployment requirements, upgrade requirements, security requirements, and so on. Functional requirements describe the features of the software and the tasks it performs. Nonfunctional requirements, also known as quality of service (QoS) requirements, describe properties that the system should display, such as performance, accessibility, or extendibility. For example, imagine a software development project that is designed to bring the organization's current accounting system into compliance with new financial legislation. A sample business requirement would be "Extend the application to support the new legislation." A sample user requirement might be "Allow authorized users to produce reports that identify the time, date, reason, and authorization for any financial data changes." A sample system requirement is "The new application code should be built in Java, connect to the existing MySQL database, and run on the existing server." A sample deployment requirement is "Establish a process for automatically deploying the modified application to a staging environment for testing, then automatically deploying the application on the mainframe." A sample upgrade requirement is "The upgrade must preserve all existing data and not require the system to be offline during business hours."

Once gathered and categorized, all requirements should be uniquely labeled, and recorded in the SRS document. This document is used later for prioritizing requirements and for entering them into the requirements management system.

Why   Requirements explain how the product vision translates into software features. Requirements definition is a critical link between creating the high-level purpose for the software development or updating and building a software product that achieves that purpose. Without requirements, it would be difficult to develop effective use cases. Having ineffective or insufficient use cases would complicate application design, and subsequently development. Additionally, it would be more difficult to develop test cases that objectively and effectively verify whether the requirements are implemented correctly and completely in the code.

A process for the requirements organization is necessary because of their quantity and complexity. Storing all the requirements gives those involved in the project a way to access them. Organizing the requirements makes it easier to identify some of the prevailing problems in requirement specifications: they can be ambiguous, incomplete, or even contradictory. For instance, a requirement that states "Implement user-friendly reports" could be considered ambiguous because the definition of "user-friendly reports" is open to multiple interpretations. A requirement that states, "The application should record purchase information in the database" is incomplete unless it is accompanied by information that specifies what purchase information should be stored. An example of potentially contradictory requirements are "Clear all inactive account information after three years" and "Save all purchase information for five years."

Many functional description and feature description defects could be prevented when requirements are properly gathered and organized. Additionally, the combination of tracking and organizing the requirements creates continuity of information, so that new team members know exactly how the project is defined.

Who   All project stakeholders should be closely involved in the requirements process. The development and testing team members should be involved from the start of the requirements process. Even if the organization has designated roles for the requirement analysts, who specialize in the gathering and organizing of requirements, the developers need to be involved in requirements definition so they will truly understand what they are responsible for implementing. The testing team needs to be involved in the requirements definition so that they can construct the appropriate tests in a timely manner.

How   First, multiple meetings with customers (for external requirements) or the system architect (for an internal project) should be held to establish which categories of requirements are needed, such as functional requirements, quality attributes, constraints, and business rules [4]. As the requirements are gathered, they should be organized into the predefined categories. In addition, each feature should be broken down into several functional requirements. For instance, returning to the earlier example of the accounting application, one feature might be "Produce a report that lists all changes made to financial data." Related functional requirements might include "Flag all changes to financial data," "Record the change made, user, time, date, reason, and approval," and "Generate an HTML report that provides a table with all change data sorted by date (starting with the most recent)."

A traditional meeting is just one of many available requirements elicitation techniques, each of which is effective in different contexts. Scott Ambler [5] ranks available elicitation techniques as follows (listed from the highest relative effectiveness to the lowest):

1. Active stakeholder participation
2. On-site customer participation
3. Joint application design, which involves a highly structured meeting
4. Focus groups with actual and/or potential end users
5. Observation of end users performing their daily work
6. Face-to-face interviews with stakeholders who have valuable information to share, but can't or won't attend meetings
7. Interviews via telephone, videoconferencing, e-mail, or meeting software
8. Legacy code analysis
9. Reading any legacy system documentation, business documentation, or material related to similar or competing systems

---

FOCUS ON SECURITY: DEFINING SECURITY REQUIREMENTS AND POLICY

Building security into an application involves designing and implementing the application according to a policy for reducing the risk of security attacks, and then verifying that the policy is implemented and operating correctly. Consequently, security becomes a requirements and specification issue. If the specification does not define how the application should be built to safeguard security, the application will be vulnerable to security attacks.

Security policies are espoused by security experts, such as the Open Web Application Security Project[b] (OWASP), and are mandated for compliance with many regulations, which require organizations to demonstrate that they have conducted "due diligence" in safeguarding application security and information privacy. A security policy is a specification document that defines how code needs to be written and tested to withstand unauthorized access. A security policy typically includes custom security requirements, privacy requirements, security coding best practices, security application

---

[b] The Open Web Application Security Project (OWASP) is an organization for developing and supporting open source projects that produce tools, documentation, and standards for application security (http://www.owasp.org).

design rules, and security testing benchmarks. Ideally, a security policy should also require that all security-related operations be located in one segment of the application, which allows for verifying and maintaining security within that one critical module. Centralizing the security code acts like a drawbridge for a castle: it isolates the area that attackers can exploit and facilitates a more focused defense strategy.

The policy should describe what types of resources require privileged access, what kind of actions should be logged, what kind of inputs should be validated, and other security concerns specific to the application. The security policy should then be converted into core rules for enforcing the organization's specific security requirements. Finally, these security requirements are added to the requirements management system so that developers can easily reference them during implementation and testing.

Measurement The system should measure the number of requirements for each section of the Vision and Scope document. If there is not at least one requirement for each section, the requirements are unquestionably incomplete. Typically, the higher the ratio of requirements per section, the more thoroughly the team has parsed the product vision into requirements. Moreover, since there should be a natural progression from Vision and Scope document to requirements and then to use cases, the use case quality and change rate measures discussed later also shed light on requirements quality and stability.

Tracking Each requirement should be stored in the requirements management system. The category to which the requirement belongs should be noted. If the requirement defines part of a feature, it should reference that feature. Each requirement should be associated with the person who defined it, so that this person can be contacted for clarification. In addition, each requirement should reference the section of more general documents (such as the Vision and Scope document) that would apply to it. For instance, if a requirement referenced section 2.1 of the Vision and Scope document, then the document reference field should have "2.1" in the requirements management system. Such labeling would enable team members to retrieve all requirements related to a specific Vision and Scope section. It would also enable team members responsible for implementing or verifying a requirement to reference the relevant part of the Vision and Scope document in order to learn its high-level purpose. Most requirements management systems offer categorization and query/filter capabilities, which help team members to efficiently access previously entered items of interest, such as all previous feature requests related to a specific category. This is exemplified in Figure 4.1.

Automation In the intermediate and expanded infrastructure, automation is provided through the requirements management system. The following tasks should be automated through the requirements management system and its

Requirement	Feature	Category	Reference	Author
Encrypt Database...		Security	Scope 2.1	A. W. Q.
Password Length...	Supplier Login	Business	Vision 3.1	G. V. S.
Manage Account...	User Account	User	Vision 3.2	D. A. B.
Select Themes...	Customizing	Interface	Vision 4.1	S. R. P.

Figure 4.1 Example of requirements data being tracked in the requirements management system.

integration with the testing system, source control system, and problem tracking system:

- Tracking of requirement modifications
- Tracking of use case modifications
- Tracking of use case implementation
- Correlating requirements and use cases
- Correlating use cases to code and to test cases
- Tracking of requirement completion

4.2.3 Prioritizing Requirements

The priority of a requirement indicates how necessary it is to the product. The priority of a requirement has two components: how necessary it is to implement it in the current release of the software, and how necessary the functionality will be in the final version of the product.

Implementation priorities indicate the importance of a given requirement in the current iteration, and therefore determine when a requirement should be implemented. The implementation priorities are therefore highly dynamic, and will be changed at the beginning of each iteration. The designations for implementation priorities are "high," "moderate," and "low":

- *High*: Must be implemented in the current iteration
- *Moderate*: Candidate for implementation in the next iteration (could be implemented in this iteration if all high-priority requirements have been completely implemented)
- *Low*: Candidate for implementation after two or more iterations (could be implemented in this iteration if all high- and moderate-priority requirements have been completely implemented)

Functionality priorities indicate what requirements/features should be in the final version of the product to make the software maximally useful to the end user, and therefore determine what must be implemented. The functionality priorities are relatively static, and should change infrequently across all iterations. The designations for functionality priorities are "core" and "non-core":

- *Core*: A requirement is considered core if the majority of the stakeholders believe the software would not be useful if the requirement was not implemented.
- *Non-Core*: A requirement is considered non-core if the majority of the stakeholders believe the software would still be useful if the requirement was not implemented.

Once assigned, requirement priorities should be reflected in the SRS document.

Why   Given short timelines and many requirements, compromises must be made about what can be implemented and when. The identification and analysis of non-core requirements may help to reveal requirements that add little value to the product. In addition, the implementation of high-priority requirements will yield early successes that will motivate the developers [6].

Who   The project manager, in collaboration with the architect and perhaps other team members, should analyze and assign requirements. Input from the customer will determine priorities based on the usability or value that each requirement adds, and will therefore mainly determine functionality priorities. Input from the developers will determine priorities based on difficulty or time of implementing the requirement, which will mainly determine implementation priorities. After balancing the input from the developer and customer, the manager can assign priorities to the requirements.

How   The priority of the feature or requirement should be determined based on usability, cost, difficulty, and/or risk. The priority of a given feature will determine the priorities of the functional specifications that comprise that feature.

The functionality priorities should be determined during the initial cycle of requirements analysis, where the project manager performs a preliminary prioritization of the requirements. This is an estimate based on her knowledge of the project and initial discussions with stakeholders. During successive passes through requirements analysis, the project manager discusses the initial prioritization with the stakeholders. This involves reviewing each requirement, one by one, and asking the stakeholders if the software would still be useful if that requirement was not implemented. If the software would not be useful without the requirement, the requirement is considered a core requirement. The project manager then makes the necessary revisions based on the feedback received.

The implementation priorities should be determined at the beginning of each iteration. The priorities should be determined based on the number of features and requirements: if, for example, the desired schedule gives 2–6 months per iteration, the requirements team must estimate how many features can be completed in that time. Core requirements should always be the first candidates for high implementation priority. During the requirements phase of each successive iteration, additional requirements will be added and then all existing and new requirements (approved change requests, discussed later in this chapter) will be analyzed. For the new iteration, high-priority requirements will come from high-priority requirements that were not implemented previously, promoting existing moderate-priority requirements, or designating new requirements as high priority.

Measurement   The ratio of the core requirements (the requirements that were not filtered out during the stakeholder review) to the total number of requirements will indicate whether the project is focused on critical issues. For instance, if more than 20% of the requirements are non-core requirements (requirements that the stakeholder can live without), then the final product may require too much work without delivering significant benefit. A large number of requirements that have not been assigned a priority may indicate that the requirements were not thoroughly analyzed and that their priorities need to be evaluated.

Tracking   Each of the requirements should have a priority assigned to it, and include who assigned the priority and when it was assigned. In addition, changes to the priority should also be tracked. The requirements management system should be able to retrieve this information and present it in tables. (See Figure 4.2.)

4.2.4   Developing Use Cases

A use case describes how someone or something would interact with the proposed system. In use cases, an actor is a representation of all users who interact

Requirement	Implement. Priority	Functionality Priority	Assigned By	Created	Modified
Requirement 7	High	Core	A. S. F.	11/24/05	12/01/05
Requirement 4	High	Core	R. S. E.	11/20/05	12/10/05
Requirement 12	Moderate	Core	W. A. I.	11/28/05	12/05/05
Requirement 3	Moderate	Non-Core	Q. L. R.	11/19/05	12/14/05
Requirement 22	Low	Non-Core	R.S.E.	11/15/05	11/29/05

Figure 4.2   Tracking priorities in the requirements management system.

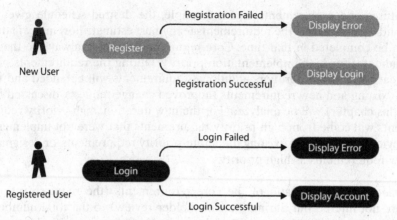

Figure 4.3   An example of a use case for a login process. A new user would first need to register successfully before logging in. A registered user would need to login successfully, and then she would be redirected to her account information.

with the system in a given role, while a persona is a specific user with a unique background and needs. The goal of the use case is to describe realistic scenarios for using the features defined in the requirements. For example, a login use case might look like Figure 4.3. Use cases should be uniquely labeled and referenced by corresponding requirements in the SRS document.

Why   Use cases illustrate how the requirements are applied to achieve goals described in the Vision and Scope document. As mentioned previously, use cases are a critical foundation for effective application design and construction. They are also an essential prerequisite for developing test cases that objectively verify whether the software meets expectations.

Who   As in other requirements best practices, the project manager is responsible for this task, but the entire team (including the architect, development team members, and testing team members) is involved in the process to ensure that they have a thorough understanding of the requirements.

It is critical to create a feedback loop with customers during the creation of use cases, since it is likely that requirements will change as the project proceeds. By interacting with a group of customers who represent actual or potential application end users, the team can begin to separate information that is useful to the application from extraneous information. The stakeholders' feedback is also important for determining if enough use cases have been made, or if more need to be created.

How   Every requirement should have two types of use cases: positive and negative. Positive use cases describe the feature's expected usage. They are constructed to elicit functional requirements of the system by describing its step-by-step desirable behavior. Their counterparts, negative use cases (also called misuse or mis-use cases), are constructed to elicit possible undesirable system behavior. This undesirable behavior is caused by either intended or unintended misuse of the system. Consequently, the primary goal of negative use cases is to elicit system security–related requirements, so the misuse of the system does not result in security breaches.

Three to four use cases per requirement are typically required to define each requirement's expected usage. However, it is desirable to have as many use cases as possible because this will provide a clearer, more detailed picture of the project's functionality.

Measurement   The first measurement is the number of use cases per requirement. Every requirement should have a positive and negative use case. Three to four use cases per requirement are needed to define each requirement's expected usage, but the more use cases created the better. Plotting how the ratio of use cases to requirements varies over time reveals how the system is being refined as it evolves.

After requirements start to change, the ratio of change in use cases (the original use cases to the number of added, removed, or modified use cases) should be tracked. A high ratio of change indicates that either the project's initial vision and scope was not well defined (for instance, as a result of misunderstanding the project needs or poor communication) or that the software requirements changed since the project's inception.

The number of use cases may change after the initial application model has been developed, as work with the project stakeholders produces additional use cases to assess the validity of the model.

In both of the former cases, changing use cases may suggest that the product vision document and requirement definitions may need updating, and that the stakeholder feedback loop needs to be improved (for instance, through more frequent communication, documenting conversations and implementing more formal approvals at each phase, etc.).

Tracking   Each use case should be stored in the requirements management system and reference a requirement (which in turn references a section of the Vision and Scope document). Use cases should be marked as either positive or negative. Additionally, the initial number of use cases should be recorded, as should the number of use cases that are added, removed, and/or modified after the initial use case definition.

Automation   When the requirements change, it should be automatically detected and reported which use cases, code, and tests need to be updated.

4.2.5   Creating a Prototype to Elicit Requirements

A software prototype is a mock-up of the desired product that shows how the software might look or work. The prototype does not need to be a functioning software application.

Why   Since customers often do not have technical background and they may be unsure what features can or cannot be implemented, they have difficulties describing their needs. One way of coping with this problem is to develop an application prototype. The prototype is used as a means to determine that the client's needs have been elicited accurately [7,8]. To paraphrase the famous quote that "a picture is worth a thousand words," we believe that *a prototype is worth a thousand words for a requirements specification.*

The prototype allows the team to understand how the requirements translate to the application's interface and flow. It also helps the team identify usability problems that are typically found much later in the process when correcting them is much more difficult, costly, and time-consuming. When viewing a prototype, people are likely to notice requirements that are missing or poorly defined.

Who   The developers on the project, led by a manager or architect, should build the prototype. Occasionally, experts such as graphic designers can be hired to help in designing prototypes for user interfaces.

How   There are two ways to approach prototyping: by building an application mockup (throwaway prototype) that will not be used for actual application development, or by building a very basic application framework (evolutionary prototype) that serves as the foundation for later development. The best solution depends on the nature of the project.

If the project involves developing a complicated user interface and it is necessary to assess and improve the usability of that interface, it is desirable to develop a throwaway prototype. A throwaway prototype is built quickly and inexpensively, but it serves no purpose other than to test the interface's usability. With a throwaway prototype, it is unnecessary to have realistic data or content because the main goal is to model and test the proposed data flow, not to verify functionality details. These prototypes can typically be built with graphical tools such as design and modeling systems.

On the other hand, the evolutionary prototype is best suited for projects that involve complex architectures, algorithms, or mathematical calculations. If technologies are available for prototyping such systems without implementing the code, they should be used. Otherwise, a skeletal, yet functional, implementation of the application should be constructed. This will help to determine how well the architecture, computations, and algorithms solve the problem that the application was designed to solve. This type of feedback could not possibly be provided by a throwaway prototype.

DEVELOPER'S TESTIMONIAL

I am currently working on developing a brand-new product for auto dealers. The business analyst in my organization wrote use cases, but they lacked the flow of the whole system. To get the initial feedback from the dealers about the final product, we hired a graphic artist to come up with a quick comp for the entire system and provide basic navigation between pages. These comps were developed as simple jpeg images, which were modified repeatedly based on the feedback from the dealers. We cannot use these comps in our code, hence they became throwaway prototypes for us. They were ideal for getting the user experience.

Then there was another problem in which we needed to export some dealer information to publish on their website, with each website taking data in a different format and using a different protocol for communication (some use form post, some use ftp, some use e-mail, etc.). Since the requirement wasn't clear and was unknown for the future customers, we had to try out a system based on Microsoft's workflow engine, which was just to show that it would be easy to change based on this requirement. Once we understood the technology better and designed the basic structure for this prototype, all the subsequent detailed implementation was based on this initial framework. This is a perfect example of an evolutionary prototype.

—Atul Menon, Solution Architect

When prototyping a research or exploratory software product, it is essential that the most critical, risky, and difficult-to-implement requirements are implemented first—especially if resources are limited. This avoids the risk of spending the bulk of the resources on secondary functionality, and not having sufficient resources left to implement the key functionality.

Measurement The measurements include *source lines of code* (SLOC) in the prototype and the developers' effort rate in SLOC/day. These measurements can be used later for preliminary estimates of the project effort and schedule based on requirements specifications.

Tracking Each prototype should have its location, date created, and owner stored in the requirements management system. For evolutionary prototypes, the size of initial code (in number of lines of code) in the prototype and the resources (number of developer hours) required to build the prototype should be tracked.

Automation As soon as an evolutionary prototype is built, it establishes a source for automating builds and the execution of the regression test suite. This seed should later grow into the full-fledged automated infrastructure.

4.2.6 Creating Conceptual Test Cases

Conceptual test cases are a skeleton of the more rigorous, executable test cases that are created in later phases. The conceptual test cases are an initial written description of the expected inputs and expected outputs, which are used to help refine the requirements. Creating conceptual test cases forms the basis for a test plan.

Why Requiring the development of the conceptual test cases before or during, and not after, the construction of the code helps in clarifying requirements and facilitates the implementation of the correct functionality. In addition, using tests to drive development prevents the writing of unnecessary code.

Who The architect and development team members are responsible for developing conceptual test cases. In some cases, requirements analysts may be involved to assure that the test cases are traceable to specific requirements.

How Conceptual test cases should be created as soon as the use cases have been developed. For each use case, where appropriate, the expected input and output should be determined, and then this information should be recorded in the requirements management system (along with the corresponding use case). For example, consider conceptual test cases for login functionality. There would need to be a set of passwords that includes valid passwords, invalid passwords, and inputs that a hacker might write to try to gain unauthorized access to the system. The use cases would define the expected behavior for each type of password (for instance, "When a valid username and password are entered, the user is logged in and the application displays a message 'Welcome [username]'").

We recommend that developers use test data to verify the code as they build it. One obstacle is that developers generally cannot run the complete test cases until later in the development life cycle. Consequently, it is important that during the detailed design phase, the conceptual test cases are correlated to the flow of the data through the objects and between the objects. Once defined, these conceptual test cases can be translated into actual test cases and used at the unit level to quickly verify the functionality of the objects before the rest of the application is built.

A throwaway prototype can be used to configure tests for the use cases before any code is implemented. Tests can be designed based on the application flow demonstrated in the prototype. The main limitation is that it is not possible to verify realistic outcomes yet because it is only the prototype. Then, when the same flow is eventually implemented in code, the test cases can be easily transferred from the prototype interface to the actual interface. At this point, the test cases need to be modified to verify the outcomes.

When using an evolutionary prototype, it is recommended that tests are generated for it as soon as possible. This yields a head start on implementing the test plan. Often an evolutionary prototype contains main paths through the code, so many prototype tests can be reused in later development.

Measurement   One of the metrics used is the number of test cases per use case. Each use case should have a set of corresponding test cases. Another measure used later in the development is the number of passed and failed tests. These metrics should be tracked and assessed by the project manager and architect periodically to evaluate project progress status.

Tracking   Each conceptual test case should be stored in the requirements management system, and should reference the related use cases and requirements. As the product implementation progresses, conceptual test cases are translated into executable test cases that can be tracked as indicators of a feature implementation status. Additionally, the above metrics should be tracked to assure that all use cases have corresponding test cases and that these test cases pass and do not regress as the implementation progresses.

Automation   Creating conceptual test cases cannot be automated. However, once conceptual test cases are translated into executable test cases, most of them can be added to the regression test suite and executed automatically. For an evolutionary prototype, manual test cases should be supplemented by automatically generated and executed test cases. Once verified, test outcomes (pass or fail) can be tracked automatically. Metrics that indicate the number of the test cases per use case and the test pass rates can be calculated and tracked automatically.

4.2.7   Requirements Documents Inspection

The final step in validating the requirements documents before they are used in later development phases is the requirements documents inspection. While all the best practices above help in preventing defects, the requirements documents inspection is a comprehensive examination of all the requirements documents to find any lingering problems, such as missed requirements.

Why   Defects discovered after the requirements phase are more costly and difficult to remedy. One study, conducted by John Kelly, Joseph Sherif, and

Jonathan Hops, showed that defects discovered in testing took from 5 to 17 hours to fix, while defects discovered in the requirements took an average of 30 minutes to fix [9]. After following the best practices listed in this chapter, project artifacts such as the Vision and Scope document, requirements documents, use cases, and conceptual and some actual test cases would have been created. These documents need to be inspected for accuracy and consistency during the requirements phase, where it is easier and less costly to make corrections, before moving to subsequent phases.

Who For requirement inspections, several groups should be represented: the authors of the general requirements documents, the authors of the specific requirements documents, developers, product testers, and people who will develop products that interface with the product being inspected [4]. Additionally, if the project is a revision of an existing application, the inspection should also involve people familiar with the previous version, including users, developers, and testers.

How Informal requirement inspection will occur in varying degrees during the requirements phase, but a formal inspection should occur before the requirements documents are finalized. Checklists of common defects should be created for each requirements document, and members of the inspection team should each be assigned a few of the defects to evaluate. Once new defects are detected, they are added to the defect list and a defect prevention process is initiated.

One critical part of the inspection is to review the team's and organization's policies to determine how well the software requirements satisfy the policies and to determine what requirement revisions are needed. Requirements analysis is the best time for this review. Performing this at the end of the requirements phase allows all parties involved to have a better understanding of the application, which is necessary to determine whether the policy requirements are satisfied. If this were done later, any problems discovered would be exponentially more costly, difficult, and time-consuming to resolve.

Inspections are most effective when all participants are able to interact in real-time; questions can be asked and answered, follow-up questions can be posed, solutions can be brainstormed, and so on. However, it is difficult to gather all participants in one location, especially with geographically distributed teams. One workaround is conference calls. A better solution is to use modern meeting technologies, which allow geographically distributed team members to demonstrate and review software and collaborate on documents.

Measurement The dates of inspection should be available so managers can see when the inspections were performed. Requirements that have not recently been inspected should be evaluated. If entire categories or large sections of requirements have not been inspected, they should be scheduled for review.

The ratio of requirements that failed inspection to the total requirements should also be measured. If there is a high percentage of failed requirements, the process of defining requirements may need to be improved and then the requirements should be reanalyzed. The cause of the problem should be treated first (poor process), before treating the symptoms (poor requirements).

Tracking After each requirement is inspected, it should be marked with the date and person who inspected it. If it fails the inspection, the reasons why should be noted and it should be marked for rework. If it passes the inspection, the item should be marked as having passed. In addition, the time needed for the inspection should be tracked, which can be used to predict the time required for future inspections.

4.2.8 Managing Changing Requirements

Requirement changes occur after the initial requirements have already been finalized. These changes occur for two reasons: to accommodate changing needs and/or to correct misunderstandings that informed the initial vision. As we said earlier, changes typically will not emerge until after completing at least one cycle of the requirements analysis phase and starting the design phase.

Why A software project team will never elicit every requirement that every user or customer wanted on the first try. Requested changes may require considerable reworking of other systems, they may not be part of the current scope, or they may be unfeasible. Therefore, these changes must be managed so they are subject to the same processes as the rest of the requirements.

Who The architect, lead developer, or her designee should be selected to manage change requests, such as receiving the requests, evaluating the request, or providing input on the approval of the request.

How First, a requirements management system that tracks change requests should be available to everyone involved in the project, such as developers, customers, and managers. If a person wants to request a change, she should submit it through the change request feature in such a system. If such a feature does not exist, a manual approval process should be established. The project members who control the change control activities must review each change request and evaluate its feasibility and cost. This will determine whether the request will be accepted or rejected. If accepted, the originator of the request should be notified, as well as any other team members who will need to update documents or code. If the team does not have separate technologies that support requirement change tracking, they can use a spreadsheet or an existing database. However, all changes in the requirements should be stored in a shared repository and available to all involved stakeholders.

Requirements should not change significantly after their final inspection and approval. If a project manager or architect decides that some existing requirements need significant changes, the project's "production line" should stop, and the team should reiterate through the requirements phase. For instance, if there is truly a need for major changes that could not have been foreseen or prevented (e.g., your main competitor just released a new version and the application needs to add a significant new functionality to keep pace), requirements specification should restart, and best practices should be applied again with these new requirements in mind. If it is necessary to start over again, the team should attempt to reuse as much of the existing work as possible to move in the new direction. This might be difficult, but it will prevent wasting much of the previous effort.

In most cases, however, the demand for major changes indicates that best practices were not applied effectively. If this is the case, the team should apply the methodology's principle of "learning from mistakes": determine what part of the requirements process failed, and improve the requirements gathering and specification process so that unexpected changes do not occur in the future. For instance, assume that requirements need to be changed during implementation because the lead developer says it is impossible to implement one of the major requested features. This could have been avoided by having the lead developer more involved throughout the requirements process and/or by trying to develop an evolutionary prototype soon after the requirements were defined. To prevent the same problem from recurring in the future, the team could require that the lead developer attend the requirements-related meetings and approve each requirements-related artifact (Vision and Scope narrative, requirements, etc.). They could also require that an evolutionary prototype be built as soon as possible to determine whether requirements for new technologies are actually feasible and then modify the requirements as needed prior to implementation.

Requested changes that occur after requirements for the current release are frozen should be recorded in the problem tracking system and scheduled for future considerations or releases. This way, they are not forgotten. They should also be assigned preliminary priorities.

Measurement   Measures should include the number of change requests, the number and percentage of requests with a given status (pending, open, rejected, closed),[c] and the number of requests per originator. An excessively high number of change requests could indicate that the requirements were not comprehensive enough, or that the customer's expectations have changed.

---

[c] Pending indicates the request has not yet been reviewed. Open indicates the request has been accepted and will be implemented. Rejected indicates that the request was reviewed but will not be implemented. Closed indicates that the request has been implemented.

When requirements analysis has been completed, the ratio of change in use cases (the original use cases to the number of added, removed, or modified use cases) should be tracked. Again, a high ratio of change in use cases indicates either that the project's initial vision and scope was not well defined (for instance, as a result of misunderstanding the project needs or poor communication) or that the software requirements changed since the project's inception.

Tracking The change request, the person who requested it, and the date on which it was requested should all be tracked. Status change request dates, the new status, the status assigner, and the status change dates should also be tracked. (See Figure 4.4.)

Request	Author	Reviewer	Status	Created	Modified
Delete user...	A. F. N.	Q. L. D.	closed	11/04/05	11/06/05
Auto update...	B. T. K.	Q. L. D.	open	11/04/05	11/15/05
E-mail notify...	L. Y. W.	A. F. R.	rejected	11/06/05	12/18/05
Daily backup...	A. F. N.	A. F. R	pending	11/12/05	11/24/05

Figure 4.4 An example of the data tracked for change requests.

Automation When a change request is submitted, the person in charge of change requests should be automatically notified. When the status of a change request is updated, the originator of the request should be automatically notified, as well as any other members on the project who would need to know about it.

4.3 BEST PRACTICES IN DIFFERENT ENVIRONMENTS

The goal of applying best practices is to ensure that developers understand the requirements and implement code that satisfies the requirements provider's expectations. However, in some situations, it is possible (and more efficient) to achieve the same goal with less formality and the best practices can be modified to meet the needs of the group.

4.3.1 Existing versus New Software Project

When revising existing software projects, it is a common and critical mistake to overlook the project's past. The first step in working on requirements for an upgraded version of an existing software product should be to review the functionality of the current version. This can be done by reviewing the user's guide, use cases, requirements, Vision and Scope documents, and other relevant project artifacts. This should also involve conversations with people who worked on or used the current product version (including the product users, developers who implemented it, testers who tested it, and QA staff members who audited it).

Next, it is important to understand the legacy code that the new code will interface with and possibly extend. If there is existing functionality that is related to the planned new functionality, its code should be reviewed and evaluated for possible reuse and extension to accommodate the new requirements. In addition, the existing modules need to be reviewed during both the requirements definition and design stages to determine how the new modules will be integrated with the existing ones.

Often, the legacy code is not well documented. In this case, it is important to focus on understanding the code just well enough to add the new functionality to the existing functionality. Documenting the interface that the new code will connect to is important, but trying to document all of the legacy code at this point could be overwhelming as well as unnecessary. The most feasible way to document the legacy code is to document each piece as it is being extended or refactored. The requirements management artifacts (Vision and Scope document, SRS document, use cases) can then define how the new functionality will fit into the existing functionality, and how the old and the new will be integrated.

When working with existing projects, an attempt should be made to optimize reuse of existing code by adding as little new code as possible. Writing only as much new code as is needed helps to reduce the risk of injecting new defects. When reviewing the requirements with the project stakeholders, the new functionality needs to be well explained, and it should be clarified how the new use cases will be implemented in the context of the existing application: Will they pass through any existing functionality, or will they require all new functionality?

4.3.2   In-House versus Outsourced Development Teams

When team members are separated geographically, the risk of miscommunication increases. Even if the distance between team members is no more than one city block, it can still cause a communication barrier. Good communication is essential over the course of the entire project, and is especially important during the requirements gathering phase. If the team implementing the product does not fully understand what the software is supposed to do, chances are high that the software they deliver will not meet customer expectations.

Thus, to compensate for distance, it is important to institute formal meetings and a formal review/approval process for each requirements artifact. The entire outsourced team does not need to be involved at each step, but someone who works closely with that team should be involved. Web-based meetings should take place to improve communication and strengthen the feedback loop.

Over time, the level of formality can be relaxed as the relationship grows closer. For instance, when the requirements provider trusts that the outsourcer will correctly implement the requirements discussed in a meeting, a written document is not always needed. Alternatively, to move the project along faster, the requirements provider may want a trusted implementer to forgo producing a working prototype, and instead quickly sketch the proposed user interface. On the other hand, when the implementer has little or no interaction with the requirements provider (for instance, if the implementer is in one country and the requirements provider is in another), many misunderstandings can be prevented by producing formal specification documents and prototypes, and by waiting for approval at each step before proceeding to the next.

4.4 POLICY FOR USE OF THE REQUIREMENTS MANAGEMENT SYSTEM

As the requirements are gathered, defined, and prioritized, they should be entered into the requirements management system. Such a system is a repository shared among all project stakeholders and, depending on the organization's needs and maturity, it can be as elaborate as a sophisticated commercial software tool or as simple as an in-house customized spreadsheet application.

The goal of the requirements management system policy is to facilitate consistent use of this system for tracking the status of requirement changes and implementation. This policy includes tracking not only the requirements but also the related use cases and tests, which can be used to assess the extent to which the code conforms to the requirements at any given time. In addition to providing an objective insight into how well the code satisfies the requirements, this type of use of a requirements management system also prevents code rewrites due to requirements misinterpretation.

The Project Manager Should Approve the Final Version of the Vision and Scope Document, Which Should Be Entered into, and Tracked in, the Requirements Management System. The Vision and Scope document contains an overall product description and should therefore be stored and tracked in the requirements managements system. The change approval process for the Vision and Scope document should be well defined and automatically traced. All involved parties should be automatically notified when the Vision and Scope document has been modified.

The Architect Should Approve the Final Version of the Requirements Specification (SRS) Document. The Requirements from SRS Should Be Entered into, and Their Changes Tracked in, the Requirements Management System. In addition to the requirements, their priorities and implementation status should also be tracked. Requirements should be cross-referenced with corresponding features, so when the features are implemented, the corresponding requirement shows implementation progress. Changes in requirements and feature requests, and their priorities, should be tracked and all involved parties in the implementation of the requirement should be automatically notified when such changes take place.

The Architect or Lead Developer Should Define the Scope and Test Requirements for each Feature to Be Implemented, and then Enter those Details in the Requirements Management System For each requirement listed in the product specification, the architect or a lead developer should define the scope of the corresponding feature and describe what conceptual test cases she believes are needed to verify that the feature is implemented completely and correctly. This information should be recorded in the team's requirements management system. For example, the architect might record that a login functionality should be added, describe how this functionality should be implemented, and then require that the feature be verified with unit test cases, database verification test cases, and system test cases that track the login procedure as it passes through the system.

The Developer Should Create Test Cases for each Feature She Is Assigned to Implement, and Add those Test Cases to the Requirements Management System After a feature is approved, and design for it completed, the developer who is assigned its implementation should create test cases as specified in the requirements management system, and, once the code is implemented and tested, the verified test cases should be added to the regression test system. Test cases should reflect all requirements corresponding to a feature. As we will explain in the chapters on design and construction, for services, modules, and units of high complexity, tests are created first, and they will fail in the absence of the corresponding code. All other tests are created during or after the code implementation.

Working in this manner ensures that feature requests are not overlooked, and that the code is considered unfinished until all features are properly implemented. The team can then track the project status by monitoring the failed requirements test cases and/or by monitoring the requirements management system's list of open features.

After the Developer Implements a Feature, She Should Modify the Test Cases to Verify the New Feature; once the Tests Pass, She Should Mark the Feature as "Implemented" Once the developer has added the code that implements a feature, she needs to modify the original test cases to reflect changes to the code and to verify that the new feature is implemented completely and cor-

Feature Implementation Overview

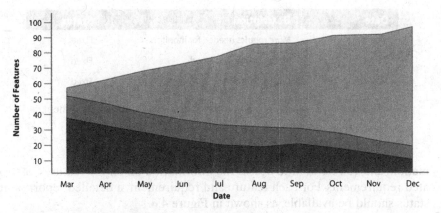

Features

Date	Unimplemented	In Progress	Implemented
Dec	15	9	98
Nov	17	11	96
Oct	21	10	92
Sep	25	12	88

Feature Details

ID	Feature Description	# Requirements	Status
1	User Customization of Interface	43	Unimplemented
2	User/Admin Login	16	In Progress
3	Loading/Saving Files	37	Implemented
4	Data Backup and Recovery	28	Implemented

Figure 4.5 An overview of the features for the product over a specified period.

rectly. If the modified test cases pass and verify all of the feature's requirements, the feature is considered complete and the developer should mark the
feature as "implemented." If the modified test cases do not pass, the developer
needs to modify the code and retest it.

4.4.1   Measurements Related to Requirements Management System

The reporting system should generate graphs illustrating the requirements
management data, such as the implementation of the features and requirements of the system. A feature graph displays the status of the features, as
shown in Figure 4.5. The table shows the number of features that are unimplemented, that are currently being implemented (in progress), and that are
implemented. Additionally, the features are listed with their overview infor-

Feature/Requirement: Feature A, Requirement 5

Date	Description	Status
May 10	More metrics needed for monitors	Fixed
May 4	Status change approved	Fixed
May 2	Changing status	Fixed

Figure 4.6   Detailed report on the status of a feature/requirement.

mation, and can be used to access the information on all the features' associated requirements. For each feature and requirement, a detailed report on its status should be available, as shown in Figure 4.6.

4.4.2 Tracking of Data Related to the Requirements Management System

The requirements management system should track the following data:

- All of the requirements and their priorities
- Use cases related to all requirements
- All features related to the requirements
- Test cases for each requirement
- Results of the test cases run

4.5 EXAMPLES

The first example shows how a customized best practice for requirements specification can be created based on defect root cause analysis and project needs. The other two examples focus on the reports for monitoring and managing requirements using the intermediate or extended infrastructure. Managers and architects should review reports to check current trends in the status of the project, and evaluate whether there are any potential problems.

4.5.1 Focus on Customized Best Practice

This example shows defect root cause analysis and a resulting customized best practice for a real-time application that communicates with external hardware and software system components.

Defect Identification   Consider an application that is supposed to monitor a computer system for possible security breaches and notify a remote security system once it detects tampering with the local system. A failure to detect tampering with an application system was observed by a system administrator. When a system was tampered with, an immediate call should have been made to the security system's remote computer, triggering an alarm. However, the alarm failed, leaving the tampered system prone to further security breaches.

Additional testing was performed, and it showed that if the initial call from the monitoring application receives a busy signal on the security system's remote computer, a second call is never made. Thus, in such situations, information about possible security breaches and tampering is completely lost.

Had the software been properly tested to see how busy signals would alter the local and remote communication routine, the problem would have been detected before the system was deployed. Communication defects of this type can be found in many applications, especially between web servers through web service calls and queries.

In this case, the root cause of the problem was a missing requirement in a description of feature interactions. While the "busy signal" was described as one of the states of the remote system, the local system response to this state was not specified. This oversight trickled down through both the system design and testing phases. (See Figure 4.7)

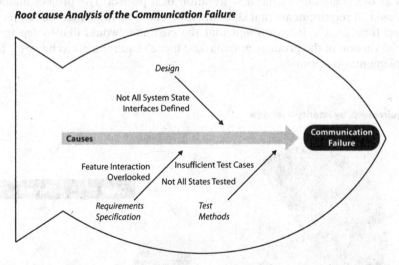

Figure 4.7   Fishbone diagram illustrating causes of the communication failure.

Customized Best Practice   A preventive action plan in this case requires a customized best practice that helps to ensure the inclusion of feature interactions in descriptions of project requirements, design, and testing. The practice would require that: "For a real-time project in which system components communicate with external components, all critical communication states must be explicitly identified, and all possible interactions between communicating components' critical states must be explicitly described."

All team members involved in the specification, design, and coding of the system communication components will be notified and trained to apply this practice. Design tools can help in verifying completeness of state representations and an automated testing system can help validate test completeness. The policy for the requirements management system would then require that use cases and test cases be entered into the system as soon as new features are added, and therefore that the status of feature interaction implementations would be tracked automatically.

4.5.2 Focus on Monitoring and Managing Requirement Priorities

This example shows how to monitor and manage requirement priorities. First, we will examine how the requirements should be divided into different priorities for a new project, and then how to monitor these requirement priorities during later iterations of an existing project.

At the beginning of a new software development project, it is important to assess the viability of the project goals and to properly assign the priority of the requirements. Figure 4.8 shows an overview of the implementation priorities at the beginning of the first iteration of a project. The project manager selected 24 requirements that she estimated could be implemented within the given time for the iteration and that the customer would like to see in the initial version of the product, and marked those requirements as having a high implementation priority.

Requirements by Priority Overview

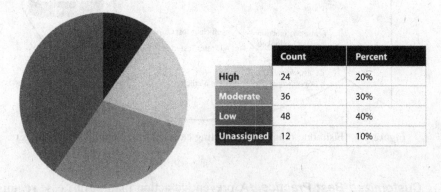

	Count	Percent
High	24	20%
Moderate	36	30%
Low	48	40%
Unassigned	12	10%

Figure 4.8 The Requirements by Priority Overview shows the counts and percentages of implementation priorities assigned at the beginning of an iteration.

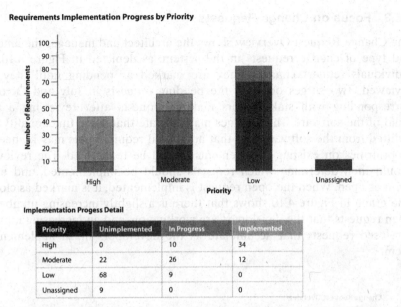

Implementation Progess Detail

Priority	Unimplemented	In Progress	Implemented
High	0	10	34
Moderate	22	26	12
Low	68	9	0
Unassigned	9	0	0

Figure 4.9   An overview of requirements implementation by priority.

High-priority requirements should be implemented first, and should meet the basic functionality needed to satisfy the customer. There should be enough high-priority requirements to keep the developers busy and to meet the needs of the customer, but not so many that the developers feel overwhelmed or that it would be impossible to complete the given iteration on schedule. Too many unassigned requirements may indicate that the requirements need to be thoroughly reviewed and prioritized.

During successive iterations of an existing software project, it is important to reassess the requirement's implementation priorities and evaluate the progress made in implementing the requirements. Figure 4.9 shows an example of the progress made implementing requirements after the first iteration of development. Almost all of the high-priority requirements have been implemented, but a few are still in progress. This indicates that slightly fewer requirements should be considered high priority for the next iteration, which would allow the developers to complete them and deliver the agreed-upon functionalities to the customer. Figure 4.9 also shows that implementation effort is being expended upon moderate and low priorities. This may indicate that some of the requirements originally identified as moderate or low priority were necessary to the project, and the priorities may need to be reevaluated to minimize the risk of missing future deadlines. As deadlines near, it may be necessary to have developers stop working on low- or moderate-priority requirements so that high-priority requirements can be completely implemented.

4.5.3   Focus on Change Requests

The Change Request Overview shows the architect and manager the amount and type of change requests in the system, as depicted in Figure 4.10. As individuals request changes, they are marked as pending until they are reviewed. Two surges occur in the pending requests in July and October, corresponding with stakeholders making requests after reviewing a new build of the software. These surges may indicate that some functionality was omitted from the software, and that additional requirements may be needed or priorities on existing requirements should be reanalyzed. The reviewers should then determine which requests should be implemented, and mark them as open. When the open request is implemented, it is marked as closed. The graph in Figure 4.10 shows that there is a slightly increasing number of open requests that the developers are working on, and an increasing number of closed requests that accumulate as the developers finish implementing them.

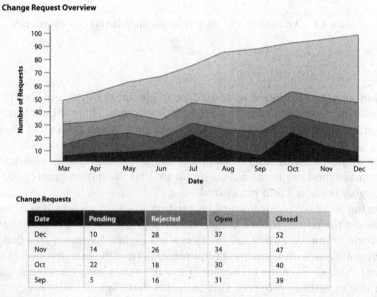

Change Requests

Date	Pending	Rejected	Open	Closed
Dec	10	28	37	52
Nov	14	26	34	47
Oct	22	18	30	40
Sep	5	16	31	39

Figure 4.10   Overview of submitted change requests. The table shows the number of pending, open, closed, and rejected requests for each month.

Having the ability to view the change requests by the users who made them can give insight into which stakeholders are providing the most useful feedback. In Figure 4.11, the first individual, A.F.N., has made several requests, but most of them have been rejected. The last user, D.T.C., has also made many requests, and most have been accepted and implemented.

Requests By	Pending	Open	Closed	Rejected
A.F.N.	10	4	2	23
B.T.K.	2	3	5	1
L.Y.W.	6	5	9	4
D.T.C.	14	12	27	6

Figure 4.11 View of change requests made by individuals. The table indicates how many of each individual's requests are pending, open, closed, and rejected.

4.6 ACRONYMS

SLOC　　　　　　　Source lines of code
OWASP　　　　　　Open Web Application Security Project

4.7 GLOSSARY

change request　A change request is a proposal submitted and evaluated to assess technical merit, potential side effects, overall impact on other configuration objects and system functions, and the projected cost of the change. [10]

conceptual test case　A high-level natural-language description of a test case. It precedes the code implementation and it is used by developers and testers to generate actual test cases.

evolutionary prototype　A fully functional prototype created as a skeleton or an initial increment of the final product, which is fleshed out and extended incrementally as requirements become clear and ready for implementation. [8]

feature　A functional or quality characteristic of a software element. It is a small block of system functionality.

inspection　A static analysis technique that relies on visual examination of development products to detect errors, violations of development standards, and other problems. Types include code inspection and design inspection. [11]*

Open Web Application Security Project (OWASP)　An organization for developing and supporting open source projects that produce tools, documentation, and standards for application security (www.owasp.org).

rapid prototyping　A type of prototyping in which emphasis is placed on developing prototypes early in the development process to permit early feedback and analysis in support of the development process. [11]*

scenario　A description of a specific interaction between a user and a system to accomplish some goal. An instance of usage of the system. A specific path through a use case. Often presented in the form of a story. [11]*

Software Requirements Specification (SRS) A complete description of expected functionality and behavior of the system. The SRS document should contain a complete list of requirements, their categories, and priorities, and it should reference corresponding use cases.

test case A set of test inputs, execution conditions, and expected results developed for a particular objective, such as to exercise a particular program path or to verify compliance with a specific requirement. [11]*

throwaway prototype A prototype that is created with the express intent of discarding it after it has served its purpose of clarifying and validating requirements and design alternatives. [8]

* From IEEE Std. 610.12-1990, Copyright 1990, IEEE. All rights reserved.

4.8 REFERENCES

[1] Jacobson, I., Booch, G., and Rumbaugh, J., *The Unified Modeling Language User Guide*. Addison-Wesley, 1999.

[2] Martin, R.C., *Fit for Developing Software: Framework for Integrated Tests*. Prentice Hall, 2005.

[3] Burnstein, I., *Practical Software Testing. A Process Oriented Approach*. Springer, 2002.

[4] Wiegers, K.E., *Software Requirements*. Microsoft Press, 2nd ed., 2003, pp. 78–90, 120–124, 242–251, 264, 333–337, 485, 488, 489.

[5] Ambler, S., "Requirements Wisdom," *Software Development*. October 2005, pp. 54–57.

[6] Venugopal, C., "Single Goal Set: A New Paradigm for IT Megaproject Success," *IEEE Software*, Vol. 22, No. 5, September/October 2005, p. 49.

[7] Boehm, B.W., Gray, T.E., and Seewaltd, T., "Prototyping Versus Specifying: A Multi-Project Experiment," *IEEE Transactions on Software Engineering*, Vol. 10, No. 5, May 1984, pp. 290–303.

[8] Schneider-Hufschmidt, M., and Zullighoven, H., "Prototyping in Industrial Projects—Bridging the Gap between Theory and Practice," *IEEE Transactions on Software Engineering*, Vol. 20, No. 11, November 1994, pp. 825–832.

[9] Kelly, J.C., Sherif, J.S., and Hops, J., "An Analysis of Defect Densities Found During Software Inspections," *Journal of Systems and Software*, Vol. 17, No. 2, 1992, pp. 111–117.

[10] Pressman, R.S., *Software Engineering: A Practitioner's Approach*. McGraw Hill, 6th ed., 2005.

[11] Institute of Electrical and Electronics Engineers, "Glossary of Software Engineering Terminology," *IEEE Standard 610.12-1990*—1990.

4.9 EXERCISES

1. Research a requirements management system. Does it offer automation, tracking, and measurements features that would help to implement the

ADP methodology? Which automation, tracking, and measurement features does it lack?

2. Do you think it would be more beneficial to buy a requirements management system, or to develop your own? Discuss why.

3. How would you deal with a customer who insists that every requirement is high priority, and must be implemented immediately?

4. In what situations would you use a throwaway prototype? When would you use an evolutionary prototype?

5. The tracking in your change request system reveals that a very important customer/manager is making considerably more change requests than any other stakeholder. What do you think this indicates, and how would you deal with this situation?

6. The tracking in your change request system reveals that all of the stakeholders are making numerous change requests. What do you think this indicates, and how would you deal with this situation?

7. An evolutionary prototype of a product has 5,000 SLOC. Calculate an estimated size and effort for the complete product (of ~50,000 SLOC) knowing that an average programmer's productivity on this prototype was 20 LOC/day.

8. How else would you estimate time and effort of a project based on the initial requirements?

9. Give examples not mentioned in this chapter of requirements-related reports that you would find useful when working on a project.

10. Name three software tools with extensive requirements management features.

CHAPTER 5

EXTENDED PLANNING AND INFRASTRUCTURE

The best way to predict the future is to invent it.

—Alan Kay

5.1 INTRODUCTION

In iterative software development, planning is in itself both iterative and incremental. Thus, beginning with the initial planning and infrastructure phase, we progress through requirements elicitation and specification, to extending both the planning and the infrastructure. *However, extended planning does not necessarily trail the requirements specification in a rigid sequential manner, but rather works **in conjunction with** the elicitation and specification of the requirements, and the design of the product architecture.*

In fact, requirements elicitation and specification is the planning of the software functionality, while the architectural design is the planning of its implementation. In its extended phase, planning also involves defining project artifacts and deliverables, assessing potential risks, estimating costs and schedules, as well as evaluating and possibly enlarging the infrastructure. As an incremental process, planning evolves as more requirements are elicited and specified, more clarity about the project functionality and its needs is attained, and the project deliverables are built. In iterative planning, cost and schedule estimations become more accurate as we progress through the successive implementations of the product iterations.

Automated Defect Prevention: Best Practices in Software Management, by Dorota Huizinga and Adam Kolawa
Copyright © 2007 John Wiley & Sons, Inc.

Planning and estimation is one of the most challenging tasks in software development. The Standish Group 2004 Report [1] validates this conjecture by stating that 18% of software projects failed completely (canceled prior to completion, or delivered and never used); another 53% were challenged (late, over budget, and/or with less than the required features and functions); and only 29% of the surveyed projects succeeded as planned.

The difficulty in estimating the costs and schedules of software projects stems not only from the fact that each product is unique, but also from the fact that perpetual technological advances very quickly render estimation models outdated.

Common planning problems fall into the following two categories:

1. Underestimation of efforts due to unforeseen project circumstances, such as an increase of project scope
2. Unplanned activities, such as the need for clarification of requirements, redesign, or additional debugging

Through the iterative approach to planning, some of the estimation problems can be alleviated. As the project progresses, a higher degree of approximation accuracy can be achieved.

The software development plan described in this chapter is a living document and its first version should be created after the core requirements have been specified and a high-level architecture has been outlined. Ideally, the plan should be reviewed after each iteration and updated as needed.

As the project progresses, the technology infrastructure might require further adjustments, customization, and expansion. At the same time, the people infrastructure might need to be reassessed and augmented to match the needs of the project. While not limited to this phase, these activities should have high priority during extended planning.

In this chapter, we explain how to create an initial software development plan and how this plan should be adjusted as the product iterations progress. We also show examples of the extended infrastructures necessary to meet the needs of applications such as embedded systems, web applications, web services, and databases.

The expected work products for this phase are:

• A software development plan
• An extended infrastructure

5.2   SOFTWARE DEVELOPMENT PLAN

The IEEE standard for Software Project Management Plans (SPMP)[a] [2] specifies the primary components of a software development plan. This

---

[a] The controlling document for managing a software project. [2]

standard provides general guidelines that are applicable to software projects of any scope or size. Based on this standard, as well as our research and experience, we have defined the following components as essential parts of the software development plan (SDP):[b]

- Defining project objectives
- Defining project artifacts and deliverables
- Selecting a software development process model
- Defining a defect prevention process
- Managing risk
- Managing change
- Defining an iterative work breakdown structure (WBS)[c]
- Estimating project effort
- Preparing the schedule
- Identifying and fulfilling additional resource requirements
- Extending the infrastructure

Planning is a team effort. All team members are involved in estimating time and effort, but the project manager is ultimately responsible both for the plan and for its execution.

While the SDP is a "living document," it is critical that it be as complete as possible early in the development phase so that no major features or deliverables are overlooked, which could cause project efforts to be grossly underestimated.

5.3 DEFINING PROJECT OBJECTIVES

The overarching goals of any project are to deliver a quality product on time and within budget while keeping all stakeholders satisfied. (See Figure 5.1.)

With these overarching goals in mind, the SDP is defined. The Vision and Scope document and the key product feature list are the basis for defining both the project objectives and the SDP.

It is important to keep project objectives simple. For example, when defining project objectives, one may think in terms of an advertising campaign that would concisely announce the key selling characteristics of the product. Project objectives are outlined in the SDP document, together with a list of product *key features* and product uses. These key features are later gradually refined into product implementation features and requirements in the SRS (software requirements specification), which is either a separate document or a list of items in the requirements management system.

[b] A project plan for a software development project. [3]
[c] An outline that organizes the tasks and activities necessary to achieve the project objective.

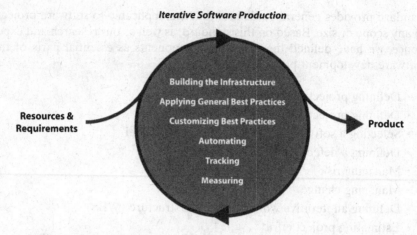

Figure 5.1   ADP's software production turns resources into goals.

If software is going to be released in phases, the features should be prioritized and divided into phases. Based on the features listed in the project objectives for the current release, the total time and effort for this release is estimated.

In the subsequent sections of this chapter, we will show how the SDP is created for an innovative, high-risk project called "FoodMagic" and for an existing low-risk project called "ParaBank."

New Project Example: FoodMagic's Objectives and Product Key Features

Project Name: FoodMagic

Objective: To provide users an online food shopping experience that will customize meal plans to their tastes. Based on user preferences, the program will find several recipes that will suit the user's tastes for each course of a meal. The users will be able to select which dishes they prefer for each meal, see the recipes for each dish, see the nutrition information for the meal, and order the ingredients for home delivery.

Intended Key Features:

- Matching Users' Tastes
  - User can select items from a list to create her taste profile
  - Program matches the taste profile to find foods the user will enjoy
- Personalizing Meal Preferences
  - User selects preferred dishes from provided samples
  - User selects any dietary restrictions (vegetarian, low sodium, low cholesterol)
  - User selects her preferred cooking tools (appliances, utensils, and so on)

- User selects type and number of meals she prepares per week
- User can rate previously selected dishes
- Automatically Generating Meal Plans
  - Program suggests several dishes for each meal based on user tastes
  - New meal plan will be generated every week
- Viewing Meal Plans
  - Ingredient lists are available for each dish in the meal plan
  - Recipes are available for each dish in the meal plan
  - Nutrition information is available for each meal
- Editing Meal Plans
  - User can customize meals from suggested dishes
  - User can request additional suggestions for dishes
- Saving Meal Plans
  - User can save meal plan
  - User can edit saved meal plan
- Ordering Ingredients for Meal Plans
  - User can view ingredients from meal plan, and select which to order
  - User can elect to receive the meal plan and a reminder as a weekly e-mail

Existing Project Example: ParaBank's Objectives and Product Key Features

Project Name: ParaBank

Objective: A realistic presentation of an e-banking application for demonstrating the functionality of web testing tools. The system is not designed to process actual banking transactions, but rather to have an e-banking interface that allows users to quickly assess the functionality of web testing tools.

Existing Key Features:

- Web server–based system is deployed on a small machine.
- Executable code runs on Apache's Jakarta Tomcat[d] server.
- Code is written in Java.
- Currently existing functionality allows users to:
  - Register for online access to existing accounts
  - Login to existing accounts
  - Open new accounts
  - Obtain an account summary

---

[d] Apache Tomcat is the servlet container that is used in the official Reference Implementation for Java Servlet and JavaServerPages technologies. [4]

- Search for previous transactions
- Update contact information
- Contact customer service

Intended New Key Feature:
- Allow the user to transfer funds from one account to another

5.4   DEFINING PROJECT ARTIFACTS AND DELIVERABLES

Project artifacts are all work products developed during the project lifetime. Project deliverables are those artifacts that are designated for the customer. The majority of the team's focus and time should be spent on the project deliverables because they present direct value to the customers. The identification of the required project artifacts and deliverables should be done by the entire team, but the final selection of the deliverables is up to the project architect and the project manager.

The list of the project artifacts includes but is not limited to:

- The Vision and Scope document and project objectives
- SRS, describing the product key features
  - Use cases or scenarios
- Architectural and detailed design documents and models
  - UML diagrams, data flow diagrams, database schemas
- List of COTS (Commercial-Off-the-Shelf Components)[e] used
- Source and executable code
- Test plan
- Acceptance plan
- Periodic reports generated by the reporting system
- Deployment plan
- User and operational manuals
- Customer training plan

5.4.1   The Vision and Scope Document and Project Objectives

Defined during the initial planning, the product Vision and Scope document, which contains a preliminary description of the product's main functionality

---

[e] Commercial Off-the-Shelf (COTS) products are hardware or software solutions that can be purchased ready for use either as a standalone solution or for integration into other applications.

and sets the boundaries of product growth, might need modifications after the core features and requirements have been specified. This document together with the project objectives should be stored in a shared repository and should provide a uniform theme and a product reference point to all team members throughout the entire product development.

5.4.2 SRS, Describing the Product Key Features

Depending on the organization maturity, product type, and external factors, the SRS can be a very detailed document included as a part of a contractual agreement and subject to external approvals for changes, or a high-level list of key features that are refined into the detailed requirements during subsequent product development iterations. For internal projects, requirements are already stored in a shared repository, so there is no need to create a separate document.

In either case, the team focuses on implementing requirements selected as high priority for the current iteration.

Use cases and scenarios help the team understand the application's desired functionality. They show the interactions between the users and the system, referred to as actors and personas. Similar to the features and requirements, high-level use cases are included in the initial SRS document and refined as needed during the implementation.

5.4.3 Architectural and Detailed Design Documents and Models

Since a high-level architectural design is performed in conjunction with extended planning, the preliminary design documents should be added to the project artifact repository during the extended planning phase. Other documents, including detailed design narratives and diagrams, are included as the project progresses. The team needs to decide what level of detail is necessary for the design of the product, and the architect should make the final decision about the required design documents. They may include UML diagrams that visualize objects and their interactions, data flow diagrams that illustrate the flow of data between modules and objects, or database schemas that demonstrate how the data is stored in a database and how data items relate to each other. In addition, an interface schema showing interactions between modules and objects may have to be included.

5.4.4 List of COTS (Commercial Off-the-Shelf Components) Used

One of the decisions that must be made during the extended planning phase is the potential use of COTS. Today's extensive use of COTS, which span a wide spectrum of products from databases to game engines, is dictated by the market shift to customization of existing commercial applications to fit project needs rather than performing in-house development of such systems. COTS promise higher quality than the equivalent systems implemented in-house because they are developed by vendors who specialize in systems providing the required functionality and are well tested by many users. The use of COTS, if affordable, is a recommended ADP practice. A list of COTS used in the project should be included in its SDP.

5.4.5   Source and Executable Code

The source code and its executable are the ultimate product artifacts. The plan should include the target hardware and software configurations for the code.

5.4.6   Test Plan

The conceptual test cases are defined when the product features and requirements are specified. They should be included in the plan, and the time for testing and debugging each feature should be added to the project estimates. In addition, the stop-test criteria for each iteration should be determined at this point. This may include the test pass rate combined with the test coverage and other quality indicators determined by the team. Both functionality and quality requirements should be considered when deciding on the transition to the subsequent iterations and deployment.

5.4.7   Acceptance Plan

The acceptance plan usually is defined by a contractual agreement. A part of this plan includes the acceptance testing that is conducted to determine whether a system satisfies the acceptance criteria specified by the customer. In iterative development, frequent interactions with the customer are important, and as successive components of the product are developed, they should become part of the system acceptance plan. This gradual progress of acceptance prevents misunderstandings and miscommunication that might take place at the end of the implementation and allows for correcting the system to the customer's satisfaction before its deployment.

5.4.8   Periodic Reports Generated by the Reporting System

The plan also should state what reports from the reporting system will be used and how often they will be reviewed. Some reports, such as code builds and test results, should be reviewed by the team daily. Other reports, such as a feature implementation status and a schedule index, could be evaluated before the end of each iteration to readjust estimations and, if needed, reallocate project resources. The reports that give a comprehensive view of the system, such as a confidence factor, can be used to determine the product's deployment readiness.

5.4.9   Deployment Plan

The deployment plan should include all steps necessary for the final product to be transferred to the production system. This may include building the intermediate staging systems so the product is tested in a simulated environment similar to the production configuration. The deployment process should be automated by scripts and programs that gradually transfer product modules to the production area.

5.4.10   User and Operational Manuals

User and other operational manuals should be created as the product is being developed and the time and effort for their development should be allotted in the plan. Ideally, the manuals should be created by those team members who are most familiar with the product. As soon as the features are implemented, their descriptions should be added to the manual. A final revision must be performed after all user interfaces have been finalized and their functionality verified.

5.4.11   Customer Training Plan

If customer training is required, the time and effort for training activities needs to be accounted for in the plan. The training schedule should be added to the plan as soon as it is finalized.

The following subset of the above artifacts constitutes the project deliverables:

- Software requirements specification
- Acceptance and deployment plans
- COTS and the executable code
- User and operational manuals
- Customer training plan

New Project Example: FoodMagic's Artifacts and Deliverables

Artifacts:

- Vision and Scope document
- SRS document describing the product's key features
- Evolutionary prototype of the software architecture
- Use cases
- Data flow diagrams
- Database schema
- Database entity relationship diagrams[f]

---

[f] A diagrammatic technique for illustrating the interrelationships between entities in a database.

- UML object diagrams
- Test plans and test cases

Deliverables:

- Database
- Executable code
- User and operational manuals

Existing Project Example: ParaBank's Artifacts and Deliverables

Artifacts for Adding the New Functionality Include:

- Use cases
- Source code and executable code
- Test cases for regression testing
- Test cases for the integrated new and existing functionality
- Revised user's manual

Deliverables:

- Executable code with added functionality
- Revised user's manual

5.5 SELECTING A SOFTWARE DEVELOPMENT PROCESS MODEL

This section of the plan describes the software development process models selected for the project. This choice depends on the nature of the application and the existing processes in the organization. As discussed in Chapter 1, modern software processes usually do not conform to one specific model, but instead often utilize elements of many approaches from waterfall, through prototyping, to agile. The team might specify a generic model such as *agile* or *unified*, and explain additional characteristics or best practices used in the development. The model defined by the ADP best practices does not rely on one specific process and it can be used with any existing approach used by the organization.

For an existing project where the organization already has a well-defined software development process model, our methodology recommends building an infrastructure that facilitates further maintenance and expansion of the product, with minimal changes to the existing process model.

New Project Example: FoodMagic's Software Development Model The ADP software development process model (explained in section 2.5) has been selected for this new project.

Existing Project Example: ParaBank's Software Development Model
The software development model used in the past and currently for this application is an *agile process*.

5.6 DEFINING DEFECT PREVENTION PROCESS

The defect detection and prevention roles were defined and assigned during
the initial planning phase. While all team members should be involved in the
defect prevention process, the primary responsibility for it is assumed by the
testers, QA staff, and the architect.

This section of the plan describes activities associated with the defect prevention process. Testers detect defects, and report them in the problem tracking system. For each detected defect, they should provide a brief description
that covers how the defect was detected. At the same time, a preliminary
decision should be made as to whether the defect should be marked as severe
and whether additional preventive action is required. If a tester deems the
defect as severe, the team should decide whether the problem is widespread
and repeatable enough for a new customized best practice to be created. The
team also should decide when the new practice should be used. For example,
if the team's current practice is to declare any defect related to possible security vulnerabilities as severe and requiring immediate attention, a new practice
that prevents a detected security problem should be implemented at once.
Otherwise, the introduction of other best practices might be postponed to the
next iteration.

Defect reports should be analyzed by the team on a daily basis, and the
team activities reassigned to resolve high-priority issues as they arise.

5.7 MANAGING RISK

Risk management is the process of minimizing chances of project failure
due to unplanned and undesirable circumstances. Since defects are both
unplanned and undesirable, defect prevention is ultimately a risk mitigation
technique.

DEVELOPER'S TESTIMONIAL

I am also a big fan of *risk management*. Many of the people I work with spend a
great deal of effort focused on what they are doing in the present. Risk management
actively thinks about the future. I consider the concept of defect prevention to be
consistent with, and perhaps conceptually fit within, risk management.
                                                    —Gordon C. Hebert, Systems Engineer

---

A risk plan is a list of all potential risks, along with a plan to mitigate some of those risks. The risk plan is developed by the project manager, who works closely with the architect and other team members. Risk planning involves brainstorming sessions to identify potential risks, estimate of each risk's impact, and create a possible mitigation plan for each risk. Once identified, the risks should be prioritized according to both the magnitude of their possible negative impact and their probability of occurrence. For each of the risks with a potentially high negative impact or with a high probability of occurrence, a mitigation plan should be developed.

The following categories of potential risk sources should be taken into account:

- Requirements ambiguity and volatility
- Design complexity
- Lack of personnel expertise
- Testing and debugging difficulties
- Difficulty in determining deployment readiness
- Technology changes and needs
- Personnel changes and needs

A key to avoiding future problems is to deal with the most complicated and highest risk problems first.

For new projects, design complexity is often one of the riskiest factors and therefore should be mitigated early. This is especially true when creating an innovative product that has never existed before, which is more common in the software industry than in other types of organizations. Creating a vertical prototype[g] is the most effective way to assess design complexity and helps to avoid future problems. If it becomes apparent that the problems that arose during prototyping cannot be solved, it is likely that the project will fail. On the other hand, if the vertical prototype is successful, the decision should be made to move forward with the project. As a side note, it is wise to assign the most capable people and advanced technology to new and complicated projects.

In maintaining and revising existing projects, there are two categories of risk that need to be considered. The first category includes the risks common to all existing projects, which should be mitigated by applying general best practices. In the second category are project-specific risks, which should be mitigated by applying customized best practices.

---

[g] A partial implementation of a software-containing system that slices through all layers of the architecture and provides evidence that the idea is feasible. [5]

New Project Example: FoodMagic's Risk Plan

Risks Specific to FoodMagic

Risk 1: It may not be possible to discern a person's tastes and correlate them to various types of foods.

Risk 1 Impact: If it is not possible to correlate tastes, it will be impossible to create a working product that fulfills the project's primary objectives.

Risk 1 Probability of Occurrence: Since this is a new technology, we cannot accurately gauge the probability of occurrence, and must therefore assume that it is high.

Risk 1 Mitigation Plan: Develop a prototype of taste correlation functionality. Assign two or three developers to this task for approximately 6 months. If the prototype cannot discern tastes and find appropriate foods to match the tastes, the project will be abandoned.

Existing Project Example: ParaBank's Risk Plan

Category 1—Risk Common to All Existing Projects

Risk 1: Possibility of introducing defects to the existing parts of application when adding new functionality.

Risk 1 Mitigation through a General Best Practice: Apply the following general best practice: review existing code and its design thoroughly, and minimize the amount of modifications to the existing code. Regression testing should be applied at each update to verify that the update has not affected existing functionality.

Category 2—Risk Specific to ParaBank

Risk 2: The screen flow is not convincing enough to achieve the purpose of providing a realistic demo to customers.

Risk 2 Mitigation through a Customized Best Practice: Customize the prototyping best practice in the following manner: Prototype screen flow to and from the screens that add new functionality, and validate the flow with customers.

Observation: Because the users of this site are not going to perform actual banking transactions with ParaBank, the potential risk impact is relatively low.

5.8 MANAGING CHANGE

Depending on the project size, and whether it is an internal development or an external contract, change management might be less or more formal. If changes require customer approvals, then the change process has to be formalized and described in the plan. In addition, if the project size is very large, change approvals might have to be formalized to keep all team members notified and to ensure that the workflow reflects all recent changes. In such formalized situations, the project manager should oversee and mandate the protocols and procedures for the requirement and design change as well as other changes in product development. Requests for changes should be stored in the problem tracking system, prioritized, and then approved or rejected by the team and, if required, other project stakeholders.

5.9 DEFINING WORK BREAKDOWN STRUCTURE—AN ITERATIVE APPROACH

Once the project's key features have been defined, the software development model chosen, and the risk and change management plan determined, the project must be divided into tasks, which will be recorded in the work breakdown structure (WBS). In the traditional top-down approach, WBS is a list of tasks that, when completed, will produce the final product. While such a global list might be originally created for the purpose of total project time and cost estimation, in the iterative approach, a detailed WBS is created only for the current iteration. Thus, in iterative development, the concept of WBS is dynamic and represents a set of current activities as generated by the CAL (Current Activity Log) report.

The dividing of the project into tasks can be based on the organization's processes or on the product features. We favor the second approach because it focuses on the product, which is what ultimately brings value to the customer. The processes that are already in place should then be adapted and extended through the application of best practices that reflect the product-based approach. A rule of thumb is that in any iteration the project can be broken into 10 to 15 primary tasks, where the task granularity depends on the project size and scope, and the iteration duration.

These tasks may include:

- Defining and managing communication with customers
- Defining additional product features
- Designing use cases for a new feature
- Developing prototypes for parts of the product that have not been prototyped, but require special attention

- Determining the feasibility of the new features
- Designing and modeling the product elements
- Refining existing features to detailed requirements
- Implementing a set of features and requirements
- Designing a test plan for a set of features
- Testing implemented features and requirements
- Debugging
- Preparing operational and user manuals
- Planning deployment and customer training

The tasks to be executed during the current iteration are assigned the highest priority and marked as active. Team members should understand what is required for each task and how they will accomplish each task. Some tasks, such as the implementation of a feature, may continue throughout the entire iteration, but others, such as removing a defect, may be finished early.

New Project Example: FoodMagic's Work Breakdown Structure

Contacts for WBS:

- Point of contact with customers and upper management: Gary (Project Manager)
- Point of contact Group A: Shu-Ping (Lead Developer)
- Point of contact Group B: Morgan (Lead Developer)
- Point of contact Group C: Anna (Lead Developer)
- Point of contact for Review Change Requests and Notification of Appropriate Groups: Sri (Architect)

Iteration 0 (Prototype of Taste-Matching Functionality) WBS:

- Prototype Taste Database: Group A, Alex (Architect)
- Prototype Taste-Matching Engine: Group B, Sri (Architect)

Iteration 1 (Taste-Matching Functionality) WBS:

- Requirements
  - Vision and Scope document: Gary (Project Manager) with all groups
  - SRS document: Gary (Project Manager) with all groups
- Design
  - Taste-Matching Database: Group A, Alex (Architect)
    - Entity relationship diagrams: Janet
    - Database schema: Tom

- Taste-Matching Application Logic: Group B, Sri (Architect)
  - Data flow diagrams: Frank
  - UML diagrams (Classes and Objects): Satoe
- Taste-Matching User Interface: Group C, Betty (Architect)
  - Use cases: Poulami
  - Customer user interface screen flow: Dexter
- Implementation and Testing
  - Taste-Matching Database: Group A, Alex (Architect)
    - Test plan: Alex
    - Database and test cases: Group A
  - Taste-Matching Application Logic: Group B, Sri (Architect)
    - Test plan: Sri
    - Source code and test cases: Group B
  - Taste-Matching User Interface: Group C, Betty (Architect)
    - Test plan: Betty
    - Source code and test cases: Group C
- Taste-Matching Documentation: Shu-Ping, Morgan, Anna (Group Leaders)

Iteration 2 (Ingredients and Recipes Functionality) WBS:

...

Iteration 3 (Meal Plan and Preferences Functionality) WBS:

...

Iteration 4 (Website Administrator Functionality) WBS:

...

Iteration 5 (Website Customer Shopping Functionality) WBS:

- Requirements
  - SRS document: Gary (Project Manager) with all groups
- Design
  - Website customer database: Group A, Alex (Architect)
    - Entity relationship diagrams: Janet
    - Database schema: Tom
  - Website Customer Application Logic: Group B, Sri (Architect)
    - Data flow diagrams: Frank
    - UML diagrams (Classes and Objects): Satoe

- Website Customer User Interface: Group C, Betty (Architect)
  - Use cases: Poulami
  - Customer user interface screen flow: Dexter
- Implementation and Testing
  - Website Customer Database: Group A, Alex (Architect)
    - Test plan: Alex
    - Database and test cases: Group A
  - Website Customer Application Logic: Group B, Sri (Architect)
    - Test plan: Sri
    - Source code and test cases: Group B
  - Website Customer User Interface: Group C, Betty (Architect)
    - Test plan: Betty
    - Source code and test cases: Group C
- Website Customer Documentation: Shu-Ping, Morgan, Anna (Group Leaders)

Existing Project Example: ParaBank's Work Breakdown Structure

WBS One and Only One Iteration:

- Development of the screen flow prototype: A.A.D.
- Validation of prototypes with customers: A.A.D.
- Design, implementation, and testing of the new functionality: A.A.D.
- Regression and system testing: C.B.L.
- Deployment and communication with customers: C.B.L.

5.10 BEST PRACTICES FOR ESTIMATING PROJECT EFFORT

The project estimates are predicted values of the total effort required to develop a complete or partial software product. Project effort is generally expressed in *person months* (PM) or *person years* (PY). A person month is the amount of effort that one person spends working on a software project for one month. Similarly, a person year is the amount of effort that one person spends working on a software project for one year.

Due to a large variety of types and the inherent uncertainty of software projects, accurate estimates of development efforts are difficult to calculate. Moreover, such estimates often have to be performed early (when little is known about the project) in order to bid on a contract, make the decision whether to proceed with product development, or to beat the competition to market.

If the project is more conventional, similar projects can be used to estimate its total effort, and these estimates can be done as soon as project key features have been determined. However, for innovative projects where little or no historical data exists, most models would require a high-level architectural design for the first level of effort estimate.

There are numerous models and automated tools that facilitate project effort estimation based on either prior historical data of the organization, parametric representations, or databases of data from similar projects. Such tools should be added to the technology infrastructure and used throughout the project to track its cost and schedule and provide estimates for successive iterations.

DEVELOPER'S TESTIMONIAL

We develop use cases, estimate the complexity of use cases, and implement prototypes to better estimate the work and complexity. Depending on the number of use cases, we evaluate high-level classes and objects. We use tools like Quantitative Software Management's SLIM[h] to input the complexity of use cases, number of use cases, objects, project deliverables, and other parameters to get graphical outputs of estimates. We come up with a Productivity Index to compare against the project database that QSM provides in order to get a high-level estimate of our project. Then, we manipulate it with various other parameters to see how the overall project schedule will vary using tools/techniques.

In one of our recent banking projects that I worked on, which is a J2EE/Websphere application, I input the following estimates into the QSM tool:

# of UC = 28, # of Biz Obj = 38, # of Biz Rules = 170

The tool estimated that with six developers, the required time would be three months, which turned out to be close to reality (with a variance of 10%).

—Ravi Bellamkonda, Business Systems Analyst

In the subsequent sections, we will describe the three categories of effort estimation that can be used for the entire project duration, or a single iteration:

1. Estimation by using elements of Wideband Delphi[i]
2. Estimation by using effort analogy[j]
3. Estimation by using parametric models[k]

---

[h] A commercial estimation and tracking software tool.
[i] A consensus-based method for estimating effort.
[j] Using experience with one or more completed projects or a project prototype to relate actual cost and development time to the cost and development time of the new project.
[k] The model calculates the dependent variables of cost and duration based on one or more estimated parameters.

The *Wideband Delphi* approach relies on multiple meetings of individuals involved in the project and a progressive convergence of their effort estimates. Estimation by *effort analogy* is based on data from similar existing projects or *a working prototype* of the current project, which are used as the basis for the total project effort estimation. *Parametric models* are mathematical representations of formulas with variables for effort-related factors such as project complexity, required product reliability, organization maturity, component reuse, and many more. These models use regression analysis, numerical analysis, or management surveys to calculate parameter values.

For small projects, simple heuristics based on the product design and developers' estimated time of effort should suffice. For medium to large projects (those that exceed $1M in costs), it is recommended that two complementary approaches be used to verify the validity of the estimates.

The project effort estimates are readjusted throughout the project's lifetime. Thus, they are a changing component of the SDP document, which is modified and validated based on the progress status of the tasks defined in the project's initial and subsequent iterations of product development.

5.10.1   Estimation by Using Elements of Wideband Delphi

A straightforward approach to effort estimation is to have the people responsible for their tasks estimate the amount of time it will take them to complete these tasks. To obtain a more objective estimate, elements of an approach called the *Wideband Delphi* estimation method can be used. In the Wideband Delphi approach, multiple team members participate in estimating each other's task efforts. The project manager selects a moderator and an estimation team of three to seven members. Two meetings occur in the Delphi approach. The first meeting is the kickoff meeting during which the complete project WBS is created and discussed. Each individual team member then creates an effort estimate for each of the tasks in the project WBS. During the second meeting, estimates from all team members are collected and reviewed, discrepancies in estimates are discussed, and then a consensus is achieved with help of a moderator. The Wideband Delphi method provides a wide perspective on task effort estimates and it reduces the chances of estimation errors by involving multiple team members, who evaluate each other's estimates. After the task estimates are collected from everyone involved in a project, a comprehensive project time and effort estimate can be created. A similar, but less formal, approach can be used for evaluating the Current Activities Log for each iteration, and reassigning the task priorities.

While relatively simple and easy to implement, the Wideband Delphi approach may prove both inaccurate and unacceptable for medium- and large-sized projects with few precedents or when more formal estimation approaches are contractually required.

New Project Example: FoodMagic's Wideband Delphi Estimations

Wideband Delphi Estimations for the FoodMagic Prototype

Two developers were assigned to the FoodMagic prototype. In the second Wideband Delphi meeting, the developers' estimates were four months and seven months. After working with the moderator, the developers decided that six months would be an acceptable estimate for the time needed to complete the prototype.

Wideband Delphi Estimations for the FoodMagic Product

Four developers were assigned to the FoodMagic product. In the second Wideband Delphi meeting, the developers' estimates were 18 months, 20 months, 24 months, and 28 months. During the first part of the meeting, the developers with the higher estimates convinced the other members that the product would take at least 22 months to develop. They revised their estimates again, and three developers agreed that the project would require 22 months, but the last developer still believed the project would take 28 months. After working with the moderator, the developers agreed that the project would require 24 months to complete.

Existing Project Example: ParaBank's Wideband Delphi Estimations

A.D.D. estimated total effort for the ParaBank's five tasks to be two weeks. C.B.L. estimated three weeks. Since the project was very small, additional meetings were not held, and the estimate of three weeks was selected.

5.10.2 Estimation by Using Effort Analogy

For projects that are more conventional, estimation by *effort analogy* can be used. This is achieved by predicting total project effort based on prior experience from developing similar products or a product's prototype, or by accessing a database with information about similar projects. In this case, the team members are building a product or components of a product similar to the ones that they or somebody else built previously, and therefore the required effort for the new project should be similar to the effort required for the past project.

For example, consider two products for testing websites, Product A and Product B. The new product, Product B, is very similar to the existing Product A. They have the same basic requirements: testing functionality of websites, load testing of the websites, and performing static analysis on the client-side code. It took a five-person team two and a half years to implement a functional version of Product A. Thus, the rough estimate of the effort for the new Product B is $5 \times 2\frac{1}{2} = 12\frac{1}{2}$ PY.

To obtain more precise estimates, the information about efforts needed for building components of similar systems in the past can be obtained from the reporting system using the reports similar to the one shown in Figure 5.2 in combination with the Wideband Delphi approach.

Project	SubProject	SLOC	Months	Developers	Person Months
Project A	User Interface	70,000	10	4	40
	Admin Interface	64,000	8	4	32
	App. Logic	144,000	12	8	96
Project B	User Interface	40,000	8	2	16
	App. Logic	54,000	8	3	24
Project C	Web Service	33,000	6	2	12

Figure 5.2 An overview panel from the reporting system shows the developers' productivity.

Estimation by effort analogy can also be used in situations where an innovative product (a product with no prior experience) is being developed after a functioning prototype already exists. In such a case, the amount of project effort can be approximated by extrapolating the prototype effort. Since the effort to develop the prototype is known (called here effortPrototype), we can estimate the effort of the entire project (effortProject) by making an educated guess about the percentage of the entire project effort that had been used for the prototype (prototypePercent).

Thus, the estimated project effort can be expressed by the following formula:

$$effortProject = (100/prototypePercent) * effortPrototype$$

New Project Example: FoodMagic's Estimation by Analogy

FoodMagic's prototype development required six months for a two-person team. Thus, effortPrototype = 12 PM.

Assuming that this prototype required about 10% of the total project effort, we have arrived at the following formula:

$$effortFoodMagic = (100/10) * effortPrototype$$

$$effortFoodMagic = 120 \text{ PM} = 10 \text{ PY}$$

Thus, assuming that four developers can work on this project in parallel, it will take approximately 2.5 years to complete it.

Existing Project Example: ParaBank's Estimation by Analogy

Both A.D.D. and C.B.L. worked on the ParaBank project before, and therefore they were able to provide the above estimation for the project duration. Thus, the project effort estimation was 3 person weeks (PW).

Another analogy-based approach for estimating the effort for a project with a functional prototype is to use the following, already-known, data:

- The number of requirements needed to complete the project (RequirementsToComplete)
- The average amount of time it took to complete each implemented requirement (AverageTimePerRequirement)
- The average number of developers needed per implemented requirement (AverageNumberOfDevelopers)

To estimate the total amount of effort for a project, the following formula can be used:

$$\text{effortProject} = \text{effortPrototype} + \text{RequirementsToComplete} * \\ \text{AverageTimePerRequirement} * \\ \text{AverageNumberOfDevelopers}$$

Some software estimation models and contractors still require input expressed in SLOC (source lines of code). In general, SLOC is not a very accurate measure either of the project effort or a developer's productivity, since it varies widely for different projects and types of development. For example, in a single product that requires development of a firmware, drivers, and a high-level language application, the number of SLOC/developer/month can vary by orders of magnitude; it can be respectively 300, 1,200, and 8,000 SLOC/developer/month.

If there is such a need for expressing software size estimates in SLOC, then an analogy-based approach to estimation is to use SLOC size as a basic measure and approximate the total project size before calculating the project effort. After a prototype is finished, the following information is available:

- The number of requirements needed to complete the project (RequirementsToComplete, expressed in Req)
- The average number of SLOC in each implemented requirement (AverageSLOCPerRequirement, expressed in SLOC/Req)
- The average number of SLOC per developer per month (AverageSLOCPerDeveloperMonth, expressed in SLOC/PM)

To estimate the total number of person months required to complete the project, the following formula can be used:

$$\text{effortProject} = \text{effortPrototype} + \text{RequirementsToComplete} * \\ \text{AverageSLOCPerRequirement} / \\ \text{AverageSLOCPerDeveloperMonth}$$

SLOC or Not SLOC

DEVELOPER'S TESTIMONIAL

We use Oracle to develop database applications that store up to several million records. It is always challenging to build web applications that access these data so the customers can use them in a meaningful way. The user-friendly web GUI must be implemented with underlying engines that extract data so only the data needed by the customers is displayed. Also, the data input and modification web screens are built so the users can manipulate data in a meaningful way.

In order to estimate the developers' productivity, we not only use SLOC/developer/month as a basic metric, but we also use a difficulty assessment of programming a web GUI or internal engine that requires advanced skills and database knowledge. We baseline the SLOC/developer/month based on the developer skills and the difficulty of programming. For example, we only baseline 300 lines of code/developer/month for a certain internal calculating engine or queries that require accessing reference tables that have many pointers. The difficulty for this type of code is high, so we assign it a difficulty factor of 10. So, we multiply $300 \times 10 = 3000$ to normalize SLOC/developer/month. We categorize tasks by difficulty and multiply the quantified number with SLOC/developer/month to give us the absolute SLOC/developer/month. In this way, we go through every task before the development starts and during the programming. We constantly discuss this estimation among our team members to exchange ideas about difficulty and solution. This improves the predictability of the estimates.

—Henry Pae, Software Engineer

Estimations by analogy are effective in low-risk projects and projects for which similar historical data exists. Unfortunately, they cannot be used in innovative projects unless a functioning prototype already exists, and even then, the estimate is just a good guess. If used for innovative projects, estimates should be corroborated by one of the other approaches.

5.10.3 Estimation by Using Parametric Models

Parametric models are mathematical representations by formulas, which use effort-qualifying variables representing either quantitative or qualitative attributes of software development. Quantitative parameters describe, for example, size, number of defects, number of violated coding rules, or number of months. Qualitative parameters can describe, for example, software complexity, team cohesion, organization maturity, or a level of process automation.

Historically, parametric approaches have their roots in Constructive Cost Model (COCOMO), which was originally developed in the early 1980s by Barry Boehm [6]. While superseded by more modern approaches, including COCOMO II [7,8], the original COCOMO was the first attempt at a comprehensive, parametric model to estimate software development effort. The following sidebar describes its basic features.

HISTORICAL BACKGROUND—COCOMO

The Constructive Cost Model (COCOMO) is a software cost and scheduling estimate hierarchy of models, which describe three types of projects developed in different modes: *organic*, *semidetached*, and *embedded*.

Organic Mode

This mode describes an in-house, relatively small project to be developed by a relatively small group, where most of the group members are already familiar with the organization's past projects and goals. Many of the group members will understand the current project and the organization's objectives, and will be able to begin effectively working on the project from its inception.

Semidetached Mode

The semidetached mode of software development represents an intermediate stage between the organic and embedded modes. The project is of medium size. The environment is less stable and less familiar to the group members than in the organic mode. Similarly, project constraints usually are more rigid than in the organic mode.

With respect to its conformance to functional and interface specifications, a typical semidetached-mode project might be, for example, a transaction processing system with quite rigorous interfaces, which must conform to regulatory demands.

Embedded Mode

A project in the embedded mode is subject to rigorous constraints. The product must adhere to constraints in the form of hardware, software, regulations, and operational procedures. These constraints cannot be relaxed or changed, usually due to cost or difficulty. Therefore, the product must be developed to conform to the constraints and to overcome any difficulties that may arise from the constraints.

The general formula, developed based on studying 56 projects, can be expressed in the following manner:

$$\text{effortProject} = A \times (KSLOC)^B$$

where A and B are project mode–related parameters defined below:

Mode	Effort
Organic	$PM = 2.4\,(KSLOC)^{1.05}$
Semidetached	$PM = 3.0\,(KSLOC)^{1.12}$
Embedded	$PM = 3.6\,(KSLOC)^{1.20}$

The quantity KSLOC is the projected number of thousands of delivered source lines of code in the software product. The quantity PM is the number of person months estimated for the software development effort.

Example of Estimates Using COCOMO I

Here is an example of an organic-mode software project. An initial study has determined that the size of the program will be roughly 32,000 delivered source lines of code (32 KSLOC). From the above parameters, we estimate the effort of the project:

$$\text{effortProject} = 2.4 \ (32)^{1.05} = 91 \text{ PM}$$

COCOMO II   COCOMO II [9][1] was developed by Boehm in 1995 to respond to the changing economic landscape in software development. COCOMO II is an extended version of COCOMO; it includes more parameters and is capable of estimate distribution across the various phases of the project. Similar to the original COCOMO, the COCOMO II model requires sizing information, such as source lines of code (SLOC).

If SLOC cannot be estimated by analogy, a technique based on *function points*[m] can be used to approximate SLOC. Function point analysis (FPA) is a method that produces project estimates based on problem size instead of code size. Function points can be derived from the requirements. To count the total number of function points, parameters such as user inputs, user outputs, files, and external interfaces are needed. Depending on the development language used, the above parameters are assigned numerical values and in turn are used to calculate so-called *adjusted function points (AFP)*.[n] Adjusted function points account for a set of complexity factors such as performance, data communication, or algorithmic processing. Once the adjusted function points are estimated, the SLOC is calculated by a predefined parameter that represents the number of lines of code per function point (SLOC/AFP) for a given programming language. For example, it is estimated that in C++, the SLOC/AFP is 64. Thus, if a program has an estimated 1,000 AFP, the function point method would calculate 64 KSLOC for its C++ implementation. COCOMO II can be applied together with FPA to assure that the estimates are reasonable and to produce a more comprehensive set of estimates. Object points are an alternative to function points. They typically represent screens, reports, and third-generation language modules. Calculating object count is

---

[1] Early papers describing COCOMO II were published during 1995 and 1996. [7]

[m] A measure of software size, based on the number and complexity of internal logical files, external interface files, external inputs, outputs, and queries.

[n] The value adjustment factor is multiplied with the number of counted function points to produce an adjusted function point total. For adjusted function points, effort measurement data from other projects is taken as estimates for the current project.

similar to calculating AFPs; adjustments are made to the raw count for complexity. In many situations [10], object points proved an effective approach to estimating efforts using COCOMO II.

Like the original COCOMO, COCOMO II is a hierarchy of estimation models that address the following three areas:

1. *Application composition model.* This model is used during the early stages of software development, when critical requirements have been elicited but before all the requirements have been fully stabilized.
2. *Early design stage model.* This model is used once the requirements have been stabilized and the basic software architecture has been established.
3. *Post-architecture model.* This model is used during the construction of the software.

Thus, the three levels of models correspond to the level of information detail available in the corresponding development stage of the project. The COCOMO II estimates rely on *scale drivers* (SD) and *cost drivers* (CD). There are five scale drivers: precedence, development flexibility, architecture/risk resolution, team cohesion, and process maturity. There are 17 cost drivers, which include product reliability, complexity, response time constrains, programmers' experience, use of software tools, and other factors.

The basic formula, subject to future parameter calibrations, for the post-architectural estimated project effort can be expressed as follows:

$$\text{effortProject} = A \times (KSLOC)^B \times C$$

$$\text{where,} \quad A = 3.0, B = 1.01 + \sum_{i=1}^{5} SD_i$$

$$\text{and} \quad C = \prod_{j=1}^{17} CD_j$$

where A, B, and C are effort-qualifying parameters; A is initially calibrated to 3.0, B is an exponent derived from scale drivers, and C is a parameter derived from cost drivers.

As an example, let us consider a project with scale drivers parameter B equal to 1.06, and cost drivers parameter C equal to 1, and an estimated 20 KSLOC. The estimated effort would be:

$$\text{effortProject} = 3.00 * 20^{1.06} * 1 \text{ PM} = 71.81 \text{ PM}$$

Parametric models are built on original project data and should be tailored to local development environments. Thus, parameters A, B and C, or at a higher level of granularity SD_i $1 \leq i \leq 5$ and CD_j $1 \leq j \leq 17$, should be calibrated based on the organization's processes and data.

One commonality between COCOMO II and ADP is that they both directly benefit from the data collected throughout the project progress. Similar to COCOMO II, ADP planning is done in the initial planning phase and then in the extended planning phase. COCOMO II can be integrated into ADP by using the formulas based on current information about the project. By using ADP's automatic collection of project data as the project proceeds through the successive iterations and phases, the collected data can be applied to the quantitative analytic framework of COCOMO II to provide increasingly better cost and scheduling estimates.

In general, parametric models such as COCOMO II are the most suitable and are the best practice recommended by ADP.

5.10.4 Estimations of Using COTS and Code Reuse

The prevailing use of COTS adds extra complexity to the estimation of project efforts. While the use of COTS saves both time and effort, the time for their customization and integration with the other components of the application is hard to predict. Some models use estimation techniques that are similar to code reuse to calculate their approximations. If COTS is used as a black box, the function points rules can be applied for integration and functionality estimates. If COTS's source code needs to be modified, the models relying on estimation of code reuse are more accurate. The estimates for code reuse considered in most models are usually based on factors such as the percentage of the code that requires redesign, modifications, and retesting. These three factors are used to evaluate the effort as a percentage of the effort to create the code from scratch.

While there is not one method that fits all situations, ADP's general best practice is that COTS be distinguished from other types of development in effort estimations.

5.10.5 Quality of Estimation and the Iterative Adjustments of Estimates

Although the initial estimates for the entire project effort might be based exclusively on the core requirements and a sketch of an architectural design, in iterative development, these efforts should be recalculated as the data from successive iterations is collected. The estimated total project effort can be viewed as the sum of efforts for all iterations.

When predicting the project effort, variance should be accounted for because not all iterations are of the same length, not all team members have the same experience and skill level, and some of them might be working on multiple projects. In the latter case, the amount of time needed to switch between projects should be added to the estimates.

Assuming that the project will go through n iterations, the estimated total project effort can be expressed as the sum of efforts in all iterations:

$$effort\ Project = \sum_{i=1}^{n} estimated\ Effort\ (iteration_i)$$

As iterations are completed, the effort estimates of project completion are adjusted to reflect work done so far. Thus, after the kth iteration, the estimated remaining effort required to complete the project could be expressed as:

$$effort\ Project_k = \sum_{i=k+1}^{n} estimated\ Effort\ (iteration_i)$$

where *effortProject$_k$* denotes the amount of effort necessary to finish the project after the kth iteration has been completed.

Estimates, however, often vary from the actual effort required to perform tasks. One of the measures that can be used to evaluate the quality of the projections as defined by DeMarco [11] is an EQF (estimate quality factor). EQF is the inverse of the absolute values of the sum of differences between actual effort and the estimated effort. We can use a more granular approach for successively evaluating past estimates and recalculating remaining project time by calculating the average estimate error of the first k iterations:

$$EstimateError_k = \frac{1}{k}\sum_{i=1}^{n} \left| estimatedEffort\,(iteration_i) - actualEffort\,(iteration_i) \right|$$

If the estimate error is large, a root cause analysis of the problem should be performed by the team, and estimates for successive iterations should be recalculated. Some common causes that should be investigated are an unrealistic number of active tasks, underestimation of the amount of time per task, and the unaccounted time for extraneous activities and switching between multiple projects.

One measure that can be used to estimate project effort is the projected number of requirements to be completed in each iteration. Figure 5.3 shows a reporting system graph that can be used for such an estimate. However, since not all the requirements are of equal size, normalizing factors that account for length discrepancies should be used. The number of use cases closed and modules implemented should provide additional feedback.

The ADP best practice is to track the work that has been completed and how much needs to be done, and update the estimates based on the most current data.

5.11 BEST PRACTICES FOR PREPARING THE SCHEDULE

Once the estimates are in place, the schedule can be prepared. There are two characteristics of any schedule to be considered: the precedence of tasks and immovable milestones.

The precedence of tasks determines the absolute order in which the tasks need to be executed. For example, the system has to be functional and fully

Iteration 1: Requirements & Testing Overview

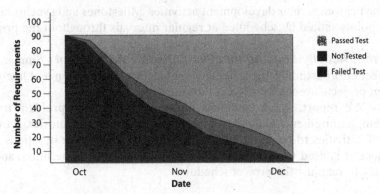

Figure 5.3   Reporting system graph of requirement status during one iteration.

tested *before* it is deployed. Thus, any testing, including system testing, takes place before deployment. At a finer level of granularity, a feature has to be defined before it is implemented. The precedence of tasks is important because it allows for determining a *critical path*[o] for the schedule, and consequently helps to estimate the shortest time needed to complete the project.

The immovable milestones are the "fixed deadlines" such as contractual delivery time, tradeshow dates, and prescheduled meetings with the customer. Such dates cannot be changed, and consequently should be placed on the schedule calendar first. The tasks should then be scheduled backward together with other milestones, such as the projected completions of iterations. The following paragraph summarizes the recommended scheduling practices:

- *Last Tasks are Scheduled First*: The delivery of the product is the last milestone, and should be placed on the schedule first. Placing the final tasks first allows for viewing the whole project in terms of a beginning and an end, and the intermediate tasks can then be scheduled and adjusted in relation to the start and end dates.
- *The Schedule is Created Working Backward*: After the last tasks have been scheduled, the second-to-last tasks are scheduled. This is repeated for scheduling all preceding tasks. Scheduling the last tasks first and working backward will help to prevent assigning the earlier tasks too much time at the expense of later tasks.
- *Project Milestones, Such as the Projected Date of each Completed Iteration, are Recorded on the Schedule*: Milestones, such as completed iterations, give the group intermediate goals. Synchronization points[p] allow

---

[o] In a graph that shows how tasks in the work plan are related, the longest path without any slack from start to finish that corresponds to the shortest time in which the project can be completed.
[p] A synchronization point allows for synchronizing cooperation between two or more processes, and/or teams.

the groups/group members to exchange information about their tasks and synchronize their development activities. Milestones and synchronization points should be scheduled at regular intervals throughout the project.

Current Activity Log and Iterative Schedule Adjustment   Similar to the project effort estimate, the schedule is subject to reevaluation and fine-tuning when project subsequent project iterations are completed.

The CAL report, which combines information from the problem tracking system, requirements management system, and other repositories, shows the list of activities to be completed during current and future iterations of the project. It is used to reevaluate the length of the current iteration, and ultimately to readjust the project schedule.

New Project Example: FoodMagic's Estimated Schedule

Based on the WBS, the following schedule was created for the FoodMagic Product:

Iteration 0 (Prototype)—6 Months:

- Prototype Taste Database—1 month
- Prototype Classifying Users' Tastes—$1/2$ month
- Prototype Classifying Taste-Matched Recipes—$1/2$ month
- Prototype Taste-Matching Engine—4 months

Iteration 1 (Taste-Matching Functionality)—6 months:

- Taste-Matching Database—2 months
- Taste-Matching Application Logic—2 months
- Taste-Matching User Interface—2 months

Iteration 2 (Ingredients and Recipes Functionality)—5 Months:

    . . .

Iteration 3 (Meal Plans and Preferences Functionality)—6 Months:

    . . .

Iteration 4 (Website Administrator Functionality)—3 Months:

    . . .

Iteration 5 (Customer Shopping Functionality)—4 Months:

- Customer Website Database—2 months
- Customer Website Application Logic—2 months
- Customer Website User Interface—2 months

Total Estimated Schedule:

- Prototype—6 months
- Product—24 months
  - Iteration 1—6 months
  - Iteration 2—5 months
  - Iteration 3—6 months
  - Iteration 4—3 months
  - Iteration 5—4 months
- Total—30 months

Existing Project Example: ParaBank's Estimated Schedule

Based on WBS and estimation by analogy, this project can be completed in three weeks.

5.12 MEASUREMENT AND TRACKING FOR ESTIMATION

When working on an existing project, the best way to perform planning for the current iteration is to look at the metrics from past iterations of the project. The following metrics can contribute to successful decision making when planning the current iteration:

- *Requirements metrics.* Requirements metrics show the number of features that have been implemented and tested. They also show how many features remain unimplemented. The number of features implemented and successfully closed (tested and approved) per iteration is an indicator of the project velocity if the features require approximately the same effort. Once normalized over features efforts, this number can be used to estimate times of future project iterations.
- *Code metrics.* Code change and size metrics show the amount of code deleted, modified, and added to the code base and the change in the total size of code. These metrics can help in making projections of the amount of work left if the estimates are based on SLOC of the final product.
- *Test metrics.* Test metrics show the percentage of passed, failed, and incomplete test cases for all unit and integration test runs. These metrics are used during extended planning to make decisions about how much effort must be put into testing activities for the current iteration.
- *Defect metrics.* Defect metrics show the number of reported bugs for the current iteration as well as the number of previously fixed bugs. These metrics can be used to estimate the time needed for debugging. Since "not all bugs are equal," the estimate of the debugging time might require normalization depending on defect type.

- *Estimate quality metrics.* These metrics calculate the quality of the time and effort estimates for each iteration by comparing them to the actual time and effort spent for each iteration. If the estimations are acceptable (e.g., within 10% error), then a similar approach is used for estimation of future iterations. Otherwise, the root cause of the estimation error should be analyzed and future estimations adjusted accordingly.

5.13   IDENTIFYING ADDITIONAL RESOURCE REQUIREMENTS

After the initial infrastructure has been built, the need for extending the people and technology infrastructures [12] in order to fulfill project-specific needs should be assessed. For implementing applications such as embedded systems, the target hardware is needed to perform testing. For web applications, web services, and databases, a staging system might be needed. The general purpose of a staging system is to provide an environment in which software can be safely tested before it is deployed to the production system. The following section outlines the factors to be considered in building a staging system.

Staging System[q] Considerations   There are two general types of staging systems: personal and shared. In many ways, the final destination of an application can also be considered a staging system because the process for deploying the final application to the production environment should be similar to the one used for staging systems.

The number of staging systems needed depends on the project size, team size, and application requirements. First, we will describe general considerations for setting up staging systems and then we will examine the two most common types of staging systems: personal and shared.

- *What is the Staging System's Purpose?* Staging systems are primarily used for integration, system, and acceptance testing. The staging system should emulate the production system as much as possible, and it should be subject to configuration modifications so that a thorough testing of the product can be performed.
- *How Many People will be Using the Staging System?* Will the staging system be used by one person, or will it be shared by multiple team members working together? In general, we recommend use of personal staging systems, where appropriate, so that developers do not interfere with each other. If it is necessary for multiple developers to use a shared staging system, then a policy for sharing a single staging system should be established to avoid possible conflicts and code regressions.

[q] An environment that mirrors the target application environment. New content is moved to the staging system and tested before it is deployed to the production area.

- *Should the Application Be Fully or Partially Deployed?* Naturally, the final application should be fully deployed, but staging systems can consist of only a well-defined subset of the deployable functionality. Often, this solid subset of the functionality is sufficient to perform effective testing. In addition, partial deployment to the production area can take place even if the application is incomplete but has a well-defined and tested subset of deployable functionality. The ADP best practice is that a staging system should be added to the project infrastructure for web applications, web services, and databases.

5.13.1　Extending the Technology Infrastructure

The precise infrastructure that will be assembled varies based on the nature of the projects that the team is working on. Fundamentally, the way that the team interacts with this infrastructure is similar, whether the infrastructure is tailored for Java code, database development, web services, or another technology. However, because different technologies demand different infrastructure components, tasks, and practices, there are slight variations in how each team member accesses the infrastructure as part of the group workflow. If it will be used as part of a web application, run as embedded software, interact with a database, or be accessed via a web service, it is necessary to extend the infrastructure as described in the following sections.

Embedded Systems Extensions　For embedded systems, the basic infrastructure described in Chapter 3 should be extended to include the *target hardware*, which serves as a staging system where the embedded software can be exercised and tested in a realistic environment and software tools can verify the software functionality on the target hardware (Figure 5.4).

As soon as a developer finishes working on a unit of code that can be deployed to the target, she checks it into the source control system. After the code is checked in, the automated build deploys it to the target, where it undergoes automated on-target testing. In addition to this automated regression testing, the code deployed to the target is manually tested by the testers, who verify the code's functionality and quality.

Web Application Extensions　For web application development, the basic infrastructure should be extended to include a staging system, as well as software technologies that can test the web application from its front end (Figure 5.5). Some files (such as images and static pages) can be thoroughly tested without a staging system, but other functionality (such as dynamically loaded pages or database updates), cannot.

The staging system should look like the actual web application and it should contain copies of the same components as used in the application under development. The staging system should contain similar databases, legacy systems, application servers, and so on, in order to perform thorough integration and

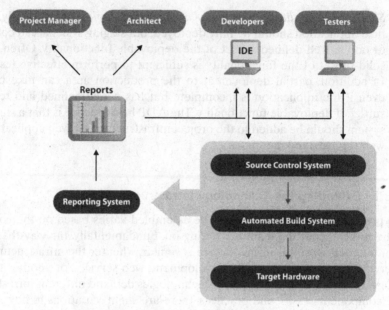

Figure 5.4 Embedded systems infrastructure.

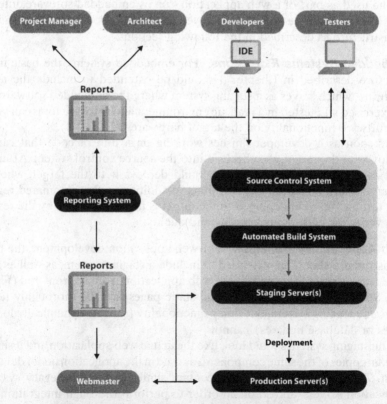

Figure 5.5 Web application development infrastructure.

system testing. However, if the components of the live web application are used in the staging system (e.g., if the staging system contains staging web servers that interface with the production database), there is a risk of corrupting the live components. In such a situation, developers and testers should actively work to prevent any potential problems.

Often, development teams establish two staging system levels: a personal staging system (a private web server containing all application components related to the application areas on which a developer is working) and a project-wide shared staging system (a directory that is essentially an internal-use-only web server shared by all developers, testers, and QA staff). The personal staging system lets developers test their work as early as possible so that they can find and fix problems before they check code into the source control system. The shared area is used to test components as they interact with parts of the system developed by other team members.

These staging systems should be used as follows: As the developer writes the code for the web application, she should apply all standard best practices used by the team. As soon as she completes a unit of code that can be exercised by a client (for example a web browser), she should deploy the code to her personal staging system, then use additional software tools to test the application from its front end. After the code is checked into the source control system, the automated build deploys it to the shared staging system, where it can be further tested by the developer and later by the testers.

The Webmaster monitors the behavior of the application that is deployed to the staging system by using test suites created by developers and augmented by testers. Only after all uncovered defects are corrected, the application is migrated to the *production server*,[r] where its functionality and performance can be monitored with the same test suites.

Web Services Extensions   Web service projects either develop client software that uses an existing web service, or develop a new web service that will be used by other clients.

For web service client development, the infrastructure is similar to the basic infrastructure and workflow described in Chapter 3. The main difference is that software tools are also needed to test the web service client, a *mock-up server*,[s] and a staging server built by the web service provider (Figure 5.6). The mock-up server should be as realistic as possible. The developers and the testers use the mock-up server to test and debug their client code. Once the client code has been fully tested using the mock-up server, the testers should run it on the staging server, which is a replica of the actual server that is built and maintained by the web service developers to allow client developers to perform a final verification before accessing the production server. This staging server should be used only to confirm that the service operates as expected. Routine testing and debugging should be performed using the mock-up server,

---

[r] This is the server that hosts the deployed application.
[s] This is a server that simulates the actual server for the purpose of testing the client.

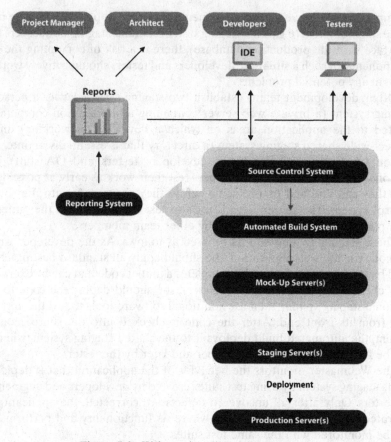

Figure 5.6   Web service client infrastructure.

not the staging server, because testing could place an unreasonable load on the staging server, which is usually shared by other client developers. Once the client application has been verified to function and perform adequately on the mock-up server and the staging server, it can be used to access the production server and perform live transactions.

For web service server development, the basic infrastructure should be extended to include a staging server, a production server, and software tools that verify the functionality and quality of the web service server.

Like the staging system for a web application, the staging system for a web service server is a private version of a complete web service server.

After the developer writes and tests a logical unit of a web service (for instance, a set of Java classes), she deploys it to a local staging server. She tests the service there and, once she is confident in its functionality, security, and basic performance, she adds the related files to source control. Once the code is checked into the source control system, the automated build deploys it to the shared staging system, where it is tested by the testers and the automated testing suite. After all defects are removed, the service is migrated to the production server, where its functionality and performance can be monitored with the same test suites.

Database Extensions For software that interacts with a database, the basic infrastructure should be extended to include a *development database* and a *production database*, as well as software tools that verify the functionality of the database. The developers work on the development database, which is located on a staging server. Once the database is tested and ready for deployment, it is moved to the application deployment server (Figure 5.7).

As the developer implements the code for the database interface, the database developer (either the same developer or a different developer) designs and implements the database. To verify the database's functionality and performance, developers use software tools to check that the database design complies with best practices, as well as to confirm data integrity, structural integrity, and database performance.

As testers test the integrated application, they also have to verify the functionality of the database. After the application is deployed, the operations manager monitors the production database to detect any emerging data, functionality, or performance problems. As databases evolve, changes made to

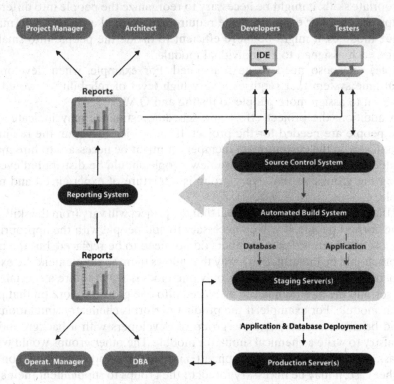

Figure 5.7 Database infrastructure.

design, structure, and content can lead to problems such as performance degradation, incorrectly stored data, and incorrect query results. For example, inefficient indexing might not have affected query performance with the small amount of test data, but it might create significant bottlenecks with the amount of data accumulated on the production database. Because of these and other potential problems, an application that performed flawlessly in tests conducted in the development or staging environment could still fail in the production environment if continuous testing and monitoring is not performed throughout the application life cycle.

5.13.2 Extending the People Infrastructure

Just as the technology infrastructure should be extended to meet the needs of the project, so should the people infrastructure. After requirements specifications have been defined, the nature and extent of the project, the estimated effort, and the schedule will determine what people resources will be needed to complete the project. Extending the people infrastructure may require reorganizing or retraining the existing people or adding people with possibly different skill sets.

Even if estimates indicate that there are currently enough people with the appropriate skills, it might be necessary to reorganize the people into different groups or roles. For example, if the requirements reveal a project with many unique modules, it might be more efficient to divide the people into smaller groups, each assigned to an individual module.

Roles may also need to be reassigned. For example, when developing a real-time system that requires a very high level of reliability, it would be beneficial to assign more people to testing and QA.

In addition, the project effort and schedule estimates may indicate that more people are needed for the project. If the project is within the realm of the skill sets of the current team members, it might be necessary to hire more people with similar skill sets. These new people should be distributed evenly among the groups, so that every group is a mixture of experienced and new people.

If the project specifications reveal that the project will vary from the skill sets of the current people, it will be necessary to add people with the appropriate skill sets. The current team members do not need to be replaced, but the new people should be integrated in a way that allows them to supplement the existing people's skill sets. In one case, only one module may require a specialized skill set, and the new people can be placed into one group to work on that particular module. For example, if the product performs chemistry simulations, it would be necessary to have one group of developers with a background in chemistry to write a chemical simulator module. The other groups would work on tasks such as database development, interface development, and so on. In another case, it may be necessary for all of the groups to supplement their skill sets by adding a new member. For example, when developing a web version of an existing desktop application, it might be necessary to hire people with web experience and then distribute them evenly among the existing groups.

Finally, any new hires added to the project need to learn the methodology and the project. After a new person has been introduced to ADP, she should become familiar with the technology infrastructure. Because all of the project and product information has been recorded in the reporting system, she will be able to look up information on the project when needed. For example, she could look up the Vision and Scope document to get an overview of the product, or look up features and requirements to understand the more detailed aspects of the product.

5.14 EXAMPLES

5.14.1 Focus on the Root Cause of a Project Scheduling Problem

Planned System   A new system was instituted for automatic toll collections based on a GPS. The system relied on placing on-board units in trucks that charged tolls automatically based on the miles traveled on toll roads. As listed in Figure 5.8, there have been a number of reported problems with this system, which caused substantial delays in its final deployment.

Missed Deadline   The first issue was a project management problem. The system was scheduled for completion within one year. However, the developing organization could not complete the system in that time. When it became clear that the deadline could not be met, the requirements were reprioritized

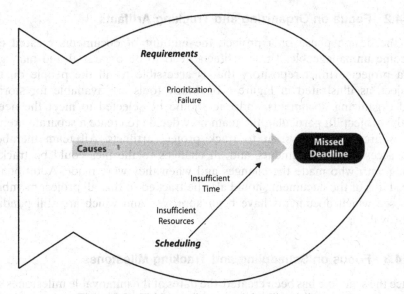

Figure 5.8   Fishbone diagram of deadline failure.

and a reduced system was delivered with a promise that a full system would be delivered the following year. (See Figure 5.9)

Root Cause Analysis and Suggested Preventive Action

Problem Description	Cause Category	Cause Description	Recommended Practice	Measurement, Tracking & Automation
Missed Deadline	Scheduling	Management failed to schedule enough time and resources to meet deadline.	Add a parametric model or a tool for project estimation; use iterative tuning for successive estimations.	Use CostXpert software to automate estimation. Add reporting on milestone iterations: planned vs. met.
	Requirements	Requirements not initially prioritized and planned to meet deadline. Architectural prototype for an innovative system not developed.	Add prioritization of requirements policy. Define core requirements first, and rank them during successive iterations. Develop a prototype to verify architecture of an innovative product.	Implement requirements review policy to include prioritization. Add reporting on requirements w/ priority, planned vs. completed.

Figure 5.9   Root cause analysis and suggested action plan for a project scheduling problem.

5.14.2   Focus on Organizing and Tracking Artifacts

By the design phase of a project, the amount of documents created can become unmanageable. These artifacts need to be organized and managed in a project artifact repository that is accessible to all the people on the project, as illustrated in Figure 5.10. Many tools are available for storing and organizing documents, and one should be selected to meet the needs of the project. In particular, the team may decide to create a separate area in the source control system to track project artifacts. All team members can access these documents, and all changes to the files could be tracked along with who made the changes and when they were made. Additionally, the status of the document should also be tracked so that all project members can see which documents have been approved and which are still pending approval.

5.14.3   Focus on Scheduling and Tracking Milestones

Once the schedule has been created, the dates of the immovable milestones set, and the lengths of the project iterations estimated, the team members should be

Project Artifact Repository: Project A

– Vision and Scope Docs	Status		
VisionAndScope.doc	approved	view doc	view log

– Deliverables	Status		
ReqSpecsForCustomer.doc	approved	view doc	view log
UserManual.doc	pending	view doc	view log

+ Use Cases	Status		

+ Class Diagrams	Status		

+ Database Diagrams	Status		

– Other	Status		
RiskManagementPlan.doc	approved	view doc	view log
WorkBreakdownStructure.doc	pending	view doc	view log

Figure 5.10 The project artifact repository showing how project artifacts can be organized.

able to see the progress of the project in relation to each milestone (Figure 5.11). This allows the team members and the manager to determine which milestones are in danger of not meeting their deadlines and gives the team enough time to take appropriate action. By seeing the progress toward all of the milestones in one screen, the project manager can determine if resources need to be reallo-

Milestone Overview Panel: Project A

Milestone	Deadline	Progress
Requirements Specified	Feb 1	
Database Designed	Mar 1	
App. Logic Designed	Apr 1	
User Interface Designed	May 1	
Database Implemented	Aug 1	
App. Logic Implemented	Sep 1	
User Interface Implemented	Nov 1	
99% Test Cases Pass	Dec 1	

Figure 5.11 An overview panel of project milestones.

cated or added to the project. For example, the milestones in Figure 5.11 show that the Application Logic has fallen behind and missed the April 1 design milestone. However, the progress for the May 1 deadline is on schedule, and the manager may be able to shift some of the effort from this on-schedule task to the behind-schedule task. If the manager does this early and carefully enough, it might be possible to make both milestones by the deadline.

5.15 ACRONYMS

AFP	Adjusted function points
CD	Cost drivers
COCOMO	Constructive cost model
COTS	Commercial off-the-shelf components
DBA	Database administrator
EQF	Estimate quality factor
FPA	Function point analysis
KSLOC	Thousands of source lines of code
PM	Person months
PY	Person years
QA	Quality assurance
SD	Scale drivers
SLOC	Source lines of code
SDP	Software development plan
SPMP	Software project management plan
TDEV	Number of months estimated for software development
UML	Unified Modeling Language
WBS	Work breakdown structure

5.16 GLOSSARY

adjusted function points The value adjustment factor is multiplied with the number of counted function points to produce an adjusted function point total. For adjusted function points, effort measurement data from other projects is taken as estimates for the current project. [10]

Apache's Jakarta Tomcat Apache Tomcat is the servlet container used in the official Reference Implementation for the Java Servlet and JavaServer Pages technologies. The Java Servlet and JavaServer Pages specifications are developed by Sun under the Java Community Process. It powers numerous large-scale, mission-critical web applications across a diverse range of industries and organizations. [4]

artifact A work item produced during software development. Some examples of software development artifacts are software designs, code, and test cases.

critical path   In a graph that shows how tasks in a work plan are related, the longest path from start to finish. This is also the path that does not have any slack, thus the path giving the shortest time in which the project can be completed.

deliverable   An artifact that is delivered to a customer or user.

entity relationship diagram   A diagrammatic technique for illustrating the interrelationships between entities in a database.

estimation by analogy   An estimation method involving reasoning by analogy, using experience with one or more completed projects to relate actual cost and development time to the cost and development time of the new project.

functioning prototype   A working prototype built to determine that the design is within the specifications requirements of the final product.

function point   A measure of software size, based on the number and complexity of internal logical files, external interface files, external inputs, outputs, and queries. [11]

mock-up server   A server that simulates the actual server for the purpose of testing the client.

parametric model   A mathematical representation consisting of formulas that use parameters as the basis of the model's predictive features. The model calculates the dependent variables of cost and duration based on one or more estimated parameters.

production server   The server that hosts the deployed application.

risk management   An approach to problem analysis that relies on identifying the risks, assessing their probabilities of occurrence and their impact to give a more accurate understanding of potential losses, and creating a plan for avoiding and mitigating them.

software development model   A model of the software development process. The process by which user needs are translated into a software product. The process involves translating user needs into software requirements, transforming the software requirement into design, implementing the design in code, testing the code, and sometimes, installing and checking out the software for operational use. [3]*

software development plan   A plan for a software development project. [3]*

software project management plan   The controlling document for managing a software project. A software project management plan defines the technical and managerial project functions, activities, and tasks necessary to satisfy the requirements of a software project, as defined in the project agreement. [2]*

staging server   A server that is a mirror of the live application server. New content is deployed to the staging server, tested, and then published to the live server.

statement of work document   The document that contains descriptions of the products or services to be supplied via a contract.

synchronization point   A point where two or more parallel activities can be brought together.

vertical prototype   A partial implementation of a software system that slices through all layers of the architecture. It is used to evaluate technical feasibility and performance. It is also called a structural prototype or proof of concept. [5]

Wideband Delphi method   A consensus-based method for estimating effort. It was originated by the Rand Corporation. Multiple team members participate in estimating each other's task efforts until they reach a consensus.

Work breakdown structure   An outline that organizes the tasks and activities necessary to achieve the project objective.

5.17 REFERENCES

[1] The Standish Group International, *2004 Third Quarter Research Report*, 2006, www.standishgroup.com (retrieved: August 2, 2006).

[2] Institute of Electrical and Electronics Engineers, *IEEE Standard 1058.1-1987— Software Project Management Plans (SPMP)*, 1987.

[3] Institute of Electrical and Electronics Engineers, *IEEE Standard 610.12-1990— Glossary of Software Engineering Terminology*, 1990.

[4] The Apache Software Foundation, *Apache Tomcat,* 2006, http://tomcat.apache.org/ (retrieved: March 13, 2006).

[5] Wiegers, K.E., *Software Requirements*, Microsoft Press, 2nd ed, 2003.

[6] Boehm, B., *Software Engineering Economics*. Prentice Hall, 1981.

[7] Boehm, B., Clark, B., Horowitz, E., Madachy, R., Selby, R., and Westland, C., "Cost Models for Future Life Cycle Processes: COCOMO 2.0," *Annals of Software Engineering*, Special Volume on Process and Product Measurement, The Netherlands, 1995.

[8] Boehm, B., Abts, C., Brown, A.W., Chulani, S., Clark, B.K., Horowitz, E., Madachy, R., Reifer, D., and Steece, B., *Software Cost Estimation with COCOMO II*. Prentice Hall, 2000.

[9] University of Southern California, COCOMO, CSE Center for Software Engineering, 2002, http://sunset.usc.edu/research/COCOMOII/index.html, updated date: 9/23/ 2002 (retrieved: March 14, 2006).

[10] Federal Aviation Administration, *FAST—Federal Aviation Administration Acquisition Toolset*, 2006, http://fast.faa.gov/pricing/c1919–4.htm (retrieved: August 7, 2006).

[11] DeMarco, T., *Controlling Software Projects: Management, Measurement and Estimation*. Prentice Hall, 1986.

[12] Kolawa, A., Hicken, W., and Dunlop, C., *Bulletproofing Web Applications*, Hungry Minds, 2002.

5.18 EXERCISES

1. A customer has asked you to create a "Photo Album" program for viewing and organizing digital photos. What are some key features you could list about this product in your project objectives? What are some features that you would not list in the project objectives and why?

2. Give examples of project artifacts and deliverables that were not listed in Section 5.4.

3. Develop an SDP for an online version of the "Photo Album" program that creates online albums that can be viewed by predefined set of users.

4. What would be the primary risks in developing the "Photo Album" project (as described in previous exercises)?

5. Create a WBS for the "Photo Album" project (as described in previous exercises).

6. Estimate a total effort for the "Photo Album" program described in the previous exercises, knowing that it took two programmers three months to develop a functioning prototype of this program.

7. What minimal, expanded, and extended infrastructure would you use for the "Photo Album" product, as described in previous exercises?

8. Discuss the key factors necessary to calibrate the COCOMO II formula.

9. Find estimates of developer productivity in SLOC/Developer/month for different types of projects such as database applications, gaming, web services, compilers, etc.

10. In general, what other types of extended infrastructure can be used in software development?

CHAPTER 6

ARCHITECTURAL AND DETAILED DESIGN

> There are two ways of constructing a software design: One way is to make it so simple that there are obviously no deficiencies, and the other way is to make it so complicated that there are no obvious deficiencies. The first method is far more difficult.
>
> —C. A. R. Hoare

6.1 INTRODUCTION

When designing a software system, the technical expertise of the architect meets her creativity. This technical expertise is required to properly define the elements of the system architecture[a] and their interactions, while creativity is essential to make the design efficient to implement. Thus, software design is as much art as engineering.

While, in its simplest description, software architecture can be construed as a high-level design, more specifically it refers to the initial definition of a system in terms of its computational elements and the interactions among these elements. At the highest degree of encapsulation, these elements include services such as those specified by an SOA (service-oriented architecture)[b]. Clients,

---

[a] The organizational structure of a system or component. [1]

[b] Service-oriented architecture is an architectural style "within which all functions are defined as independent services with well-defined invokable interfaces which can be called in defined sequences to form business processes." [2]

Automated Defect Prevention: Best Practices in Software Management, by Dorota Huizinga and Adam Kolawa
Copyright © 2007 John Wiley & Sons, Inc.

servers, databases, filters, layers, and components or modules[c] are the building blocks of the architectural design, and interactions among these elements could be interface contracts in SOA, client/server protocols,[d] multicasts[e] and piped streams,[f] or at a finer level of granularity, function calls or shared variables.

Once the high-level architecture is defined, the *detailed design* takes place. We will refer to the detailed design as a gradual process of refining the architectural blueprint by mapping services to components or modules, and modules into classes, objects, and functions, and by specifying interactions among those components, modules, classes, objects, and functions. Most of the detailed design is performed at the beginning of each iteration after the features and requirements for the current iteration have been selected and refined.

The realm of software design is vast and spans many techniques including pattern[g] [3] and model-driven[h] [4,5] approaches at the architectural level, and object-oriented and structural approaches at the detailed design level. Regardless of the design method used, defects can occur at all of its levels.

Design defects can be the result of incorrect or incomplete requirements or can be injected independently during creation of design artifacts such as diagrams of modules or pseudocode descriptions of algorithms or data structures. We have expanded Ilene Burnstein's [6] classification of design defects to include the following categories:

- *Service, Module, and Object Functional Defects*, which include flawed or missing design elements, due either to incorrect requirements specifications or inaccurate interpretations of these requirements
- *Service, Module, and Object Interface Defects*, which result from incorrect descriptions of messages, or parameter types, or incomplete parameter numbers passed between services, modules, or objects
- *Algorithmic Defects*, which are caused by inaccurate depictions of algorithmic steps in the design of the pseudocode
- *Control, Logic, and Sequence Defects*, which result from the improper design of branching or nesting and wrong use of logic operators or Boolean expressions

[c] Architectural elements that are discrete and identifiable with respect to their encapsulated functionality, structure, interaction with other elements or compilation, or loading. [1]

[d] A communication protocol in which a client process interacts with users, allowing the users to request services from server processes. A server process waits for a request to arrive from the client process and then responds to those requests.

[e] A communication protocol in which data is delivered to all hosts that have expressed interest. This is one-to-many delivery.

[f] An interprocess communication protocol in which output streams from one thread become input for another thread exchanging information between programs or system resources.

[g] Design based on identifying of existing, relevant design patterns, so that complex structures can be constructed from these design patterns.

[h] Design based on the idea of identifying high-level models that allow designers to specify and analyze interactive software applications from a semantic-oriented level.

- *Data Defects*, which stem from flawed design of data structures, such as wrong variables or pointer types, missing fields, or improperly allocated storage space
- *External Hardware and Software Interface Defects*, which are the result of the incorrect design of interfaces with external hardware components, such as I/O devices, external services, or other software components such as legacy code or COTS
- *Usability Defects*, which stem from improper design of user interfaces such as missing or erroneous navigational elements, or a lack of consistency in navigational graphics

Not only is the design often rushed or even neglected, but it also frequently lacks consistency in carrying critical system attributes throughout the entire project, and consequently defeats its original goals.

We try to solve the problem by rushing through the design process so that enough time is left at the end of the project to uncover the errors that were made because we rushed through the design process.

—Glenford J. Myers

Maintaining design integrity throughout the entire product is a challenging task. For example, if scalability is one of the critical quality attributes, and the architectural design accounts for it, the application might still fail to scale if the detailed design does not include proper memory management for objects and data. Moreover, this lack of consistency in design applies not only to software internals but also to user interfaces. User interface design is often neglected because developers tend to focus on implementing internal system functionality while overlooking human–computer interactions. This is partially due to the current training of computer professionals concentrating on technical aspects while frequently ignoring the human factors that must be understood to design effective user interfaces.

Thus, to alleviate the above problems, one of the key elements of our methodology described in this chapter is the definition of *design policies*. These policies facilitate consistency in design of both system functional and nonfunctional requirements, throughout the organization on a project-by-project basis. These policies specify the best practices that should be followed to avoid previously encountered problems and to meet critical design attributes such as efficiency, scalability, or security.

While there is no universal cure-all, in this chapter we will describe a set of general best practices that help avert these common design problems.

All systems obviously require the development of code, and most systems require the development of a user interface. We will therefore consider the best practices for the design of the system functionality and the user interface together, encapsulating these in design policies.

The expected work products for this phase are:

- Policy to manage functional design and quality attributes
- Design documents for system functionality and quality attributes
  - Architectural patterns used
  - Module diagrams
  - Module interaction diagrams
  - Class diagrams
  - Class interactions diagram
  - Pseudocode
  - Service and module tests
- Policy to manage design of graphical user interfaces
- Graphical user interface design documents
  - Interface prototype
  - Usability tests

6.2   BEST PRACTICES FOR DESIGN OF SYSTEM FUNCTIONALITY AND ITS QUALITY ATTRIBUTES

The goal of the software design is to create a blueprint of the system that, when implemented, would fulfill user requirements. While achieving the correct system functionality is a primary objective of the design, it is the non-functional requirements, such as performance or security, that often make the design a challenge.

Jan Bosch [7] points out that the architectural solution affects system quality attributes such as performance, robustness, distributability, and maintainability. Thus, both functional and nonfunctional requirements should serve as inputs to the system design.

In order to maintain the design integrity throughout the entire product, its critical quality attributes should be identified during the initial architectural design phase and applied to creating detailed design policies by the team. Once such policies are defined, the architectural solution can be consistently and progressively refined during successive project iterations.

At the architectural level the design is performed by the product architect. Most of the detailed design is conducted by developers, who should closely follow the architectural blueprint and design policies.

6.2.1   Identifying Critical Attributes of Architectural Design

When creating a software architectural design, it is important to identify the most critical system quality attributes first. Some attributes are highly desirable in all software systems, while others are more applicable to certain types of systems. Once these attributes have been identified, they become the guideposts of the design process. It is therefore crucial that they be considered at every step, and that they play a pivotal role in all decisions, from creating the top-level architectural view to the detailed design work at the algorithmic and data structure levels. These critical attributes will also be used to create the design policy, which will serve as a reference document that contains the design guidelines for all team members of the project.

DEVELOPER'S TESTIMONIAL

In my current project I work on backend services. We write prototypes to validate architecture, design concepts, and some quality attributes such as performance, security, scalability, etc. If the prototype shows the architecture or design to be viable, usually the prototype evolves into the deliverable product. In other words, we prototype architectures that are not well-understood or for which there is no pattern of usage in our industry.

—Enrico Lelina, Software Engineer

The following sections define a set of architectural attributes and explain their impact on design.

Correctness   The ultimate goal of any project is to build a product that meets the customer's needs and specifications. Correctness[i] is the measure of how well the design matches the specified requirements. Thus, because the customer was, and preferably still is, involved in defining and approving the requirements, correctness is also a measure of how well the design matches what the customer expects from the product.

To ensure that the software design is correct, the requirements should be viewed as the primary input into the design process. Each step in developing the high-level and detailed design should begin with reviewing the requirements to identify the specifications, such as functionality or constraints, that apply to the current design task.

Modularity   Modularity[j] describes how well the requirements have been separated into unique entities based on their function. Modularity reduces the complexity of the interactions in the code by dividing it into several manageable functional units, which then interact with each other through well-defined interfaces. A solid modular design has a positive impact on the resulting code: first, it facilitates its extensibility because it is easier to add more modules, and second, it makes maintenance easier because modular code is more comprehensible and modifiable, since changing code inside a module should not affect other modules.

[i] The degree to which a system or component is free from faults in its specification, design, and implementation. [1]
[j] The degree to which a system or computer program is composed of discrete components such that a change to one component has minimal impact on other components. [1]

Defining modules begins with categorizing the requirements based on their functionality, data usage, and interactions. It then proceeds through the abstracting of common functionalities to facilitate reuse of the code within the application, and ends with delineating module boundaries and describing their interfaces.

Reusability   Reusability[k] describes how well parts of the code can be reused with little or no modification. In a design that ignored reusability issues, many sections of the code would perform the same or similar tasks, and any updates to these tasks would require rewriting of all these sections of code. Reusability is intimately related to modularity: by separating the repetitive functionalities into modules, their functionality can be reused as needed in the code. Additionally, the code is more concise because redundancies have been removed and any changes to the reused functionalities need only be performed on their respective modules.

Carefully reviewing the requirements will reveal repeated functionalities, and these functionalities should be separated into reusable modules. A reusable module will be shared by many other modules and should therefore contain only the common functionality required by all other modules that will share it. Additionally, considering reusability during the design of all modules increases the likelihood that individual modules or collections of modules could be reused if the need arises.

Efficiency and Scalability   Efficiency[l] describes how well the application uses resources, such as CPU time, memory space, or network resources. Scalability is the ability of the program to adapt to increased demands. Many applications start with a small data set that grows over time, thereby increasing the demand on system resources. If such growth in the usage of system resources is expected, scalability is one of the important quality attributes that must be considered during design. Scalability and efficiency are related because inefficient systems do not scale well. However, while efficiency is always a desired attribute, scalability may not be. For example, in many embedded applications, efficiency is very important because quick response time is vital but scalability is irrelevant because the demands on these programs do not grow.

Both algorithmic complexity[m] and data growth need to be evaluated, as even polynomial algorithms will have scaling problems if the input size is large. Consequently, algorithms need to be designed to minimize program complexity. If it is expected that data will grow substantially, memory management[n]

---

[k] The degree to which a software module or other work product can be used in more than one computer program or software system. [1]
[l] The degree to which a system or component performs its designated functions with minimum consumption of resources. [1]
[m] The complexity of an algorithm describes the number of computational steps that it takes to transform the input data into the result of computation.
[n] Memory management involves identifying used and available physical memory units, managing virtual memory mapping onto physical memory and swapping the virtual memory pages to disk while performing the appropriate address translation.

might be affected. For example, keeping too much data in memory will cause excessive paging[o] while reading too little data would cause too many disk accesses, both of which can hinder system performance.

Portability   Portability[p] is the ability of a program to be transferred from the environment in which it was created to different environments with little or no modifications. This is important for applications that will be run on different hardware, operating systems, and so forth, but not important for systems that are designed for a specific platform or applications that run in an environment that is intrinsically portable, such as Java.

If portability is a critical attribute, then the design needs to accommodate the heterogeneity of the underlying systems with which the code interacts. This is done by restricting the design to features that are available on all systems or by designing a common set of functionalities defined for all systems and then adding separate system-specific modules.

Interoperability   Interoperability[q] is the ability of a program to interact with other programs, especially by using the same procedures, file formats, or protocols. If the product must work with other entities, then it is necessary to design modules for transmitting and receiving data from the entities and any additional processing that is required to make the data usable by either the product or the external entities. All interactions with other entities or data should be defined during the design phase, and a method for exchanging information for each of the interactions should be identified.

To achieve interoperability in a product, the types of data that will need to be passed between applications should first be determined. Next, commonly used procedures, file formats, or protocols for the specific type of data transmission should be identified. Finally, the data and any additional processing that needs to occur should be defined to meet the standards that have been identified for each type of transmission.

Maintainability and Extensibility   Maintainability[r] is a measure of how easily a program's existing code can be repaired or updated without adversely effecting existing functionality. Extensibility[s] is the ability of a program to have functionality added to it later without having to modify the current architecture of the system. In modern iterative software development, both of

---

[o] A storage allocation technique in which programs or data are divided into fixed-length blocks called pages, main storage is divided into blocks of the same length called page fames, and pages are stored in page frames. [1]
[p] The ease with which a system or component can be transferred from one hardware or software environment to another. [1]
[q] The ability of two or more systems or components to exchange information and to use the information that has been exchanged. [1]
[r] The ease with which a software system or component can be modified to correct faults, improve performance or other attributes, or adapt to a changed environment. [1]
[s] The ease with which a system or component can be modified to increase its storage or functional capacity. [1]

these attributes are critical because applications are frequently updated and their functionality is extended in each iteration or release.

Both of these are highly dependent on how well the original architecture has been divided into modules, and therefore should be considered when designing modules. When designing the modules, it is important to consider how extensible and maintainable the modules are by looking at their relationships. Modules that are highly dependent on each other may be affected by any change to either module, and therefore an attempt should be made to reduce the dependencies.

Security   The security[1] of an application reflects how well the application protects its data in case of unexpected or malicious use. Issues such as how the application should log information, how the application will verify identities, and how it responds to incorrect input should all be considered. An application for which security is critical should have security built into it at all levels. In such cases, security should be an intrinsic part of the application, not just an afterthought in the form of fixes or add-on features.

First, the critical assets of the application data that must be protected need to be identified. Next, the operations that take place on these critical assets should be defined, and the means of protecting them from being compromised should be designed. Categories of internal and external users need to be established, their authority to use and possibly misuse the data evaluated, and the methods of deterring possible security violations determined.

6.2.2   Defining the Policies for Design of Functional and Nonfunctional Requirements

The critical attributes are the basis for defining the design policies. Having such a design policy in place is vital to controlling design complexity and enforcing the consistent application of design guidelines across all parts of the product. While based on the critical goals of the architectural design, this policy should also include general best practices dependent on accepted design rules and customized best practices derived from the organization's prior experience. Identifying prior problems and avoiding their recurrence by defining design policies is an essential part of ADP. Thus, a design policy should include both the general and specific guidelines needed to meet the overall objectives of the development team in building a functional and reliable application.

Why   Organizations may have a large number of developers working on different parts of an application implementation at any given time. Thus, there is a high probability of errors such as duplication, lack of compliance, and lack

---

[1] The establishment and application of safeguards to protect data, software, and computer hardware from accidental or malicious modification, destruction, or disclosure. [8]

of interoperability if the development group does not take proper measures to follow specific guidelines and best practices. Additionally, policies are used to help in carrying out critical design attributes from iteration to iteration when a new set of detailed design artifacts is prepared.

Who The developers, architect, and project manager should work together to define the design policy. The final approval of this policy should be done by the architect or by the lead developer.

How The design policies should be brief and technically specific. Each policy should include the critical quality attributes addressed by the policy, and it should describe specific design rules that need to be followed so that the implemented application exhibits the predefined requirements.

The design policy should contain:

- Critical quality attributes that apply to the project
- Possible problems and design rules to avert each problem
- References to the functional or nonfunctional requirements to which the policies apply
- Automation of policy verification (if applicable)

Examples

Policy for Memory Management

Critical Attribute: Efficiency and scalability in handling data

Possible Problems: Data overload. All applications utilize main memory that is managed by an operating system. The concept of virtual memory and paging enables applications to run when not all of their code or data is currently in physical memory. Breaking up large amounts of data into smaller, more manageable parts is an ideal way to manage limited resources such as memory. Relatively inactive virtual pages can be temporarily removed from physical memory. If those pages are later referenced, a page fault[u] will occur, and the pages will be remapped and reread into physical memory. Although operating system paging strategies often attempt to optimize performance, paging can become excessive and hinder system performance.

Specific Design Rules to Avert Excessive Paging: All global memory allocations shall be made during the system initialization phase only. Thereafter, memory allocation from a global memory heap shall be avoided. The minimum amount of memory should be used for objects and data. Memory

---

[u] An event that occurs when an accessed page is not present in main memory.

should be allocated only when needed and deallocated thereafter (Note: C++ can support this behavior by providing mechanisms for class-specific new and delete operators).

Requirements Related to This Policy: The deployed software shall be run on hardware containing at least 1 GB RAM. The system shall handle data sets up to 16 GB.

Automation of Policy Verification: Once the corresponding pseudocode or code has been developed, a static analysis system can be used to check conformance to this policy by identifying all global variables and whether each memory allocation is followed by its deallocation.

Policy for Using Inheritance in Class Definition

Critical Attribute: Maintainability and reusability of the code

Possible Problems: Excessive class complexity. Inheritance[v] is the concept of creating a general class of objects that define common functionality and specific subclasses to extend their functionalities. The general class is called the base class, and the specific subclasses that inherit from it are called the derived classes.[w] Therefore, an object in a derived class does not need to have its own definition of all data and methods, because it can inherit them from the base class. This is meant to accelerate program development and to ensure an intrinsic validity in the defined subclass object: what works for the base class should also work for the derived class.

Even though inheritance is meant to simplify the design, there are many instances where inheritance can add complexity to a program. For example, multiple inheritance (inheritance from more than one base class) can be very error-prone. For example, a developer might create a variable class "Food" with the properties "calories," "fat," "fiber," and "sugar." A derived class "Vegetable" would inherit the properties from the "Food" class, and would add the properties "vitaminC," "vitaminE," and "vitaminK." However, if the developer wants to utilize a completely different class hierarchy simultaneously, such as allowing "Vegetable" to inherit from the "Plant" class as well as the "Food" class, it is likely that the mixed hierarchy will cause confusion or logical errors.

Specific Design Rules to Avert Excessive Complexity Due to Inheritance: Typically, inheritance shall be used only when the derived class is a refinement

---

[v] Inheritance is a form of software reusability in which programmers create classes that inherit an existing class data and methods, and enhance them with new capabilities.
[w] A derived class inherits from one or more (possibly unrelated) base classes.

of the base level class (or classes). The relationship of two classes can be clarified by expressing it in a sentence. If the sentence "B is a kind of A," accurately represents the relationship between two classes, then class "B" can be derived from "A." For example, an apple is a kind of fruit, so an apple class should be derived from a fruit class. However, if the sentence "B is a part of A" is clearer than "B is a kind of A," a "using" relationship should be used, not inheritance. For example, seeds are a part of a fruit, so their classes should be related with a "using" relationship.

In general, no more than two levels of inheritance should be used. Before deciding on using multiple inheritance, alternatives that take into account the effect that multiple inheritance will have on the system, especially its maintainability, should be considered. Because changes to high-level base classes affect all child classes, deep inheritance trees (greater than about two ancestors) should be avoided.

Requirements Related to This Policy: There is no specific requirement related to this policy. This is strictly a design issue.

Automation of the Policy Verification: Once the code is implemented, the depth of the inheritance can be verified by a static analysis tool.

Policy for Code Reuse

Critical Attribute: Reusability of the code

Possible Problems: Interfaces between existing legacy modules may not be compatible with modules designed for the new application.

Specific Design Rules for Reuse: Only the modules marked for reuse in existing applications shall be reused. When designing new modules, interfaces to the existing code shall be designed first, and then the new module's functionality.

Requirements Related to This Policy: All new system features will be compatible with the specified components of legacy systems.

Automation of the Policy Verification: The legacy code marked for reuse can be automatically verified. Interface design has to be inspected manually.

6.2.3 Applying Design Patterns

Design patterns[x] are language-independent strategies for solving common design problems. Developers can apply design patterns when working on elements similar to existing solutions that have proven both efficient and

---

[x] A design pattern is a documented best practice or core of a solution that has been applied successfully in multiple environments to solve a problem that recurs in a specific set of situations. [9]

effective. Learning and properly applying design patterns not only improves code quality, portability, and maintainability, but also helps people to communicate their ideas and designs with others effectively, especially in the world of OOD (object-oriented design).

Similar to the design itself, patterns span multiple levels of granularity ranging from architectural to detailed design. There are a number of common design patterns available to developers. The book, *Design Patterns*, by Erich Gamma, Richard Helm, Ralph Johnson, and John Vlissides (1995) [3] serves as a groundbreaking reference to a variety of design patterns that are on a middle level of granularity. They could easily be used across many application areas and encompass several objects.

The authors of the above book divide these patterns into three categories: creational, structural, and behavioral.

- *Creational patterns* control how objects are created. They make an application independent of how its objects are created, composed, and represented. For example, the *singleton* pattern is used for a class where only one instance should ever be instantiated.
- *Structural patterns* help to compose groups of objects into larger structures, such as complex user interfaces or accounting systems. For example, the *façade* pattern is used to create a single high-level interface for a collection of subsystem interfaces.
- *Behavioral patterns* are concerned with algorithms and the communication between objects in a system and how the flow is controlled in a complex program. For example, the *observer* pattern is used to create dependencies between objects so that when one of the objects is updated, all of its dependents are updated.

Example For example, consider an application that uses a load balancer. Only one instance of the load balancer should ever exist. Therefore, the singleton design pattern should be used for the load balancer class because it guarantees the class will create only one instance of itself. When the class is instantiated, it checks if it already exists and, if so, returns the existing instance. Otherwise, it creates a new instance and returns it.

These patterns provide a standardized way of solving common problems and offer a number of benefits to design teams. Because developers can choose from a number of design patterns and alternatives, they can add considerable flexibility in creating their code.

How The design should start from identifying the architectural patterns relevant to the application. These are determined by context, problem, and solution schema: [10]

- *Context* is the design situation giving rise to a design problem. The context can be quite general, such as "a distributed application with heterogeneous cooperating components," or it can be more specific, such as "processing streams of data," which is done with pipes and filters. As specifying a correct context for a pattern is challenging, Buschmann et al. [10] recommend listing all known situations where a problem that is addressed by a particular pattern can occur. Design policies for a project could include a list of such situations applicable to the product under development.
- *Problem* describes a specific repeatedly occurring design issue that the pattern addresses. For example, the *view handler* pattern can be used to design a part of the user interface that manages the user's view of the data. This would include activities such as opening and closing windows, brining data to the foreground, and manipulating data in the foreground window.
- *Solution* describes how to solve the above recurring problem. It specifies a special configuration of the pattern elements, their relationship, and runtime behavior. For example, a *proxy* pattern, which makes the clients communicate with a representative rather than the original component itself, would identify all the functionalities of the original component to be implemented in the proxy. It would also show the structure of the proxy in its relationship to both the original component and the client, and the data flow between the client, proxy, and the original component.

Some examples of architectural patterns found in [9,10,11] include the *layered architecture*, which is a decomposition of services such that most interactions occur only between neighboring layers, the *subsystem interface*, which manages the dependencies between cohesive groups of subsystems, and the old but useful *microkernel*, which places the minimum functionality in a kernel and coordinates parts that are added onto it. The *broker* pattern can be used to structure distributed software systems with decoupled components that interact by remote service invocations. The *blackboard* pattern is useful for problems for which no deterministic solution strategies are known, where several specialized subsystems assemble their knowledge to build a partial or approximate solution.

At the class and object design level, perhaps the most enlightening patterns in the context of defect prevention are the so-called *anti-patterns*, also referred to as *pitfalls* [12]. These are examples of commonly used bad solutions to problems. An example of such an anti-pattern is a Blob class, which consists of too many methods. The excessive number of methods makes the Blob object difficult to maintain and therefore a poor programming practice.

DEVELOPER'S TESTIMONIAL

You can't forget anti-patterns. What is an anti-pattern? An anti-pattern is a pattern that spins off a negative result. For example, one of my favorite anti-patterns is Blob. (I once had a software lead whose code was a perfect example of a Blob pattern.) A Blob pattern is a class that has an excessive number of methods and attributes in it. Some people set this at 50, while I have always thought having a combination of 30 attributes and methods was too much. One of the solutions to eliminating a Blob pattern is to break the class into two or more smaller classes.

—Curt Martin, Software Engineer

6.2.4 Service-Oriented Architecture

An architectural superpattern that provides the highest level of functional abstraction in design is SOA. Mike Papazoglou and Dimitrios Georgakopoulos [13] refer to services as "self-describing, open components that support rapid, low-cost composition of distributed applications." The concept of SOA was originally proposed by Gartner analysts Roy Schulte and Yefim Natis in response to the growing need for a closer alignment of the organizations' business processes with their IT capabilities [14].

Why SOA facilitates agility, reuse, and interoperability because services are autonomous and are platform and technology independent. They interoperate based on a formal definition of a communication protocol and/or contract, such as WSDL[y] (Web Services Description Language) [15], that is independent of the underlying operating system, platform, or the application programming language used. The service provider offers the service by defining its interface and implementing the service functionality. A service requestor binds that service into its application [16]. For example, if an existing service provides real-time stock market data, the service requestor may choose to query only those stocks that pertain directly to its business.

How The SOA pattern can be applied both to existing applications, such as external web services, or to new projects within a single organization. In general, the SOA pattern should be considered when there is a need for utilizing an existing external service, or when code reusability, modularity, and interoperability are critical design attributes of the system. In such cases, the product requirements should be mapped onto services first, and then refined for the design of components and modules.

6.2.5 Mapping Requirements to Modules

Once the high-level architecture has been created, the design proceeds to the definition of the system components and modules. A module is a collection

---

[y] WSDL is an XML format that describes how to communicate using web services including the protocol bindings and message formats required to interact with the web services.

of related elements that provide a cohesive functionality. For large systems, it may be necessary to subdivide modules into smaller submodules until the appropriate level of granularity is attained. Normally, a module consists of a set of classes that encapsulate a common functionality.

Why   Before determining the modules' interactions or their detailed design, it is necessary to create a high-level view of the modules. This overview of the system will serve as a framework for subsequent design steps, allowing the project groups to know what areas they must attend to as they delve deeper into the design of the system. In addition, as the system is divided, and possibly subdivided into modules and submodules, this view also provides a natural way to break up project work between groups and their members. Each module can be assigned to a group, which may in turn define submodules to assign to group members, who can then work on the detailed design. This subdividing of tasks and effort is essential for optimizing team productivity and preventing problems, such as module interface defects.

How   To begin defining modules, it is necessary to identify the major categories of functionality, those that are the most general and essential, by reviewing the requirements and the use cases. Next, the requirements and use cases should be assigned to the appropriate module based on common functionality. If the modules require further subdivision, this process should be repeated for each module's submodule.

Very often, use cases contain multiple actors—users or entities with specific roles and characteristics within the application. Some actors will have the same needs and duties while others will not. For example, a use case for a school's library software may have five actors: a librarian, a student, a professor, a teaching assistant, and a school administrator. Each of these actors will take part in the use cases depending on her duties and roles. These multiple roles may share the same functionality such as logging in and out, viewing a catalog, or searching for citations.

Often multiple use cases that span a product reflect a tangled web of data and control through an application. Each unique use case represents a logical passage through the application, which may overlap and intersect with other use cases within the same application. In the above example, librarians should be the only user group having the authority to add new items to the online catalog. Students should be allowed to check out books, but, for example, not journals. Professors could have the authority to check out both the books and journals as well as place those items "on reserve" for the exclusive use of students in a specific course. However, everybody, regardless of her position, should be able to view the school catalog. Thorough system analysis should help identify points of common functionality. By separating unrelated use cases and identifying common functionalities, it is easier to achieve a high level of modularity.

Modules for Use Case 1

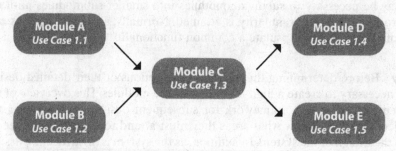

Figure 6.1 A simple block diagram of modules and their relationships for use case 1, which has been broken into sub–use cases 1.1 through 1.5.

After the major categories of functionality have been defined, the modules should be modeled using a simple block diagram that demonstrates compliance with project requirements. A block diagram depicts system structures and their interactions (Figure 6.1). Each block in a block diagram represents a different module and allows the team to understand how the requirements map to these modules and their interfaces, which ultimately helps to define the overall application logic.

When examining the block diagrams and the modules, it needs to be verified that the set of modules is complete in the sense that each use case is represented in the proper sequence. Therefore, the blocks must be arranged in sequential order corresponding to the control flow of use cases. In addition, the modules should be reusable so that they can be used in multiple use cases. After defining and arranging the modules, there should be enough blocks to build any use case possible for the application. Ideally, the number of blocks/modules can be reduced even further after viewing the entire information flow within the application as modeled by the block diagram. Ultimately, there should be a smooth information flow along the use cases, and one should be able easily to define the interfaces between them.

Measurement A helpful measure is the number of use cases per module. It is important to have each module used in multiple (five to ten) use cases. This measure indicates which modules are highly used and which are not. To track how this measure changes over time, the number of use cases per module should be plotted. During the design, the number of use cases per module is a measure of code reuse.

After the application is implemented, this measure can be derived directly from analyzing the source code. In some cases, well-functioning code can be reused in another application. If there are two separate applications that each comprise 1 million lines of code but share 800,000 lines of code, there is a high ratio (80%) of code reuse. In either case, the more code that is reused, the less code will need to be written, which reduces the likelihood of introducing new defects.

Tracking The architectural definition documents that describe the blueprint of the product architecture, including the modules and their interfaces, and any associated text that explains the design should be stored in the project artifact repository.

Each time the document is edited, the change and its author should be recorded. Whether the document is approved or pending approval, and who approved it and when should also be tracked.

6.2.6 Designing Module Interfaces

Once the modules have been defined, it is necessary to determine how the modules will interact. A module's interface is the set of parameters, methods, and attributes that a module exposes for interaction with other modules or entities. This determines what data can be accessed and what activities executed by each module, and what restrictions exist for the ways the modules can communicate or act upon one another.

Who The architect or lead developer should work with the developers to define the interfaces for the modules.

How First, the requirements and use cases that are associated with each module should be reviewed to make a list of desired functionalities for each module. For each pair of modules, which we will call Module A and Module B, it should be determined whether either module will depend on the data or functionalities of the other module. If Module A depends on Module B, then it should be noted on Module A that it uses Module B. Then, it should be noted on Module B what data or functionalities are used by Module A. This process should be repeated until all possible pairs of modules have been reviewed. When this is completed, all of the potential dependencies between the modules will have been mapped. After viewing how the modules are dependent on one another, it may be necessary to remap some of the requirements to different modules, create new modules, and divide or merge existing modules.

When all of the dependencies have been mapped, it is possible to create interfaces for each of the modules. If a module has dependent modules, the interface of that module should expose the data and functionalities that are needed by the dependent modules. These data and functionalities should be marked as public, while all other data and methods not used by any other modules should be marked as private.

This is an excellent time to verify how well the modules meet the critical design attributes, especially modularity, reusability, maintainability, and extensibility, and to make any additional necessary adjustments.

6.2.7   Modeling Modules and Their Interfaces

The Unified Modeling Language (UML) [5] is a visual language for the modeling of business processes, software applications, and system architectures. Used as a standard by the Objects Management Group [17], UML is particularly suited for object-oriented design. UML provides a standard visual notation to describe a system's blueprints, including high-level concepts such as business processes and system functions, as well as more specific items such as classes and objects. UML diagrams can be divided into two types: structure diagrams and behavior diagrams. Structure diagrams depict the static organization of the elements and include component, class, and object diagrams. Behavior diagrams describe the flow of activities through dynamic actions of the system and include use-case, activity, collaboration, and sequence diagrams (Figure 6.2).

UML should be applied in concert with other modeling/design best practices, starting with mapping use cases to modules, continuing on to defining interfaces, and then to defining application logic.

Why   Most importantly, UML is used to document the architecture and detailed design of the system, which can then be used by all members of the project. The design documents can succinctly convey information about how the system will be built and can be referenced by all of the project members.

Additionally, UML aids in evaluating and improving the logic of the designs, thus helping to prevent algorithmic and logic defects. Creating structure and behavior diagrams of the system allows for viewing the system at each stage

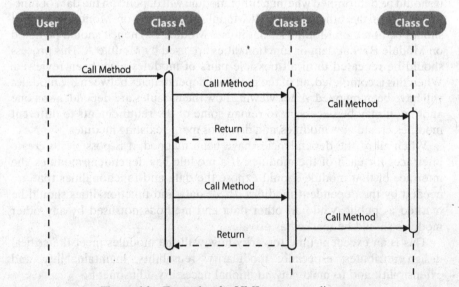

Figure 6.2   Example of a UML sequence diagram.

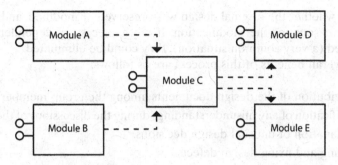

Figure 6.3 A diagram for the module and use case interactions.

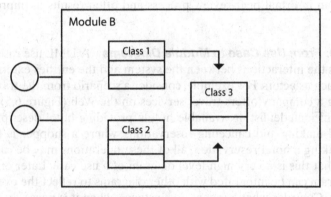

Figure 6.4 A diagram of the classes in a module in a lower-level view of the system.

of granularity, from a high-level architectural design to a low-level object view. The design diagrams can be navigated by "zooming in" to a lower-level diagram to see a more specific view of the system, or "zooming out" to a higher-level diagram to see a more general view of the system. This zooming technique is useful in gaining perspective on the data and activity flow of the different levels of granularity. Diagrams in Figures 6.3 and 6.4 show a progressively detailed view of the design.

Who The architect or a lead developer should determine which UML and other diagrams will be used for different views in the project. The architect should also specify for what parts of the modules diagrams are necessary and which standards should be used for each type of diagram.

How When designing a completely new module, a designated person from the team can create the diagrams and then distribute the diagrams to the rest of the team. The team can then review the designs and discuss them with the original design author. If any questions arise, the author has the opportunity to answer questions and defend any of her design decisions. The review helps to detect whether the original design was preserved or modified, and if modified, the reasons for the modification. If any unnecessary dependencies are introduced (a very common situation), they could be eliminated.

The overall benefits of this process are as follows:

- Distribution of the design documents among the group members.
- Clarification of any misunderstandings during the discussions of the design.
- Explanation of unusual design decisions.
- Finding and fixing design defects.

Additionally discussing the UML diagrams with the development team provides an informal peer-review process and often results in improving the design.

Example: From Use Case to Module Diagrams   A UML use case diagram illustrates the interactions between the system and the entities external to the system, such as actors. For example, consider a scenario from the travel industry, where a company offers travel services on the Web (Figure 6.5). The services might include: listing available hotels, providing hotel descriptions and rates, and making and canceling reservations, where a shopper is the actor. When making a hotel reservation, all of these operations may be called.

Note that this is a very high-level diagram of a use case. Later on, this use case diagram can be integrated with other diagrams to reflect the overall business logic. Consider what happens, for instance, when it is necessary to create a reusable service that represents searching for and booking a hotel room. Several services will be invoked, some in a particular order. For example, first

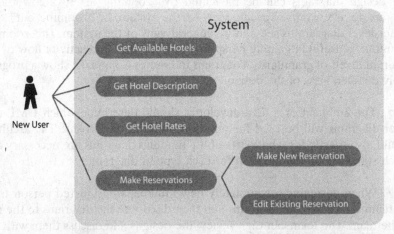

Figure 6.5   A use-case diagram for the hotel web service.

a list of hotels near a given airport should be generated, then a request for rates for the hotels should be sent. In other cases, operations may be performed in parallel. There may be conditional logic, such as making a reservation only if the rate is within the budget. All such situations can be modeled using UML diagrams.

Once the use cases are modeled, the team should begin to create diagrams for increasingly detailed design levels in the system.

Using the travel example, we can zoom in to the "get available hotels" module of the use case. Next, different modules would be merged with and separated from one another according to their commonalities and dependencies. For example, the "get hotel description" module can be merged with the "get hotel rates" module, while "make reservation" will be a separate module. Once the modules are determined, and their interfaces are defined, the detailed design of the application can start.

6.2.8   Defining Application Logic

Once all the use cases that will be executed by a particular module have been determined, the module's logic should be defined.

Why   If the application logic is not defined prior to implementation, there is a risk that the developers will waste time writing redundant code, and that the resulting objects will not represent the most effective design. Moreover, if application logic is modeled using UML, the application logic framework can be generated automatically, minimizing the amount of the manual code required and thus decreasing the chance of defects.

Who   The developers should work under the supervision of the architect or lead developers to define the application logic. The lead developers should also delegate detailed design tasks to other team developers, and then review them.

How   The starting points of this step are the already-created component and class UML diagrams. Each module should be broken into classes with well-encapsulated functionality. After that, class interactions should be defined, which may be described by sequence and collaboration diagrams. State diagrams can be used to represent object behavior. Often, however, detailed design is performed directly by coding, and only the most algorithmically complex classes require additional diagrams or pseudocode.

Measurement   An excessively high ratio of objects per module usually produces an increased defect rate. Ideally, one module should be managed by one developer. While building bigger modules that are maintained by multiple team members may prove necessary, it often complicates module implementation.

6.2.9 Refining Test Cases

Conceptual test cases defined in the requirements phase should be modified to reflect the product design. Properly defined test cases help to ensure that the requirements are traceable at each level of the design. In the design phase, generation of tests starts with services and modules and continues through classes and methods. All tests defined in this phase should map onto the conceptual tests defined in the requirements, and conversely each requirement should have multiple corresponding test cases.

Why Use case–based test cases are the most accurate technical description of the user requirements. By requiring the refinement of conceptual tests during design, but before the development of the services and modules, both the design and implementation can be traced back to the product requirements, assuring that the correct functionality is being implemented. In addition, by using tests to drive development, writing of excessive code is avoided.

Who Developers are responsible for creating test cases.

How Developers should generate test cases for services and modules and refine them further during detailed design and coding. It is important that during the detailed design phase, the test cases reflect the flow of the data between and through the objects, and that they verify that parameters are passed correctly between the objects. This can help validate the functionality of the objects before the rest of the application is built and prevent interface design defects.

The application should be designed in such a way that each module, and consequently its interface, can be isolated and tested separately. This is especially important when developing web services because they are comprised of big modules defined with XML (Extensible Markup Language) [18] and other types of interfaces. A web service may need to process customer requests, database information, client responses, and other data. For each of these cases within the web service, it is necessary to define the proper set of inputs, outputs, and design that will facilitate the correct information flow. Tests must be created for each module to verify its functionality and ensure that the application can handle both positive and negative inputs.

Positive test cases should return expected values, and a number of different positive test cases should be constructed to flush out any defects. A positive test case is said to succeed when the expected and the actual output is the same. For example, the SOAP (Simple Object Access Protocol) responses from the web service should be captured and compared against the expected responses.

Additionally, the application should fail gracefully upon receiving negative test cases that simulate abnormal and malicious uses. The span of the unit tests, which are created at the time of code construction, should be such that each predefined functionality is verified and traceable back to the requirements stored in the requirements management system.

Measurement   The number of passed tests shows the progress of product implementation: more tests succeed as the code nears completion. Another measure that is important to observe at this time is the ratio of test cases to use cases. Every use case should have both positive and negative test cases.

Tracking   Each test case should reference the relevant use cases and requirements. As the code is being built, the implemented features, use cases, and requirements should be tracked. This will help to determine the status of the product implementation.

Refined test cases, including unit tests, should be stored in the requirements management system. If the infrastructure consists of both an automated testing system and a requirements management system, generation, storage, and tracking of test cases should be integrated between these two systems.

Automation   Test cases can be executed automatically as the application is being built. Originally, the services and modules are not implemented so the test cases would fail. During the construction phase, the code is being implemented and the number of "passed" test cases would gradually increase. Test case outcomes (pass, fail, or incomplete) can be measured automatically.

6.2.10   Design Document Storage and Inspection

As design artifacts are being created, they should be stored in the project artifact repository that is accessible to all relevant stakeholders. The development group should then review the design documents and ensure that the design is complete and consistent. The architectural design should be reviewed before detailed design starts. Detailed design documents should be reviewed at the beginning of the iteration in which the design is implemented.

Who   The developers that are most familiar with a specific part of the system, or that are the most experienced with the specific type of software, should be responsible for reviewing the respective design documents. Each developer is responsible for thoroughly reviewing all the class diagrams, use cases, test cases, and so on that she created, and should perform additional detailed reviews with the architect or lead developer to verify that her designs meet the specifications for the application's architecture. The developer should be able to describe the design and its use cases, and explain how these use cases are to be implemented in the code.

How The development group should review each module and class to determine whether the objects represent all the required functionality and data. The key to design review is to ensure that the objects will allow for maintainability and extensibility. The group must consider the extent to which the code will be refactored [19] and changed in the future, and whether the objects are flexible enough to accommodate this change. Use cases must also be simulated through the objects in order to find and prevent any interaction problems. At this point, many defects can be found, fixed, and prevented by discovering problems with module interactions, class and object definition, and data and control flow.

In addition, a review of test cases should also be performed while the modules and classes corresponding to use cases are reviewed. Test cases force development group attention to detail and they ensure that the requirements are satisfied at each level of design.

This is an excellent time to review how well the design adheres to both the critical goals defined in the design policy and the high-priority requirements. The review should start from the high-level design to determine how well it meets all of the critical goals and requirements, and it should be repeated for each step of refinement in the design.

6.2.11 Managing Changes in Design

Because the design reflects all the elements and relationships that exist in the product requirements specification, it evolves as each requirement is implemented. Therefore, the very process of designing the system is one of constant expansion, adaptation, and refinement.

Why System design is an inherently iterative process, where the design grows and changes as each requirement is realized. Incorporating specifications and team member suggestions adds new material to the design and often requires modifying material already present in the design. Additionally, the architecture and detailed design should be updated during successive passes through the design phase. It is therefore necessary to track the design document changes and relationships with requirements.

Who Any team member who creates or modifies a design document is responsible for adding it to the project artifact repository. The architect and any developers who worked on a design document are responsible for making changes to that document, and should decide whether requested changes can be made.

How   Design documents should be stored in the project artifact repository. They should contain records of design document changes, and their relationships to the requirements. This will allow all team members to access each other's designs and see what designs are changing or have stabilized. When a team member updates a design, it may be necessary to request that other team members update their designs also. Depending on the project, these changes could be requested through a formalized process or done informally by talking with the architect and other involved developers. Either way, the architect and all developers involved in the affected designs should work together to approve or reject the proposed change. If accepted, the originator of the request should be notified, as well as any other team members who will need to update their designs. If the team does not have separate technologies that support design document change tracking, they can use a spreadsheet or an existing database.

If the change is in response to a serious design defect, the team should apply the methodology's principle of "learning from your mistakes": determine what part of the design process failed, and improve the process so that unexpected changes do not occur in the future. Requested changes that occur after design for the current release is frozen should be recorded in the problem tracking system and scheduled for future considerations or releases.

Measurement   Measures should include the number of change requests, the number and percentage of requests with a given status (pending, open, rejected, closed), and the number of requests per originator. An excessively high number of change requests could indicate that the there were defects in the original design and a closer look at the original design might be advisable.

Tracking   The change request, the person who requested it, and the date on which it was requested should all be tracked. Status change request dates, the new status, the status assigner, and the status change dates should also be tracked.

6.3   BEST PRACTICES FOR DESIGN OF GRAPHICAL USER INTERFACE

The architectural and detailed design of the system shows how the software should be constructed but it does not describe how the user will interact with it, and therefore it should not be relied upon to determine the design of the user interface. The design of the user interface is especially important because even the best functionality will not compensate for a poor user interface, and people will not use the system unless they can successfully interact with it. Unfortunately, design of user interfaces often is given very low priority or even neglected by developers. While the power of software seemingly improves on a daily basis, user interfaces seem to lag behind. Frustrated users are often faced with hostile software interfaces when trying to perform routine tasks.

If the organization does not have trained user interface designers, the developers should be trained in interface design. The policies for user interface design should be created, customized by product, and followed by all team members involved in the design and implementation of the user interface.

6.3.1   Identifying Critical Attributes of User Interface Design

When designing user interfaces, basic cognitive models of how humans perceive and learn should be considered at every step of the process. Complexity and ambiguity are the two biggest enemies in designing an effective interface. The following attributes determine how successfully a user can interact with an interface and therefore whether the user will continue to use the system (or if use is mandatory, the ease of continued use).

Ability to Understand   Understanding occurs when a user is able to link the words and symbols presented on an interface to the actions that the program could perform. This is the most fundamental and critical goal that an interface must achieve: if a user cannot understand the interface, it will greatly impair her learning and remembering (if she even continues to use the software at all). An *intuitive* interface gives the user meaningful words and symbols that accurately describe the actions or results of actions.

How

- The icons/symbols used should be meaningful.
- The words or terminology used in the interface should be understandable by the target audience.
- If the program mimics an activity in the real world, the interface should use analogies to the activity. For example, "add to cart" and "checkout" buttons in a shopping application would be understood by anyone who shops at a grocery store.
- Terminology, symbols, and organization should be the same or similar to those commonly used in other programs, especially existing programs that are similar to the program being developed.
- If the user cannot immediately understand the items on the interface, she should be able to easily access appropriate help files.

Ability to Learn   Learning occurs when a user acquires the ability to perform actions by studying or gaining experience with the user interface. The first component of learning is the user's ability to relate an action to a reaction of the system. For example, by clicking a button labeled "smaller," the user learns that the application makes the text smaller. The second component of learning is the user's ability to apply her acquired knowledge to similar situations. For example, if the user has already learned what the "smaller" button does, she will quickly be able to learn what a button labeled "larger" does. Consistency and repetition are invaluable methods in helping the user learn how to use the system.

How

- The action a user selects on the interface should always be followed by the same reaction of the system.
- Similar actions should be grouped together and have similar names. This allows the user to infer the function of unused actions based on the actions she has already learned.
- Each entity/action should have a name that is used consistently wherever it may appear in the interface.
- Similar actions should trigger similar processes.

Ability to Remember   Remembering occurs when a user is able to return to an interface and repeat actions that she had previously learned. How well the user remembers the interface is highly dependent on interface complexity and frequency of use.

How

- The interface should remain the same between usages. If the user had customized the interface previously, this customized interface should always be displayed to the user.
- Revisions/updates to the program should not completely reorganize the interface. While some small changes may be necessary, the user should not open the new version to find a completely different interface.

Ability to Navigate   Navigating occurs when the user moves through different screens in the program. Navigation is especially important in applications that allow the user to move freely through large amounts of content or processes with many branching decision points, such as websites. When using these programs, users move many steps through the program and may feel lost if the interface does not provide a comfortable system for navigating.

How

- The program should have a "home" screen, preferably as the first screen that is displayed. The user should be returned, or have an option to return, to this screen after completing other actions. Additionally, the user should be able to reach this screen whenever she feels lost in the program.
- There should always be some form of top-level navigation that does not drastically change and allows the user to return "home" if needed. For web applications, this navigation should appear on every web page.
- If there are several sections that require sublevels of navigation, the navigation format should remain consistent across all subsections.

Usability The term *usability* has several interpretations, but we will define it as the ease with which a user can use the program to achieve her goals. This is therefore the most subjective of the critical goals, as it relies on the users' interpretation of how easy a system is to use and how well the program performed in meeting their goals.

How

- An effort should be made to reduce the complexity or number of the steps required for the user to reach her goal.
- User experience and actions should be anticipated when designing the interface by asking, "Is this easy to use?," and "Does this accomplish the user's goal?"
- Feedback of the usability of the interface should be gathered from the customers.

Accessibility Accessibility is the concept that a program should be usable by as many people as possible, regardless of impairments or disabilities. While this critical attribute should be considered by all software developers, it is mandated that all federal agencies give comparable access by Section 508 in the Rehabilitation Act. This act enforces the removal of barriers in accessing information when technologically possible, and encourages the development of new technologies for overcoming accessibility barriers.

How

- Accessibility standards for the type of product being developed should be incorporated into the user interface design policy.
- Disabilities or impairments that might exist in the target audience, such as cognitive, motor, or visual impairments, should be considered, especially if the product is intended for an audience with accessibility concerns. For example, a website that fills orders for prescription glasses

should allow users to adjust the font sizes in case the default font size is illegible for some users.

- If the program cannot incorporate certain accessibility features, designing alternative methods of access should be considered.

6.3.2   Defining the User Interface Design Policy

The user interface design policy is a document that contains all decisions and standards that will be followed during the design and implementation of the user interface, and serves to enforce consistency for the user interface. During the design phase, this document will be used to store and refine policies about the user interface, and during implementation, this document will serve as a reference for the implementers of the user interface.

Who   The project architect and project manager should work with the customers and developers to develop the design policy for the user interface. If there is a human–computer interaction expert, she should lead the development of the design policy. Additionally, feedback from the customers is especially important because their experience with the interface will greatly influence their opinion about how well the product meets their specifications.

How   The design policy for the user interface should contain the following:

- List of terminology including definitions, spelling, capitalization, etc.
- List of icons and their titles, descriptions, and associated actions
- List of actions, their title and description, and a reference to any requirements to which they apply
- Navigation
- Accessibility issues and their solutions
- Profiles of the intended users

Understanding the User   Creating profiles of the target audience is one of the most important factors in understanding the user. For example, if the end user is a working professional who chooses to do online shopping, she will have a very limited amount of time and would have to be able to navigate through the system very quickly. If she is not successful in accomplishing these tasks in a short period of time, she is not likely to use the system again.

Many systems will have users who vary in their technical skills, professional expertise, and frequency of system use. For example, an ultrasound machine at a hospital is used on a daily basis by technicians, often by radiologists, but only occasionally by doctors of other specialties. However, when a doctor who is an infrequent user needs to perform an ultrasound, it is probably because the patient requires urgent attention. Having an interface that is not intuitive will hinder the examination, and might put the patient's health or even life in danger.

USER'S TESTIMONIAL

You would think that if a new ultrasound machine cost so much, it would be user friendly. Wrong! Nobody in the hospital knows how to navigate it, because the user interface is very counterintuitive. When I try to perform the most basic functions, I am required to move constantly between irrelevant screens. For example, even before I start the patient's evaluation, the image is flipped, and I have to switch menus in order to correct its position!

The interface is so cumbersome that not only does it increase the time needed to perform a patient's evaluation, it also causes a great deal of frustration. This is intensified by the fact that I only have a couple of minutes in my schedule to do it. Moreover, as I do not use the ultrasound machine on a daily basis, I have to relearn this complicated interface every time.

And, by the way, you would think that they would consult us, the doctors and technicians who will be using this equipment, when they design it. We could make suggestions that would facilitate conducting more accurate examinations and enhance patient safety.

—Catherine Warner, MD

Thus, the following factors need to be considered in order to understand the user and create her profile:

- *Subject Knowledge*: How much does the user know about the subject that the software is presenting?
- *Technical Experience*: How much experience does the user have with this particular kind of software?
- *Frequency of Use*: How often will the user work with the program? Consider two tax programs: one designed for accountants who use it every day and one designed for nonaccountants who do their own taxes once a year. While the programs may have identical functionality, the non-accountants will need to be given help in selecting the appropriate forms and guided through the process of filling them out. Additionally, infrequent users may want to circumvent more complex or refined options, and just be able to use default options.
- *Goals*: What does the user want the program to do? How quickly will the user need to achieve these goals?
- *Need*: Will the user be using the software for work or for fun? Many kinds of software are used for fun or luxury, such as games, public websites, or

utilities for managing household tasks. Software that is designed for fun or luxury must be exceptionally intuitive and easy to use. The user wants something that entertains her or makes basic tasks easier, and will not be willing to invest time in learning how to use the software before seeing results. Remember that these kinds of software are optional to the user, and will be quickly abandoned if the interface makes the task more difficult or diminishes the entertainment value.

6.3.3   Identifying Architectural Patterns Applicable to the User Interface Design

Some architectural patterns facilitate design of user interfaces by the explicit separation of the user interface design from the application functionality or by depicting the user interface pattern of a common functionality, such as managing the display of multiple windows. The MVC (Model-View-Controller) [10] is an example of such a pattern; it relies on functionality separation. MVC divides an interactive application into three distinct components: application's data model, user interface, and control logic. The model contains the core functionality and data. Views display information to the user. Controllers handle user input. Views and controllers together comprise the user interface (GUI). Modifications to one component can be made with minimal impact to the others. A change-propagation mechanism ensures consistency between the user interface and the model.

A more specific pattern for design of the user interface (mentioned in Section 6.2.3) is the *view handler* pattern, which describes how to manage the user's view of the data.

6.3.4   Creating Categories of Actions

When a proposed product has hundreds of features, it would overwhelm the user to display a complete list of these features and ask her which she would like to perform. It is therefore necessary to group features together based on their functionality and present them to the user in meaningful categories. The user can then answer the question "What kind of actions can I take?" by simply viewing the categories. The design focus is on organizing the interface so the user can find her desired action.

To create meaningful categories, first all the features/functional requirements that represent actions a user can take should be listed. To identify possible categories, user-centric requirements and use cases should be reviewed for common functionalities. For example, "insert picture," "insert text," and "insert file" could be part of an "insert" category. "Add task," "view task," "edit task," and "delete task" could all be part of a "manage tasks" category. Once there is a preliminary list of possible categories, the relationship and number of requirements in each category should be assessed. If there are many requirements or they are not closely related, the category should be separated into two distinct categories or divided into subcategories. To create the subcategories, this process should be repeated for all of the requirements within the given category. For modeling and documenting the categories, hierarchal diagrams should be used.

In summary, categories should contain similar user actions and be easy to navigate. Therefore, the names and divisions of the categories should use terms and concepts familiar to the user. The importance of the task to the users should also be considered: actions most frequently used should be readily available.

6.3.5   Dividing Actions into Screens

Once the user actions have been defined, system reactions should be defined in the form of a screen. Screens are what is displayed to the user, such as windows in graphical desktop applications or pages in web applications. A series of screens answers the user's question of "How can I do this action?" by moving her through the process, and the design focus is on how to present the action and its functionality to the user. For simple actions that require no additional input from the user, the system will respond by performing the action and showing the result in an updated screen. For complex actions that require additional input from the user, additional screens should be provided.

To design screens for each of the actions, consider first what the user needs to start the action and then what the user expects to happen at the end of the action. At the end of an action, the user should always be able to see that something happened, by either giving a confirmation or showing the actual change. Any problems that arise during the action should be displayed to the user to inform her not only that a particular type of error occurred, but also what actions she can take to safely complete or exit the action. For simple actions that do not require additional screens, the resulting action could be documented with text describing how the change will update the screen. During the design of the user interface, sketches should be used to help designers quickly exchange and refine their ideas, as illustrated in Figure 6.6. As the design becomes finalized, these sketches should be scanned into or recreated in electronic format for documentation purposes.

For users who have little experience with the action, or will use the action infrequently, it may be necessary to have a series of screens with directions to lead them step-by-step through each action. They may also require more directions at each step, and might be overwhelmed if too many options are given. Experienced or frequent users want to move through the process quickly, and they know what options they want to select. Therefore, they usually want the action to be performed with as few screens as possible and minimal directions. They also want to see all of their options. For example, consider the difference between the "setup wizard" and the "advanced settings" screens in many desktop applications.

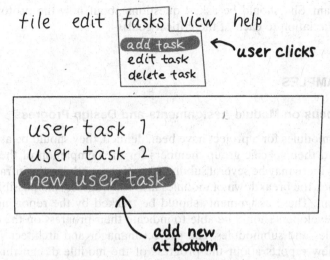

Figure 6.6   A quick sketch of a screen for an action.

6.3.6 Prototyping the Interface

A prototype of the interface can be as simple as "paper prototype" sketches, or as detailed as screen builds linked together to simulate the user interface. For programs that require considerable navigation or have many screens, it may be necessary to create a prototype with active navigation elements for clicking through all of the screens for each of the actions. Developers can then use the prototype interface to test the interface for usability and navigation. This will also help to expose any problems or difficulties with the interface, so the design flaws can be remedied before the developers start implementing the interface and its underlying functionality.

6.3.7 Testing the Interface

When developing a system, it is very difficult for developers to remove themselves from the process of building software to see how a user would actually interact with the software. Therefore, the best way to get feedback about a user interface is to show potential users the interface prototypes and evaluate their responses. For interfaces with few screens, it may only be necessary to give a user some "paper prototype" sketches of the screens. For large systems with many screens, it is better to give the user an interface prototype that they can click through to see how the system works.

The user should interact with the interface without prompting from the developers, but the developers should ask the user questions as she uses the prototype. Observing the user will help to determine interface effectiveness.

Additionally, the user should be able to document her experience as she uses the program and should fill out a questionnaire when she is finished using the program. She should be asked questions about how the prototype performed in relation to each of the critical goals.

6.4 EXAMPLES

6.4.1 Focus on Module Assignments and Design Progress

Once the modules for a project have been defined, they should be assigned to groups and then specific group members for the completion of the detailed design. As there may be several subdivisions of the modules, the infrastructure should track the breakdown of modules into submodules, and possibly further subdivisions. These assignments should be tracked by the reporting system, and the developers should be able to indicate their progress on the design of the modules and submodules. The project manager and architect should be able to view reports about the progress of the module design through the reporting system, such as in the panel shown in Figure 6.7.

Module		Assigned To	Design Progess
Module A		Group A	70%
	Submodule A1	G.A.V.	75%
	Submodule A2	M.E.D.	65%
	Submodule A3	C.T.S.	70%
Module B		Group B	80%
	Submodule B1	R.I.L.	85%
	Submodule B2	Y.J.K.	75%
Module C		Group C	65%

Figure 6.7 Overview panel for the project manager and architect showing the assignment of modules to groups and group members.

6.4.2 Focus on the Number of Use Cases per Module

The number of use cases per module is an important measure because it indicates design efficiency: in general, more use cases per module means greater design efficiency. Once all the modules are tracked by the infrastructure, each use case that employs the module should also be tracked. This information should then be available as a panel through the reporting system. This allows project members to view the number of use cases per module, as shown in Figure 6.8. A similar panel showing number of modules used for each use case could be used to show design completeness (i.e., that all use cases are being implemented), as illustrated in Figure 6.9.

Module	Used By	# Use Cases
Module A	Use Cases: 1, 2, 4, 6, 8, 9	6
Module B	Use Cases: 3, 6, 7, 9	4
Module C	Use Cases: 2, 5, 6, 9	4
Module D	Use Cases: 1, 3, 5	3
Module E	Use Cases: 4, 5, 7, 9	4

Figure 6.8 List of project modules and their associated use cases.

Use Case	Uses	# Modules
Use Case 1	Modules: A, D, G, K	4
Use Case 2	Modules: A, C, H, I, J	5
Use Case 3	Modules: B, D, F	3
Use Case 4	Modules: A, E, G, H, I	5
Use Case 5	Modules: C, E	2

Figure 6.9 List of project use cases and their associated modules.

6.4.3 Focus on Module Implementation Overview

Once all the modules have been tracked in the infrastructure, the developers, project manager, and architect should be able to assess the progress of the project based on the overall module implementation status as displayed in Figure 6.10.

6.4.4 Focus on Customized Best Practice for GUI Design

Background This example, drawn from real experience, uses a website that provides interior house paint samples. To select a particular color the user must first select a broad color grouping, for example, red, blue, green, and so forth. Selecting green, for example, would then expose the user to a range of green color groupings, ranging from blue-green to yellow-green. Selecting one of these, say blue-green, would expose the user to 20 or so individual shades of blue-green. Selecting a shade of blue-green, say aquamarine, would allow the user to print a sample, add this particular color to a palette of colors for a complete interior decoration, and so on.

In summary, then, the user should be able to select any available color with three clicks, for example, green, then blue-green, and then aquamarine.

Problem Regarding the second choice, in this example the selection of a green color grouping, the user was forced to start with the middle grouping, the greenest green, and then to advance only to either of the two adjacent

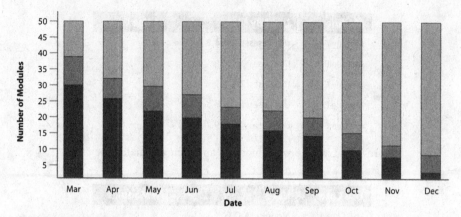

Module Implementation Details

Date	Unimplemented	In Progress	Implemented
Dec	3	5	42
Nov	7	4	39
Oct	10	5	35
Sep	14	6	30

Figure 6.10   Module implementation status.

color groupings. Given a range of 15 green color groupings *and a user who knows she wants a color from an extreme color grouping*, for example, from the bluest greens, the user will be forced to click through seven different color groupings, requiring several unnecessary clicks and causing user frustration.

Customized Best Practice   The customized best practice for the design of the user interface includes the following two rules:

1. *Providing for the Maximum Navigational Freedom to the User.* When required to make a selection from a range of options, the user shall not be forced to evaluate any mandatory options. This facilitates the knowledgeable user's experience, while allowing the uncertain user free rein to explore as desired.
2. *Providing for the Horizontal Selection Space.* A user selection space should be traversable in three moves/clicks or less. Selection spaces requiring more than three moves/clicks require an explanation from the developer and approval from the architect.

6.5   ACRONYMS

HTTP   HyperText Transfer Protocol
OOA   Object-oriented analysis

OOD	Object-oriented design
SOA	Service-oriented architecture
SOAP	Simple Object Access Protocol
WSDL	Web Service Description Language
XML	Extensible Markup Language

6.6 GLOSSARY

abstraction   (1) A view of an object that focuses on the information relevant to a particular purpose and ignores the remainder of the information. (2) The process of formulating a view as in (1). [1]*

algorithm complexity   The number of computational steps required to transform the input data into the result of the computation.

architectural design   (1) The process of defining a collection of hardware and software components and their interfaces to establish the framework for the development of a computer system. (2) The result of the process in (1). [1]*

architecture   (1) The organizational structure of a system or component. (2) The structure of components, their interrelationships, and the principles and guidelines governing their design and evolution over time. [1]*

block diagram   A representation of a system, computer, or device in which the principal parts are represented by suitably annotated geometrical figures to show both the functions of the parts and their functional relationships. [1]*

class   A description of a set of objects that have common properties and behaviors, which typically correspond to real-world items (persons, places, or things) in the business or problem domain.

class diagram   An analysis model that shows a set of system or problem domain classes and their relationships.

client/server protocol   A standardized method for allowing client processes and server processes to communicate. A client process interacts with users, allowing the users to request services from server processes. A server process waits for a request to arrive from the client process and then responds to those requests.

correctness   (1) The degree to which a system or component is free from faults in its specification, design, and implementation. (2) The degree to which software, documentation, or other items meet specified requirements. (3) The degree to which software, documentation, or other items meet user needs and expectations, whether specified or not. [1]*

derived class   A derived class inherits from base classes.

design   (1) The process of defining the architecture, components, interfaces, and other characteristics of a system or component. (2) The result of the process in (1). [1]*

design pattern   A documented best practice or core of a solution that has been applied successfully in multiple environments to solve a problem that recurs in a specific set of situations.

efficiency   The degree to which a system or component performs its designated functions with minimum consumption of resources. [1]*

encapsulation   A software development technique that consists of isolating a system function or a set of data and operations on those data within a module and providing precise specifications for the module. [1]*

extensibility   The ease with which a system or component can be modified to increase its storage or functional capacity. [1]*

functional design   The process of defining the working relationships among the components of a system. [1]*

information hiding   A software development technique in which each module's interfaces reveal as little as possible about the module's inner workings and other modules are prevented from using information about the module that is not in the module's interface specification. [1]*

inheritance   A form of software reusability in which programmers create classes that inherit an existing class data and methods and enhance them with new capabilities.

interface   A hardware or software component that connects two or more other components for the purpose of passing information from one to another. [1]*

interoperability   The ability of two or more systems or components to exchange information and to use the information that has been exchanged. [1]*

library   Also called software library. A controlled collection of software and related documentation designed to aid in software development, use, or maintenance. Types include master library, production library, software development library, software repository, system library. [1]*

maintainability   (1) The ease with which a software system or component can be modified to correct faults, improve performance or other attributes, or adapt to a changed environment. (2) The ease with which a hardware system or component can be retained in, or restored to, a state in which it can perform its required functions. [1]*

memory management   It is a technique that involves identifying used and available physical memory units, managing virtual memory mapping onto physical memory, and swapping the virtual memory pages to disk while performing the appropriate address translation.

model-based approach to design   Design based on the idea of identifying high-level models that allow designers to specify and analyze interactive software applications from a semantic-oriented level. MDA provides a set of guidelines for structuring specifications expressed as models.

modularity   The degree to which a system or computer program is composed of discrete components such that a change to one component has minimal impact on other components. [1]*

module   (1) A program unit that is discrete and identifiable with respect to compiling, combining with other units, and loading; for example, the input to, or output from, an assembler, compiler, linkage editor, or executive routine. (2) A logically separable part of a program. [1]*

multicast   A communication protocol in which data is delivered to all hosts that have expressed interest. This is one-to-many delivery.

object   A specific instance of a class for which a set of data attributes and a list of operations that can be performed on those attributes can be collected.

object-oriented design   A software development technique in which a system or component is expressed in terms of objects and connections between those objects. [1]*

page fault   An event that occurs when an accessed page is not present in main memory.

paging   A storage allocation technique in which programs or data are divided into fixed-length blocks called pages, main storage is divided into blocks of the same length called page frames, and pages are stored in page frames. [1]*

package   A separately compilable software component consisting of related data types, data objects, and subprograms. [1]*

pattern-based approach to design   An approach that identifies important and relevant design patterns, so that a complex design can be constructed from these design patterns. [10]

piped stream   A communication protocol allowing output from one thread to become input for another thread for communication between programs or to system resources.

portability   The ease with which a system or component can be transferred from one hardware or software environment to another. [1]*

protocol   A set of conventions that govern the interaction of processes, devices, and other components within a system. [1]*

refactoring   A reorganization technique that simplifies the design (or code) of a component without changing its function or behavior. [19]

reusability   The degree to which a software module or other work product can be used in more than one computer program or software system. [1]*

scalability   The ability of a program to gracefully adapt to growing demands on the system resources.

Service-oriented architecture   is an architectural style "within which all functions are defined as independent services with well-defined invokable interfaces which can be called in defined sequences to form business processes." [2]

security The establishment and application of safeguards to protect data, software, and computer hardware from accidental or malicious modification, destruction, or disclosure. [8]

Simple Object Access Protocol Simple Object Access Protocol is a protocol for exchanging XML-based messages over a computer network.

unit test Testing of individual hardware or software units or groups of related units. [1]*

WSDL is an XML format that describes how to communicate using the web services, including the protocol bindings and message formats required to interact with the web services.

XML is a markup language for documents containing structured information. [18]

* From IEEE Std. 610.12-1990, Copyright 1990, IEEE. All rights reserved.

6.7 REFERENCES

[1] Institute of Electrical and Electronics Engineers, *IEEE Standard 610.12-1990— Glossary of Software Engineering Terminology*, 1990.

[2] Channabasavaiah, K., Holley, K., and Tuggle, E., "Migrating to a Service Oriented Architecture," *IBM Developer Works*, December 16, 2003.

[3] Gamma, E., Helm, R., Johnson, R., and Vlissides J., *Design Pattern: Elements of Reusable Object-Oriented Software*. Addision-Wesley, 1995.

[4] Kleppe, A., Warmer, J., and Bast, W., *MDA Explained—The Model Driven Architecture: Practice and Promise*. Addison Wesley, 2004.

[5] Rumbaugh, J., Jacobson, I., and Booch, G., *The Unified Modeling Language Reference Manual*. Addison-Wesley, 2 ed., 2004.

[6] Burnstein, I., *Practical Software Testing: A Process Oriented Approach*. Springer, 2002.

[7] Bosch, J., *Design and Use of Software Architectures*. Harlow: Addison-Wesley, 2000.

[8] Thayer, R.H. and Dorfman, M., *System and Software Requirements Engineering*. IEEE Press, 1990.

[9] Kuchana, P., *Software Architecture Design Patterns in Java*. CRC Press, 2004.

[10] Buschmann, F., Meunier, R., Rohnert, H., Sommerlad, P., and Stal, M., *Pattern-Oriented Software Architecture: A System of Patterns*, Vol. 1. John Wiley & Sons, 1996.

[11] OpenGroup, *Architecture Patterns*, 2006, http://www.opengroup.org/architecture/ togaf8-doc/arch/p4/patterns/patterns.htm (retrieved: August 8, 2006).

[12] Brown, W.J., Malveau, R.C., McCormick III, H.W., and Mowbray, T.J., *Anti-Patterns: Refactoring Software, Architectures, and Projects in Crisis*. John Wiley & Sons, 1998.

[13] Papazoglou, M.P. and Georgakopoulos, D., "Service-Oriented Computing," *Communications of the ACM*, Vol. 46, No. 10, October 2003.

[14] Schulte, R.W. and Natis, Y.V., "Service Oriented Architecture," *Gartner*, April 12, 1996.

[15] Web Services Description Language (WSDL) Version 2.0, Part 1: *Core Language*, 2006, http://www.w3.org/TR/wsdl20 (retrieved: August 21, 2006).

[16] Sommerville, I., *Software Engineering*. Addison-Wesley, 8th ed., 2007.

[17] The Object Management Group (OMG), 2006, http://www.omg.org (retrieved: August 12, 2006).

[18] Walsh, N., *A Technical Introduction to XML*, 2006, http://www.xml.com/pub/a/98/10/guide0.html (retrieved: August 12, 2006).

[19] Pressman, R.S., *Software Engineering: A Practitioner's Approach*. McGraw-Hill, 2004.

6.8 EXERCISES

1. What other design attributes not mentioned in this chapter could be considered in defining design policies?

2. Give examples of software applications for which security would be a critical attribute. Define a security policy for each.

3. Describe at least two architectural patterns not mentioned in this chapter, and explain what problems they solve.

4. Give examples of commercial or noncommercial software tools that perform autocode generation from design models.

5. Define an architecture for the FoodMagic application described in Chapter 5.

6. Why is it important to define test cases for modules during design and before the actual implementation of the modules?

7. Explain the primary reasons for the unfriendliness of many user interfaces, and propose means for alleviating it.

8. Define a policy for FoodMagic's user interface.

9. In addition to what is described in this chapter, what do you think should be tracked and measured during the software design?

10. What should be tracked and measured during the design of the software user interface?

CHAPTER 7

CONSTRUCTION

I'm not a great programmer. I'm just a good programmer with great habits.
—Kent Beck

7.1 INTRODUCTION

The key product of architectural and detailed design is the blueprint of the system under development. This blueprint delineates product services, describes components and modules with their interfaces, and serves as a guide for further design and implementation.

Developers refine architectural design by modeling classes and objects, creating algorithms, and constructing software. Their work revolves around the source code, which is continually changing. They write the new code, test it, debug it, rewrite it, and integrate it with other parts of the code. The excitement of adding new capabilities to the product is often combined with the much less rewarding, error prone, and tedious tasks of editing and debugging the existing code. Moreover, the algorithmically complex parts of the design require a high level of prolonged concentration and creativity, which is hard to maintain if the developer is repeatedly interrupted by more trivial activities. Additionally, since the code is shared among multiple team members, construction opens the door to problems resulting from a lack of communication

Automated Defect Prevention: Best Practices in Software Management, by Dorota Huizinga and Adam Kolawa
Copyright © 2007 John Wiley & Sons, Inc.

and synchronization of tasks. A small piece of defective code could adversely affect the whole project. For example, improper versioning of a module by a single team member could cause the complete failure of a regression test, and unnecessarily delay project progress. Poor modularization of the design combined with a lack of task synchronization can cause the same piece of code to be inadvertently modified by two or more developers, leading to hours of frustration attempting to successfully merge the code if parallel development[a] is not supported by proper infrastructure and well-defined policies.

Similar to prior development phases, coding defects either can be traced to the earlier stages of the project or they can be injected independently during code construction and integration. Since much detailed design work is done directly by coding, coding defect classification is similar to detailed design-level defect classification. Based on Ilene Burstein's [1] and Cem Kaner's [2] categorizations, we have adopted the following classification of coding defects:

- *Initialization defects,* which stem from omitted or incorrect variable initialization statements.
- *Algorithmic and processing defects,* which stem from incorrect implementation of algorithmic design, improper progression of steps in processing data, or incorrect coding of arithmetic operations, and Boolean expressions, or inadvertently lost precision.
- *Control, logic, and sequence defects,* which are caused by incorrect implementation of conditional statements such as "if-then-else," expressions of "case" statements, or loop boundary problems.
- *Error handling defects,* which stem from the failure to properly anticipate invalid inputs to the program, and the omission or incomplete implementation of error handling routines. These types of defects often predispose the system to security vulnerabilities.
- *Code reuse defects,* which result from the failure to account for the reused code constraints in the implementation of its interfaces and in its use.
- *Data defects,* which result from the incorrect implementation of data structures, such as wrong variable types, pointer mismatches, or improper allocation of memory or secondary storage elements.
- *Data flow defects,* which are caused by improper data sequence. For example, a variable should be initialized first, then used, and then disregarded. If a variable is disregarded before it is used, a data flow defect occurs.
- *Service, module, and object interface defects,* which result from a faulty message format between services, improper parameter type declaration, or incorrect parameter numbers passed between modules or objects.

---

[a] A planning decision that allows multiple developers to work on the same configuration item at the same time.

- *External hardware and software interface defects,* which stem from the erroneous coding of interfaces with external hardware components, incorrect implementation of contracts or communication protocols with external services, wrong parameters passed to system calls, or improper access of COTS.
- *Usability defects,* which stem from missing, incorrect, or improper implementation of elements in the user interface, mostly due to missing or improper use of the graphical user interface design and its policy.
- *Code documentation defects,* which occur in situations when the code documentation does not reflect code functionality or if it is too cryptic to help in understanding code functionality.
- *Configuration and version defects,* which result from incorrect versioning of source code components, improperly linked libraries, and other parts of the system under the development.

In this chapter we will describe general best practices for code construction that help to avoid the above problems. We will also explain a set of generic policies for the use of the source control system and automated build system. The goal of the infrastructure in this phase is to automate repetitive activities, such as the build process and regression testing, as well as to give the developers freedom to experiment with their code without negatively affecting the work of others, and to help in the synchronization of their tasks by providing an adequate control of basic daily development activities.

The expected work products for this phase are:

- Best practices for code construction
- Source code
- Test cases
- Policy for the use of the source control system
- Policy for the use of the automated build system

7.2 BEST PRACTICES FOR CODE CONSTRUCTION

Code construction requires many decisions, such as the software development process model, the order in which features and their corresponding design elements are implemented, and the use of language- and technology-dependent coding conventions. The best practices for code construction are based on organization processes and standards combined with project-specific requirements. Since organizational standards are applicable to nearly all projects, they would primarily include rules for code maintainability such as readability and documentation. For example, naming conventions for configuration items and the rules for the organization of project artifacts would belong to this category.

Project-specific standards will depend on the product requirements, the process model adopted, the architectural model, the design policies, and the development environment. For example, in SOA development, the contract-first approach, which facilitates proper interface implementation and data exchange, should be used. Similarly, in a web application, Java coding standards that help to implement secure code should be considered.

We have identified six categories of best practices for avoiding detailed design and coding defects that are process and project independent:

1. Application of Coding Standards throughout the Development
2. Test-First Approach at the Service, Component, and Module Level
3. Implementation of Contracts and Interfaces before the Corresponding Services, Components, and Modules
4. Test-Driven Development Approach for the Algorithmically Complex and Critical Code Units
5. Application of Unit Testing after Implementing Each Unit and before Checking in the Code to the Source Control System
6. Verification of the Code's Consistency with the Requirements and Design Policies

Since code construction and testing are intertwined, these practices should be applied in conjunction with the best practices for software testing.

7.2.1 Applying Coding Standards throughout Development

Coding standards, which are the rules for structuring and formatting the code, have long been recognized as a best practice when developing software. Developers know that programming languages have tendencies to attract problems that are not visible to compilers. In his bestselling book [3], first published in 1992, Scott Meyers pioneered a new programming paradigm by explaining how to avoid common pitfalls in C++ and make the best use of this language's object-oriented features, such as constructors, destructors, inheritance, virtual functions, and per-class allocators. Since then, coding standards have been defined for all modern programming languages, including Java™ [4], and their use is a mature practice today.

The overall purpose of coding standards is to produce code that has a consistent style and structure and that conforms to required quality attributes. In addition to correct functionality, code quality attributes include proper factoring, appropriate use of language features, data structures, ability to handle invalid inputs, as well as adherence to predefined style, format, and language-specific conventions. In several cases these standards are documented and formalized as part of company's general best practices for developing software.

ARCHITECT'S TESTIMONIAL

There are more than 50 coding guidelines used in my organization. Some of the basic coding practices include:

1. *Do Not Use Hungarian Notation or Add Any Other Type Identification to Identifiers*. This practice prevents language dependency that complicates maintenance activities.
2. *Use Pascal and Camel Casing for Naming Identifiers*. This helps readability and use of multiple words to name an identifier. For example, InventoryEntry specifies that the identifier stores an inventory entry.
3. *Use Namespaces According to a Well-defined Pattern*. This helps avoid conflict of similar names in different modules and classes.
4. *Use a Noun or a Noun Phrase to Name a Class*. This helps identify real-world objects.
5. *Prefix Interfaces with the Letter* I. This helps identify and logically group all the interfaces.
6. *Use Verbs for Class Methods*. Usually methods perform some action and actions can be described only by verbs.
7. *Each File Shall Contain a Header Block*. This helps identify the author of the file and also the intent of it.

In general, the coding guidelines help developers to move from one project to another with ease. They also create a common vocabulary that can help developers understand code much faster and make it easier to modify.

—Atul Menon, Solution Architect

Once adopted, coding standards should be stored and made available in a shared repository, and should be updated when they evolve as the organization matures and the project progresses through iterations.

Why   In addition to improving code readability and maintainability, application of coding standards prevents functionality, performance, security, and usability defects.

How   Many coding standards are based on the lessons that industry experts learned by examining developers' mistakes. These experts already performed the most difficult tasks of defect prevention by identifying which defects are common for each programming language, determining the root causes of these defects, and defining best practices that prevent these defects from occurring.

Coding standards should be always followed when working with a language or technology with a well-defined syntax. This includes not only programming languages such as Java, C++, C, JavaScript, and VBScript, but also HTML, XML, and platforms such as .NET.

One reason why code construction conventions historically fail is due to the excessive amount of information that typically is delivered when developers first apply new coding standards to their source code. Another reason is the complexity of static analysis tools that are used for verification of standards application. The key to overcoming these challenges is to introduce coding standards in phases. Consistent with ADP principles and the psychology of flow, this step-by-step approach prevents the team members from being overwhelmed by an unmanageable number of new standards at once, in addition to performing their normal job responsibilities.

One approach to phasing in coding standards is to divide them into three levels, *mandatory*, *highly recommended*, and *recommended*, and then introduce each level incrementally. Once the team members master the "mandatory" standards, they should follow the "highly recommended," and after that the "recommended" set. It is important to measure the extent to which a practice is used before phasing it in to estimate a baseline against which trends and improvements can be assessed.

Categories of coding standards are described in the subsequent sections.

Style, Layout, and Formatting Standards   Style, layout, and formatting conventions make the code readable and consistent, and thus help in avoiding defects related to code reusability. They describe the rules for use of white spaces, indentation, the maximum length of a line, and how to separate long expressions and parameter lists into multiple lines. For example, a rule might require the use of tabs for white spaces. Another rule may require line wrap at 80 characters. Additionally, the rules may include common editor setups for handling tabs versus spaces for indentation. In this category also are conventions for layout of braces and parentheses that separate logical blocks of source code.

The fundamental premise of applying formatting conventions is that good visual layout should show logical structure of the code. An example is the "Begin-End" layout style [5]:

```
void tryThis( )
{
   switch (condition)
   {
    case Option_1:
        actionOne();
        break;
    case Option_2:
        actionTwo();
        break;
   }
}
```

Code Structure Standards Code structure standards are the rules that define the internal organization of components, modules, classes, and objects by specifying quantitative measures of recommended maximum complexity, enforcing proper sequence of data flow, and facilitating testing and debugging through program assertions. We identified the following categories:

- Structural complexity rules
- Functional and data flow rules
- Use of assertions
- Code cross-correlation rules
- Usability and accessibility rules

Structural Complexity Rules The guiding principle for code structural complexity rules is the following statement: "Never make code more complex than necessary." The structural complexity rules pertain to code refactoring, modularization, and levels of nesting. They specify parameters such as the recommended maximum number of methods per class, and the maximum McCabe [6] or Halstead [7] complexity of the code. *McCabe's complexity*, also known as *cyclomatic complexity*, measures the number of independent paths in a program unit. The *Halstead complexity* measure is derived from the number of operands and operators in a module. For example, if the code is algorithmically straightforward, its cyclomatic complexity should not exceed 10. Similarly, Halstead measure can be used to assure code modularity and readability in computationally complex implementations.

The rules for restricting code complexity depend greatly on the project type and the algorithmic complexity of each code unit. Programmers who exceed the recommended maximum values are usually asked either to redesign the code to conform to the required rules or to justify the need for increased complexity by properly documenting the relevant parts of the code.

The code structural complexity rules help avert algorithmic and processing defects by enforcing proper modularization and by requiring close attention to the design prior to coding.

Functional and Data Flow Rules Using data flow coding standards helps to ensure that the code implements the call sequences described in the functional or nonfunctional requirements and in the overall application design. For example, a rule that facilitates the implementation of a security requirement protecting against unauthorized account changes might involve verifying that a change account function can be called only after the login function. Applying this standard might also involve mapping steps of the corresponding use case to a proper sequence of function calls during development. Functional and data flow rules help in avoiding initialization, data flow, and error handling defects.

Use of Assertions An assertion is a Boolean expression that should always be true and, therefore, will be false only if a fault occurs. For example, if a method calculates the velocity of a fast-moving object, the assertion would verify that the calculated velocity is less than the speed of light. Many programming languages support assertion constructs that enable testing of program behavior [8]. By verifying that the Boolean expression is indeed true, the assertion confirms assumptions about the intended program behavior, increasing the confidence that the program is free of defects.

```
void foo(){
        for (...){
            if (...)
            return ;
        }
assert false; // Execution should never reach this point
}
```

Assertions are used in development, testing, and debugging to facilitate verification of program expected behavior, but they are usually disabled in the production system. One of the most effective uses of assertions is their application in verifying the code preconditions, postconditions, and invariances as suggested by *Design-by-Contract*™. The concept of Design-by-Contract was proposed by Bertrand Meyer [9,10,11] and first described in his articles in 1986. Meyer redefined the traditional defensive programming approach that expected programmers to create additional, often redundant lines of code to include as many checks as possible for error handling, regardless of whether such checks already took place in other parts of the code. In Design-by-Contract, assertions, which are either executable statements or design documentation or both, are used to verify the state of the code before it runs (its precondition), the expected state after the code runs (its postcondition), and its invariants.

A powerful defect-prevention practice, assertions verify and document expected behavior and fail only in presumably logically impossible situations. They are also used in design of tests and in automated testing. A major advantage of using this approach is that when the assertion fails, the problem can be analyzed and resolved immediately rather than later through hard-to-diagnose side effects. In addition, code reuse defects can be prevented using assertions, since preconditions and postconditions can be verified for the reused code.

Cross-Code Correlation Rules   Cross-code correlation rules are used to help ensure that independently developed pieces of the code that are related to the same feature remain consistent as the software evolves. If two or more developers work independently on the same feature, their code often becomes less compatible as the work progresses.

Cross-code correlation rules require documenting correlations in the code. When a developer writes code that is correlated with another developer's code, she adds a comment that indicates the appropriate correlation. For instance, in Java she can mark the code by inserting a new type of comment, `@correlate filename`, to indicate that the code is related to the code in another file and therefore it needs to be inspected.

Cross-code correlation rules help prevent module interface defects and assist in merging related pieces of code, as developers can easily identify correlated code and inspect its compatibility.

Usability and Accessibility Rules Usability and accessibility rules are defined to ensure that the application follows general rules for avoiding usability problems and to guarantee that the application is executable on a wide variety of devices. Foremost, usability rules should be consistent with the definition of the user interface design policy. Second, general best practices known to facilitate application usability should be applied. For example, in web applications, rules based on Jakob Nielsen's [12] web usability recommendations[b] could be used, such as the following suggestion for screen resolution:

Optimize web pages for 1024 × 768, but use a liquid layout that stretches well for any resolution, from 800 × 600 to 1280 × 1024.

If the application is being developed for a United States Government agency, it must comply with the Section 508 amendment to the Rehabilitation Act, which mandates that any technology produced by or for U.S. government agencies be accessible to people with disabilities [13]. To satisfy this requirement, the product must follow all applicable standards outlined in Section 508 legislation.

Language and Technology Specific Standards Language- and technology-specific coding standards are conventions that are language syntax dependent. They are a set of rules for the use of the language constructs that help to avoid possible execution faults or system vulnerabilities. Such conventions are defined for Java, C++, C, C#, HTML, JavaScript, VBScript, and XML, and can be found in sources such as [3,4,5] or in Joshua Bloch's guide on effective Java programming [14]. The following types of coding rules can be identified:

Reliability Rules Recommend a Specific Use of Language Constructs to Prevent Ungraceful Application Failures For example, in Java, `try`, `catch`, and `finally` blocks with empty bodies should be avoided. These blocks are used for handling exceptions and the code inside these blocks should prevent sudden system exits due to unexpected faults or resource unavailability. The proper use of these blocks helps in preventing error handling defects.

---

[b] The main recommendations are that text should be concise and easy to scan.

Security Rules Help Avoid Code Vulnerabilities For example, in C++ they may include the rules to avoid passing user input directly into methods as a parameter, or not to use the random number function from a library known to generate a predictable sequence. In Java, a secure way to build SQL statements is to construct all queries with `PreparedStatement` instead of `Statement` and/or to use parameterized stored procedures. Parameterized stored procedures are compiled before user input is added, making it difficult for a hacker to modify the actual SQL statement.

Performance Rules Help to Efficiently Manage System Resources such as Network Connections, Memory, or Secondary Storage For example, in C++ they may require that developers not pass objects as function parameters by value. In Java, the rule to close input and output resources in `finally` blocks can be used to prevent potential resource leaks. The `finally` block allows the programmer to avoid having to clean up code accidentally bypassed by a `return`, `continue`, or `break`. Putting cleanup code in a `finally` block is always a good Java practice.

Maintainability Rules Facilitate Code Readability and Increase Ease of Future Modification They may include rules such as the requirement to initialize all data members in the class constructor, which helps to prevent variable initialization defects, and not to use hard-coded constants, which facilitates future code modifications. Providing Javadoc[c] comments and descriptions for classes and interfaces and declaring package-private methods are other examples of rules in this category.

DEVELOPER'S TESTIMONIAL

Each programming language has its own set of coding standards from naming convention, rules in functions, formatting, do's and don'ts, etc. Take SQL coding standards, for example. We used standard prefixes such as `pkc_` as primary key clustered, `TB_` as table, `fk_` as foreign key, etc. Naming convention is one of the best practices that can reduce confusion and help increase readability and maintainability.

Examples of other rules that we use are:

- *Always Specify the Owner When Creating a Procedure*: This is to increase maintainability and integrity of the code.
- *Enumerate All Column Lists*: Do not use the * wildcard. This is for a faster execution speed and consequently better performance.
- *Use Parentheses to Increase Readability*: Especially when working with branch conditions or complicated expressions.

—Bin Li, Stay-at-Home Mom and Former Software Engineer

---

[c] A tool for generating API documentation in HTML format from comments in source code [15].

Language- and technology-specific standards can be subdivided into very fine categories, such as initialization rules, exception handling rules, threads and synchronization rules, or interoperability rules. Having such a fine level of detail might prove necessary for applications that heavily rely on specific language features. For example, a multithreaded application, which requires statements from different threads to be synchronized, may have to apply "thread and synchronization" rules that prevent deadlocks.[d] If not avoided, deadlocks may cause the application to halt. In an attempt to synchronize, threads could execute in an indefinite cycle waiting for each other's response.

Documentation Standards   Documentation standards are among the most commonly used coding standards, as they are often defined at the organization level to improve code readability, maintainability, and reuse. They fall into three main categories: naming conventions, code descriptions, and comments format.

Naming Conventions   Naming conventions specify how developers name their variables, data members, methods, classes, events, and parameters, files, and configuration items. For example, a rule for naming Java [16] packages states that the prefix of a unique package name is always written in all-lowercase ASCII letters and should be one of the top-level domain names, such as com.sun.eng. A rule for naming methods is that they should be verbs, in mixed case with the first letter lowercase, with the first letter of each internal word capitalized, for example: getData(). Rules for naming variables are that unless they are temporary such as iterators controlling loops, they should have short and descriptive names such as width, or velocity.

Code Descriptions   Comments are written descriptions in the code that explain the logic of the code. Quality code should be somewhat self-documenting and comments should fill in the gaps. Sample comment rules are outlined in the bulleted list below.

- Source code documentation should include for each source file at least the following:
  - Brief description of the purpose of the file
  - A change history of the source file
  - A source control string identifying the source control file and version
- Class definitions should include at least the following:
  - Brief description of the class and its purpose
  - Brief description of each of the class methods and attributes

---

[d] *Deadlock* refers to a condition when two or more processes or threads are each waiting for another to release a resource, or perform an action, creating a circular "wait-for" chain.

- Member function comments should include at least the following:
  - Brief description of the member function and its purpose
  - Brief description of the function's arguments and return values
  - Brief description of all unusual and error conditions
  - Brief description of the operation of the function
  - Brief description of all local variables, excluding loop iterators and temporary variables
- Global shared data and object declarations should include at least the following:
  - Brief description of the item
  - Brief description of the item's users

Comments Format   The format of the comments depends on the language and available constructs for the comment insertions. For example, Java programs can have four styles of implementation comments: block, single-line, trailing, and end-of-line.

- *Block Comments*: Block comments should be used at the beginning of each file and before each method, to provide descriptions of files, methods, data structures, and complex algorithms.

```
/*
 * This is
 * a block comment.
 */
```

- *Single-line Comments*: These are short comments that appear on a single line describing the code that follows.

```
if (x>0) {
    /* Calculate square root */
    . . .
}
```

- *Trailing Comments*: These are very short comments that can appear on the same line as the code they describe, but should be shifted far to the right to separate them from the rest of the code.

```
if (isEven(a)) {
    return false;        /* Can't be prime */
} else {
    return isPrime(a);  /* Check if it's prime */
}
```

- *End-of-line Comments*: These are short comments that use "//" delimiter. They can comment out a complete line or only a partial line.

```
if (bar > 1) {
    // Do a double-flip.
    . . .
}
else {
    return false;              // Explain why here.
}
```

DEVELOPER'S TESTIMONIAL

"Codes within Code"

We have two rules in programming:

1. Use only the English language in your code, including naming of variables and writing comments.
2. No hard-to-decipher abbreviations or slang.

Background Scenario:

I used to work with a company where a majority of the programmers are 18- to 21-year-olds. At that time, text messaging using cell phones was the trend and all of us were accustomed to abbreviating words in order to save text message space. You could have only 160 characters in a message. We would send, on average, 100 texts per day.

Here is an example of what was in our codes as a comment:

   /* Dis func s usd 4 w8tin 4 usr 2 clik accept bu2n */

Translation: "This function is used for waiting for user to click accept button."

                                               —Lesley Ku, Systems Analyst

---

Selecting Coding Standards The first step in selecting the appropriate set of coding standards for a project is compiling a list of potential categories applicable to the project (Figure 7.1). The next challenge is determining which of the several available standards should be mandatory, highly recommended, or recommended. One helpful strategy is to review the available standards categories and eliminate those categories that do not apply to the current project. For example, for an application that is supposed to manage a centralized, multithreaded human resources database, categories of interoperability such as EJB (Enterprise Java Beans), which enable rapid development of distributed applications, or J2ME (Java 2 Micro Edition), which are aimed

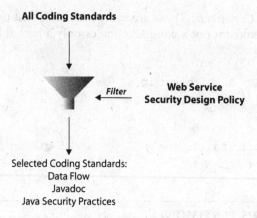

Figure 7.1 Selecting appropriate coding standards for a specific project.

at platforms with limited hardware such as cell phones or embedded systems, can be eliminated as they are not applicable.

After removing categories that are not applicable, the critical design attributes of the application should be reviewed and the remaining categories should be evaluated. For instance, in the above example of a human resources database, product security is a critical attribute, and therefore the Code Structure Standards for functional and data flow as well as language- and technology-specific security rules should be used. If the developers are new to implementing multithreaded applications, the rules for synchronizing threads should be considered. In each category, the rules should be classified by the severity of a possible defect resulting from the rule violation. A mandatory status should be given to the rules with high severity of possible defect rankings, highly recommended rules should match other organization guidelines, and recommended rules should help prevent other common defects.

Measurement The following measures should be used in conjunction with coding standards:

- The amount of code that is required to follow the standard
- The number of coding standards violations in the code that is required to follow the standard
- The total number of coding standards violations in all project code

Tracking The number of coding standards violations should be measured and tracked, as shown in Figure 7.2.

Detailed information about the violations should be available, such as the most common types of violations (Figure 7.3) and the number of violations per file (Figure 7.4). Viewing the coding standards violations by type will point to specific coding standards that are especially difficult for developers to apply.

Coding Standards Violations

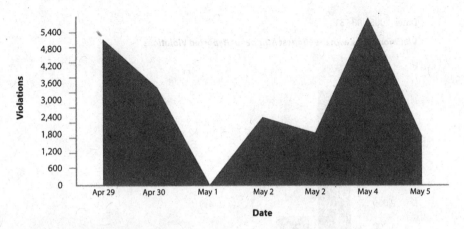

Coding Standards Violations Detail

Date	Violations
May 5	1726
May 4	5876
May 3	1815
May 2	2364

Figure 7.2 An overview of coding standard violations.

The violations by file will help to isolate any files that are not amenable to the coding standards or have been neglected when applying the standards.

The developers can reference a report that shows them the number of their own violations, as shown in Figure 7.5. This report can help the developer to find which standards she needs to improve on and where she might need additional training.

Automation In an expanded infrastructure, conformance to coding standards can be verified by static analysis tools, which include style checkers[e] and complexity analyzers. Static analyzers do not execute the program. Program execution and verification of its execution results against expected results fall into the dynamic analysis category. Static analyzers scan the code for patterns, and report on types, locations, and the number of rule violations. One of the first static analysis tools was Lint, developed by Stephen Johnson [17] in the 1970s for the C programming language. Lint worked by searching the code for patterns known to cause common problems. Similar principles are used in modern static analysis tools, which now support many different technologies and often, in addition to a set of built-in patterns, have interfaces for program-

[e] Static analysis tool that verifies conformance to style and format rules in code.

Coding Standards Violations by Violation Type

Date: 2005 - 08 - 31

Violation Types with the Highest Number of Reported Violations

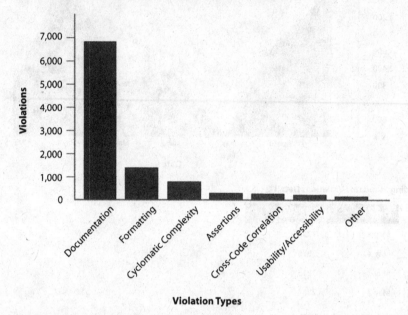

Violation Types

Details:

Documentation

File	Violation #
AddJob_en.java	623
Frequency.java	323
Settings_en.java	283
HDMLUtil.java	258

Figure 7.3   The number of coding standards violations by violation type.

mable rules. Present static analysis tools are sophisticated and can be customized to fit project needs. They can verify style and format, identify language-specific or data flow inconsistencies, or look for vulnerabilities in SQL injections.

In most cases, it is possible to check whether the code complies with the applicable standards by having a static analyzer scan the code as the developer is writing it. Developers usually employ static analysis after compiling but before dynamic testing of the code. Such practices have been proven to improve several aspects of code quality, including the undesirable use of hard-coded constants and design modularity [18]. Joseph Sant reports [18] that, in a classroom environment, when programming course students were required

Coding Standards Violations by File

Date: 2005 - 08 - 31

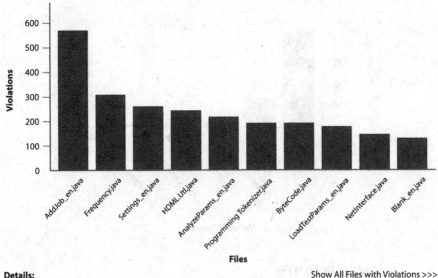

Files with the Highest Number of Reported Violations

Details: Show All Files with Violations >>>

Addjob_en.java

Violation Type	Violation #
Assertions	575
Formatting	1

Frequency.java

Violation Type	Violation #
Cross-Code Correlation	305
Cyclomatic Complexity	1

Figure 7.4 The number of coding standards violations per file.

to perform static analysis of their assignments to verify adherence to maximum allowed cyclomatic complexity, they paid more attention to refactoring.[f] He says: "This was the first time in this author's experience where students from several sections asked for help in refactoring their code before submitting an assignment."

Automated tools can be used to check whether code contains sufficient comments, indicate where more comments are needed, and flag comments that use incorrect syntax. They also can be used to identify copies or similar code and to flag correlated pieces of code. Many of the usability and accessibility standards—especially standards for web technologies—can be verified automatically with a static analysis tool and record/playback tools.

[f] A reorganization technique that simplifies the design (or code) of a component without changing its function or behavior (see Chapter 6).

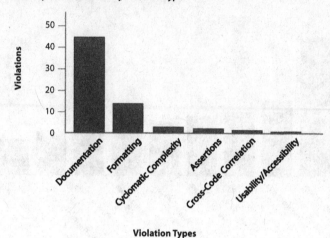

Developer Coding Standards Violations

Date: 2005 - 08 - 31
Developer: A.C.D.

Your Reported Violations By Violation Type

Violation Details By File:

Addjob_en.java

Violation Type	Line #
Formatting	128
Cyclomatic Complexity	492

Frequency.java

Violation Type	Line #
Usability/Accessibility	1056
Documentation	1397

Figure 7.5 Developers' report of their own coding standards violations.

FOCUS ON PREVENTION

To maximize the benefits of coding standards analysis, it is critical to recognize coding standards as a means of *preventing* defects—not detecting them. Many developers are disappointed if a coding standards violation does not point them to an obvious bug. When they explore a violation and find a defect-prone construct rather than a defect, they think that the coding standards are not useful. Consequently, they eventually stop investigating violations or even cease to apply coding standards analysis altogether.

For a coding standards analysis practice to be effective, developers need to understand that coding standards analysis is designed to identify defect-prone code, not full-fledged defects. Coding standards analysis should not be perceived as a substitute for defect detection practices, but rather used in conjunction with them.

If the code is constructed dynamically (as in, for example, HTML code that is built dynamically as servlets execute), static analysis verification cannot be performed until at least part of the application is deployed to a staging server.

Additionally, calculating measures for coding standards conformance and tracking these measures can be done automatically.

7.2.2   Applying the Test-First Approach at the Service and Module Implementation Level

Once the coding standards for the project have been selected and defined, the code construction should start with implementing test cases for services and modules. Known for several years [19] and used sporadically in the past, the test-first approach was popularized by Ken Schwaber in TDD (test-driven development) [20] as an enabling practice of XP. In TDD, tests are written prior to the code and thus originally fail in the absence of the corresponding code.

Why   TDD is the ultimate technique for preventing requirements-related defects since tests can be viewed as the most accurate technical descriptions of product requirements. Additionally, applying TDD for services and modules prevents module interface defects.

How   The conceptual test cases defined during the requirements definition phase were refined in the design phase. During code construction, these tests are implemented, correlated with corresponding requirements and use cases, and added to the testing system, so they can be executed automatically. Since they are implemented prior to the code that they are testing, these are *black box*[g] *tests*. For services and modules these tests will originally fail. However, as the implementation moves forward, they should show a steadily increasing pass rate and will become indicators of project progress.

Measurement   For an existing external service used by the application under development, the number of passed tests is an indicator of the status of contract and interface implementation. For a new service or a module under implementation, the number of passed tests indicates the status of service/module implementation. Since modules are correlated to use cases, this metric can be further extrapolated to calculate the status of use case implementation.

Tracking   All of the above measures should be tracked and the test pass rates should increase. Also, once the test results stabilize, the tests should be added

---

[g] Tests that consider a functional design specification to design test cases without regard to the internal program structure. The tested element is treated as a black or opaque box.

to the regression suite to continue verifying code base correctness as new features are added in subsequent iterations.

Automation Since they are created before the code is implemented, the original service and module test cases are developed manually. Automated tools can be used to facilitate generation of these tests through insertions of assertions for expected behaviors such as preconditions and postconditions. Also, record and playback technologies can be used to save test cases and execute them automatically in the future. Once the implementation is sufficiently mature, test cases can be generated automatically and added to the test suite.

Measures pertaining to the test pass rate can be calculated automatically, and tracking of these measures also can be done automatically by retrieving data stored in the infrastructure and displaying it in the reporting system.

7.2.3 Implementing Service Contracts and/or Module Interfaces before Their Internal Functionality

Once tests have been developed for services and/or modules, the corresponding contracts and interfaces should be implemented. In SOA, services describe themselves as interface contracts. The contract-first approach requires that the message formats between participating services are designed and implemented before code construction, which reflects the application functionality details. Similarly, module interfaces should be implemented before the module functionality is developed.

Why Implementation of interfaces before the service or module functionality is a natural extension of the test-first approach. As soon as interfaces are implemented, tests can be run to validate the interface correctness. Through this approach, service and modules public data can be clearly decoupled from private implementation details, ensuring that only the information specified in contract and interface is made available to external entities. Moreover, isolation of interfaces from the internal details of services and modules facilitates consistency of the architectural design implementation, and reduces the amount of rework and time necessary for merging needed during system integration.

How Service and module interdependencies should have been mapped during the design phase. These interdependencies should be examined carefully before contracts and interfaces are implemented. Exact message formats and parameter types should be defined and tested at this point. The data and functionalities that are used by other services and modules should be made public, while all other data and methods should be implemented as private.

7.2.4   Applying Test-Driven Development for Algorithmically Complex and Critical Code Units

In addition to the test-first approach at the service and module levels, algorithmically complex code and critical code units[h] should be implemented using TDD. Algorithmically complex code may involve a unique computationally intensive solution or a large data processing problem. A critical code unit is referred to as the unit responsible for an application's critical state, for which failure may have disastrous consequences, such as a malfunction of a medical device or an intrusive access to high-security data. Both algorithmically complex code and critical code units require special attention in development.

Why   Creating test cases before implementing an algorithmically complex or a critical code unit assures that the code is lean and that its required functionality, as specified by test cases, is implemented. Black box unit tests written prior to the implementation of the code are the technical description of the requirements at the finest level of granularity. Moreover, recent research, such as a case study of TDD practice conducted at IBM by Laurie Williams et al. [21], shows a 40% defect reduction rate compared with a baseline prior product development.

How   First, algorithmically complex code and critical application code units need to be identified. This should be done during detailed design, based on application-critical attributes and the design policies. Later, these code segments can be found using static analysis tools. For each of the identified units, positive and negative test cases should be developed and added to the test suite.

Measurement   The number of passed and failed tests should be measured for each unit.

Tracking   The number of passed and failed tests should be tracked and the test pass rates should steadily increase. In addition, once the tests results stabilize, the tests should be added to the regression suite.

Automation   Tests are generated manually, but automated tools can be used to facilitate the generation of unit tests. Measures pertaining to the test pass rate can be generated automatically, and tracking of these measures can be done automatically, too.

---

[h] A unit is the smallest testable piece of code such as a method, function, class, or a subsegment of a long segment of code.

7.2.5 Conducting White Box Unit Testing after Implementing Each Unit and before Checking the Code into the Source Control System

For code that is not algorithmically complex and not critical, *white box*[i] *unit tests* should be developed as soon as the code is implemented and compiled. Regardless of whether TDD was used or the tests were developed after the code was implemented, only code that passes all its unit tests should be added to the source control system.

Why The goal of unit tests is to uncover possible defects early in the development and prevent defects from propagating to other parts of code. Results of unit tests give immediate feedback to developers and pinpoint problems that otherwise would require time-consuming and tedious debugging.

How For each unit, test cases executing both valid and invalid inputs should be created and added to the test suite.

Measurement In addition to the number of tests passed and failed per unit, the total number of passed and failed unit tests should be measured. Unit tests are part of module testing and, as such, they can be used in extrapolating the implementation status indicators of the module and its corresponding use cases.

Tracking Tracking of the pass rate of unit tests provides steady feedback of product implementation progress. Test results should indicate whether to run more tests or focus on correcting uncovered defects.

Automation Most unit tests can be generated using automated testing tools. Both automatically and manually created tests should be added to the test suite and automatically executed on a daily basis. Both measurement and tracking of test results can be done automatically by scanning test results, and the test metrics can be displayed by the reporting system.

7.2.6 Verifying Code Consistency with the Requirements and Design

As the code construction progresses, developers should periodically review both the requirement and design documents and check whether there are any recent changes. The developers should verify whether their code implements the up-to-date version of the application as reflected in these documents.

Why A fundamental question of software validation asks: "Are we implementing the right product?" Indeed, the code developed during each

---

[i] Tests that require knowledge of the internal structure of a program to design test cases. The testing element is treated as a white or glass box.

iteration should be traceable back to both the requirements and the design. If the requirements or design changed, appropriate modifications should be embodied in the code immediately to minimize the amount of necessary rework.

Who Both the architect and the developers should conduct periodic manual reviews of the code to verify its consistency with requirements and design.

How The scope of the code review is usually determined by use cases: when developers complete implementation of a use case, all the related code should be subject to a manual walkthrough. Alternatively, code can be reviewed incrementally—for example, as it is added each week while more granular requirements are implemented. The extended infrastructure can facilitate this process by automatically alerting reviewers about newly modified and not-yet-reviewed code.

7.3 POLICY FOR USE OF THE CODE SOURCE CONTROL SYSTEM

The source control system is one of the fundamental components of the infrastructure; in fact, without a properly configured source control system, quality software is difficult to create. This is due to the fact that source code is in the state of perpetual modification through the project life cycle. Often programming teams lose track of recent changes, compile old versions of the code, or find that old bugs have resurfaced. To avoid these problems, proper use of the source control system is essential. Thus, it is important to establish comprehensive guidelines for the developers' use of the source control system, and to ensure that the developers understand and follow them. Technologies that support organization and control of source code, such as version and configuration management tools, come with detailed manuals describing their effective use and a wide-ranging set of features.

The following list provides basic guidelines for the use of such systems. These guidelines should be treated as an initial step in the gradual process of phasing in a technology infrastructure, and they should be expanded as the organization's ADP processes mature.

Each Developer Should Have a Local Copy (Sandbox) of Files Related to Her Current Work A sandbox[j] is an area where copies of project-related files can be stored and manipulated without affecting the master source code base. Before source control is used, the team should establish an individual sandbox for each developer. In addition, each developer's sandbox should be cleanly shadowed (e.g., receive read-only copies of the master files stored in the

---

[j] A copy of the project's files.

source control system) from the source control system and cleaned after major revisions (see the policy "Each developer should clean the sandbox and re-shadow relevant files after major changes," discussed below in item 6).

The developer's sandbox provides an environment where the developer can freely modify and experiment with the code, without negatively affecting the base code.

Each Team Should Have a Sandbox with Copies of all Files Needed to Build Each Application Before the source control system is used, the team should establish one build sandbox for each application that the team is going to build. This build sandbox should also be cleanly shadowed from the source control system and deleted on a daily basis. Ideally, once the build sandbox is established, it is used according to the policies described in Section 7.4, "Policy for Use of Automated Build."

Similar to the developer's sandbox, the team's sandbox provides an environment where the team can freely modify and experiment with the code without affecting the base code.

Parallel Development Practices Should Be Well Defined and Understood by Participating Developers The parallel development feature available in most configuration management systems allows two or more developers to work on the same configuration item simultaneously. After the developers make their modifications to this item, they check it into the source control system, and the system will attempt to merge the modifications. However, often such a merge can cause unpredictable results and prove to be counterproductive. In fact, parallel development can actually introduce defects into a product because the source control system is merging two very different editions of code that were modified without regard for each other. The success of merging two independently updated files depends on the sophistication of the merging tool and the developers' experience both in parallel development and in using such a tool. Therefore, by default this feature should be disabled, unless the appropriate technology has been tested and proven successful, and developers are familiar with it.

Should developers find it necessary to perform parallel development, for example, because a file is very large, the recommended practice is to inspect the merged code after checking it in.

DEVELOPERS' TESTIMONIALS

Parallel Development or Not?

My company uses Perforce. It has very good branching, merging, and parallel development tools. But I still run across areas where a careless merge will wipe out files. It seems a lot of people are pro parallel development. I accept it as a necessary evil. If the project is properly decomposed there should not be a need for two people to be working on the same module at the same time for the most part. There are, of course, exceptions to any rule, though.

My team usually runs about three major branches and several smaller branches at any given time. We try to keep them to separate areas of the code, but occasionally we have a project that touches just about everything. Recently we had a denormalization project to improve our front-end performance. Since this changed the schema for some of the core application tables it affected many areas of the code, including our batch process. We had two other projects that were also affecting the schema and batch process. After the denormalization project was merged to the main line, a smaller project was merged overwriting several of the stored procedures. They contained everything but the last few days' changes to the denorm branch, so they still succeeded and passed the tests, but they were not as efficient and a few columns were not moved properly. It was a subtle enough error that it was not caught until right before the release. This was mostly human error due to a careless merge, but parallel development offers many opportunities for human errors.

I will agree that the tools make a huge difference. Without all of the modern source control systems, parallel development is almost impossible. So my conclusion would be to avoid it if you can and be careful if you can't.

—Scott Sanford, Software Engineer

Even though at work this is the type of development we do, I cannot stand it one bit. If minor changes are made to a file, when someone else working on the same file merges their changes, it usually is going to cost them more time than if they had just waited to work on it until someone else was done. I do not know many developers who don't have a ton of stuff to work on, so in my opinion it is better if the project manager schedules work so that only one person is working on a single file.

I have had so many bad experiences with merges—in some cases, it could take days to get everything working again—so I don't feel the time saved by using this method is actually all that great. Not to mention merging-introduced unexpected behavior all the time, since there is so much potential for merges doing weird things.

—-Jason Obermeyer, Software Engineer

I don't see any problem with a parallel development approach. In our company we use it in everyday life. There are two senses of parallel development that we need to focus on: multidevelopers (with their own environment setup) that work on the same version of software, and multidevelopers that work on multiversions of software. We used separate environments for each developer, a branching version for handling multiversions of software/multiprojects, and definitely a CM, test suites, and issue tracker.

I never see any problems with merging and checking back in, as well as the build results from all of that—either manual build, nightly build, or release build. We automatically track all builds including manual build in the issue tracker, so any issue caused by parallel development will be noticed immediately, which is none in our case.

—Ricky, Senior Software Engineer

Each Developer Should Check out only Code That She Is Actively Modifying. Before a developer can modify a file that has been shadowed to her sandbox, she must check out that file from the source control system. If no parallel development is allowed, once a file is checked out it is locked by that developer, and no other developers will be allowed to modify the file until the first developer checks in her changes (e.g., adds the modified file back into source control and removes the revision lock). During any given day, each developer should check out only the files that she is actively modifying. This practice is essential so the developer does not prevent other group members from modifying their work files and contributing to a development bottleneck.

Each Developer Should Check into Source Control only Code That Complies with the Required Coding Standards and Passes the Designated Quality Checks. As soon as a developer is certain that new or modified code satisfies the required coding standards and passes its unit tests, she should add that code to the source control system. When developers follow this practice, the only code that is not available in the source control system is the code that a developer is actively modifying. This policy guarantees that the developer is checking in only source code that adheres to the best practices, which makes the process more efficient. Additionally, other developers rely on this code, so it should be checked in as soon as it complies with the best practices.

The implementation of the above source control policies 1 and 2 is illustrated in Figure 7.6.

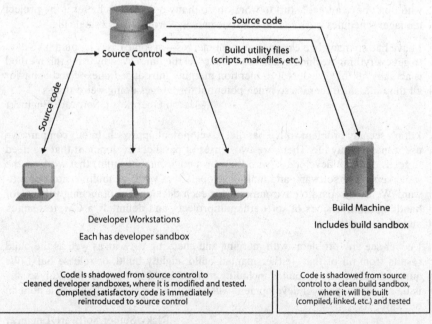

Figure 7.6 Developer's and team's interactions with the source control system.

***Each Developer Should Clean the Sandbox and Re-Shadow Relevant Files
after Major Changes*** After significant structural changes are made to the
directories shadowed in a developer's sandbox (e.g., many files are added,
removed, or renamed), it is a good practice to remove all the files from
the sandbox and then re-shadow the code from the source control system.
This ensures that the sandbox is synchronized with the code in the source
control system. The build sandbox also undergoes a similar cleaning and re-
shadowing to ensure that it also stays synchronized with the main source code
base.

This policy helps the developer to avoid possible version mismatch or
working on outdated copies of the files.

***The Entire Team Should Store Code for Different Software Versions in Physi-
cally Independent Locations of the Source Control Systems*** Once the code for
a software version is finalized, it should be physically separated from the
working code base and placed in an independent location of the source control
system (Figure 7.7). By physically separating the code base for each "final"
software version, the possibility of day-to-day source code modifications
affecting the "final" versions of the software is avoided. In addition, this
approach prevents any emergency fixes of the "final" version from affecting
the current version. When a version is no longer supported, the entire source
control system for this version should be archived and stored in a backup
system.

Not separating the versions can yield two serious risks. First, if a file is
modified in the old version of the software, it could cause unexpected side
effects in the current working version of that software. Second, as the files are
modified in the new version of the software, the changes could affect the old
versions, and it might be difficult to determine exactly what code is being used
in the old versions.

***The Entire Team Should Use Versioning Features only for Small Variations
within one Software Version*** Many developers are under the impression that
versioning features allow them to safely modify different versions of
code. However, defects may occur by modifying files without paying appropriate attention to the version the changes will affect. A developer may fix a
problem in one version, while introducing numerous defects into another
version.

These versioning pitfalls can be averted by moving each completed software version's code base into an independent source control system, as
described in the preceding policy.

Although versioning features are typically error-prone when used
to separate code from different sequential releases (e.g., 2.0 from 2.01 and
2.1), versioning features could be useful when there are minor
differences in a software version (e.g., different versions—with slightly different files—for different devices).

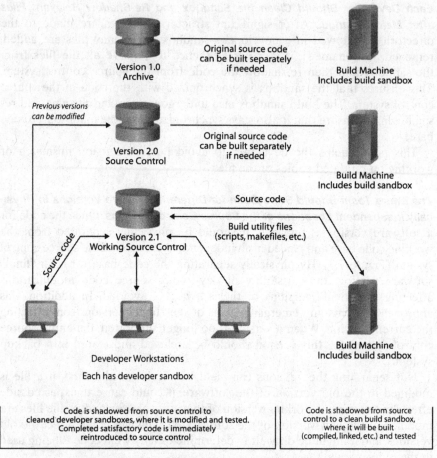

Figure 7.7   Versioning for the source control systems.

Minor releases do not affect as many files as major releases. Thus, it is acceptable to use versioning for minor releases, but not for major releases when a large number of files are affected.

7.3.1   Measurements Related to Source Control

Measures related to the source control system should be available through the reporting system. Overview reports will allow the project manager and architect to view the growth and changes occurring in the source code, such as the size of the code base or the number of revisions over a given period. Detailed reports will allow the project manager and architect to see the number and types of changes in individual files or by individual developers.

The *code base size* is the total number of lines of code contained in every file for a project. The size of code base should be viewable from the reporting system in a graph format for a given period, such as in Figure 7.8.

Code Base Size

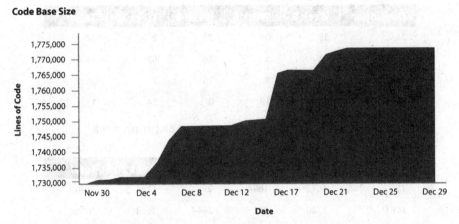

Figure 7.8 Code-base-size graph as presented by the reporting system.

Revisions to Source Code

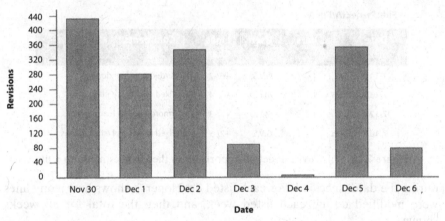

Figure 7.9 The number of revisions made to the source code, in lines, for a given period.

The reporting system should also generate graphs of the *number of revisions* that were made to source control files associated with a specified project (or all projects) each day during a specified date range, as shown in Figure 7.9.

The *revisions by user* report in Figure 7.10 lists all developers and the number of source control files they modified on the specified project(s) during the dates specified. For each listed developer, it shows how many revisions were made during each listed week, and then the total for all weeks shown.

The *lines of code modified by user* report in Figure 7.11 lists all developers and the number of lines of code they modified on the specified project(s)

Developer	Week 7	Week 8	Week 9	Week 10	Total
J.L.C.	35	24	26	2	87
M.E.D.	72	5	48	67	192
T.R.R.	12	4	13	7	36
G.V.S.	80	19	0	24	123

Figure 7.10   Files revised by each developer per week.

Developer	Week 7	Week 8	Week 9	Week 10	Total
J.L.C.	4673	1894	293	1286	8146
M.E.D.	3726	361	2844	3928	10859
T.R.R.	2735	47	4501	3728	11011
G.V.S.	237	3928	1748	2837	8750

Figure 7.11   Lines of code revised by each developer per week.

File: ProjectA/FileA

Date	Vers.	User	Lines Changed	Comments
7/14 2:15 pm	1.4	G.V.S.	+6/-2	Added new function for…
7/13 11:00 am	1.3	M.E.D.	+3/-4	Fixed error for reading …
7/12 2:30 pm	1.3	M.E.D.	+7/-3	Ignore error for loading files…
7/10 11:30 am	1.2	G.V.S.	+2/-5	Fixed location of existing files…

Figure 7.12   File revision details report shows the changes made to a file.

during the dates specified. For each listed developer, it shows how many lines were modified during each listed week, and then the total for all weeks shown.

The *file revision details* report in Figure 7.12 shows the history of the selected file, including all the modifications made to that file beginning from the date it was created.

7.3.2 Tracking of Source Control Data

The following data should be tracked:

- All code-check-in-related measures described above
- Requirements related to the code checked in
- Comments entered by the developer that describe each check in, feature implementation status, etc.

7.4 POLICY FOR USE OF AUTOMATED BUILD

By applying the following policies, an automated build process should provide early detection of incompatible changes in the application components, ensure that the application continues to run as expected, and detect any defects introduced by newly integrated code.

At regularly scheduled intervals (e.g., every night), the automated process should access the most recent set of source files from the source control system, and then perform all tasks needed to build the application (including compilations, initialization, linking, transfers, and other tasks needed to construct the application). Depending on the nature and complexity of the application being built, the automated build could take a long time and involve multiple machines. If multiple versions of the product must be built, the build should automatically construct all required versions. The messages related to build completion should be tracked by the infrastructure and made available through the reporting system. Additionally, the build information could also be made available to a designated team member by alternate routes (e.g., results could be directed to a file or e-mailed to that team member).

Creating a Special Build Account. Before implementing an automated build, a special administrative account should be created for running the build. If the build is run from a special account, the possibility of developer configuration errors is eliminated and the builds are portable.

Creating a special account protects the build system from inadvertent misconfiguration.

Cleaning the Build Area before Each Build. Cleaning involves removing all elements of the previous build(s)—including source files, binary files, and temporary files. Old files should always be removed before a new build begins, avoiding situations where old files are inadvertently used to build a new application.

Shadowing or Cloning the Source Code to the Build Directory. After the build area is cleaned, the source code that needs to be built must be copied to the build account. This copying can occur through shadowing or cloning.

Shadowing involves copying the latest project sources from the source control system. The sources should be stored in a directory that is accessible across the network. This way, if there are multiple machines running builds, all build scripts can access the archived source (or individual files) that were shadowed on the original machine.

Cloning involves copying previously shadowed source files over any existing files in the build directory. This process is called *cloning* because the same source archive is used for multiple machines (or multiple platforms). Cloning is performed to speed up the build or to perform the build on multiple platforms.

If there is more than one machine using the same code for a nightly build, it is a good idea to shadow it on only one machine, then clone that shadowed code on the other machines. This way, the same code is used for all builds, even if changes are introduced into the source control system between the time the first machine shadows the code and the last machine accesses the code. If a source tar file[k] is created to archive all the latest sources, the other machines can clone the build environment by getting the archive tar files.

Building the Application at Regularly Scheduled Intervals after Cleaning the Build Directory and Shadowing or Cloning the Source Code. Building is the process of constructing the application. It can be as simple as executing the make[l] utility on the build directory, or as complicated as executing a hierarchy of scripts. The builds should occur automatically at regularly scheduled intervals (e.g., nightly), so that the team has up-to-date build results that include the most recent source code modifications and that the team knows immediately when source code modifications cause the build to fail.

Completely Automating the Build Process. Scripts,[m] Makefiles,[n] and build tools can be mixed and matched to automate the process to the point where all necessary cleaning, shadowing/cloning, building, and testing steps can be executed from a single command. Once there is a process for automating all build tasks, it is possible to use utilities such as cron[o] (for UNIX[p]) or the Windows scheduling utility to ensure that the necessary tasks are performed automatically at scheduled intervals.

Manually performing all of the necessary steps correctly, day after day, is not only tedious, but also error-prone. When the build process is fully automated, all the necessary steps are performed correctly and consistently.

Creating Hierarchies for Makefiles and/or Other Build Files. If supported by the build system, creating hierarchies of files can save time and prevent many build-related version and configuration defects. When a hierarchy of files is used, there is one build file at the bottom of the hierarchy for each part of the application, and a file at the top of the hierarchy that invokes low-level files

---

[k] By using a general-purpose archiving utility, many files are packed into a single archive file called a tar file.

[l] The utility that keeps a set of executable programs current, based on differences in the modification times of the programs and the source files that each is dependent on.

[m] A sequence of computer commands written in the batch language.

[n] A file that contains a description of the relationships between files, and the commands that must be executed to update the derived files to reflect changes in their relationships.

[o] A program that enables UNIX users to execute commands or scripts automatically at a specified time/date.

[p] UNIX® is a registered trademark of The Open Group.

in the designated order to build the entire application. Each developer should create a low-level file to build her work within her sandbox. If a developer modifies her build file, the change will automatically be applied when the entire application is built without a need to modify other build files.

A hierarchy of Makefiles or other build files assures reliable builds throughout the subsystems because all changes propagate consistently throughout the build process.

Parameterizing Scripts and Build Files. Scripts and Makefiles should be parameterized. For example, one way to parameterize these files in UNIX is to use $BLDROOT as the environment variable that represents the root location of the nightly build source. When this location is a relative or parameterized project root path, the build process will work on any machine that has the correct $BLDROOT environment variable—even on machines that do not have the same directory structure as the initial build machine.

Using parameterized scripts, Makefiles, and other build files will make the builds portable in a multimachine/multiuser environment, preventing build problems due to different directory structures.

For n-Tier Applications, Establishing and Creating a Build on a Staging Area as well as A Production Area. When teams are working on n-tier applications such as web-based applications or web services, the automated build process should be capable of building the application on a staging server as well as on the production server. For example, with web applications, some files (such as static web pages[q]) can be thoroughly tested without a staging area, but dynamic functionality (such as login functionality or checkout operations) cannot. Testing web services also requires a staging area that includes a staging server, a production server, and software tools that mimic the client or server (depending on which is available and which is being tested).

Without a staging area, there is a chance of corrupting the application on the production server.

Fully Integrating Automated Builds with the Source Control System. All configuration items related to the automated build, including scripts, build files, and other resources that are required to automate the complete build process, should be stored in the source control system. This assures that the proper version of the system is built because configuration files, scripts, and the source code are in the same location.

Integrating Testing into the Automated Build Process. To be truly effective, the automated build processes should be fully integrated with the testing

---

[q] A static web page is a web page that is completely created in advance, with all text and images in place, and housed on a web server, ready for use.

system; it should run all available test cases and report any failures that occur. Integrating testing into the build process assures that the entire code base is tested and provides immediate feedback in case of unexpected regressions.

Often during development, teams tend to shy away from integrating testing into the build. They assume that as code is added and modified, defects will inevitably be introduced into the application, and tests will fail frequently. Thus in order to avoid the negative psychological effects of experiencing such failures, developers often choose not to run tests altogether. However, it is important to build a development culture that views these build failures as a blessing, not a curse; if there is a problem with the code, it is best to uncover that problem as soon as it is introduced, when it is easiest, fastest, and least costly to fix it. Thus, the status of the application in terms of possible defects should be assessed daily.

7.4.1 Measurements Related to Automated Builds

To measure the team's automated build system usage, the reporting system should generate build results graphs, as shown in Figure 7.13. This graph

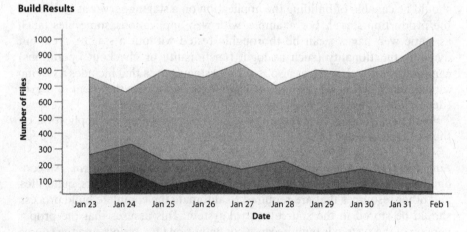

Build Results Detail

Date	Failed	Incomplete	Passed
Jan 23	120	250	750
Jan 24	130	320	680
Jan 25	90	220	800
Jan 26	100	250	750

Figure 7.13 Build results as shown by the reporting system.

Date: January 15, 2005

Total Modules/Files: 25 / 715

Failed Modules/Files: 4 / 16

Warnings Modules/Files: 5 / 23

Passed Modules/Files: 16 / 676

Module Name	Failed	Warning	Passed
Module A	2	4	11
Module B	0	0	12
Module C	0	5	10
Module D	5	2	17

Figure 7.14 Build results for an individual file.

shows the number of files that compiled successfully, failed to compile, or were incomplete for the builds during the selected period.

The reporting system should also show the build results details for the modules/files in the project, as shown in Figure 7.14.

7.4.2 Tracking of Data Related to Automated Builds

The following information related to automated builds should be tracked:

- Files and modules that passed the compilation
- Files and modules that failed the compilation
- Files that contain warnings and are incomplete during the build for the selected day
- Builds run per day

7.5 EXAMPLES

7.5.1 Focus on a Customized Coding Standard Policy

This example shows a defect root cause analysis and the resulting customized coding policy for a medical records system application that interacts with a legacy system.

Defect Identification   Consider an application that displays real-time patient care information in a hospital. The system was built based on a legacy database with an existing patient record system, and intermittent, hard-to-reproduce system failures were observed by the hospital IT team. Additional testing was performed and the legacy code was scanned, which showed both low coverage and high cyclomatic complexity of the code.

Root Cause Analysis of the Intermittent Failures A review of the high-complexity components (those having a cyclomatic complexity greater than 10) found that many nested conditional statements were unnecessary. Two functions in the legacy code with high cyclomatic complexity had paths that did not exit gracefully under invalid input, causing a memory access violation and ultimately system failure.

In this case, the root cause of the defect was the original design and coding that allowed unnecessarily deep nested conditionals. These conditionals formed paths reachable only from a rare combination of invalid inputs, making it difficult to test and subsequently isolate the problem.

Customized Best Practice A preventive action plan requires a policy that would limit the depth of nesting conditionals by specifying a maximum cyclomatic complexity. A new customized policy is shown in Figure 7.15. The new policy states that any segment of code with cyclomatic complexity greater than 10 must be additionally documented and with complexity greater than 20 is also subject to peer review. All team members involved in the specification, design, and coding of the system will be notified and trained to apply this practice. Additionally, the static analysis system will be updated to automatically verify the source code's compliance with this rule.

Cyclomatic Complexity	Customized Best Practice
1–10	A simple program; standard program documentation is required.
11–20	More complex; additional documentation explaining complexity is required.
21–50	Complex; additional documentation and peer review of the code is required.
51+	Very complex, untestable, unmaintainable; redesigning and refactoring of the code is required.

Figure 7.15 Customized best practice for code complexity.

7.5.2 Focus on Features/Tests Reports

The following examples show reports that combine information from the testing system with the requirements management system or the defect tracking system.

Features/Requirements Testing Overview

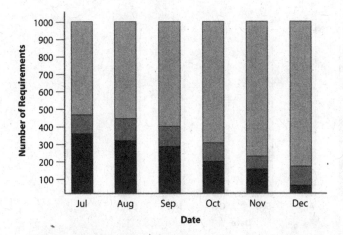

Features/Requirements Testing Details

Date	Failed Test	Not Tested	Passed Test
Dec	65	110	825
Nov	123	96	781
Oct	186	105	709
Sep	265	118	617

Figure 7.16   Overview of the testing of features/requirements.

A requirements/feature testing graph displays the status of testing the requirements, as shown in Figure 7.16. The table shows the number of requirements that have passed testing, failed testing, and have not been tested.

The defect testing graph displays the status of tests run to verify defect removal, as shown in Figure 7.17. The report shows the number of defects that have been successfully removed and therefore passed testing, are unresolved, have not been tested, and have failed testing.

7.6   ACRONYMS

DbC   Design by Contract
EJBs   Enterprise JavaBeans
SQL   Structured Query Language
TDD   Test-driven development

Defects Testing Overview

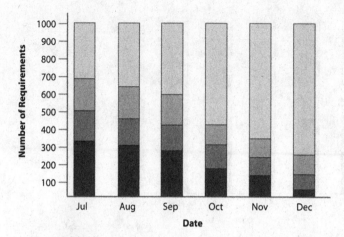

Defects Testing Details

Date	Failed Test	Not Tested	Unresolved	Passed Test (Fixed)
Dec	65	105	78	752
Nov	123	136	81	660
Oct	186	149	107	562
Sep	265	163	128	444

Figure 7.17   Overview of the testing of defect removal.

7.7   GLOSSARY

black box testing   A testing strategy that considers a functional design specification to design test cases without regard to the internal program structure. The tested element is treated as a black or opaque box.

code freeze   A period of time when access to the current code baseline in the version control system is restricted so that only critical changes can be made to the code.

checkpoint   A point in a computer program at which program state, status, or results are checked or recorded. [22]*

cron   The program that enables UNIX users to execute commands or scripts automatically at a specified time/date.

cyclomatic complexity   Also called McCabe's complexity [6]; a measure of code nesting and complexity based on the number of independent program paths.

deadlock   A condition when two or more processes or threads are each waiting for another to release a resource, or perform an action, creating a circular "wait-for" chain.

defensive programming   The practice of trying to anticipate where errors can occur in programs, and then adding code to identify or work around the issue to avoid program failures or security holes.

Design-by-Contract   A design technique that focuses on documenting (and agreeing to) the rights and responsibilities of software modules to ensure program correctness. It is developed by Bertrand Meyer for the language Eiffel. [9]

false positive   A test result of yes, when the correct answer is no.

make   The utility that keeps a set of executable programs current, based on differences in the modification times of the programs and the source files that each is dependent on.

Makefile   A file that contains a description of the relationships between files, and the commands that must be executed to update the derived files to reflect changes in their prerequisites.

parallel development   A planning decision that allows multiple developers to work on the same configuration item at the same time.

sandbox   A subset copy of the project's files.

script   A sequence of computer commands written in batch language.

SQL injection   A technique to inject crafted SQL into user input fields that are part of web forms. It can also be used to log into or even to take over a website.

static web page   A web page that is completely created in advance, with all text and images in place, and housed on a web server, ready for use.

style checker   A static analysis tool that verifies conformance to style and format rules in code.

tar file   A single archive file containing many other files.

test-driven development   A programming practice that instructs developers to write tests of the code before the code is implemented.

unit   A unit is a logically separable part of a computer program. [22]*

unit testing   Testing of individual hardware or software units or groups of related units. [22]*

white box testing   A testing strategy that requires knowledge of the internal structure of a program to design test cases. The testing element is treated as a white or glass box.

* From IEEE Std. 610.12-1990, Copyright 1990, IEEE. All rights reserved.

7.8   REFERENCES

[1] Burnstein, I., *Practical Software Testing: A Process Oriented Approach*. Springer, 2002.

[2] Kaner, C., Falk, J., and Nguyen, H.Q., *Testing Computer Software*. John Wiley & Sons, 2nd ed., 1999.

[3] Meyers, S., *Effective C++: 55 Specific Ways to Improve Your Programs and Designs*. Addison-Wesley Professional Computing Series, 3rd ed., 2005.

[4] King, P., Naughton, P., DeMoney, M., Kanerva, J., Walrath, K., and Hommel, S., *Code Conventions for the Java Programming Language*, 2006, http://java.sun.com/docs/codeconv/html/CodeConvTOC.doc.html (retrieved: August 21, 2006).

[5] Macadamian, *Coding Conventions for C++ and Java*, 2006, http://www.macadamian.com/index.php?option=com_content&task=view&id=34&Itemid=37 (retrieved: August 21, 2006).

[6] McCabe, T., "A Complexity Measure," *IEEE Transactions on Software Engineering*, Vol. 2, No. 4, 1976.

[7] Halstead, M. H., *Elements of Software Science, Operating, and Programming Systems Series*. Elsevier, New York 1977.

[8] Java Developers Network, *Programming with Assertions*, 2006, http://java.sun.com/j2se/1.4.2/docs/guide/lang/assert.html (retrieved: August 21, 2006).

[9] Meyer, B., "Design by Contract: Technical Report TR-EI-12/CO," *Interactive Software Engineering Inc.*, 1986.

[10] Meyer, B., "Design by Contract," in *Advances in Object-Oriented Software Engineering*, Mandrioli, D. and Meyer, B., eds., Prentice Hall, 1991, pp. 1–50.

[11] Meyer, B., "Applying Design by Contract," *IEEE Computer*, Vol. 25, No. 10, October 1992, pp. 40–51.

[12] Nielsen, J., *Jakob Nielsen on Usability and Web Design*, 2006, http://www.useit.com (retrieved: March 26, 2006).

[13] Government Services Administration, "Section 508," *Summary of Section 508 Standards*, January 23, 2006, http://www.section508.gov/index.cfm?FuseAction=Content&ID=11 (retrieved: April 3, 2006).

[14] Bloch, J., *Effective Java Programming Language Guide*. Addison-Wesley Professional, 2001.

[15] Sun Developers Network (SDN), *Core Java Javadoc Tool*, 2006, http://java.sun.com/j2se/javadoc/ (retrieved: August 27, 2006).

[16] Sun Developers Network (SDN), *Code Conventions for the Java Programming Language: Naming Conventions*, 2006, http://java.sun.com/docs/codeconv/html/CodeConventions.doc8.html (retrieved: August 27, 2006).

[17] Johnson, S., "Lint: A C Program Checker," *Technical Report 65*, Bell Laboratories, December 1977.

[18] Sant, J., "Using Mark Previews to Improve Quality of Student Programs," *Proceedings of the 2005 International Conference on Frontiers in Education: Computer Science and Computer Engineering*, Las Vegas, Nevada, June 2005, pp. 62–68.

[19] Gelperin, D. and Hetzel, W., "Software Quality Engineering," *Proceedings of the 4th International Conference on Testing Computer Software*, Washington, D.C., June 1987.

[20] Beck, K., *Test Driven Development: By Example*. Addison Wesley Professional, 2002.

[21] Williams L., Maximilien, E.M., and Vouk, M., "Test Driven Development as a Defect-Reduction Practice," *Proceedings of the 14th International Symposium on Software Reliability* (ISSRE'03), Denver, Colorado, November 2003, pp. 34–45.

[22] Institute of Electrical and Electronics Engineers, *IEEE Standard 610.12-1990— Glossary of Software Engineering Terminology*, 1990.

7.9 EXERCISES

1. What other types of coding standards would you add to those described in this chapter?

2. Give examples of use of assertions in coding, and explain why use of assertions is consistent with the ADP methodology.

3. List the advantages of having a proper security policy and give an example of such.

4. What open source style checkers are available and what are their features?

5. Why is the contract first approach a good practice in the development of SOA?

6. Give examples of situations for which you would recommend TDD.

7. What source control systems are available? What about open source systems?

8. When would you recommend and not recommend use of parallel development? Give examples.

9. How would you deal with developer resentment of automated testing systems, or any other tools that would show coding inadequacies, which are perceived as "negative reinforcement" undermining developer confidence?

10. What other policies for the use of the technology infrastructure would you add to those described in this chapter?

CHAPTER 8

TESTING AND DEFECT PREVENTION

Software is written by humans and therefore has bugs.

—John Jacobs

8.1 INTRODUCTION

Testing is the process of revealing defects in the code with the ultimate goal of establishing that the software has attained a specified degree of quality. Testing takes place throughout the life cycle of the product, and as we discussed in prior chapters, test design should start as soon as use cases and requirements are defined. In our methodology, testing plays a special role because it leads to the root cause analysis of detected defects and it initiates the process of defect prevention for subsequent iterations of software development.

Testing is both a challenging and laborious task. Indeed, studies [1,2,3] report that testing is second [1] only to maintenance in software development costs, accounting for 34% [2] and even up to 50% [3] of the initial (prior to the release) effort. Nikolai Tillman and Wolfram Schulte state: "In many projects in Microsoft, developers have written more lines of code for the unit tests than for the implementation they're testing [4]."

A major contributing factor to the high cost of testing is the lack of the appropriate testing infrastructure in software organizations. The survey data

Automated Defect Prevention: Best Practices in Software Management, by Dorota Huizinga and Adam Kolawa
Copyright © 2007 John Wiley & Sons, Inc.

reported by NIST in 2002 [5] indicates that the national annual costs due to inadequate software testing infrastructure are estimated to range from \$22.2 to \$59.5 billion. The report states the following: "Over half of these costs are borne by software users in the form of error avoidance and mitigation activities. The remaining costs are borne by software developers and reflect the additional testing resources that are consumed due to inadequate testing tools and methods."

While the primary goal of testing is to reveal defects in the code, incorrect testing may introduce defects into the code. The categories of testing defects are:

- *Test design and implementation defects*, which stem from incorrect or incomplete definition or implementation of test input or output data
- *Test harness*[a] *design or implementation defects*, which stem from defect injection during design or implementation of the code necessary to create test cases

In this chapter, we will explain the best practices for software testing as well as for avoidance of testing defects. We will also describe policies for use of the regression testing system and problem tracking system. Additionally, we will show how defect analysis and classification facilitates the prevention of defect reoccurrence.

Expected work products of this phase are:

- Tests
- Policy for use of problem tracking system
- Policy for use of regression testing system
- Defect reports and customized best practices

8.2 BEST PRACTICES FOR TESTING AND CODE REVIEW

During code construction, testing proceeds from small code segments through increasingly larger interacting elements, to completed modules and multimodule components. Thus, the testing process progresses through several levels: starting from white box and black box unit testing, through integration[b] to system[c] and acceptance testing.[d] At each level, several tests are generated and

---

[a] The auxiliary code supporting execution of test cases. It consists of drivers that call the tested code and, if needed, the stubs that represent elements it calls.
[b] Testing in which software components, hardware components, or both are combined and tested to evaluate the interaction between them. [6]
[c] Testing conducted on a complete, integrated system to evaluate the system's compliance with its specified requirements. [6]
[d] Testing conducted to determine whether a system satisfies specified acceptance criteria, by which the user determines whether to accept the system. [6]

executed and their outcomes verified. However, during this laborious process it is often not clear whether sufficient testing has already been performed and what rules should be used to guide developers and testers to proceed to the subsequent levels. To alleviate this problem, we have defined test progression criteria. Each criterion is a value of a measure or a set of measures that, when satisfied, permits both development and testing to advance to the subsequent level. Conversely, all testing practices discussed in the following sections should be measured and the predefined test progression criteria should be used to prevent code from prematurely moving to successive phases.

White box and black box unit testing as well as regression testing starts with the project's first iteration and is conducted throughout most of the subsequent iterations. Integration testing begins later, when module implementation is advanced, and class and module interactions need to be exercised. System testing takes place when all modules and multimodule components are completed and put together. Finally, acceptance testing, which usually involves end users, is conducted. However, progressive acceptance testing of selected product features should be performed as early as possible, so that customer feedbacks and requests can be contemplated, and possibly accommodated, in subsequent iterations of the product implementation.

8.2.1 Conducting White Box Unit Testing: Bottom-Up Approach

As opposed to black box testing, white box unit testing is a strategy that requires knowledge of the internal structure of a program to design test cases.[e] Based on this structure, white box testing, also called *glass box testing*, exercises statements, branches, paths,[f] loops, and data flows in order to expose construction defects and security vulnerabilities. Because of the level of detail required to implement and verify its results, traditionally this type of testing has been performed for relatively small code elements. However, with the use of the modern technology facilitating automatic generation of test cases, white box unit testing can now span multiple classes and even submodules. (See Figure 8.1.)

As described in the previous chapter, white box unit testing is one of the recommended best practices used during code construction. It should be conducted as soon as units are implemented and before the code is checked into the shared source control system.

Why   Performed as one of the very first testing activities, white box unit testing provides immediate feedback to the developers about code quality. Its purpose is to exercise a wide number and variety of branches and paths

---

[e] A set of test inputs, execution conditions, and expected results developed for a particular objective. [6]
[f] A sequence of instructions that may be performed in the execution of a computer program. [6]

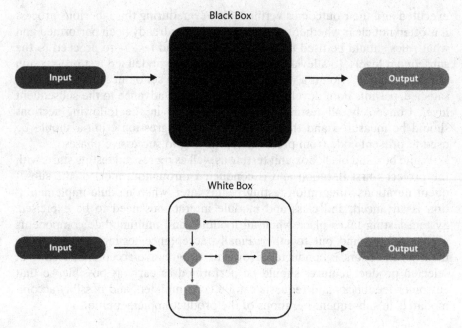

Figure 8.1 Black box versus white box tests.

(including perhaps unintentional paths) and uncover construction defects resulting in faults such as runtime exceptions[g] or invalid memory accesses. By identifying and correcting these faults early in development, defect propagation to other parts of the code is minimized, and it is ascertained that the code can process a wide variety of permissible inputs without faulty execution, exposing security vulnerabilities, or behaving unpredictably.

Code construction robustness becomes increasingly important with new technologies such as web services, where system interfaces are exposed to the outside world. If code in these systems is not tested properly, unpredictable behavior not only can lead to functionality and performance problems, but also can provide intruders with pipelines to enter and manipulate the system.

Who Developers conduct white box unit testing.

How White box unit testing starts at the function, method, and basic class level and progresses through complex classes and sometimes submodules. However, not all methods and classes require separate unit tests. If the code is not very complex, it is much more efficient to generate unit tests for a set of interacting classes instead of each individual class.

[g] An exception is a software interrupt caused by an unexpected program behavior.

White box testing is much like posing a series of "what-if?" questions that determine whether the application continues to behave appropriately under unusual or exceptional conditions. Its success hinges on the developer's ability to create a set of test inputs that is wide and varied enough to cover the unit's branches and paths as fully as possible and perhaps expose unexpected behaviors. However, creating such a set of tests is a challenge since the number of possible program paths could be prohibitively large, and testing all paths is often not only impractical but simply not feasible. As elegantly exemplified by Glen J. Myers [7], even a short program with 20 lines of code can have 100 trillion paths.

For white box testing, the focus should be on exercising branches and statements, rather than paths. Additionally, variables used in calculations and predicates should be tested, as well as possible outcomes of Boolean expressions.

All unit tests must be repeatable. Once executed, their expected results are manually compared with actual results, as depicted in Figure 8.2. The tests are marked as passed only if these results match.

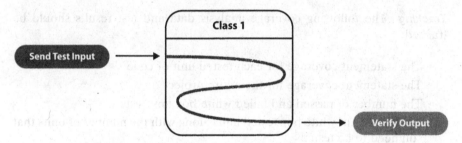

Figure 8.2   Verifying the results of a white box unit test.

Once the unit's white box testing results meet their test progression criteria, such as 90% statement coverage, and all white box unit tests pass, the unit can be checked into the source control system. At this time, the unit's white box tests are converted into black box tests. This is done by developers performing the following tasks:

- Verifying results of white box tests
- Selecting a subset of these tests that focuses on the unit's functional requirements
- Adding other tests that verify unit functionality
- Marking all verified tests as black box tests

Thus, the end product of white box testing is a set of test cases that capture the unit's intended behavior.

If an expanded infrastructure is used for the project, these verified test cases should be then added to the automated testing system. Additionally, these test cases can be used as a baseline to detect changes introduced by code modifications, and once the code development stabilizes in the current iteration, they should be included in the automated regression testing system.

Measurement   White box testing measures belong to the broad category of code coverage analysis.[h] In coverage analysis, test adequacy indicators such as coverage criteria[i] [8] are used to define test stopping rules. Test stopping rules answer the fundamental question, "How much testing is enough?" For example, if a goal is to assure that all statements in the unit are executed at least once, the criterion is 100% statement coverage. Similarly, a requirement might be to achieve 100% condition decision coverage, in which all possible outcomes of every condition are tested. Other important measures in this category include variable *c-uses*, which are uses of variables within computational expressions, and variable *p-uses*, which are uses of variables within conditional expression predicates. For each of these tests, the expected and the actual results are compared to determine whether the test has passed or failed.

Tracking   The following coverage analysis data and test results should be tracked:

- The statement coverage for each tested unit of code
- The statement coverage for the entire project
- The number of passed and failed white box unit tests
- The number of white box tested units along with the number of units that still need to be tested

A graph such as the one depicted in Figure 8.3 shows the increase in the unit's statement coverage as more white box test cases are generated and executed.

The graph in Figure 8.4, which plots passed and failed white box tests per day, provides a quick way to monitor the extent and the results of the team's white-box testing efforts. Additional reports can provide a more detailed view of the test coverage, as well as help in identifying the source of any problems. Once the white box test cases are verified and marked as black box tests, the line on this graph goes down. This is normal as long as test cases are moving to black box testing.

Automation   Unit testing tools can automatically generate a wide variety of inputs designed to thoroughly exercise the unit, execute test cases with those inputs, and then report results including the exceptions that occur during test case execution. Automation of both test generation and execution not only

[h] A set of techniques used to measure how much of the code was exercised with respect to a predefined criterion.
[i] Test adequacy criteria pertaining to code coverage and used to define test stopping rules. For example, 100% statement coverage.

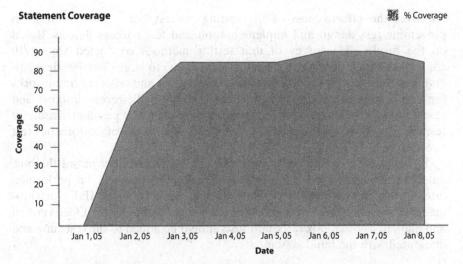

Figure 8.3 White box testing coverage graph for an individual unit.

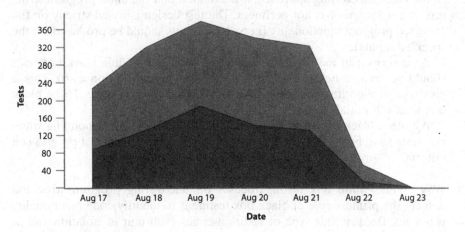

White Box Tests Details

Date	Failed	Passed
Aug 23	0	0
Aug 22	16	36
Aug 21	133	188
Aug 20	145	192

Figure 8.4 White box test results.

improves the effectiveness of the testing process but is also essential in preventing test design and implementation and test harness defects. Based on the results of a survey of unit testing methods conducted among 19 companies, ranging from extra small (1 developer) to large (100–999 developers), Per Runeson [9] reports that "test automation and tailoring frameworks for unit testing are successful practices." Additionally, recent interest and research in the fields of symbolic program execution and parameterized unit testing [4] show considerable promise in the area of automatic test generation.

Typically, 60–70% statement coverage can be achieved by out-of-the-box, automatically generated test cases. Test case execution can be performed interactively (by the developer while working on code in the IDE), or automatically (in batch mode, as part of the automated testing suite). Once verified and marked as black box tests, unit tests should be added to the test suite and integrated with the build system.

8.2.2 Conducting Black Box Testing and Verifying the Convergence of Top-Down and Bottom-Up Tests

In the black box testing approach, it is assumed that the inner program structure is not known or is not pertinent. The test design is based strictly on the expected program functionality (i.e., what outputs should be produced for the specified inputs).

As described in the previous chapter, service and module black box tests should be created before service and module implementation starts. This is also true of algorithmically complex and critical units of code. These black box tests will initially fail.

All other black box tests should be created after the corresponding white box tests have been generated, executed, and have met their test progression criteria.

Why While white box testing focuses on uncovering program structural defects, the primary role of black box testing is to identify code functionality problems. Because this type of testing verifies each unit in isolation and as part of the system, it allows developers to reconfigure the functionality of each piece of code that does not conform to its requirements, and identify any potential defects that could negatively impact system behavior.

Who Developers conduct most of the black box testing. Testers create and execute black box tests at the system and acceptance levels, and sometimes at the integration level.

How Black box testing involves generating a set of inputs and corresponding expected outputs based on the unit's functionality specification. Both valid and invalid inputs should be exercised by test cases. Valid inputs should produce expected outputs while invalid inputs should generate error messages or cause graceful application exits. Since the range of inputs to be tested can be prohibitively large, in order to effectively perform black box testing, a technique called equivalence class partitioning[j] [7,11] is often used.

Equivalence class partitioning divides the input domain into distinct subsets in such a way that a single test case can reveal defects for the entire subset of possible inputs. For example, if all integer inputs greater than zero are supposed to generate the same output, and all integer inputs less than or equal to zero are expected to produce the same, but different from positive integers output, two classes of equivalence can be defined: one for positive inputs and the other for zero and negative inputs. Thus, only two test cases are needed to cover a wide range of possible inputs. Equivalence class partitioning not only eliminates the need for exhaustive testing but also facilitates effective test case creation, because defects can often be found on the boundaries of the equivalence classes. Thus, when creating black box tests, or converting white box tests to black box tests, the test cases should check the boundary conditions of each equivalence class as listed below:

- BLB—a value just below the lower boundary
- LB—the value on the lower boundary
- ALB—a value just above the lower boundary
- BUB—a value just below the upper bound
- UB—the value on the upper bound
- AUB—a value just above the upper bound

In the above example, test cases would have to cover at least the following inputs:

- For the positive domain: 0, 1, 2, and MAXINT–1, MAXINT, MAXINT+1
- For zero and the negative domain: 1, 0, –1, MININT+1, MININT, MININT–1

Usually developers start black box functional testing by writing unit-level test cases, extending them to the submodule level, and then extending and linking them again into module-level tests that exercise use cases through the application. However, in our approach, black box testing proceeds simultaneously from both ends: the top (from services and modules) and the bottom (from methods and classes). On one hand, service and/or module test cases are executed continuously and keep failing in the absence of the

---

[j] A technique for dividing input domain into distinct subsets of inputs, which are processed in the equivalent way by the target software.

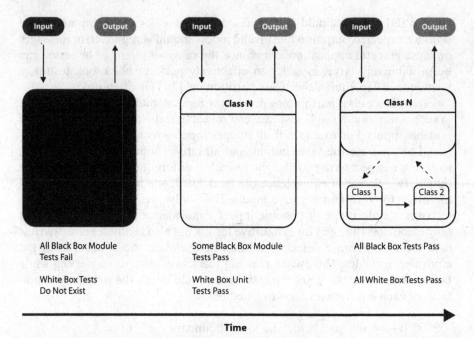

Figure 8.5 Progressive pass of the module black box tests.

corresponding code. On the other hand, once the code is developed and the units pass the corresponding white box tests, they are checked into the source code control system, the white box tests become black box unit tests and the black box module tests start progressively passing. Figure 8.5 shows such a progressive pass of the module tests as the code is developed and more classes are implemented.

Each unit test will need a test harness that allows the unit to be exercised independently of the rest of the application, stubs[k] for calls to external resources such as databases or other modules, test inputs that exercise the unit, and a means of verifying whether the expected results were obtained. If the unit has any special requirements in addition to its basic functionality (e.g., one function should call another function no more than once), supplementary tests should be added to verify these special requirements. Ultimately, the conceptual test cases defined during the requirements phase should dictate the nature and the number of the black box test cases created.

The next step is testing the functionality of submodules, which are multiple units that interact but do not yet form a complete functional module. At this point, the unit test cases should be extended so that they verify not only the functionality of each unit, but also the interactions between the related units. At each level, there should be at least one test case for each applicable equivalence class in the application's valid and invalid input domains. The test cases

---

[k] A piece of code that stands in for a full-fledged element. A stub may simulate the behavior of existing code or be a temporary substitute for yet-to-be-developed code.

should then be extended to encompass the modules. These tests should match the tests that were originally created before module implementation started.

Therefore, the final step is the verification of the convergence of the original module black box test cases with the test cases generated through the bottom-up approach. If these tests do not converge, then either the original module specification has changed but its test cases have not been updated, or the module does not implement the expected functionality.

Measurement   The total number of black box tests as well the number of tests that passed and failed per unit, submodule, and module should be measured on a daily basis. Also, the ratio of the passed tests to the total number of tests should be measured. This ratio should approach 100% as the module implementation progresses. Another important measure is the rate of convergence of bottom-up unit tests with the originally created module black box tests. This measure is an indicator of the module functionality correctness as originally specified and designed.

The total number of units and the number of units that still need to be tested should be measured. As the units are added to the source control system, the number of tests grows, and it is important to monitor the test pass rate in order to observe the correct pattern of growth in the ratio of passed to the total number of tests. During black box testing, it is common to observe the "sawtooth" pattern, which indicates that defects are being found, code is being fixed, and then the fixed code is being checked in.

Black box testing introduces a concept of code coverage testing different from that of white box testing. The black box test coverage is the ratio of the number of units exercised by test cases to the total number of units. Therefore, it is a measure of the completeness and correctness of requirements implementation. At a minimum, each requirement should have at least one black box test that exercises both valid and invalid inputs for each equivalence class. The number of units successfully tested should approach the total number of units.

These tests then should be correlated to the corresponding use cases and should become indicators of use case implementation. The black box unit tests should have a 100% pass rate before they are added to the regression suite and used in verifying existing functionality when the new code is being added to the source control system.

Tracking   The following measures should be tracked:

- The total number of units and the number of units that have yet to be tested.
- The number of units without test cases in all project code.
- The passed, failed, and the total number of black box test cases.
- The ratio of passed tests to the total number of black box tests.
- The level of the convergence of the bottom-up unit tests with the originally created module black box tests. (The level of the convergence is the

Black Box Tests Details

Date	Failed	Passed
Aug 23	0	327
Aug 22	15	312
Aug 21	26	301
Aug 20	30	297

Figure 8.6 Black box tests table generated by the reporting system.

number of the bottom-up module tests that match the original module black box tests divided by the total number of the original module black box tests.)

• The black box test coverage, which is the ratio of the number of units exercised by test cases to the total number of units.

• The number of failed tests and total tests for all project code.

Figure 8.6, which shows passed and failed black box tests per day, provides a quick way to monitor extent and results of the team's black box testing efforts.

Automation As described above, software tools can be used to automatically generate unit tests. Also, once the submodule or module construction is completed, additional functional black box test cases can be automatically generated by exercising a running application and recording its behavior. This type of test generation is based on the so-called *record/playback* feature of the tool: the application execution is recorded and, based on this execution, test cases are created and replayed automatically.

Another approach to the automatic generation of black box test cases is based on the assertions used for the preconditions and postconditions of units as defined in the Design-by-Contract specification.

8.2.3   Conducting Code Reviews as a Testing Activity

Types of code reviews include informal walkthroughs, formal inspections, and the recently popularized paired programming. In paired programming, two developers participate in a combined development effort at one workstation. For example, one creates a unit test for a class while the other thinks of the design and implementation of the class that will pass the test. The partners frequently (at least once a day) switch roles.

Regardless of the approach used, the purpose of code review is to manually evaluate a segment of software (by an individual or a team) in order to identify potential coding and design defects.

Why Code reviews facilitate detection of defects early in development. Additionally, they motivate developers to write manageable code. When developers know that the code will be reviewed by their peers, they tend to create more clear and concise programs and to properly document their code. This role of reviews is especially important because writing documentation is often psychologically resented during code construction. Code reviews also improve the technical knowledge of the participants since developers are given an opportunity to learn from each other about the latest coding patterns and new programming tips. Another positive side effect of code reviews is the fact that they facilitate the building of a common team culture through face-to-face interactions. During such meetings the developers are more likely to pressure the "odd man out" to follow the team's standards and practices.

Conducting code reviews to increase both software quality and development productivity began in the 1970s, and was originally described by Michael Fagan [12] and Glen Myers [13]. Recent studies, such as the work reported by Jeffrey Holmes [2], show that traditional code reviews are indeed value-added tasks; they increase development productivity of the current project and they can facilitate future productivity improvements up to 20%.

Results of research on the productivity of paired programming are less conclusive. Popularized recently by Kent Beck in *Extreme Programming Explained: Embrace Change* [14], paired programming was first reported in the workplace by Larry Constantine in 1995 [15], and discussed by Edwin Hutchins [16]. Laurie Williams and her colleagues conducted the study [17], which provided quantitative evidence that paired programming improves product quality and reduces time to market. However, more recent research, described by Kim Man Lui et al. [18], presents a rigorous scientific experiment and indicates that productivity improvements depend on the experience and skills of the individuals forming pairs. For example, novice–novice pairs compared with novice solos are much more productive than expert–expert pairs compared with expert solos.

DEVELOPER'S TESTIMONIAL

Code reviews should be scheduled for new modules and major modifications of existing code. Minor revisions should be reviewed solely by the change reviewer, rather than multiple engineers.

Code reviews serve multiple purposes:

- Detect code defects, including adherence to coding standards.
- Expose other developers to different parts of the system.
- Serve as a learning experience to gain knowledge from more experienced developers.
- Serve as a team-building experience.

—Nick Stamat, Software Engineer

Who   Developers and the architect should conduct code reviews.

How   Code reviews allow developers to evaluate the implementation of their co-workers in hopes of turning up possible defects. The scope of the code review is usually determined by use cases: when a developer completes the code required to implement a use case, all the related code should be submitted for review. Alternatively, code can be reviewed incrementally—for example, as it is added to the source control system. The expanded infrastructure can facilitate this process by automatically alerting reviewers about newly modified lines of code once a week. In the latter case, the reviews should be performed after the code is checked in and demonstrated to satisfy coding standards as well as white box testing and black box test progression criteria.

Those parts of the code that show coding standards violations, as identified by the automated coding standards analysis, are a natural starting point for a code review. The violations should be assessed to determine whether they are warranted, and therefore whether the code should be exempt from the required standard, whether the standard should be modified to permit the reported type of violations, or whether the code should be modified to comply with the standard.

In addition, a code review should occur each time a regression test failure is reported. The goal of this inspection should be to determine whether the code behavior change was intentional. If the change was intentional, the test cases should be modified to allow for the new expected behavior. Otherwise, the code should be corrected.

Code reviews should be performed on the new, modified code and on the most critical parts of the application.

This type of approach indicates a sense of priority. While focus should be on defect detection, code reviews should also help to identify bottlenecks and performance problems in program segments.

DEVELOPER'S TESTIMONIAL

The parts of code to be reviewed most often should be the critical parts. The critical parts of the code are dependent on the type of application and the programming language used. I suggest making a review checklist for every project. The checklist itemizes the parts of the code that are required to be reviewed (e.g., all global variable instantiations, and "go to" statements, all database queries involving more than three tables, etc.).

Let me add to the purposes to code reviews Nick had stated [see previous sidebar]:

- *Code Optimization*: This is needed when coding software with resource limitations such as a Java game for cell phones.
- *Adherence to Code-Level Design Qualities*: For example, the system should be fault tolerant such that the code should catch errors. The review should check if the programmer implemented exception handlers or if the code is validating the user inputs.

—Lesley Ku, Systems Analyst

The seriousness of the defects identified during code reviews should be assessed, and severe defects should be reported in the problem tracking system and used in defect analysis and prevention.

Measurement The amount of code that has been reviewed and that still needs to be reviewed should be measured. This number should be used in assigning priorities to the developers' tasks as reported in the CAL (Current Activity Log) report, and in estimating the time needed for testing activities. All code subject to the review should be approved by the architect or a lead developer before the integration testing starts.

Tracking The new and modified code that needs to be reviewed should be tracked. Once reviewed and approved by the architect and/or a lead developer, the code should be marked as accepted.

Automation As explained in the previous chapter, in an expanded infrastructure, conformance to coding standards and project-specific programming rules can be verified automatically by static analysis tools. However, review of the algorithms and complex parts of code should be done manually. While these types of code reviews cannot be automated, the code covered by reviews can be tracked automatically. Static analysis can be used to help in identifying parts of the code that need to be reviewed, such as segments of code with high cyclomatic complexity. A code review tool should identify new and modified code in the source control system and notify a reviewer (the architect or the lead developer on a particular module) about the required reviews. The developers should be provided with a list that tracks the review status (accepted, pending, or needs revisions) of all relevant pieces of code.

8.2.4 Conducting Integration Testing

After the test progression criteria for units, submodules, and modules have been met, it is necessary to verify that these elements work correctly together. The role of integration testing is to conduct such a verification by an orderly progression of testing in which all the individually tested software parts are combined and tested together until the entire system has been integrated.

Why The goal of integration testing is to detect defects that occur on the interfaces of the interacting elements: units, submodules, modules, and multimodule components. This type of testing verifies the formats of messages sent between services, the types and the number of parameters passed between interacting elements of code, and whether these elements are consistent with respect to their expected mutual functionalities. Depending on the nature of the test cases, integration testing may additionally expose functionality, security, and usability defects.

Who Developers perform most of the integration testing. Testers conduct integration tests of multiple modules and multimodule components.

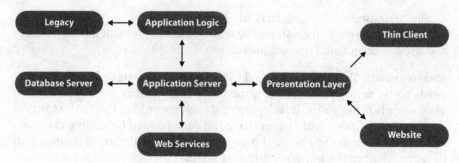

Figure 8.7   Elements of integration testing and the involved interfaces.

How   Integration testing should be performed in an iterative and incremental manner. The gradual process facilitates early isolation of possible interface inconsistencies. All module interfaces should be progressively exercised and the integrated elements should be tested for both valid and invalid inputs. Callable interfaces made available by an integrated code segment should be invoked by other units that are part of the integrated system. Where multiple units invoke a unit under an integration test, integration testing should cover calls from at least two different calling units.

Integration test cases are built by extending the existing module tests so they span the multiple modules and multimodule components until the entire system is included. By extending the unit, submodule, and module test cases to span the entire system, a test suite is established that records and tracks the results at every checkpoint[1] that was previously verified, and instantly notifies the team when a code modification introduces a problem into any part of the system.

An alternative way, recently made possible by new technology, is to exercise a set of integrated elements with realistic use cases, and then have unit test cases generated automatically. The results of these tests should be then manually verified.

To be effective, integration testing should be applied to each element of the integrated application, as exemplified in Figure 8.7.

Integration tests should be repeatable so that they can be used to verify the system after it is modified in current and/or future development iterations. Even if integration tests require partial or full manual testing, they can be made repeatable if they are recorded carefully. This can be done either by documenting each step in detail or by using an automated test record/playback tool.

Measurement   Integration tests are black box tests. Therefore, measures applied to black box testing apply to integration tests. A more specific measure, which can be tracked during integration testing, is the number of passed and

---

[1] A point in a computer program at which program state, status, or results are checked or recorded, (See Chapter 7.) [6]

failed service, component, and module interaction tests. These are the tests that verify the proper parameters passed and the calling sequences between the interacting modules. The interface coverage should be measured and used as a test progression criterion. At the module level, interface coverage for the test progression to the next integration level or to the acceptance testing should be 100%.

Tracking Integration tests and their pass and failure rates should be tracked as a subset of black box tests. Interface coverage should be tracked and used to determine progression to the next testing step.

Automation Using record/playback technology, the developer or tester can exercise the application functionality targeted for testing while the tool automatically designs test cases with real data that represents the paths taken through the application. In such situations, no coding or scripting is required. The result is a library of test cases against which new code can be tested to ensure it meets specifications and does not break existing functionality.

The following are the key advantages of using technology to automate integration testing:

- *Fast and Easy Generation of Low-Maintenance Test Suite.* Developers, testers, or QA staff members can automatically create realistic unit test cases by simply exercising the application.
- *Automated Creation of a Thorough Regression Test Suite.* Developers can verify new code functionality as soon as it is completed, and then the team can run the generated test cases periodically to determine whether new or modified code impacted previously verified functionality.
- *Ability to Test a Full Range of Application Functionality on a Single Machine Independent of a Complex Testing Environment.* For applications that contain database interactions or calls to other external data sources, processes, services, etc., automated tools generate test cases that represent those behaviors and develop test case stubs as needed. These test cases can be used to test complex application behavior from a single machine (which may be a developer's or tester's desktop) without requiring live data connections or a fully staged test environment.

8.2.5 Conducting System Testing

System testing[m] is the process of testing integrated hardware and software to verify that the system meets its specified requirements. Both functional

---

[m] Testing conducted on a complete, integrated system to evaluate the system's compliance with its specified requirements. [6]

and nonfunctional requirements should be tested. In some situations, several quality attributes such as configuration, performance, security, stress, reliability, recovery, and usability have to be tested. However, since not all types of systems undergo such thorough testing, the following sections address the three categories of the most frequently conducted system testing: functional, performance and load stress, and security.

Functional Testing   The goal of system functional testing is to verify the application functional requirements at the highest level of abstraction. System functional tests often correspond directly to the application use cases, and with ADP they are designed as early as use cases are created.

Performance and Load Stress Testing   The objective of the performance and load[n] stress testing is to verify whether the system continues to function correctly under nominal and extreme loads, and whether the response time under those loads is satisfactory. The load is the amount of work performed by a system, and in testing it is expressed as a series of inputs to execute a group of transactions. Performance testing focuses on fine tuning system response time and throughput under its nominal loads. Load stress testing, on the other hand, concentrates on creating extreme conditions that would break the system due to the resource exhaustion.

Security Testing   Security testing involves designing and executing tests to expose possible application vulnerabilities to intentional and unintentional system security violations. The focus is on those segments of code that are responsible for protecting access to the system and where sensitive data is stored.

Why   System testing is necessary to verify both the functional and quality requirements of the application before it undergoes acceptance testing and, more importantly, before it is deployed. Since system testing requires a large amount of resources, this might be the first time that all system components are tested together and on various target platforms. Problems such as resource limitations, data overflows, and other external constraints might not surface until this phase, and therefore they should be a focal point of system tests.

Who   Testers conduct system testing.

How   System functional testing takes place after successful integration testing has been completed and all the application modules and components have been connected. System functional tests are black box tests corresponding to the application use cases. For example, if an online library catalog must be

---

[n]   A series of inputs that simulates a group of transactions. [10]

able to add new users, login existing users using user name and password, and perform various types of searches, all these features should be exercised during system testing. All functional requirements should be verified for both valid and invalid inputs. Black box testing techniques such as equivalence class partitioning and boundary value analysis should be used to narrow down the number of required tests.

In order to properly conduct performance testing, its requirements have to be articulated explicitly and they should be quantifiable. For example, the requirements could state: "The system shall handle at least 10 transactions per second," or "An average response time of a search shall be less than three seconds." In order to verify these requirements, performance is measured under nominal system conditions.

The following questions should be answered when defining system nominal conditions:

- How many users should be able to access the application simultaneously?
- How much data is expected to be processed?
- Will the load be distributed among multiple systems?
- How much will the data grow?
- Can the application cope with short periods of overactivity (due to, for instance, a mention in a news article)?

In stress testing, the loads should be extreme (e.g., twice as large as under nominal conditions). Performance and stress testing is typically performed on the same staging system as is the integration testing. However, in some cases (e.g., with QA), it might not be possible to construct a realistic staging system in order to perform load and performance testing. In such cases, performance and load stress testing need to be conducted on the live application.

Security tests should cover equivalence class domains for valid and invalid password inputs, test for known encryption weaknesses, and check for trap doors[o] and Trojan horses.[p] For authorized access, security tests should also verify the levels of authorization for protected data. For example, in a hospital patient record system, a staff member responsible for making appointments should be able to pull the patient's visit history but not medical records. Additionally, security tests should look for ungraceful system degradations due to resource constraints, such as a limited number of memory or network connections. Such ungraceful degradation might provide an application entry to intruders.

If a failure is observed during system testing, it would require immediate attention and assessment of problem severity.

---

[o] Unprotected entries to the system.
[p] A disguised, malicious code embedded within a legitimate program.

Measurement The total number of system functional tests as well as the number of tests that passed and failed per use case should be measured. Also, the ratio of the passed tests to the total number of tests should be calculated. With the exception of noise, which reflects *false positive* results due to, for example, stale data in a tested record, the system functional testing pass rate should approach 100%, and this value should be used as a test progression criterion to move to acceptance testing.

System performance tests should measure average response time and throughput under system nominal conditions. Stress test results should provide information about the maximum loads that the system can handle and continue to function properly. Additionally, the system throughput under stress loads should be measured. For a new system, the load and performance test criteria can be passed after a sufficient number and range of tests that exercise realistic usage for the entire application have been developed and executed producing acceptable response times, *without* negatively affecting system functionality.

The security test pass rate should be measured, and unless its value is 100%, testing should not move to the acceptance level.

Tracking In addition to tracking the pass test rates during system testing, tracking of performance and load stress testing should be started as soon as the corresponding modules are completed. If the results of such tests are collected over an extended time and compared against a baseline, undesired performance drops can be easily detected and eliminated as soon as they are introduced. For example, before adding the security layer to a module, performance testing should be conducted and the results should be saved as a baseline. After adding the security layer, performance testing should be repeated, and the results compared with the baseline to see whether the added functionality degrades the performance. If the performance degradation is unacceptable, the security layer may need to be modified.

Automation System functional and security tests can be automatically generated using techniques described above in the automation sections on white box, black box, and integration testing. Performance and load stress testing can be automated by using load generators [19]. Load generators simulate system interactions by using patterns similar to realistic use cases. They continuously access the application and automatically record system response as a function of a tested load.

8.2.6 Conducting Regression Testing

Regression testing[q] is the process of retesting software that has been modified to ensure that no defects have been introduced by the modification and that previously verified code continues to meet its specifications.

---

[q] Selective retesting of a system or component to verify that modifications have not caused unintended effects and that the system or component still complies with its specified requirements. [6]

Why   Regression testing verifies whether each unit, submodule, module, and multimodule component continues to function as expected when the code base grows and evolves. Regression tests are useful for checking which parts of the application need to be additionally retested. For instance, if regression tests reveal that certain parts of an application are affected by a code change, it is strongly recommended that extra testing be performed to verify the continued functionality of those parts. Since the functional tests that were used to build the regression test suite correspond to segments of use cases, the regression test suite is essentially verifying that use cases are correctly implemented as the application evolves.

Who   Developers start building the regression test suite, but regression test cases can also be added by testers or QA professionals.

How   The initial regression test suite is built when the team performs white box and black box functional unit testing. As black box tests are extended to span submodules, modules, and components, they are added to the regression test suite. Each test case created for this purpose should be saved and executed after each build.

Additionally, each time a new defect is detected, a test designed to uncover this type or a similar type of problem should be added to the regression test suite. This should include not only unit tests, but also the integration-level and system-level tests. Having a robust regression test suite that runs periodically prevents the same types of defects from recurring, and over time will result in significantly fewer faults slipping into the code.

Once the regression test suite is built, effort must be made to ensure that it is maintained. Test results should be reviewed on a regular basis to determine if any testing failures occurred. If test results reveal that code modifications reintroduce previously corrected vulnerabilities or introduce new ones, the team should be alerted immediately.

Measurement   The pass rate of the regression tests should be measured and, with the exception of a small percentage of noisy data (no more than 10%), regression test results should approximate 100% pass rate.

Another important measure is the regression test failure rate delta. The delta is calculated by subtracting from the current failure rate the failure rate obtained after the last iteration. In subsequent iterations, newly added test cases are frozen, and the delta measures the differences from this new frozen state.

Any failure of a regression test suite should be viewed as a roadblock that prevents the team from moving to the next logical step in the software development life cycle. Rather than continuing, the team should analyze and correct the problems reported.

Tracking   The regression test pass and failure rate should be tracked. The regression test failure delta should be tracked and reviewed daily since it is much easier to focus on reviewing the difference from the frozen state than to assess the system "from scratch" each day.

The system response time should be measured as a function of a number of users accessing the application simultaneously. When a new piece of functionality is added to a currently deployed system, the criteria changes: passing the progression criterion should require acceptable load/performance test results for the new module, and regression test results that demonstrate that the addition of the new features did not cause either regression of previous functionality or performance degradation.

When a performance test is completed, its results should be saved and leveraged for regression testing.

Automation   Regression tests can be automatically generated using techniques described above in the automation sections on white box, black box, integration, and system testing. The measures pertaining to regression testing should be calculated and tracked automatically.

8.2.7   Conducting Acceptance Testing

Acceptance testing refers to testing conducted to determine whether a system satisfies acceptance criteria agreed upon by the customer, and to enable the customer to evaluate the system [6]. Acceptance testing often involves additional reviews of system test results by the customer as well as alpha[r] and beta[s] testing.

Additional Reviews of System Test Results   While customer representatives should be involved in inspections related to system requirements definition and system testing, an additional review period is usually allocated to allow the customer to provide documented specific concerns regarding the results of system testing. A previously agreed-upon period of time (e.g., four weeks) following completion of system testing should be allocated for this purpose.

During this time, additional review and analysis of the test results is conducted by the development team. Specific customer concerns should be documented during this period. Action items may result in a patch to the current release, or in a modification in the future release.

Alpha Testing   Alpha testing takes place at the organization that developed the product. Developers and testers conduct most of this testing. However, during this time customer representatives are allowed to access the system to execute their own defined usage scenarios. These scenarios should be described

---

[r] Part of the acceptance testing conducted by the developing organization in a laboratory setting.
[s] Part of the acceptance testing conducted both by the customer at the customer's site and by the developing organization.

in brief documentation that consists mainly of previously defined use cases and was previously made available to the development organization. Development organization representatives should be available to support customer representative execution of these predefined usage scenarios.

To obtain a quantitative metric for progression criteria of alpha testing results, each tester should complete surveys that rank key factors (such as ease of use, usefulness of existing functionality, overall satisfaction, etc.) on a scale from 1 to 10. In addition, this data can be tracked and used for historical comparisons during subsequent rounds of acceptance testing. Criteria for achieving acceptance test results can be set according to the number and results of survey responses. For instance, a team might decide that to pass the acceptance tests, they should have at least 50 tests with an average overall satisfaction score of eight or above.

Beta Testing   During beta testing, the customer usually has the option of requesting installation of the software at its place of business to test it under operational conditions. The developing organization should be given access to the beta system and should be able to observe the system in use. The tests are conducted according to prior contractual agreements and their results form the basis for final system acceptance.

8.3 DEFECT ANALYSIS AND PREVENTION

Defects uncovered during testing are subject to root cause analysis, which then leads to creation of the customized best practices that prevent those defects from recurring in subsequent iterations of software development. When testers uncover defects during integration, system, and acceptance testing, they assess defect severity and report severe defects in the problem tracking system. Defects should be considered severe if they cause intermittent or long-term system failures, or produce incorrect outputs, or if frequency of occurrence warrants a customized practice to prevent them. Customized best practices are then created based on the root cause analysis of these defects. The life cycle of a defect detected by a tester is depicted in Figure 8.8.

Furthermore, a more comprehensive defect analysis can be conducted after a series of implementation iterations or a beta release. In addition to assessing defect severity, defect reports include a defect ID, the date that it was uncovered, a brief description of the defect and the system condition when the defect occurred, an explanation of the test case code that uncovered the defect, and a link to the code segment that caused test failure.

The first step in this comprehensive analysis is the classification of the reported defects. This classification depends on the type of products developed by the organization and existing practices. In this book we have expanded on Ilene's Burstein's [10] categorization of defects and showed what are the best practices to prevent defects in those categories. There are several other

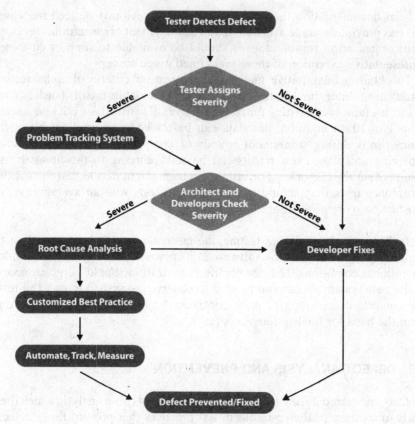

Figure 8.8 Life cycle of a defect.

sources that can be used for defect classification. Boris Beizer [11] provides an elaborate "taxonomy of bugs." Cem Kaner and his colleagues [20] divide defects into the following categories: user interface, error handling, boundary related, calculation, initial and later states, control flow, race conditions, load condition, hardware, source and version control, documentation, and testing. A formalized classification of defects by categories can also be found in the *IEEE Standard Classification for Software Anomalies* [21].

By conducting a comprehensive defect analysis and classification, patterns and trends can be identified and the cause of each defect, or class of defects, can be isolated. As an outcome of defect analysis, a table such as the one exemplified in Figure 8.9 containing information about the cause of each defect and the recommended action should be created.

Note that the root cause analysis may reveal that some defects should have been prevented by an existing practice or policy that is already used (e.g., the table in Figure 8.9 shows defects that should have been prevented by an automated build system, already in place). This indicates that the implemented practice or policy needs to be tightened or modified. In other words, for each

Defect Cause	Recommended Action for the Corresponding ADP Practice or Policy
Requirement incomplete	Review best practices for Gathering and Organizing Requirements.
Algorithm incorrect	Review design and construction best practices for Defining Application Logic and TDD for the Algorithmically Complex Code.
Variable initialization problems	Create a new Coding Standard Practice and verify it with a static analysis tool.
Metadata not updated	Review the policy for use of the automated build system.
Prohibited function calls used	Create a new Coding Standard Practice and verify it with a static analysis tool.
Shared function modified	Review Coding Standard Practice for cross-code correlations.
Interface type mismatch between modules	Review integration testing test progression criteria.
Code reuse problems	Review use of assertions in Coding Standard Practice.

Figure 8.9 Example of a table listing defect causes and recommended actions.

severe defect that eludes the standard defect prevention practices, the testers, developers, and the architect should try to establish how the defect occurred and how to prevent it.

Next, it needs to be determined how best practices can be modified or extended to implement new defect prevention mechanisms. In many cases, the defect prevention mechanism involves changes in the way the team writes code, and therefore relies on customizing the best practices by adding new coding standards. Regardless of whether a general or customized new practice is needed, this practice should be implemented in the same way as all other practices, that is, phased in incrementally and supported by the infrastructure.

Once a new or modified best practice is defined, the technology infrastructure should be configured in such a way that measurement, tracking, and automation are used to facilitate the application of this practice and provide feedback of the extent to which this practice is properly followed.

8.4 POLICY FOR USE OF PROBLEM TRACKING SYSTEM

We refer to the problem tracking system as a database used to store and track defects, feature requests, and developer ideas. We recommend the following three-tier use of such a system (listed below). First, it should be used to track severe defects detected during integration, system, and acceptance testing, and should be used as a repository for the developer's ideas about what should be added or changed in current and future releases of the product. Second, it should record all defects not detected by the test suite, but reported by end users. Tracking of these defects provides valuable data about the types of defects the teams or developers tend to make. This data can be used to hone defect prevention efforts. Ideally, the system should ensure that the relevant people are automatically notified about the problem, and it should correlate defects to source code versions. The system should record and track feature requests. Third, it should be used to prioritize requests for new features. A reliable method for tracking feature requests facilitates the design phase of the next release of the product. If recorded in this way, details of features can be easily and quickly recalled when it is time to define the next feature set.

DEVELOPER'S TESTIMONIAL

One example of a software best practice would be having a "defect tracking database." This would be a place where both bugs and requests for enhancements (extra features) would be kept. This should be accessible in one form or another by both developers and customers.

I said extra features, because the requirements document should contain all required features. These extras are "if we have time, we'll get to them." Both customers and developers should have access so that both know exactly where the software is at any point.

—Nathan D. Blomquist, Software Engineer

During Development, the Problem Tracking System Should Be Used to Store Only Severe Defects, Feature Requests, and Developer Ideas When the product is in the development stage, developers build test cases as they build code. They start by creating test cases that verify that each piece of code they add or change works correctly. These test cases are collected into a regression test suite that is run on a regular basis (preferably, every night). Each time a defect is found at this stage of the development process, a developer or a tester creates a test case to verify whether the defect is fixed, and then adds this test case to the regression test suite. Test suites are thus constantly expanded and can be used to ensure that previously detected defects do not resurface as code is modified.

At this stage in the development process, the problem tracking system should be used to track only severe defects. Test cases identify each uncovered defect, so entering the same information in the defect tracking system would be superfluous. Severe defects should be stored in the problem tracking system until they are analyzed and customized practices are created to prevent them from recurring.

Exceptions to this policy should be made when the development team is finding problems with software near the release or deployment, but lacks the resources (time, tools, expertise, etc.) to write test cases for these defects. This policy holds that writing a test case and adding it to the regression test suite is the best practice for defects found during development. If this is not practical, the next best thing is to ensure that key information—such as "how to replicate" and "how to prevent" details—is not lost. All known information about the defect can be recorded in the problem tracking system and the entry can be marked with a label such as "remind" so the team does not forget to add a test case when time and resources permit. For instance, assume that a customer support representative or technical writer noticed an error while exploring the unfinished product, but is not qualified to write a test case that captures the problem. It is better to record the problem and add the test case later than to risk the problem being forgotten because a test case is not readily available.

More importantly, the problem tracking system should be used to store developer ideas at this point; every time someone has an idea for a new feature or for a better way to implement an existing feature, this idea should be recorded in the problem tracking system as a feature request.

DEVELOPER'S TESTIMONIAL

I have always thought that using a wiki board would be a good idea to cultivate ideas. The board should have a section where developers could toss their ideas up and let them get critiqued by their peers and managers. Ideas that passed the critique of peers should be seriously looked at by management.

Allowing developers to work on new ideas in a separate sandbox development area is worthwhile. If the work in the separate work area could be used in the current project it would be merged back into the main code branch. If the new code is used for a new project, this could lead to additional benefits for the company. Fred Brooks noted that software development companies should only work their employees to 80% capacity. The advantage of this is that when crunch time came the extra 20% could be used to pick up the slack and when not in crunch mode employees could be investigating new ideas that could be used to spin off new money-making projects.

—Curt Martin, Software Engineer

***After a Code Freeze,[']* the Problem Tracking System Should Be Used to Record All Defect Reports and All Feature Requests** Once the product enters the beta testing phase, the source code is typically frozen. Because code in this stage cannot be immediately modified in response to feedback, there is an added need for a problem tracking system. Thus, the problem tracking system should now include all defect reports and all feature requests. Companies often

---

['] A period of time when access to the current code baseline in the version control system is restricted so that only critical changes can be made to the code (See chapter 7).

record only "real bugs" in their defect tracking system, and soon find that there is a fine line between bugs and feature requests. While several system malfunctions are obvious results of coding defects, classification of other "problems" is more difficult. For one person, a program lacking an expected user interface functionality might be a high-priority defect, while for another it is just a new feature request.

We recommend that instead of quibbling over definitions, all feedback and change and feature requests should be recorded in the problem tracking system so they can be easily accessed later. For classification purposes, it is useful to refer to a "defect" as a product issue that prevents a user from using the system as specified, and to call everything else a feature request. As described earlier in Section 8.3 on defect analysis and prevention, defects recorded during this time are classified, analyzed, and used for the development of new practices.

Change and feature requests should be recorded in the problem tracking system throughout the code freeze stage. As feedback is received, the demand for each feature can be tracked. The first time a feature is requested it is entered in the problem tracking system. Each subsequent time a user asks for this feature, another request for this feature is recorded. If requests are tracked in this manner, it will be easier to separate the must-have features from the unusual requests.

During Release Planning, Recorded Feature Requests Should Be Prioritized and Their Implementation Scheduled When it is time to start gathering and organizing requirements for the next release, the stored information can be leveraged to improve the product. All feature requests from the problem tracking system should be evaluated and prioritized. Priority should reflect market feedback, including the count of requests received for each feature.

After determining a features hierarchy, the order of their implementation should be decided. If a feature cannot be implemented within the time allotted for the next release, that feature needs to be saved for future releases. The feasibility of implementing a feature can be determined by considering how its implementation would affect the existing design and code base. If implementation of a high-priority feature would require only minor changes to the code base, this feature should be added to the next release. However, if implementation of the most highly demanded feature would require a major redesign and rewrite of the code base, there are two choices: either the feature could be saved for a later release, or the release timeline of the product could be changed to allow sufficient time for its implementation.

Once the decision is made to implement a new feature, the related entry should be removed from the problem tracking system and incorporated into the requirements documents or, in case of an intermediate or expanded infrastructure, requirements management system, so it can be referenced by use cases and design documents. Next, the conceptual test cases should be created, which will be converted to actual test cases during design and construction to verify whether the feature is implemented thoroughly and functions correctly. Once the feature is implemented, the regression test suite will help to determine whether it meets expectations and is ready to be given to customers.

PROBLEM TRACKING SYSTEMS AND GROUP CULTURE

Problem, issue, and defect tracking systems can play a significant role in building a positive group culture. Very few people think about these systems in this way because they are primarily used to keep track of developers' mistakes. However, if these systems are used for other purposes, they can help encourage code ownership. Developers will use and grow to value a defect tracking system if it provides valuable information about their products, and allows them to express their ideas. Thus, one important, but often overlooked, use for a problem tracking system is as a repository of developers' ideas for current or future releases. This shows developers that they are the driving force behind future projects/releases and increases their investment in its success.

When deciding which ideas to include and which to leave out, one should keep in mind the following: not respecting the developers' ideas will stifle their creativity. While not every idea is great, every idea should be evaluated. As time passes, people will think about and discuss the ideas that were recorded; flawed ideas will be exposed as such, and either be replaced with better ideas or just die away. Good ideas will persevere and most probably be incorporated into the code. The developer's ideas should never be discounted. Such an attitude undermines developers' creativity and can limit a group's success.

8.4.1 Measurements of Data Related to the Problem Tracking System

The number of severe defects reported by testers in the problem tracking system should be calculated together with the corresponding new practices developed based on the analysis of these defects.

Also, the number of defects reported by the customers should be used as an indicator of the released product quality. The count of customer requests for each feature should be used as an indicator of the implementation priority of this feature in the next product release.

8.4.2 Tracking of Data Related to the Problem Tracking System

In addition to the above measures, the following information should be tracked: the number of defects reported by the customers together with the number of defects fixed, and unresolved. Also, the number of defects detected but not retested, and tests that failed should be tracked.

8.5 POLICY FOR USE OF REGRESSION TESTING SYSTEM

The regression testing system is a part of an intermediate or expanded infrastructure. It consists of a suite of tests, developed gradually as the white and black box tests pass. Once in place, the regression suite verifies that implemented functionality continues to work properly after each new code addition to the application.

The policies described below are designed to ensure that the regression system is used effectively to identify all code regressions as soon as they are diagnosed and that the timely removal of regression defects is properly facilitated.

The Regression System Should Be Configured so that It Provides Detailed Result Information The regression system should be configured to provide sufficient detail for an architect or developer to review the regression report and be able to investigate the problem without having to run any additional tests. For example, for unit testing regressions the results should indicate the type of problem that occurred (unexpected outcome, uncaught runtime exception, etc.), the inputs that uncovered the problem, the unit, and the stack trace.[u] The stack trace is especially useful to identify defects causing abnormal program termination, as the exact instruction that caused the failure is displayed.

In all cases, the regression system results should provide more detail than the data tracked by the other components of the infrastructure, and the amount of information should be sufficient to identify the location and the cause of the regression.

Regression Tests Should Be Executed Automatically After Each Build The earlier that regression problems are detected, the faster, easier, and less costly it is to fix them. Therefore, the regression test execution should be integrated with the automated build system and executed immediately after each build. As a result of this approach, regression defects will be uncovered soon after they are introduced, and they can be fixed before they propagate to other parts of the code.

Regression Test Results Should Be Reviewed at the Beginning of Each Work Day and the Test Suite Should Be Updated as Needed Each regression test failure should be examined to determine whether the reported problem indicates a defect in the code or in the test suite. If the failure indicates a problem with the code, the developers should fix the code immediately, before starting work on new functionality.

---

[u] This is a backtrace of stack activities during the program execution.

If the failure indicates a problem with a regression test, for example, as uncovered by a false positive result, the developers should correct the test immediately to avoid the reporting of subsequent false positive results, which in the long run can desensitize the team to all reported defects. For example, assume that a test case failed because the code functionality intentionally changed, and the expected test case outcome should have been modified. The developers responsible for that test case should update the test case with the new expected outcome.

This review process should occur at the beginning of each day. Otherwise, the team members reduce their opportunity to learn from their mistakes. If the team does not recognize the problem, and the architect and testers do not immediately work to prevent it from recurring, developers may repeat the same mistake in successive developments, because they are unaware of the problem and/or because the process has not yet been improved to prevent that mistake.

Regression Tests Results Should Be Used to Assess the Deployment Readiness of the System. When the project nears release, the manager and architect should determine the ratio of regression test passes to the total number of regression tests executed that must be achieved before the software could be considered deployment ready. For example, this ratio could be 95% if the architect has developed a good understating of the product and the test status, and estimates that approximately 5% of failures are due to false positive results.

8.5.1   Measurements Related to the Regression Testing System

The number of passed, failed, and incomplete test cases for all the regression tests that were run should be calculated after each execution of the regression suite. Figure 8.10 shows a graph from the reporting system that tracks this measure over several days.

8.5.2   Tracking of Data Related to the Regression Testing System

The following information should be tracked:

- Test cases that were executed
- The number of passed, failed, and total regression tests executed
- The percentage of the code covered by regression tests

8.6   EXAMPLES

8.6.1   Focus on Defect Tracking Reports

The reporting system should generate graphs illustrating the number of reported defects that are fixed, are currently being fixed (in progress), or are unresolved, as shown in Figure 8.11. As the iteration nears its completion, the

Testing Overview

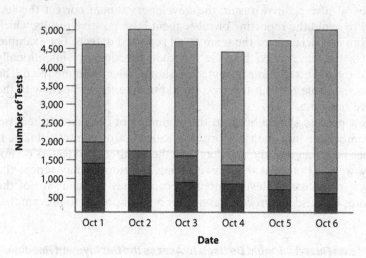

Testing Details

Date	Failed	Incomplete	Pass
Oct 6	659	583	3872
Oct 5	748	402	3932
Oct 4	803	423	3293
Oct 3	927	612	3302

Figure 8.10   Testing overview from the reporting system.

number of fixed defects should approach the total number of defects uncovered.

8.6.2   Focus on Test Type Reports

The reporting system should also generate a comprehensive graph showing the number of failed, passed, and incomplete tests for each type of testing conducted, as shown in Figure 8.12.

8.6.3   Example of a Root Cause Analysis of a Design and Testing Defect

This example [22] is inspired by a real event [23], which took place at one of the busiest airports in the United States. However, the root cause analysis of the defect is strictly hypothetical and its sole purpose is to serve as an example of a defect prevention process. (See Figures 8.13 and 8.14.)

Defects Overview

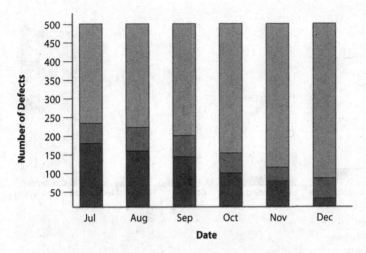

Defects Details

Date	Unresolved	In Progress	Fixed
Dec	30	50	420
Nov	70	40	390
Oct	100	50	350
Sep	140	60	300

Figure 8.11   Defect graph from the reporting system.

Defect Identification

Background   Airport baggage scanning systems randomly insert threat images of items such as "bags with weapons" to keep the screeners alert. Normally, when such an image is inserted, after a short delay, a flashing message on the screen appears stating: "This is a test." The Threat Image Projection System (TIPS) is an embedded component of such a baggage scanning x-ray machine. TIPS, which contains a threat image library, randomly selects and projects threat images.

There are four levels of access authority for the TIPS users:

Level 1 are Transportation Security Administration (TSA) screeners.

Level 2 are checkpoint supervisors who may review the performance of the TSA screeners.

Level 3 are site manager and airline guard firm authorized personnel members who may review or download reports and add/delete and modify user authorization.

Tests by Type

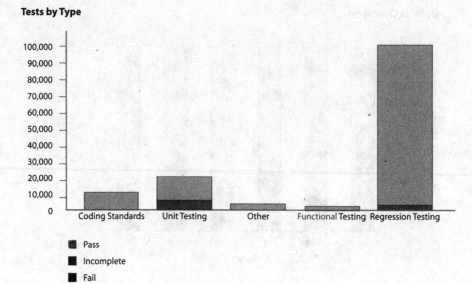

Figure 8.12   View of the types of tests and counts of failed, passed, or incomplete tests.

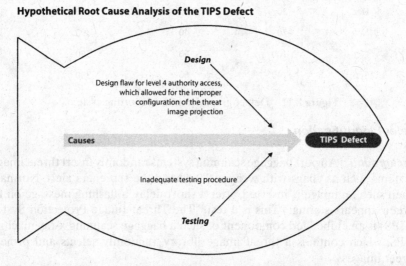

Figure 8.13   Fishbone diagram illustrating possible causes of the TIPS defect.

Level 4 are Federal Aviation Administration representatives who have all three levels of privileges and additionally can schedule test threat image insertions and administer the threats image library.

Software Defect   During routine screening, the TIPS in the x-ray screening system inserted a test image "baggage with explosive weapon," but it failed

Problem Description	Cause Category	Cause Description	Recommended Practice	Measurement, Tracking, and Automation
Failure to display "This is a test" message	Design	Design did not include configuration verification and checks for the test message displays.	Add a feature synchronization policy to the design. Review time synchronization of the thread image and test message.	Track whether the code corresponding to synchronized features has been inspected.
	Testing	Testing did not check for TIPS configuration defects.	Add test cases that verify time synchronization between corresponding features. In this case a thread image should be displayed at the same time as the test message.	Use record/playback tools; measure and track the number of passed tests. Pass rate on synchronized features should be 100%.

Figure 8.14 Preventive action plan and best practices to prevent synchronization problems.

to indicate that it was a test. The message "This is a test" did not appear on the screen. Therefore, the TSA screeners proceeded to perform a routine search looking for the suspicious bag in the conveyor belt. Since they did not find it, the entire security area was evacuated, the flights were grounded, and a police bomb squad was called.

8.7 ACRONYMS

ALB   A value just above the lower boundary of an equivalence class
AUB   A value just above the upper bound of an equivalence class
BLB   A value just below the lower boundary of an equivalence class
BUB   A value just below the upper bound of an equivalence class
LB   The value at the lower bound of an equivalence class
UB   The value at the upper bound of an equivalence class

8.8 GLOSSARY

acceptance testing Testing conducted to determine whether a system satisfies specified acceptance criteria, by which the user decides whether to accept the system. [6]*

alpha testing Part of the acceptance testing conducted by the developing organization in a laboratory setting.

beta release The official release of a prerelease version of software that is sent out to a small group of users for testing.

beta testing   Part of the acceptance testing conducted both by the customer at the customer's site and by the developing organization.

code review   A meeting at which software code is presented to project personnel, managers, users, customers, or other interested parties for comments or approval. [6]*

coverage analysis   A set of techniques used to measure how much of the code was exercised with respect to a predefined criterion.

coverage criterion   Test adequacy criteria pertaining to code coverage and used to define test stopping rules. For example, 100% statement coverage requires that 100% of the statements be executed by tests in question.

equivalence class partitioning   A technique for dividing the test input domain into distinct subsets, which are processed similarly by the target software.

integration testing   Testing in which software components, hardware components, or both are combined and tested to evaluate the interaction between them. [6]*

load stress testing   Testing to determine whether the system continues to function properly under extreme loads that cause maximum resource allocations.

path   A sequence of instructions that may be performed in the execution of a computer program. [6]*

performance testing   Testing conducted to evaluate the compliance of a system or a component with specified performance requirements. [6]*

regression testing   Selective retesting of a system or component to verify that modifications have not caused unintended effects and that the system or component still complies with its specified requirements. [6]*

runtime exception   An exception thrown when incompatibility is detected at runtime.

stub   (1) A skeletal or special-purpose implementation of a software element, used to develop or test a unit that calls or is otherwise dependent on it. (2) A computer program statement substituting for the body of a software element that is or will be defined elsewhere. [6]*

system testing   Testing conducted on a complete, integrated system to evaluate the system's compliance with its specified requirements. [6]*

test case   A test-related item that contains the following information: (1) A set of test inputs (data items received from an external source by the code-under-test; the external source can be hardware, software, or human); (2) execution conditions (conditions required for running the test, for example, a certain state of a database, or a configuration of a hardware device); (3) expected outputs (the results to be produced by the code-under-test).

test harness   The auxiliary code supporting execution of test cases. It consists of drivers that call the tested code and stubs that represent called elements. [10]

trap doors Unprotected entries to the system.

Trojan horse A disguised, malicious code embedded within a legitimate program.

user testing Testing that requires users to perform required system functionalities. [4]

8.9 REFERENCES

[1] Zelkowitz, M.V., Shaw, A.C., and Gannon, J.D., *Principles of Software Engineering and Design*. Prentice-Hall, Englewood Cliffs, NJ, 1979.

[2] Holmes, J.S., "Optimizing the Software Life Cycle," *Software Quality Professional*, Vol. 5, No. 4, 2003.

[3] Deiß, T., Nyberg, A., Schultz, S., and Willcock, C., "Industrial Deployment of the TTCN-3 Testing Technology," *IEEE Software*, Vol. 23, No. 4, July/August 2006, pp. 48–54.

[4] Tillman, N. and Schulte, W., "Unit Tests Reloaded: Parameterized Unit Testing with Symbolic Execution," *IEEE Software*, Vol. 23, No. 4, July/August 2006, pp. 38–47.

[5] National Institute of Standards and Technology, *The Economic Impacts of Inadequate Infrastructure for Software Testing*, Washington D.C., 2002, http://www.nist.gov/director/prog-ofc/report02-3.pdf (retrieved: July 7, 2006).

[6] Institute of Electrical and Electronics Engineers, *IEEE Standard 610.12-1990—Glossary of Software Engineering Terminology*, 1990.

[7] Myers, G.J., *The Art of Software Testing*. John Wiley & Sons, New York, 1979.

[8] Zhu, P., Hall, P., and May, J. "Software Unit Test Coverage and Adequacy," *ACM Computing Surveys*, Vol. 29, No. 4, 1997, pp. 366–427.

[9] Runeson P., "A Survey of Unit Testing Practices," *IEEE Software*, Vol. 23, No. 4, July/August 2006, pp. 22–29.

[10] Burnstein, I., *Practical Software Testing: A Process Oriented Approach*. Springer, 2002.

[11] Beizer, B., *Software Testing Techniques*. Van Nostrand Reinhold, 2nd ed., 1990.

[12] Fagan, M., "Design and Code Inspections to Reduce Errors in Program Development," *IBM Systems Journal*, Vol. 15, No. 3, 1976, pp. 182–211.

[13] Myers, G. "A Controlled Experiment in Program Testing and Code Walk-throughs/Inspections," *Communications of ACM*, 1978, pp. 760–768.

[14] Beck, K. and Andres, C., *Extreme Programming Explained: Embrace Change*. Addison Wesley, 2nd ed., 2004.

[15] Constantine, L., *Constantine on Peopleware*. Yourdon Press Computing Series, Prentice Hall, 1995.

[16] Hutchins, E., "Cognition in the Wild," *MIT Press*, Cambridge, MA, 1995.

[17] Williams, L., Kessler, R.R., Cunningham, W., and Jeffries, R., "Strengthening the Case for Pair Programming," *IEEE Software*, Vol. 17, No. 4, July/August 2000, pp. 19–25.

[18] Lui, K.M. and Chan, K.C.C., "Pair Programming Productivity: Novice—Novice vs. Expert–Expert," *International Journal of Human-Computer Studies*, Elsevier, Vol. 64, No. 9, September 2006, pp. 915–925.

[19] Manascé, D.A., "Load Testing of Web Sites," *IEEE Internet Computing*, July/August 2002, pp. 70–74.

[20] Kaner, C., Falk, J., and Nguyen, H.Q., *Testing Computer Software*. John Wiley & Sons, 2nd ed., 1999.

[21] Institute of Electrical and Electronics Engineers, *IEEE Standard 1044-1993—Classification for Software Anomalies*, 1993.

[22] Shui, E., Blackboard Online Discussion Posting, CPSC 542, "Software Validation and Verification," Department of Computer Science, California State University—Fullerton, June 2006.

[23] Cable News Network, *TSA: Computer Glitch Led to Atlanta Airport Scare*, April 21, 2006, http://www.cnn.com/2006/US/04/20/atlanta.airport/index.html (retrieved: September 22, 2006).

8.10 EXERCISES

1. What is the primary goal of white box unit testing?

2. What is the primary goal of back box testing?

3. Why are code reviews necessary and what parts of the code should be reviewed most often?

4. What kind of defects should integration testing reveal?

5. What criteria should be defined by management for progression through testing levels and why it is important to have such criteria?

6. What is role of regression testing and how can regression testing be automated?

7. What measures should be used to evaluate the status of the system testing?

8. Why is it important to record developers' ideas and suggestions for product enhancements and how can this process be facilitated?

9. What is the difference between alpha and beta testing?

10. Give a complete and detailed example of the defect prevention cycle: the defect that is identified, how its root cause is determined, where in the process it occurred, how the process is modified to prevent the defect from recurring, and how the modified process is monitored.

CHAPTER 9

TREND ANALYSIS AND DEPLOYMENT

One accurate measurement is worth a thousand expert opinions.
—Grace Hopper

9.1 INTRODUCTION

Throughout this book, we have illustrated the importance of measurements and tracking, and shown how they can be used to monitor the progress and status of the system under development. With the appropriate infrastructure in place, the process of collecting data is automated and seamless. Moreover, the infrastructure's reporting system should not only serve as a repository of the collected data, but also produce indicators that facilitate management decisions.

One of the fundamental problems that managers face today is information overload [1] and "analysis paralysis." A multitude of reports provide detailed indicators of the project progress, but often it is quite unclear whether the data is correct, and even more so, how to interpret it. Automation of data collection ensures that human errors of data entry are avoided, but it does not guarantee the correctness of the system that generated the data. In addition, some of the data generated is immaterial or simply just noise. Thus, when analyzing the data, team members should look for *trends* rather than absolute values.

Automated Defect Prevention: Best Practices in Software Management, by Dorota Huizinga and Adam Kolawa
Copyright © 2007 John Wiley & Sons, Inc.

The ability to discern relevant information from extraneous data, and properly interpret it, is one of the most important skills of the architect and project manager. This skill is developed through both training and the experience of observing and assessing data trends throughout project development. Interpreting trends and taking appropriate action in response to any revealed problems is critical to ensuring that project costs remain acceptable, the project schedule is followed, and development activities stay under control.

The intent of this chapter is to help develop such an intuition in observing and evaluating trends, and to facilitate decision making based on those tendencies. While evaluating trends, managers and architects should be able to assess project progress and make relevant decisions, including those related to release readiness.

9.2 TRENDS IN PROCESS CONTROL

Software processes measured and tracked throughout the project lifetime should be treated as statistical processes [2]. The data generated by the project infrastructure and presented by the reporting system should be used to evaluate trends in these processes. Eventually, a predefined level of stabilization and capability should be achieved. We have introduced the notions of stable and capable processes in Chapter 2. This section provides more detail and examples of these concepts in the context of ADP.

9.2.1 Process Variations

Variations in a process are observable, temporal changes in the expected values of its metrics. Deming [3] lists two primary reasons for variations: those that result from common causes and those that stem from special causes. A common cause, for example, is a reassignment of task priorities and teamwork based on analysis of reports from the last build. Interfering with a process that shows a common-cause variation is detrimental and it may have a negative impact on the team, its cohesion and culture, by being perceived as micromanagement. However, special causes of variations, such as a sudden steep increase in regression test failures, should be investigated because they might indicate that a process is out of control.

9.2.2 Process Stabilization

A *stable process* is predictable in the sense that its variation is limited. For example, when the process measure variations are plotted on a control chart, they fall between the upper control limit (upper threshold) and the lower control limit (lower threshold). These limits should be defined based on statistical quality control models such as Six Sigma [4]. Six Sigma is a quality management program that measures and improves a company's operational

Coding Standards for Files

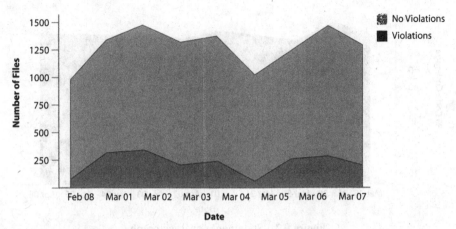

Figure 9.1 Coding standards for files.

performance by identifying and correcting defects in its processes and products. A process whose variations are due to common causes should be considered under control even if its measures are temporarily outside of the control limits.

As the project progresses, the trends in its processes should stabilize. For example, the ratio of failures to the total number of test cases that were run should continue to decrease. The sawtooth pattern on a graph would indicate that tests are being added and executed, while defects are being fixed.

Similarly, substantial variations will be initially observable in the coding standards reports. However, the ratio of files that failed coding standards to the total number of files should continue to decrease. Again, the sawtooth pattern should be perceptible, as shown in Figure 9.1, which indicates that files are being added, tested, and fixed to meet coding standards. The variations should eventually level off to indicate process stabilization.

9.2.3 Process Capability

For a process to be considered *capable*, it must be stable and the expected value of its plotted measures must fall within specified limits. A process that is under control, but does not meet its target levels, would be considered stable but not capable.

For example, if a *code coverage* graph shows stability around 40%, the process is not capable. The statement coverage should be approximately 90% or above to be considered capable, as shown in Figure 9.2. All of the measures pertaining to product quality and the status of its implementation should be deemed capable before the application is released.

Code Coverage

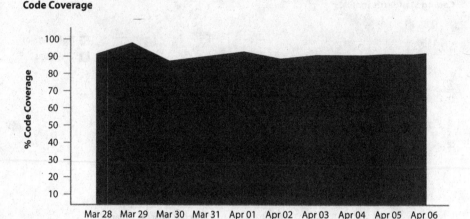

Figure 9.2 Statement coverage graph.

9.3 TRENDS IN PROJECT PROGRESS

This section describes measures that can be used to evaluate project progress. Specifically, it explains how to analyze trends in data related to the implementation of features and requirements, changes in code base size, test results and the number of reported defects, as well as project cost and schedule. We describe both desirable and undesirable trends, and suggest actions that need to be taken in response to those trends.

9.3.1 Analyzing Features/Requirements Implementation Status

Trends in data related to the implementation of features and requirements indicate the progress of the project. Analysis of these trends helps the team members to understand the current implementation status and to estimate the amount of work that still needs to be completed either in the current iteration or before the product can be released.

The following questions regarding features/requirements implementation status should be answered:

- How long will it take to implement currently scheduled features/requirements?
- Are features/requirements being properly implemented or are they migrating into defects because requirements were not thought through or were incorrectly described?
- Are features becoming more complex?

Features/Requirements Testing and Implementation Overview

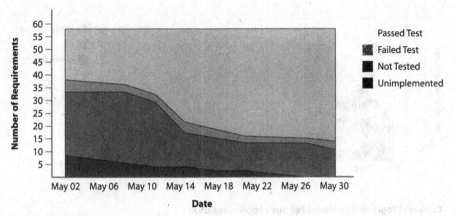

Figure 9.3 Features requirements graph showing the number of requirements that are unimplemented, are not tested, have failed testing, and are implemented and passed testing.

The features/requirements testing and implementation overview graph helps to answer these questions. If the project is progressing well, the number of new features/requirements should steadily increase before eventually leveling off. As implementation and testing advance, the number of implemented features/requirements should lag slightly behind, but ultimately approach the total number of features/requirements upon the completion of the project.

Figure 9.3 depicts a graph that tracks the implementation status of features/requirements for the project. The graph values correspond to the total number of planned features/requirements, the number of features/requirements that are unimplemented, implemented but not tested, as well as those that failed testing, and the number of features that are implemented and passed testing.

A quick and less-detailed view of the features implementation status is provided by the graph in Figure 9.4, which illustrates the number of unimplemented, in-progress, and implemented features.

It is important to note that the trends exhibited by a features graph will vary depending on the software development process model used by the team. For instance, if a traditional waterfall [5] model is used, a graph will show a rising trend in unimplemented features until the requirements phase is completed, followed by a steady decline in unimplemented features coupled with an increase in in-progress and completed features. On the other hand, a team using the extreme programming [6] approach would see a rising trend in uncompleted features/requirements almost immediately followed by a rise in in-progress and completed features.

These are illustrative trends and they do not show any unexpected or special-cause variations that may arise. However, if the total number of

Waterfall Model Features Implementation

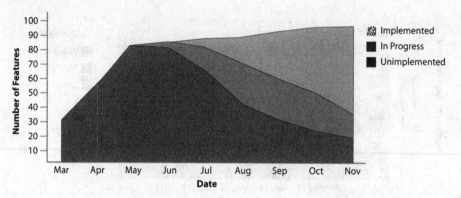

Extreme Programming Model Features Implementation

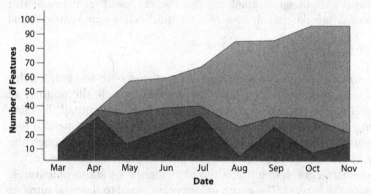

Figure 9.4   Features implementation status comparison of waterfall and extreme programming process models.

features does not stabilize as the product is nearing release, this might be an indication of a flaw in the requirements gathering process, and possible failure to comply with the best practices for requirement specification and management described in Chapter 4.

For teams using an intermediate or expanded infrastructure, another factor that will influence the patterns exhibited by this graph is the manner in which the team members use the requirements management system. If it is used solely to record and track features and requirements scheduled for implementation in the upcoming iteration or product release, the number of unimplemented requirements should stabilize very close to zero prior to release, as shown in Figure 9.5.

However, if the requirements management system is being used to record requests and ideas for later releases as well as requirements for the immediate release, it should be expected that some requirements would remain uncom-

Requirements Implementation Overview

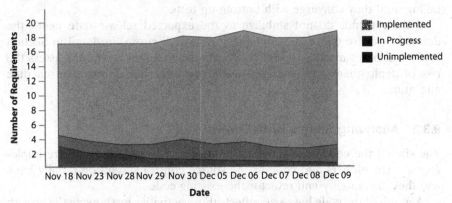

Figure 9.5 Stabilization of feature/requirements graph with the number of unimplemented features/requirements approaching zero.

Requirements Implementation Overview

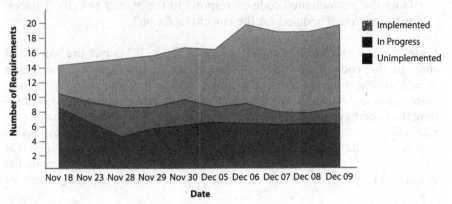

Figure 9.6 A feature/requirements graph that stabilizes with the number of unimplemented features above zero.

pleted before the release. This will result in a graph with a greater number of unimplemented features, as shown in Figure 9.6.

As requirements are implemented, correlated activities represented in corresponding graphs should be examined. For example, if the team creates test cases each time a new requirement is implemented, the number of tests should increase. If the team is adding the tests *after* the requirements are implemented, these tests should show a progressing trend in passing. However, if the team is creating the tests *before* the requirements are implemented (as, for instance in TDD [7]), these tests will initially fail and then gradually start to pass as the corresponding code is built. For the teams using the approach described in this book, top-down service and module-level tests will keep failing until they converge with bottom-up tests.

If these trends do not stabilize as the expected release date nears, the derived measure called the *confidence factor* (discussed in detail in Section 9.4.3) and other metrics should be closely examined to accurately assess the risk of deployment and to make an informed decision concerning schedule alteration.

9.3.2 Analyzing Source Code Growth

The size of the code base grows over time as new requirements are implemented. Developers add code to the source control system on a daily basis and they also modify and refactor the existing code.

A graph of the code base size reflects those activities by showing the growth rate and revealing long-term trends. When analyzing the size of the code base, the following questions should be asked:

- How fast is code being constructed?
- Does the implemented code correspond to the highest priority features/requirements scheduled for the current iteration?

Code base size graphs like the one shown in Figure 9.7 depict the amount of code in the code base stored in the source control system. This graph should exhibit different trends depending on the project's current development phase and iteration. During initial planning and requirements specification, the code base graph is level, reflecting the amount of code in the project retained from the previous release. However, as soon as the construction begins, the code base size should start increasing, with occasional dips that result from code being removed for refactoring or reuse. For example, the graph in Figure 9.7 has a dip on April 5. Such dips are typically a sign of

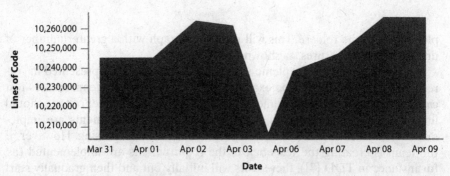

Figure 9.7 Code base size graph.

a healthy development process: developers are actively revising the code to make it more efficient. However, it is recommended that dips be investigated to confirm that they are the result of routine code cleanup rather than accidental deletions or other problems. This investigation requires carefully examining related reports. The first step is to review the *code check-ins* graph, which displays how many files were checked in on a given date, as shown in Figure 9.8.

The increase of check-ins on April 6 and 7 indicates that the developers are committing revised files after refactoring the application. Normally, a significant number of checked-in files are expected after changes due to code reuse, refactoring, or even accidental deletions, all of which result in new or modified files being copied to the source control system. From there, it is helpful to review the *modified files source control details* report, shown in Figure 9.9, and then to review the comments that developers entered to describe the changes.

As the project nears deployment, the total number of lines of code should level off (resulting in a relatively flat graph, as shown in Figure 9.10). On the

Check-Ins

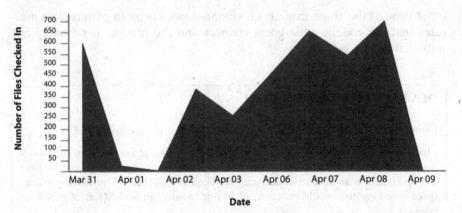

Figure 9.8   Code check-ins.

Date	Version	Group	Lines changed	Comment
4/5/06 1:21 PM	1.7	Group A	+54/-26	Remove jar shadow
4/3/06 4:24 PM	1.6	Group A	+12/-10	Fix property name
3/20/06 12:05 PM	1.5	Group B	+15/-36	Excludes added
2/17/06 12:26 PM	1.4	Group B	+10/-50	New excludes
2/16/06 1:17 PM1.2	1.2	Group A	+110/-10	Minor fix
1/5/06 11:42 AM1.1	1.1	Group A	+8/-48	Original source code

Figure 9.9   Source control details.

Code Base Size

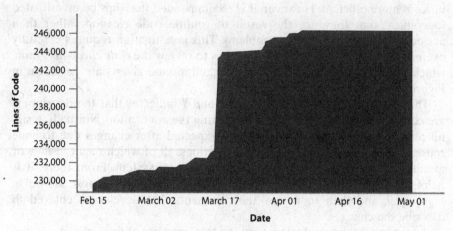

Figure 9.10 Stabilization of the code base size.

other hand, if the graph exhibits an up-and-down sawtooth pattern, this indicates that the code is undergoing changes and the product is probably not stable enough to be released.

DEVELOPER'S TESTIMONIAL

I would worry about a high amount of check-ins past the testing period.

I have seen situations where code has passed the testing phase but then the developer continues working on the code, making minor tweaks here and there. If there is a spike in the amount of code being checked in but there is no corresponding spike in testing, that would concern me. Minor tweaks can lead to lots of problems later on.

—Eugene Ngo, Software Developer

9.3.3 Analyzing Test Results

Test results should be collected daily and include outcomes of coding standards analysis, unit, integration, regression, and eventually acceptance tests. The following are the questions to ask when evaluating test results:

- Are new test cases being added at the expected rate as features/requirements are being implemented?
- Is the test failure rate decreasing?
- Is the test failure rate too high?

Tests result graphs, as shown in Figure 9.11, address these questions.

The general trend should be an increasing number of passed tests and decreasing number of failed tests. However, within these general trends, small variations of increasing failed tests and decreasing passed tests are expected. These variations are caused by large code check-ins and can be correlated with peaks in the code base size graph.

The overall number of files checked in may decrease if the code size dip resulted from file deletions. The number of coding standards violations will typically remain stable or decrease (often because of developers fixing coding standards violations in legacy code as part of their refactoring efforts), as shown in Figure 9.12. However, regression test failures typically would increase because of code modifications.

Tests

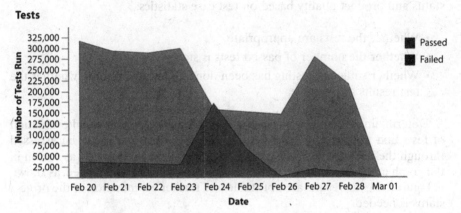

Figure 9.11 Test results graph showing the number of tests passed and failed.

Coding Standards Violations

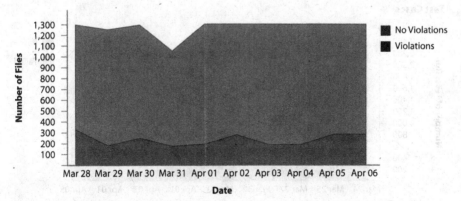

Figure 9.12 Coding standards violations, which shows the number of files with no violations and files with one or more violations.

Failures that occur after large code check-ins may result from intentional or unintentional code functionality changes. If code functionality modifications were intentional, because of a new feature implementation or specification change, test cases related to this functionality are expected to fail because the new outcomes are different from those recorded in the baseline regression suite. In this case, the test cases should be updated. However, if the code functionality changes are unintentional, this indicates defects in the code. In this case, the code needs to be repaired immediately. For subsequent tests after the test failures are addressed (by updating the test case expected outcomes or by modifying the code), the graph should resume its expected pattern of increasing number of passed tests and decreasing number of failed tests until the next significant change in the code size takes place.

There are three important factors to consider when evaluating project status and product quality based on test case statistics:

- Whether the tests are appropriate
- Whether the number of passed tests is stable
- Whether sufficient testing has been done, or, in other words, whether the test results are capable.

Determining whether the tests are appropriate requires manual evaluation of tests and their results. The stability of passed test cases can be assessed through the tests graph; if the passed test cases have leveled off (as shown in the graph in Figure 9.13), the results are stable. If the graph is jagged, as shown in Figure 9.14, the results are not stable and further examination of the project status is needed.

Test progression criteria defined in Chapter 8 should be used to determine whether a sufficient amount of testing has been conducted and therefore test results are capable.

Test Cases

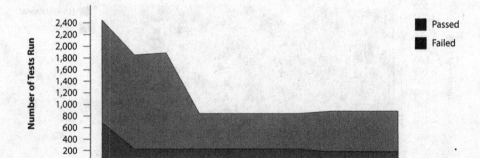

Figure 9.13   Stabilization of test results.

Test Cases

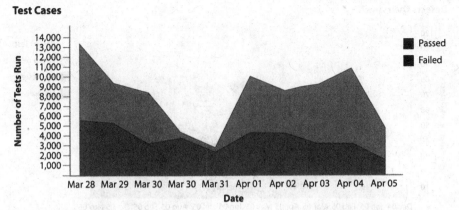

Figure 9.14   Fluctuating test results for passed and failed test cases.

Defects Overview

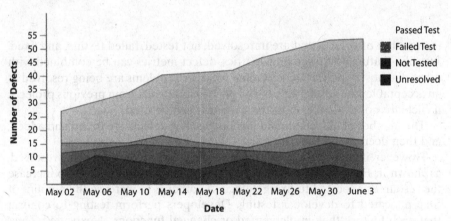

Figure 9.15   Defects overview graph shows the number of defects that are unresolved, are not tested, have failed testing, and are fixed and passed testing.

9.3.4   Analyzing Defects

Defect metrics reflect the number of discovered defects that need to be resolved before a project can be declared complete and ready to be released. As the features/requirements are being implemented, defects are found. The following questions regarding defects need to be answered:

- Is the total number of defects steadily decreasing?
- Are there any undesirable trends that may indicate that the number of defects is not under control?

A *defects overview* graph, shown in Figure 9.15, reveals the total number of defects that developers need to fix in the current iteration. It also shows

Defects Overview

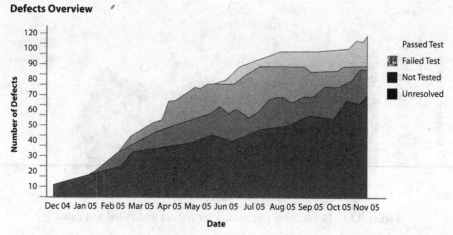

Figure 9.16 Undesirable trend of defect discovery rate being higher than defect fix rate.

the number of defects that are unresolved, not tested, failed testing, and fixed. Just like features/requirements metrics, defect metrics can be combined with other diagnostic metrics to determine whether problems are being resolved at an acceptable rate (preferably based on measurements from previous projects; if such are not available, industry standards can be used).

The number of defects should increase as new defects are found and added, and then decrease as they are fixed.

However, if defects are being discovered faster than they are being resolved, as shown in Figure 9.16, this indicates a problem. One solution is to increase the resources allocated to fixing defects. Another is to increase the amount of time allocated to developer testing. Developers perform testing to confirm that each feature they implemented or changed functions as expected. Thus, it is reasonable to expect that if more time is spent in testing, fewer defects will remain in the code after it is checked into the source control system.

As the project progresses, the defect metrics will show whether the number of resolved defects is increasing, which indicates the defects are being assigned and resolved soon after they are discovered. Once defect metrics are under control, the line reflecting fixed defects in the graph will fluctuate, resembling a sawtooth pattern. Slight variations in this pattern are acceptable.

However, other patterns can exist. Perhaps the line representing the unresolved defects is steadily increasing without any dips, which shows that many defects are being found, but few, if any, are being resolved. This could mean that many defects are not being identified and resolved during development, before code is checked in. If a sawtooth pattern is not reflected in the graph, the problem should be investigated and remedied. Once the problem is identified, it needs to be determined whether the feature affected by the defect should be included in the upcoming release or whether it should be scheduled for the next release. If fixing the defect requires substantial code change, it may be necessary to delay including this feature until the next product version to avoid missing the deadline for the current release.

To aid in isolating the causes of defects, the reporting system should be able to correlate defect fixes with the source code. The system should insert comments inside the code to differentiate which files were fixed or modified due to a specific problem.

9.3.5 Analyzing Cost and Schedule

In addition to the implementation status of the product, measures for calculating project cost and schedule should be tracked. The earned value management (EVM) [8] is a technique that objectively tracks physical accomplishment of work. Using this technique, cost and schedule measures can be calculated at the project or at a composite organization level. Cost performance index (CPI) and schedule performance index (SPI) are such measures. CPI is calculated by dividing the budgeted cost of work performed by the actual cost of work performed. SPI is calculated by dividing the budgeted cost of work performed by the budgeted cost of work scheduled.

The chart in Figure 9.17 [9] shows an example of earned value for a process. The upper and lower thresholds of the control chart can be specified by management or can be based on statistical calculations.

If the limits are based on statistical calculations, they should be calculated from a large set of data, such as data across a dozen projects each of at least 6 months' duration. This chart indicates the process SPI falls within the normal common variance levels; it is basically on schedule and it should be considered capable. The CPI indicates a trend toward overspending, as a number of points are trending toward the lower threshold. The cost trend should be investigated.

9.4 BEST PRACTICES FOR DEPLOYMENT AND TRANSITION

Deployment is the process of copying the application to a location where it can be exercised—either for actual in-the-field usage, or to permit advanced testing, such as system testing, load and performance testing, and acceptance testing.

The application readiness for release, which is the deployment to its production environment, is one of the most difficult management decisions to make, as many factors need to be taken into account.

9.4.1 Deployment to a Staging System

Although teams often delay deployment planning and execution until the later phases of the development process, in our approach both the deployment plan

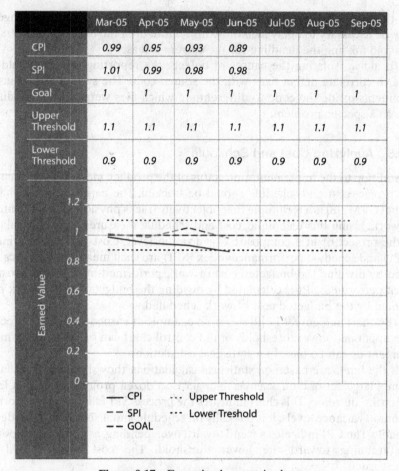

	Mar-05	Apr-05	May-05	Jun-05	Jul-05	Aug-05	Sep-05
CPI	0.99	0.95	0.93	0.89			
SPI	1.01	0.99	0.98	0.98			
Goal	1	1	1	1	1	1	1
Upper Threshold	1.1	1.1	1.1	1.1	1.1	1.1	1.1
Lower Threshold	0.9	0.9	0.9	0.9	0.9	0.9	0.9

Figure 9.17 Earned value metric chart.

and its implementation start during the extended planning and infrastructure phase, when staging systems are created.

Frequent and iterative deployment to the staging system is a recommended practice of ADP. As soon as a module or component is completed and passes the required test progression criteria, it should be deployed to the staging system, so the testers can start conducting integration- and system-level tests.

If a severe defect is found while code is still being constructed, the team can perform root cause analysis and create a new practice to prevent the introduction of similar defects. If integration- and system-level testing are delayed until the end of the construction process, an important source of mid-project defect prevention is reduced.

9.4.2 Automation of the Deployment Process

The process of deploying an application to a staging or production system can be performed manually, but such an approach is error-prone and it is likely to result in inconsistencies or defects that affect the functionality of the application. If manual deployment takes place, it is crucial to develop detailed documentation that specifies all file locations, as this will help in repeating the process in the future.

Generally, to attain higher levels of robustness and repeatability it is necessary to use an automated procedure. Fine-tuning the automation of the deployment process itself is another essential practice. If an application is not built correctly at the deployed location (files are missing, outdated versions of source files are retrieved, compilations do not use appropriate flags), there is a high risk that the application will not meet expectations of functionality and quality. Also, the longer the delay between starting deployment and developing the application, the more problems are likely to accumulate. The recommended approach is to create a minimal deployment infrastructure as soon as possible, then update and extend it as necessary.

In the past, when an application consisted of a single executable file, the only necessary step for deployment was to copy it to the target location. Modern applications are generally much more difficult to deploy because they are comprised of multiple, interdependent elements. Thus, deployment of such applications often requires the copying of multilevel directory structures and system-level configuration.

The ideal deployment process to a staging system should involve the following steps:

1. The source of the application should be stored in the source code control system.
2. The staging system should be cleaned. This is helpful in determining whether the deployment infrastructure can successfully create or recreate the application from scratch.
3. The deployment technology should automatically access the most recent versions of the files from the source control system, and then perform all necessary operations to build the application such as configuring the build process and compiling and linking all needed files.

Perhaps the most common deployment solution is to use a mix of scripts or batch files, along with some written notes about problems that resurfaced in past deployments. Scripting languages can be used to create a custom deployment process.

A faster, easier, and less error-prone method of deployment is to use a tool that automates all the tasks required for deployment (i.e., performs all transfers, compilations, and other operations necessary to build the application and the target location). If such a technology is used, a deployment infrastructure that allows for recreating or updating the staging system on demand with a click of a button (or automatically as part of a periodically scheduled build) can be established. Automating the deployment process should also record all essential deployment information in a script or file so that it can easily be passed on to testers and developers looking to create a similar deployment infrastructure.

9.4.3 Assessing Release Readiness

Release is the process of deployment to the production environment. The reporting system data and the calculated measures should provide a comprehensive view of the system under development and facilitate release-readiness decisions. Release readiness should be determined by tracking and assessing these multiple indicators over an extended period, evaluating their correlation, and obtaining a thorough understanding of the application's functionality and quality status. (See Figure 9.18.)

In addition to the previously discussed metrics, one of the most important measures in determining release readiness is the product status *confidence factor* (CF). The confidence factor is a derived measure calculated as an aggregate of the individual metrics. A sample list of such metrics contributing to the value of the confidence factor is shown in Figure 9.19.

Each of the indicators p_i is scaled from 0 to 100 and assigned a weight, w_i, which represents the indicator's significance. Using this notation, and assuming that there are n indicators, the confidence factor (CF) is expressed in percentile form by the following formula:

$$CF = \sum_{i=1}^{n} w_i \times p_i, \quad \text{where} \quad 0 \le p_i \le 100, \quad \text{and}$$

$$\sum_{i=1}^{n} w_i = 1, \quad \text{where} \quad 0 \le w_i \le 1$$

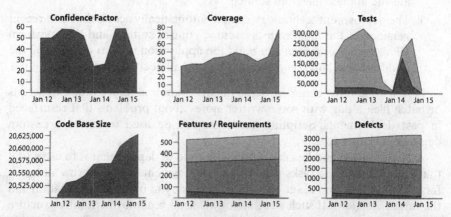

Figure 9.18 Architect panel showing graphs used in evaluating deployment readiness.

Acceptance tests pass rate	Code check-in stability metric
Coding standards pass rate	Code coverage metric
White box testing pass rate	Feature implementation metric
Black box testing pass rate	Security features implementation metric
Convergence rate of white and black box tests	Inverse of code complexity metric
Performance test metric	Inverse of defect discovery rate
Cost Performance Index	Integration test pass rate

Figure 9.19 A sample list of project status indicators.

The confidence factor is a weighted average of the values of the individual metrics, and is thus the most comprehensive of all metrics. The values of the weights should be based on project priorities and prior experience of running similar projects.

DEVELOPER'S TESTIMONIAL

I prefer the following percentages—my rationale is that more bugs are uncovered and fixed as more testing is performed. For example, white box testing reveals only unit-level defects, black box testing reveals functional defects that weigh more than white box tests. If different functionalities work together along with individual functionality, our confidence will still increase. Similarly performance—if integration tests are working fine but performance is poor, we will not be very confident. If performance is also fine and passes through acceptance testing, then we will be very confident that our system can be released. I would use the following weights:

Confidence Indicators (p_i)	Weight in % (w_i)
Coding standards pass rate	5
White box testing pass rate	10
Black box testing pass rate	15
Integration test pass rate	18
Performance test pass rate	22
Acceptance tests pass rate	30
Total	**100%**

—Ravi Bellamkonda, Business Systems Analyst

The recommended strategy for evaluating the project status is to begin by checking the value of the confidence factor to determine if the project is on track. The following questions should be asked regarding the confidence factor:

- Is the confidence factor increasing?
- Is the confidence factor stable and capable?

If the confidence factor dips drastically after code is checked in, it is likely that there is a design problem with the application.

The confidence factor might be stable, but at a low level. Raising the confidence factor first requires identifying the reason for its low value. The weakest point should be found by studying all the indicators that contribute to it. Once the weakest point is identified, the next weakest point should be located and analyzed. For example, if the weakest point turns out to be violations of coding standards, the code quality should be increased. This would increase the confidence factor, but further work might be required. Other problems might exist, such as too many code modifications and uncompleted features with their consequent failing tests. Continuing the cycle of identifying and fixing problems until the confidence factor reaches the appropriate level is necessary to attain product stability and capability and arrive at an informed release decision. (See Figure 9.20.)

The confidence factor should stabilize as the projected release date nears. Once the minimum capability level is reached (e.g., 80%), depending on the schedule, the team may choose to raise it to a higher level. If the confidence factor fluctuates considerably (for instance, if there is not at least a two-week period of stabilization), the application is less likely to be ready for release.

After the confidence factor and other measures indicate that the product is ready for release, the application should be automatically deployed to the production area. In some cases, it is possible to perform an incremental release, that is, redeploy only files that have changed. This is more efficient but requires great confidence in the release process.

Confidence Factor

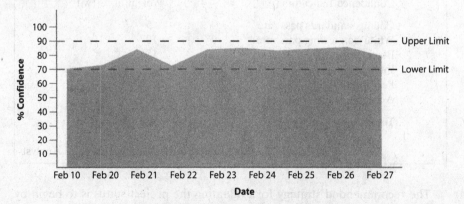

Figure 9.20 Confidence factor graph.

DEVELOPER'S TESTIMONIAL

Very often the deployment to production readiness involves solely the technology readiness. But another important factor that needs to be addressed is whether users and other stakeholders are ready to accept the new system. Often, a new product or new release is perceived with suspicion and it is thought that it would not be better than the old system. The user readiness can be improved by communicating benefits of the new system. Frequent reminders about the upcoming release should alleviate apprehension and ease users' adaptation to the new system. User readiness could be measured by surveying the users about their attitudes and could be used as one of the Confidence Factor parameters.

—Henry Pae, Software Engineer II

9.4.4 Release: Deployment to the Production System

Once the application in the staging system is deemed ready for release, the staging system is cleared and the application is deployed to the production system. Note that the production servers and the staging servers may contain different source code. For example, production servers may contain the current application while the staging servers contain the code for a modified version of the application.

The final deployment to the production system can be performed in two ways. The first and more popular method is to transfer the files from the staging servers to the production servers. The second method is to repeat the complete deployment process used to assemble the application on the staging system in order to reassemble it on the production system.

Although the second method might seem less efficient, it is usually more reliable. When using the first approach, it is necessary to create and fine tune a new repeatable deployment process that accurately transfers files from the staging system to the production system. When the application changes, it is then necessary to modify and debug two processes: the process that assembles the application on the staging system and the process that transfers files from the staging system to the production system. If a similar deployment procedure for the staging system has already been developed and debugged, using the second method to deploy the actual application requires only changing the destination directories from the staging system to the production system.

9.4.5 Nonintrusive Monitoring

After the application has been deployed to the production system and used, it is essential to ensure that the application continues to function properly. This can be accomplished through nonintrusive monitoring.

The purpose of such monitoring is to detect problems users might encounter when using the system. To detect and then prevent problems, in addition to recording application downtimes, monitoring should take place from three perspectives:

1. The user perspective, to verify whether users receive correct data within an acceptable response time
2. The development perspective, to verify whether the software components function and interact according to specifications
3. The system perspective, to verify whether all needed elements of the system supporting the application (such as network connections, load balancers, servers, etc.) are functioning as expected, and to evaluate how fast data moves throughout the system

Many organizations rely solely on basic monitoring to diagnose system problems. However, even the most complex set of measures cannot provide a comprehensive view of the system's health by itself. Assuming that a system is 100% healthy because its infrastructure components respond appropriately to heartbeat tests and other basic infrastructure "vital sign" tests is like assuming that any person with a pulse and no obvious visible bodily injury is 100% healthy. If only these types of vital signs were used to assess a patient, then even a patient in a coma would be considered 100% healthy.

Similarly, performing a full battery of tests is a valuable technique used for monitoring application health. Data from these tests can help to expose production system problems (such as offline application servers or a lost network connection) that can cause users to experience bottlenecks or system failures. In addition, this data can be used to analyze the source of an existing problem. For example, if the user perspective data showed that performance slowed dramatically after 8 A.M., and a glance at the heartbeat test results revealed that half of the web servers went offline around 8 A.M., the probable source of the problem becomes immediately obvious.

User perspective tests might include the following tests:

- Verifying whether user click paths through critical transactions deliver the expected content
- Verifying whether user click paths through critical transactions complete within an acceptable period
- Verifying whether user actions prompt the system to correctly retrieve information from the database or store information in the database

The development perspective tests should verify whether application elements continue to function properly and interact with each other according to specifications. They should include tests created during the application implementation and testing, such as:

- Black box and white box tests created by developers during module and component testing
- Integration and system tests created by testers and/or QA professionals

The system perspective tests should verify whether system elements that the application depends on continue to function according to specifications. For example, they should check whether a web service or other third-party data provider delivers a valid response in the expected format. They should also verify if the response time of these external entities is acceptable and it does not hinder the application functionality.

9.5 ACRONYMS

CPI   Cost performance index
EVM   Earned value management
SPI   Schedule performance index

9.6 GLOSSARY

CPI   A measure calculated by dividing the budgeted cost of work performed by actual cost of work performed.

EVM   A technique that objectively tracks accomplished work.

SPI   A measure calculated by dividing the budgeted cost of work performed by the budgeted cost of work scheduled.

9.7 REFERENCES

[1] Pandian, C.R., *Software Metrics: A Guide to Planning, Analysis, and Application.* Auerbach Publications, 2004.

[2] Humphrey, W., *Managing the Software Process.* Addison Wesley Publishing, 1990.

[3] Deming, W.E., *The New Economics: For Industry, Government, Education.* MIT Press, Cambridge, 2nd ed., 1994.

[4] Breyfogle III, F.W., *Implementing Six Sigma: Smarter Solutions Using Statistical Methods.* John Wiley & Sons, April 2003.

[5] Royce, W.W., "Managing the Development of Large Software Systems: Concepts and Techniques," *Proceedings of IEEE WESCON*, Vol. 26, August 1970, pp. 1–9.

[6] Beck, K. and Andres, C., *Extreme Programming Explained: Embrace Change.* Addison-Wesley, 2nd ed., 2004.

[7] Beck, K., *Test Driven Development: By Example.* Addison Wesley Professional, 2002.

[8] Fleming, Q.W. and Koppelman, J.M., *Earned Value Project Management.* Project Management Institute, 2nd ed., June 2000.

[9] Haack, L., private communication.

9.8 EXERCISES

1. How would you encourage your team to use an infrastructure, especially the reporting system?

2. What project trends need to be observed and evaluated on a regular basis?

3. Give examples of processes that are stable and those that are not stable.

4. Give examples of processes that are capable.

5. Why does a process have to be capable before it is used in making a release-readiness decision?

6. What parameters should contribute to the confidence factor? Which should be assigned the highest weight?

7. What are the steps of deployment to a production system?

8. Why is deployment of a modern system so difficult that it often needs to be done incrementally?

9. What is a release and how it can be automated?

10. What is the monitoring system used for?

CHAPTER 10

MANAGING EXTERNAL FACTORS

> In large organizations the dilution of information as it passes up and down the hierarchy, and horizontally across departments, can undermine the effort to focus on common goals.
>
> —Mihaly Csikszentmihalyi

10.1 INTRODUCTION

While many factors have a direct or indirect impact on the success of software projects, we believe that recent economic developments, legislative actions, and standardization efforts have made three categories particularly deserving of our discussion: offshore outsourcing, regulatory compliance, and quality initiatives.

Until recently, outsourcing has been considered a choice that many software organizations elected to pursue in order to increase operational efficiency. However, as the practice of outsourcing software development has become prevalent, many companies currently consider it a matter of survival, not merely preference.

The facts that outsourced work is performed by individuals who do not have direct allegiance to the organization sponsoring their work, cultural and language barriers are the norm, and contractual agreements often cannot be

---

Automated Defect Prevention: Best Practices in Software Management, by Dorota Huizinga and Adam Kolawa
Copyright © 2007 John Wiley & Sons, Inc.

enforced, pose many challenges to both sides of such complex arrangements. The organization's decision makers find themselves pondering the possible disastrous consequences of many unknowns: lack of understanding of company business, geographical distance, and communication difficulties. Even more so, one of the most devastating scenarios is the compromise or loss of the company's most treasured commodity: the organization's core business data and its intellectual property value. Should the company proprietary data be compromised during an outsourcing effort, all the advantages that outsourcing promises can be erased in an instant.

Similarly, adhering to government regulations that affect IT departments inevitably poses another set of unavoidable challenges for the software industry. These regulations are often complicated, confusing, and their compliance difficult to verify. As mentioned in Chapter 1, for example, the Sarbanes-Oxley (SOX) Act of 2002 [1] requires that publicly traded companies implement effective internal, auditable controls for their financial reporting systems, which might place a great burden on IT departments of such companies.

At the same time, several standardization and compliance organizations and initiatives, such as SEI CMMI (Software Engineering Institute Capability Maturity Model Integration) [2], ISO IEC (International Organization for Standardization/International Electrotechnical Commission) 90003-2004 [3], and Six Sigma [4], have been created to address the challenges of modern software development and to counter poor software quality. Unfortunately, many organizations have failed to achieve the desired quality goals because of the difficulty of implementing and sustaining them in a realistic development environment.

In this chapter, we will describe our approach to managing external factors such as outsourced projects, regulatory compliance, and quality initiatives. Specifically, we will define the customized minimum infrastructure for each of these external factors and we will explain how ADP practices should be applied to facilitate their management.

10.2   BEST PRACTICES FOR MANAGING OUTSOURCED PROJECTS

Increased globalization of the economy, ease of long-distance communication and data distribution combined with operational effectiveness have made offshore outsourcing an inevitable reality in the software industry. While the potential cost savings are large, poor management of an outsourced project can have disastrous consequences. Despite its recent prevalence, in many ways the management of outsourced software projects is experiencing the trials of infancy, as shown by studies conducted by DiamondCluster [5] that found that more than 70% of companies surveyed have prematurely terminated a prior outsourcing agreement.

The opinion of many is that the software industry is currently going through the growing pains that mature industries have already experienced. For example, a look at the auto industry of the 1960s reveals many similarities with the software industry of the 2000s—learning how to specialize and reduce costs, improve quality, and accelerate production.

Such industrial progress normally occurs over an extended period. Herein lies the myth of outsourcing. While it is often viewed and implemented as a short-term cost-saving approach, in actuality outsourcing should be part of a long-term management strategy.

In the next section we will describe a set of ADP best practices to implement a software development outsourcing process that facilitates such a long-term outsourced management strategy.

10.2.1 Establishing a Software Development Outsource Process

The framework presented in this section is the basis for our discussion of risks and strategies for project outsourcing. The model used structurally resembles the waterfall approach and it is based on Kevin Haw's [6] and Gene Marks's [7] representation of generic process phases for outsourcing:

Phase 0: Decision to outsource
Phase 1: Planning
Phase 2: Implementation
Phase 3: Termination

An overview of these phases and their mapping onto the ADP life cycle can be seen in Figure 10.1. The subsequent sections describe ADP's best practices for each of these generic phases.

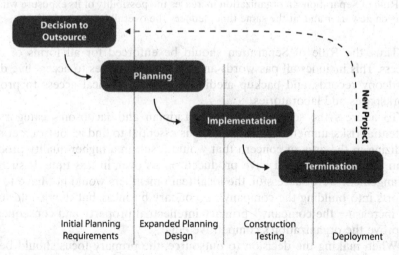

Figure 10.1 Phases in a GSDOP (generic software development outsource process) mapped onto ADP.

10.2.2   Phase 0: Decision to Outsource

Despite its many benefits, not all tasks are suitable for outsourcing. Therefore, the first phase of the process is determining whether outsourcing is a viable alternative to performing the task in-house. Research, analysis, and strategy are all involved in deciding whether to outsource parts of a project, or even an entire project. Ultimately, the potential advantages and disadvantages of project outsourcing need to be carefully considered. Svante Lidman and Ivar Jacobson [8] identify two categories of potential risk:

1. Loss of intellectual property and control over proprietary data by the company seeking outsourcing
2. Unmet business needs of the outsourced software product

The first concern should be addressed by determining the company's primary focus and deciding what is and is not appropriate for outsourcing. In general, only the products or parts of the products that are *not* the company's core business should be considered for outsourcing. Otherwise, the company can compromise its own interests and lose market competitiveness by inadvertently disclosing its most valuable intellectual property.

Additionally, a basic security principle known as the *Rule of Separation* should be taken into account when determining what can and cannot be outsourced. Kevin Day [9] presents the concept and the consequences of failing to heed it in this manner:

> The Rule of Separation states that to secure something, it must be separated from the dangers and threats of the world around it.... By not practicing the Rule of Separation, an organization increases the possibility of its exposure with each new user and, at the same time, reduces the overall level of security.

Thus, the Rule of Separation should be enforced for all forms of data access. This includes all passwords and account privileges to access live data, hardcopy records, and backup media, as well as physical access to project workspaces and laboratories.

To address the second concern of Lidman and Jacobson's category of potential risks, unmet business needs, it is essential to find an outsourcer specializing in the area of concern that would result in a higher-quality product than the company could have produced on its own, in less time. If such an arrangement were successful, the local team members would not have to put efforts into building the company's secondary business, but they could focus on increasing the company's primary intellectual property and consequently improve the organization's competitive edge.

When making the decision to outsource, the primary focus should be on improving product quality and the resulting increase in the local company's productivity. Direct cost savings can be explored later, and they should be secondary benefits derived from both the increased quality and company's productivity. Once the decision about outsourcing has been made, we can move to Phase 1 of the outsource process: planning.

10.2.3 Phase 1: Planning

Good planning is crucial in outsourcing and it involves at a minimum the following tasks: definition of outsource project scope and requirements, identification of potential outsourcing providers, generation and distribution of RFIs[a] and RFPs,[b] selection of the best solution, award of the contract, identification of the stakeholders and project manager, identification of risks, and definition of a contingency plan.

Definition of Outsource Project Scope and Requirements An initial draft of the project scope and its requirements should be created. This document should be used to select potential outsourcers who can fulfill the needs of the company in building the defined product.

Identification of Potential Outsourcing Service Providers Outsourcers should be selected based on their ability to provide services that will fulfill the requirements of the product. To make an informed decision of such a selection, diligent assessments of a prospective outsourcer's prior projects, its success rates, and its ability to sustain long-term relationships with the outsourcing company are necessary.

Generation and Distribution of RFPs Formal *requests for proposals* (RFPs), which define the project in greater detail, should be developed and distributed to the prospective outsource providers to invite them to bid. If the project is very large in scope, an earlier cycle of *requests for information* (RFIs) may be performed to allow outsource providers to give some input in defining the later, more formal RFPs.

Selection of the Best Solution Once responses to RFPs are received, an analysis is performed to compare the outsourcers' replies, expertise, and project costs. Based on the results of this comparison the most suitable outsourcer is selected.

Award of the Contract Details of the *statement of work* (SOW[c]) are resolved with the winning bidder and the contract is finalized. It is important to set expectations with an outsourcer at the beginning of a project through a solid

[a] Request for information. A process whereby questions are asked by the contractor and answered by the owner's authorized agent. [10]
[b] Request for proposal. The solicitations used in negotiated procurements. [10]
[c] A document that establishes the contractual foundation of the project. [11]

contractual agreement. Those expectations, defined in a contract and agreed upon by both sides, set the tone for a mutually beneficial relationship. Good working relationships are based on mutual respect and trust, which can be built only gradually over an extended period. The contract forms a foundation for such a long-term relationship. If a contract is biased toward one party or circumvents the ability of one party to ask questions about the scheduling, costs, or project status, the relationship is likely to fall apart.

The following should be included in written contracts: approved written requirements document, requirements change process, project plan including the model for the outsourcer's software development process, schedule and budget, definition of a minimum technology infrastructure that will be used by both parties to assess project progress status, and an approved process for system acceptance. These topics will be further explained in subsequent paragraphs.

Approved Requirements   Communicating a complete and correct requirements specification to the subcontractor, a challenging task in itself, is exacerbated in outsourced projects because of cultural differences between teams, language barriers, and the novelty of the outsourcing relationship.

DEVELOPER'S TESTIMONIAL

Lost in Translation—an Outsourcing Nightmare

I once had the misfortune of experiencing an outsourcing disaster due to poor communication and misunderstanding of software requirements. Our company outsourced a section of a system we were trying to create to a contracting company abroad. Through the contracting company's onsite representative, we outlined what we wanted in the vision statement, and in the requirements specification document for the system section they were to develop. We provided them with all the necessary documentation that we had for the system and made sure that they understood that if they had any questions, they would check with us. The representative assured us that he understood what we wanted and that the requirements were clear. Since this was a foreign contracting company, we discovered through our postmortem that certain language nuances did not translate very well. The representative forwarded the documents to the outsourcer's development center, and when their programmers called with questions, the representative felt that he understood the requirements well enough to answer the questions instead of bothering us. The problem was that they communicated in their native language and the requirements written in English were inadvertently misinterpreted.

Consequently, we had much back-and-forth finger pointing by management and business as to who was right or wrong. We ended up coming up with a settlement that neither party was happy with, and our in-house development group had to *rewrite most of what we had contracted out to do, putting us way behind schedule.*

—Michael, Software Developer

In addition to the best practices for requirements specifications delineated in Chapter 4, we recommend the following steps when dealing with an outsourced project:

Step 1: Providing the Outsourcer with Ample Time to Study and Clarify the Written Requirements Document. A well-defined and detailed requirements specification should be provided in written form to the outsourcer. The outsourcer should be given an opportunity to study the documents at her own pace and ask questions to clarify parts that are ambiguous or vague.

Step 2: Requesting the Outsourcer to Rewrite Project Requirements. To minimize possible miscommunication problems, it is in some cases advisable to request the outsourcers to rewrite the requirements in their own words. The outsourcer should reiterate both verbal and written communications in order to close the communication loop. The local team should work with the outsourcer to resolve any ambiguities or differences. Good communication relies on the clarity of the speaker/writer and the careful attention of the listener/reader, and, because these roles are continually reversed throughout the outsourcing process, both parties should strive to be as clear as possible in expressing their ideas as well as in paying attention to the other side's comments and questions.

Step 3: Requesting an Outsourcer-Created Prototype. Prototyping allows geographically separated developers to visualize the user interface and validate functional requirements. Therefore, the outsourcer should first create a prototype, and then the local and outsourced teams should evaluate it to discover whether any additional requirements need to be further discussed or refined.

Project Plan Including an Approved Methodology for the Software Development Process   This is a systematic plan of action, with the responsibility for each step divided between the two parties. The software development methodology is decided upon, interdependencies between the steps are documented, and lists of deliverable artifacts for each step are developed here. It is recommended that an incremental and iterative software development model with well-defined delivery milestones be used to facilitate assessment of progress and early identification of possible risks. A budget and schedule need to be prepared at this stage and included in the contract.

Definition of a Minimum Technology Infrastructure   Both parties should agree upon the installation of an identical technology infrastructure at each location. At a minimum, this infrastructure should consist of:

- A source control system
- An automated build system

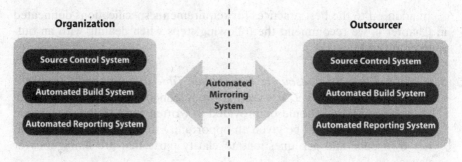

Figure 10.2   Automated mirroring system together with the elements of the minimum infrastructure for outsourced projects provides a *window* between the organization and the outsourcer.

- An automated reporting system
- An automated mirroring[d] of project data

By implementing automatic mirroring of project-related data, the infrastructure would serve as a window through which both partners can view the project progress and status, as shown in Figure 10.2. It is critical that both parties have the same versions of the technology infrastructure installed on both sides so no information is lost in converting and transferring data. Use of the reporting system that enables local managers to evaluate the project progress and run periodic reports to verify status of the implementation should be well defined.

Approved Process for System Acceptance   Additionally, it is necessary to have an approved process for system acceptance of the outsourced work, including very detailed technical descriptions of acceptance and other tests and even, if possible, mutually agreed-upon numerical values of metrics for acceptance indicators.

As the contracts are written, it is important to remember that laws pertaining to such contractual agreements vary from country to country. Translated into a working relationship with an outsourcer, a written contract might not be followed to the same extent by everyone. In many situations, a contract might prove to be just a *suggestion*, and therefore the ability to assess the status of the project frequently and to establish a solid long-term relationship is very important.

Identification of Stakeholders and an Assignment of a Dedicated Project Manager   In addition to the stakeholders that were identified during the initial requirements definition, the company should create a list of all internal

---

[d] Direct copying of a data set.

and external stakeholders and their roles. Moreover, a dedicated project manager needs to be assigned. This individual will be responsible for the outsourcing management, including allocating resources correctly, making sure that the progress of the work is monitored, and maintaining effective communication.

Identification of Risks and Definition of Contingency Plans As outsourcing introduces new risks into software development, risk management becomes even more important. In addition to possible communication barriers, there are many potential unknowns, including the outsourcer's software development processes and organizational and team culture, that need to be taken into account. Therefore, a common infrastructure that facilitates periodic assessment of the project status, as agreed in the contract, is the key to remedy some of these potential risks.

10.2.4 Phase 2: Implementation

During Phase 2, the subcontractor starts the software development process. Refined requirements, design, code, documentation, or other artifacts defined in the project plan are progressively delivered. In addition to the above mentioned necessity to maintain a stable and positive relationship with the outsourcer, the following tasks need to be performed on the customer site: frequent monitoring and assessing of the project progress and timely communication of concerns and change requests, with the ultimate goal of reaching system-acceptance status.

Establishing and Maintaining Positive Relationships in Blended Teams It is critical to find a subcontractor with whom a healthy working alliance can be cultivated and maintained. Without such a solid partnership, outsourcing projects will not be successful. Factors such as personal relationships, geographical location, and cultural differences need to be considered.

The key to success in outsourcing is understanding that the quality of a final product can be greatly improved when a healthy working relationship is developed with an outsourcer who specializes in a product that is needed, but that does not overlap with the focal point of business of the local company. It is important to communicate these objectives of specialization and improved quality to team members at the local organization so that they can understand the company's long-term mission.

A subcontractor can be of long-term benefit because of its proficiency level in a field. Thus, outsourcing forces organizations to not only establish contacts, but also build long-term partnerships in order to implement projects more efficiently. The result of these collaborative efforts is a worldwide network of companies that can rely on each other.

Building a Common Culture   When companies go outside the confines of their organization to implement a project, they inevitably need to bring two or more different groups of people together into a working relationship. Whether this working relationship is congenial, productive, and efficient greatly depends on how well both groups of employees are integrated.

The greatest challenge to overcome is the initial unfamiliarity between the two teams. Both physical separation and group differences due to cultural background and knowledge base make such bonding difficult. Cultural differences can exist at the corporate level, the technical level, or both. For example, development groups can have democratic or hierarchical structures and some may require more direct supervision than other types of groups. In some cultures, problems might not be easily verbalized and confronted because it is not polite to do so. Differences in knowledge base exist because the groups specialize in distinct areas. Because of these distinct areas of specialization, bonding at the technical level might be also difficult. For these reasons, there is a great chance that initially both teams will feel distant from each other.

Unifying two separate teams is essential for the success of an outsourcing project. It is imperative to instill a common organizational culture by creating a sense of mutual respect and shared goals. The following two practices can help build cohesion among the two groups:

1. Conducting member exchanges between both teams
2. Involvement in mutual activities, such as training sessions.

Conducting Member Exchanges between Teams   A step toward unifying the two distant teams is to start each new project with employee exchanges. It is important to select a few team members who are capable of quick learning and willing to spread the company's philosophy, infrastructure, and practices among the other team members.

Of concern might be the large expense of such exchanges. However, this might prove to be a worthwhile investment, since after face-to-face communication is established, the teams are more likely to refine and improve their working relationship. These two groups, the company's employees and the outsourcer's employees, need to connect at a human level, which can be done only face to face. This step is critical in achieving team integration.

To maintain this strong connectedness between the company's team and the outsourcer's team, multiple exchanges should take place. Remote videoconferences (such as webcasts) help in maintaining relationships, but nothing replaces direct contact.

Involvment in Mutual Activities   Next, it is critical to teach the outsourcer's team members about, and involve them in, the company's practices and use of the technology infrastructure. Similarly, it is imperative to learn the outsourcer's values and organizational culture. Such mutual learning lays a common foundation for group bonding, and helps the groups to work together as a team. This can be accomplished, for example, by having common seminars during which interesting design or coding problems are presented, new technology is explained, or brainstorming ideas are exchanged.

Monitoring and Assessing Project Status   With the project data being mirrored, the technology infrastructure in place, and a positive relationship between both parties, the project status can be easily assessed on a periodic basis. Use of the automated reporting system to assess project progress, as defined in the contract, should not pose a threat to the outsourcer and its team, but instead provide an additional assurance to both parties that they are adhering to their contractual obligations.

Decision of System Acceptance   In general, system acceptance is one of the most difficult management decisions, and many factors need to be taken into account when considering it. Proper interpretation of data collected during software development can facilitate such an informed decision. Pursuant to the contractual agreement, system acceptance should be determined by evaluating project status indicators and their trends over an extended period, and obtaining a thorough understanding of software functionality and quality status. Because of the many possible unknowns in outsourcing projects, the terms of system acceptance have to be well defined in the contract.

10.2.5   Phase 3: Termination

In this phase, work on the project is concluded per the terms defined in the contract and project plan. Any outstanding issues are resolved and loose ends tied up. The termination phase consists of the following steps:

Verification of Contract Fulfillment   At the time of termination, acceptance testing needs to be completed and all required feature implementations validated. Reporting system indicators combined with a series of audits should verify compliance with all the terms laid out in the contract and allow final financial settlements to be calculated and paid out.

Moving On   From this point, there are two possible outcomes of a successful project:

1. If further maintenance for the product is required (i.e., the maintenance period on the original project expired or none was included in the project plan), a new, dedicated maintenance contract should be negotiated. New projects may be developed under the above model for upgrades to the product or for entirely new products.
2. If the project does not require further maintenance by the outsourcer, the contract and relationship is terminated according to the original contractual agreement.

10.3 BEST PRACTICES FOR FACILITATING IT REGULATORY COMPLIANCE

Much recent government legislation places more responsibility on companies for maintaining accurate financial records, protecting employee and customer privacy, assuring proper accessibility to offered services, and validating the integrity of their software products. The broad scope of these requirements and the lack of specific development guidelines make compliance implementation a difficult task to accomplish.

Proper customization of ADP practices can facilitate both the implementation and verification of such compliance. In the following sections, we will exemplify such an adaptation of ADP's practices by defining the *minimum customized infrastructure and best practices* for the following mandates: Section 508 of the U.S. Rehabilitation Act [12], and the Sarbanes-Oxley (SOX) Act of 2002 [1].

10.3.1 Section 508 of the U.S. Rehabilitation Act

According to data from the 2000 United States Census, over 19% of the U.S. population has some type of disability [13]. People with disabilities often require adapted means for accessing software applications. Such adaptations may include:

- Changing font configurations for improved readability
- Using special devices or software (such as voice-recognition software) for navigation and input
- Using text-to-speech browsers that vocalize web page text
- Using devices that instantly translate web page text into Braille

Many existing websites cannot be properly presented or used in these contexts. As a result, much site content and functionality are not available to a sizable number of actual or potential site visitors.

According to the U.S. Food and Drug Administration, "General Principles of Software Validation" [14], the Section 508 amendment to the Rehabilitation Act of 1973, requires that any technology produced by or for federal agencies be accessible to people with disabilities. Section 508 guidelines cover 16 specific requirements that a website must satisfy to comply with Section 508 legislation. Most of these guidelines focus on ensuring graceful page transformations to adaptive devices and making content understandable and navigable on adaptive devices. Although these guidelines were originally created for government agencies and their technology vendors, they have become the standard for site accessibility.

There are two main sources of website accessibility guidelines: Section 508 Web Guidelines [15] and Web Accessibility Initiative Web Content Accessibility Guidelines [16]. Both sets of guidelines prompt website designers and developers to improve accessibility by adding elements such as optional labels and extra content to their code (rather than removing potentially inaccessible features or content).

ADP facilitates implementation of Section 508 by recommending technology infrastructure and a set of best practices to verify its compliance. This minimum infrastructure should consist of:

- A source control system
- An automated build system
- A static analysis system
- An automated reporting system

Most of the regulatory mandates can be automatically verified through static analysis of the code, and therefore the customized minimum ADP's infrastructure for Section 508 includes an automated static analysis system. Application of such technology would streamline the accessibility verification process by automatically identifying parts of the code that violate Section 508 and WAI web accessibility guidelines.

10.3.2 Sarbanes-Oxley Act of 2002

The Sarbanes-Oxley (SOX) Act of 2002 is designed to oversee the financial reporting systems for publicly traded organizations. Its purpose is to protect investors by improving the accuracy and reliability of corporate disclosures. The act also significantly tightens accountability standards for officers, auditors, and legal counsel.

As part of this legislation, a company must certify not only that the IT systems used to collect and process the organization's financial data have proper functionality but also that they are secure and reliable. Thus, the company executives, who ultimately are responsible for approval of all financial reports, need comprehensive and objective data verifying the correctness of internally developed software applications that affect such reports. Moreover, should the approval decisions be later audited and challenged, company leaders need to have a documented record of the system details that formed the basis for their approval decisions.

The main sections of the SOX legislation that influence IT are:

- *Section 302—Corporate Responsibility for Financial Reports*, which requires executives to certify that quarterly and annual financial reports are complete and accurate
- *Section 404—Management Assessment of Internal Controls*, which requires executives to annually certify that they have effective internal controls for their financial reporting and requires that auditors confirm the effectiveness of these controls

- *Section 802—Criminal Penalties for Altering Documents*, which requires the protection/retention of financial audit records

SOX Compliance   A customized ADP infrastructure can be used to facilitate verification of internally developed financial and record-keeping software for SOX compliance. This customized SOX compliance infrastructure consists of:

- A source control system
- An automated build system
- A requirements management system
- A static analysis system
- An automated testing system
- An automated reporting system

This infrastructure facilitates automatic collection of data validating implementation of the mandated requirements.

Moreover, each time a new software application or feature affecting the organization's financial system needs to be approved, the reporting system can be used in recording approval details by storing a *snapshot*, which is a time-stamped log of the application data. Thus, the snapshot data provides documented evidence of a company's due diligence in implementing SOX-mandated requirements and a time-stamped log is an important reference point in case a rollback to the previous version is needed.

Best Practices for Addressing Common SOX Problems   The ADP customized infrastructure defined above facilitates implementation of SOX compliance when used with the following best practices:

- Tracking and monitoring implementation of mandated requirements
- Streamlining executives' verification and approval work by providing objective data that is collected automatically
- Generating reports that demonstrate SOX compliance to auditors
- Assisting in verification of system security
- Assisting in verification of the sustainability of the system's compliance

In subsequent sections, we will elaborate each of these best practices.

Tracking and Monitoring Implementation of Mandated Requirements   As soon as the SOX-mandated application requirements are defined and approved, they are entered and tracked in the requirements management system. During the subsequent software design and construction phases, test cases are developed, and associations between test cases and the corresponding requirements are recorded both in the requirements management system and the automated testing system. At that time, some tests verifying these requirements can be generated automatically. For tests that cannot be automatically generated, testers either can add them manually to the testing system to be automatically executed or can record test results by hand. Therefore, both the manual and automated test data are collected by the reporting system. Consequently, the status of the implementation of each requirement is validated by the results of the tests corresponding to it, and recorded by the automated reporting system.

Streamlining the Executives' Verification and Approval Work by Providing Objective Data That Is Collected Automatically The tasks of the preliminary approval of system compliance are usually delegated to a member of the IT department. However, because executives might be held liable for inaccurate financial reports or inadequate IT internal controls, they need to be able to assess system compliance status and determine whether they are confident about approving the IT recommendation.

The infrastructure's reporting system provides a means for executives to access, review, and validate the IT member's preapproval decisions. Once the designated IT member decides that all the mandated requirements have been implemented and code vulnerabilities have been corrected, she recommends system preapproval. At this point, the reporting system *takes a snapshot* of the application under development. The snapshot is a time-stamped log of all relevant data, including the status of requirements implemented and results of the tests that verified requirements implementation, and source code contents. The snapshot is a key feature supporting approval decision. Should the functionality and security of an approved application be questioned, this snapshot can be used to instantly recall the data that formed the basis for the approval decision, even if the application has changed since the time of approval.

The next step in the review process is to have the executives review the data logged by the reporting system snapshot. The reports shown in Figure 10.3 are the natural starting point for this review. The vertical line in the middle indicates the time of the last snapshot.

Should the executive desire to explore test details before approving the application, she can view a particular aspect of the snapshot by selecting additional reports.

Once the executive is ready to approve the application, she registers her approval in the reporting system, and the reporting system adds this approval to its *project approval status* report, as shown in Figure 10.4.

Generating Reports That Demonstrate SOX Compliance to Auditors One key requirement for SOX compliance is the ability of auditors to verify that the company has correctly implemented appropriate internal controls for its financial reporting systems. The company must provide auditors with documented evidence of functioning controls and the documented results of testing procedures. However, it is often difficult to demonstrate to the auditors that

Requirements Testing Overview

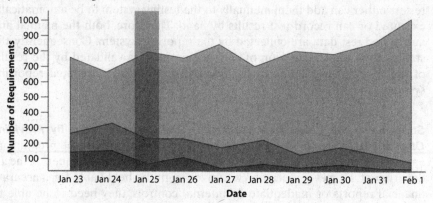

Requirements Testing Details

Date	Failed Test	Not Tested	Passed Test
Jan 23	120	250	750
Jan 24	130	320	680
Jan 25	90	220	800
Jan 26	100	250	750

Figure 10.3 The vertical bar on January 25 represents the time that the snapshot of the system was taken.

	Design	Beta	Release
Preapproved	**Sign-off** by J. Doe 2/1/2003 with comments	**Sign-off** by J. Doe 4/21/2004 no comments	**Not started** start due: 11/1/2004
Verified	**Sign-off** by J. Doe 6/15/2003 with comments	**Sign-off** by J. Doe 6/12/2004 with comments	**Not started** start due: 12/1/2004
Approved	**Sign-off** by J. Doe 9/7/2003 with comments	**Pending** started: 6/30/2004	**Not started** start due: 2/1/2005

Figure 10.4 Project approval status report.

the company has not only defined and implemented appropriate controls, but also verified their proper functionality. It is especially difficult for auditors to review and reproduce the effectiveness of manual tests, such as user acceptance tests, which are typically performed ad hoc and rarely documented. In addition, the auditors must be informed of any changes made since the previous audit that could have affected the company's internal controls.

Again, data generated by the customized SOX infrastructure provides necessary documentation and evidence of implementation of such internal controls. Moreover, because the snapshots are time stamped and changes that occurred since the previous audit are clearly marked in reports, the auditors can quickly determine what has changed, explore change details, and determine whether the most recent changes influenced the effectiveness of the company's internal controls.

Assisting in Verification of System Security   Vulnerabilities in the application itself can make the system just as prone to security attacks as unprotected networks, operating systems, or servers. Thus, a financial system is not truly SOX compliant unless it is secure.

To address this problem, ADP's security policy should be used and its implementation should be automatically verified by the infrastructure. ADP's security policy describes best practices for secure application design rules, secure coding standards, and security testing benchmarks. After this policy is customized for the specific application and implemented by the team, system security should be automatically verified at multiple levels. First, the application code should be statically analyzed to validate conformance to secure application design and coding standards. Next, functional testing should be performed to confirm that the policy has been implemented correctly and that the system operates properly. If violations of the policy are detected during either static analysis or dynamic test execution, an informed decision needs to be made whether there are possible vulnerabilities in the system and corrective steps are required.

Assisting in Verification of the Sustainability of System Compliance   After implementing internal controls for their financial systems, companies need to ensure that these systems *continue* to operate correctly, that internal controls do not break down, and that unauthorized changes to financial records do not take place. This is why Section 302 of SOX requires that executives certify the completeness and accuracy of financial reports each quarter.

ADP's infrastructure facilitates the sustainability of this compliance implementation. The reporting system shows not only project trends and status but also anomalies that may require urgent attention, such as unexpected changes in financial database records. When the status of the system is regularly monitored, problems are immediately identified so they can be remedied before they negatively influence the company's financial operations.

Addressing Key Sarbanes-Oxley Sections   The above best practices can be used to implement and verify compliance with specific SOX mandates. The following sections explain which practices are most suitable for specific requirements in key SOX sections.

Section 302 Section 302 requires executives to certify that financial reports are complete and accurate.

- The best practices for tracking and monitoring implementation of mandated requirements, assisting in the verification of system security, facilitating implementation, and verifying mandated compliance help in verifying the correctness of system requirements implementation.
- The best practice for automatically collecting and tracking data helps in assuring that the financial records are properly secured.

Section 404 Section 404 requires executives to annually certify that they have effective internal controls for their financial reporting and requires that auditors confirm the effectiveness of these controls.

- Best practices are used for streamlining the executives' verification and approval work by providing objective data that is collected automatically, generating reports that demonstrate SOX compliance to auditors, and assisting in the verification of the sustainability of the system's compliance. These facilitate the implementation and verification of compliance with Section 404.
- The snapshot feature of the reporting system helps in both decision making for approval of system compliance and automated documentation of data for audits.

Section 802 Section 802 requires the protection/retention of financial audit records.

- The best practices for assisting in the verification of system security and assisting in verification of sustainability of the system's compliance facilitate implementation and verification of this mandate.
- While static analysis and automated testing are used to verify that data is protected from undesirable security attacks, the infrastructure's task automation is crucial in sustaining system compliance.

10.4 BEST PRACTICES FOR IMPLEMENTATION OF CMMI

ADP can alleviate some of the concerns in implementing CMMI and other related initiatives by defining a technology and people infrastructure that facilitates the implementation and long-term sustainability of these programs. In the following sections we will take a closer look at CMMI and its relationship to ADP. We will also show the mapping of ADP practices to CMMI levels and describe how these practices facilitate the achievement of goals set for the corresponding CMMI process areas. Using the approach described below, similar mappings can be developed for other quality initiatives such as ISO IEC 90003-2004 and Six Sigma.

10.4.1 Capability and Maturity Model Integration (CMMI)

CMMI is a model for product and service life cycle management and process improvement. It merges technical and management activities with a focus on improving business performance. With a set of recommended best practices for its continuous[e] and staged[f] representation, it describes mechanisms for organizational culture change. CMMI encompasses software engineering, systems engineering, integrated product, and (in version 1.2) hardware engineering along with process development as well as supplier sourcing and acquisition, and it can be applied to a wide range of products such as video games, automated teller machines, digital cameras, or airplanes [2].

In order to evaluate the company's CMMI level, Carnegie Melon University Software Engineering Institute's (SEI) trained assessors conduct appraisals using Standard CMMI Appraisal Method for Process Improvement (SCAMPI®). Results of these appraisals are reported at the SEI website under the "List of Published SCAMPI Appraisal Results" [17]. The CMMI appraisal is not considered a "certification" process in terms of the ISO certification; however, organizations provide results to the SEI and may choose to have this information made available on the SEI website. Organizations typically conduct CMMI appraisals for three main reasons:

1. Support internal process improvement activities.
2. Earn a rating level required for bidding on a government contract.
3. Comply with existing contracts.

The Department of Defense, Federal Aviation Administration, and other government agencies often specify CMMI requirements as part of contract acquisition or maintenance.

At the same time, CMMI embraces those companies that want to optimize their processes without necessarily going through a formal appraisal process of their entire organization. This per-process area focus in CMMI is reflected in its continuous representation concept. Continuous representation is easier to implement than staged and has many practical benefits. Factors such as organizational culture, legacy processes, and the requirements for a formal organizational appraisal need to be considered in selecting a continuous or staged approach to process improvement.

---

[e] A comprehensive process model that is predicated on a set of system and software engineering capabilities. It defines process areas and five levels of capability.
[f] A comprehensive process model that is predicated on the staged representation and five levels of maturity. To achieve a specified level of maturity a set of goals in predefined process areas must be met.

It is worth noting that ADP can be used in facilitating either type of CMMI implementation. In the final section, we will discuss the similarities between the two approaches and show how ADP helps to bridge the practical gaps when moving from a continuous to a staged CMMI model.

10.4.2 Staged Representation

Staged representation has five *maturity levels*, each of which is a foundation layer for the subsequent level:

1. Initial
2. Managed process
3. Defined process
4. Quantitatively managed process
5. Optimizing process

With the exception of the first level, each of these levels encompasses clusters of best practices called *process areas* (PAs). Within the process areas are specific goals and practices, as well as generic goals and practices. Each PA thus contains a list of goals and practices related to planning, implementing, and controlling the project and organizational processes for that process area. As organizations achieve subsequent levels of CMMI, they evolve, mature, and expand from disciplined task fulfillment at the project level to a sustainable process improvement at the organization level.

The CMMI *maturity levels and process areas* (v1.1.) are listed in Figure 10.5.

10.4.3 Putting Staged Representation–Based Improvement into Practice Using ADP

This section outlines the implementation steps of ADP, in particular its infrastructure, which facilitate staged improvement of CMMI as illustrated in Figure 10.6.

Level 1: Ad Hoc. This level does not have designated process areas. However, ADP practices can be applied to selected areas based on the project and organization needs.

Level 2: Practices and Policies, and Tracking and Measuring at a Project Level: Implementation of disciplined processes for a development team and project by applying ADP's principles. This step includes defining and applying uniform practices and policies for the use of the technology infrastructure and ADP's *generic best practices* for software requirements management, design, construction, and testing at a group level.

Level	Focus	Process Areas
1—Initial	Ad hoc	
2—Managed	Project Management	Requirements Management
		Project Planning
		Project Monitoring and Control
		Supplier Agreement Management
		Measurement and Analysis
		Process and Product Quality Assurance
		Configuration Management
3—Defined	Standard, Consistent Process	Requirements Development
		Technical Solution
		Product Integration
		Verification
		Validation
		Organizational Process Focus
		Organization Process Definition
		Organizational Training
		Integrated Project Management
		Risk Management
		Integrated Teaming
		Integrated Supplier Management
		Decision Analysis and Resolution
		Organizational Environment for Integration
4—Quantitatively Managed	Predictable Process	Organizational Process Performance
		Quantitative Project Management
5—Optimizing	Continuous Process Improvement	Organizational Innovation and Deployment
		Causal Analysis and Resolution

Figure 10.5 CMMI maturity levels and the corresponding process areas.

Level 3: Practices and Policies, and Tracking and Measuring at the Organization Level. Expanding the implementation of processes to the entire organization by establishing organization-level standards through automated tracking and measurement. This step entails transferring the ADP techniques and methods implemented for individual groups or projects to the entire organization.

Level 4: Process Control and Trend Analysis: Implementation of statistical process control. Data collected during software development and measures generated by the reporting system make quantitative process management

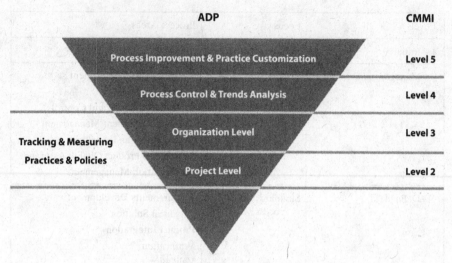

Figure 10.6   High-level mapping of ADP to CMMI.

possible. Several metrics of product quality and the confidence factor, described in Chapter 9, facilitate tracking of trends and monitoring of process stabilization as well as assessment of effectiveness of processes.

Level 5: Process Improvement and Practice Customization: Implementation of process improvement. Defect prevention is the focus here. This step entails defect causal analysis and process improvement by taking actions to prevent defects from recurring. The defect repository used throughout the project life cycle, combined with the reporting system, facilitates the tracking, analysis, and prevention of defects.

In CMMI, the *staged representation–based improvement* works best for those companies that need organization-wide process control and improvement. Normally, when implementing CMMI, the PAs at all lower levels have to be satisfied before moving to higher levels. The Level 2 and 3 requirements entail the most work at the project level, such as building the infrastructure, planning, executing a plan, and monitoring and controlling processes. Similarly, Level 3 has the greatest impact on organization processes because it entails the establishment of organization standards, measures, and training. This time-consuming set of tasks leaves a great deal of room for error at the lower levels of the CMMI pyramid. ADP infrastructure and automation can facilitate the process of climbing the CMMI ladder through comprehensive integration of technology into project and process management.

The tables in Figure 10.7 list some of the ADP practices that can be used to facilitate the fulfillment of the various PAs in the CMMI maturity levels.

CMMI Level 2 Managed (Disciplined Processes)

Process Area	ADP Support
Requirements Management	• Setting up minimum infrastructure, including a problem tracking system. • Connecting requirements management and automated test system. • Generating tests for all requirements. • Reviewing test cases for requirements with customer, and modifying test suite respectively. • The requirements management system helps to automate requirements tracking and traceability and changes.
Project Planning	• Defining a project plan according to ADP initial and extended planning best practices. • Tailoring ADP generic best practices for project planning to organizational needs. • Defining which standard practices are required for the organization's software development life cycle model. • Setting up a group stencil by defining roles in the group (Developer, Tester, QA Staff Architect, Project Manager, and so on). • Uniformly configuring technology infrastructure for all team members. • Determining a phase-in period for all practices. • Automated tracking of historical project data, such as size of code and developer productivity, for use in creating estimates for new projects. • Establishing plans for measures of spending rates, schedules, earned value, productivity, defect rate, and other attributes.
Project Monitoring and Control	• Using reports from the reporting system to evaluate trends and project status, which can be compared to the plan data. • Altering practices as needed to ensure standardized use of ADP infrastructure across the group. • Monitoring of measures established in the plan including earned value, size, and defect rates.
Supplier Agreement Management	• Mirroring the ADP technology infrastructure at the subcontractor/supplier's development location to ensure that the same practices and policies are followed by the subcontracting teams. • Automated tracking and measuring of the subcontractor/supplier's project progress using the reporting system pursuant to the prior contractual agreement. • Automated tracking of historical supplier data to use as part of the supplier selection decision.
Measurement and Analysis	• Establishing project objectives and corresponding measures. • Automated data collection. • Utilizing data to fulfill project monitoring and control requirements.
Process and Product Quality Assurance	• Using the people and technology infrastructure to inject quality requirements into processes by setting up maximum failure rate thresholds, coding standards implementation, test progression criteria, etc. • Establishing periodic audits of products and processes and ensuring that the processes are being followed. (Project follows processes per tailoring, which could be partially enforced through our automated approach.)
Configuration Management	• Setting up practices and policies for groups to use common configuration files for development technologies, a source code system, static analysis, automatic builds, regression tests, and reporting system. • Requirements management system and change request tracking and management help to enforce appropriate configuration management, and integrate change management into other processes.

CMMI Level 3 Defined (Standard, Consistent Processes)

Process Area	ADP Support
Engineering Process Area Requirements Dev. Technical Solution Product Integration Verification Validation	• Utilizing the infrastructure and best practices implemented in CMMI Level 2 to create a product. • Using ADP's general best practices in the product development cycle to meet the best practices expectations of both the customers and the industry at large. • Adding new customized best practices as needed and expanding them to the entire organization. • Automated testing tools support verification and validation.
Organization Process Focus	• Establishing organization-level ADP infrastructure by active integration of technology and people. • Extending the group ADP template (practices and policies) to the organization. • Ensuring that the group processes set up in CMMI Level 2 are consistently defined and sustainable for the entire organization and extended to support CMMI Level 3.
Organization Process Definition	• Differentiating between group practices and organization practices. • Ensuring that management has control over group processes that must deviate from the organizational standard.
Organizational Training	Training involves: • People roles. • Technology use. • Policies and practices for use of technology infrastructure. • Phase-in schedules for practices and policies. • Establishing training for new policies and procedures as well as for the software infrastructure tools—uniform training for uniform procedures across the organization. • Establishing a list of required training mapped to skills. • Automated training database tool to track training taken and to track training required versus taken. • Updating training based on defects found to prevent future defects.
Integrated Project Management/ Organizational Environment for Integration	• Gathering and tracking information from the ADP infrastructure through the reporting system. • Changing the infrastructure by appropriate parties when needed.
Integrated Teaming/ Integrated Supplier Management	• Ensuring integrated teaming (intergroup coordination) by providing each group in the organization with the same ADP infrastructure. • Mirroring the ADP technology infrastructure at the subcontractor/supplier's development location to ensure that the same practices and policies are followed by the subcontracting teams. • Tracking and measuring the subcontractor/supplier's project progress using the reporting system pursuant to the prior contractual agreement.
Decision Analysis and Resolution	• Scheduling periodic reviews of project status and inspection of artifacts. • Using data from the reporting system to analyze trends and make informed decisions.
Risk Management	• Identifying potential risks and defining contingency plans for risks identified in the extended planning phase. • Automated tracking of past risks helps in early identification of possible future risks.

Figure 10.7 *Continued*

CMMI Level 4 Quantitatively Managed (Predictable Processes)	
Process Area	ADP Support
Quantitative Project Management	• Establishing organization-level baselines for process measures and upper and lower control limits based on statistical analysis of automatically collected data. • Automated tracking and comparison of program and project level charts with the organization-level standards. • Calibrating of parametric models (such as COCOMO II) based on automatically collected historical data. • Analyzing trends described in Chapter 9 to facilitate deployment schedule and budget estimation and adjustments. • Using data and measurements from the reporting system to analyze the project status quantitatively. • Using the confidence factor to assess the overall quality of applications on a periodic basis.
Organizational Process Performance	• Introducing each practice individually and then stabilizing the key organizational practices using the data and measures generated by the reporting system. • Focusing on quality attributes and goals, and utilizing the ADP infrastructure to measure progress and to meet these goals.

CMMI Level 5 Optimizing (Continuous Process Improvement)	
Process Area	ADP Support
Organizational Innovation and Deployment	• Adding new practices and measuring their effectiveness. • Expanding the infrastructure, both people and technology, to improve organizational productivity and products quality.
Causal Analysis and Resolution	• Conducting root cause analysis of severe defects. • Implementing ADP defect prevention practices. • Analyzing trends and organization-level charts. Points outside of limits that stem from special-cause variations are subject to investigation and improvement.

Figure 10.7   *Continued*

10.4.4 Putting Continuous Representation–Based Improvement into Practice Using ADP

The continuous representation targets process capability instead of organizational maturity. Similar to maturity levels, *capability levels* demarcate what types of activities should be a focus of attention when driving selected practices to full implementation and optimization. In the continuous approach, individual processes [18] are advanced through the capability levels to full optimization. Therefore, it is possible to determine which defect prevention practices are needed in the development process and then concentrate on those practices.

Example of Implementing Coding Standards Practices in Continuous Representation For example, if a decision has been made to implement a set of coding standards in the development process, the first step is to select the development group that will practice this set of standards. The process would involve verifying the standards this group currently uses and possibly adding new rules to the existing set. In addition, the importance of the coding standards pass rate as a criterion for checking new code into the shared source control system needs to be determined. Personnel decisions would involve assigning responsibilities for coding standards selection, including the addition of new practices when needed by the project architect, manager, or lead developer.

Once coding standards are successful with one group or project, the next step is to introduce them to the entire organization, which moves the organization into Defined Level 3. Next, it needs to be determined which rules are to be used by the entire organization and which rules are to be used only by specific development groups.

Being able to quantitatively manage coding standards utilization helps to stabilize the process. Using a reporting system facilitates the measurement of coding standards effectiveness and whether other rules may be needed. Empirical data collected from the development process, such as nightly automated builds, regression tests, and other components of the infrastructure, will help diagnose additional problems and develop rules to counter them. Confidence factor values allow project managers and architects to determine coding standards effectiveness and stability. Once stable, the coding standards processes need to be optimized for the entire organization.

Note that the goal is not to configure the development group and life cycle for a set of practices, but rather for only one practice, which in this example is a set of coding standards advanced through all the levels to optimization. Overall, the organization might be only at CMMI Level 2 in a *staged representation*, but at Level 5 with respect to coding standards (which is a subset of the *technical solution* process area).

Once the selected coding standards practice in this example reaches Level 5, another practice could be selected and the process repeated. Whichever practice is chosen, the process should be similar to the one for advancing the coding standards to Level 5. For example, if the earned value analysis is chosen, it needs to be applied to a group, then to the organization, stabilized, and finally optimized.

The Advantages of Continuous Representation–Based Improvement
The advantage of the continuous approach is that the focus is on those practices and techniques that are immediately needed by the organization. The effectiveness of ADP with respect to continuous representation stems from the fact that once the group roles are defined, along with the technology infrastructure, very little work is required to drive a selected practice to Level 5. Driving a selected set of practices to Level 5 in the continuous model entails defining how the group will apply practices and use technology to ensure that those practices follow uniform policies.

Despite its immediate benefits, the continuous model is not recommended for organizations that require formal CMMI appraisals, because it focuses only on a limited set of practices.

10.5 ACRONYMS

ERP	Enterprise resource planning
FAA	Federal Aviation Administration
FDA	Food and Drug Administration
GSDOP	Generic software development process
RFIs	Requests for information
RFPs	Requests for proposals
SCAMPI	Standard CMMI Appraisal Method for Process Improvement
SOW	Statement of work
SOX	Sarbanes-Oxley Act of 2002
WAI	Web accessibility initiative

10.6 GLOSSARY

CMMI continuous model A comprehensive process model that is predicated on a set of system and software engineering capabilities. It defines process areas and levels of capability.

CMMI staged model A comprehensive process model that is predicated on the staged representation and five levels of maturity. To achieve a specified level of maturity a set of goals in predefined process areas must be met.

mirroring Direct copying of a data set.

statement of work A document that establishes the contractual foundation of the project. It provides the project team with a clear vision of the scope and objectives of what they are to achieve. [11]

web accessibility initiative WAI develops strategies, guidelines, and resources to help make the Web accessible to people with disabilities. [16]

10.7 REFERENCES

[1] The American Institute of Certified Public Accountants, *Sarbanes-Oxley Act of 2002*, January 23, 2002, http://frwebgate.access.gpo.gov/cgibin/getdoc.cgi?dbname=107_cong_bills&docid=f:h3763enr.txt.pdf (retrieved: Jun 15, 2006).

[2] Chrissis, M.B., Konrad, M., and Shrum, S., *CMMI: Guidelines for Process Integration and Product Improvement*. Addison Wesley, February 2005.

[3] International Organization for Standardization/International Electrotechnical Commission 90003-2004, *Software Engineering: Guidelines for the Application of ISO 9001:2000 to Computer Software*, ISO, 2004.

[4] Breyfogle III, F.W., *Implementing Six Sigma: Smarter Solutions Using Statistical Methods*. John Wiley & Sons, 2003.

[5] DiamondCluster, *IT Outsourcing: Following the Leaders May Well Lead to Failure*, October 30, 2002, http://www.diamondcluster.com/press/pressreleases/pressreleases285.asp (retrived: June 8, 2006).

[6] Haw, K., "Protecting Sensitive Data While Outsourcing Software Development Projects," Master's Degree Project Report, Computer Science Department, California State University, Fullerton, CA, May 2006.

[7] Marks, G., *The Complete Idiot's Guide to Successful Outsourcing*. New York, Penguin, 2005.

[8] Lidman, S. and Jacobson, I., *Controlled Offshore Outsourcing with an Active Process*, 2006, http://www.jaczone.com/papers/OutsourcingWithActiveProcess7.pdf (retrieved: June 8, 2006).

[9] Day, K., *Inside the Security Mind: Making the Tough Decisions*. Prentice Hall Professional Technical Reference, Upper Saddle River, NJ, 2003.

[10] Edwards, V.J., *Source Selection Answer Book*. Management Concepts, November 1, 2000.

[11] Martin, M.G., *Delivering Project Excellence with the Statement of Work*. Management Concepts, January 1, 2003.

[12] Government Services Administration, *Summary of Section 508 Standards*, January 23, 2006, http://www.section508.gov/index.cfm?FuseAction=Content&ID=11 (retrieved: April 3, 200 6).

[13] U.S. Census Bureau, *Persons with a Disability, Age 5+*, 2000, http://quickfacts.census.gov/qfd/meta/long_101608.htm (retrieved: June 8, 2006).

[14] U.S. Food and Drug Administration, *General Principles of Software Validation. Final Guidance for Industry and FDA Staff*, January 11, 2002, http://www.fda.gov/cdrh/comp/guidance/938.html (retrieved: Jun 8, 2006).

[15] U.S. General Services Administration, *Subpart 1194.22 Web-Based Intranet and Internet Information and Applications, Section 508: Section 508 Standards*, March 23, 2006, http://www.section508.gov/index.cfm?FuseAction=Content&ID=12#Web (Retrieved: June 15, 2006).

[16] The World Wide Web Consortium (W3C), *WAI Resources on Introducing Web Accessibility*, http://www.w3.org/WAI/gettingstarted/Overview.html (retrieved: June 8, 2006).

[17] Carnegie Mellon University Software Engineering Institute, *List of Published SCAMPI Appraisal Results*, http://seir.sei.cmu.edu/pars/pars_list_iframe.asp (retrieved: October 3, 2006).

[18] Shrum, S., *Choosing a CMMI Model Representation*, July 2000, http://www.stsc. hill.af.mil/crosstalk/2000/07/shrum.html (retrieved: October 3, 2006).

10.8 EXERCISES

1. Explain the phases of an outsourced software development project and its relationship to ADP.

2. Why is the decision to outsource so vital to many companies' future missions?

3. What is the role of the infrastructure in implementing a successful outsourced project?

4. Why is maintaining a good working relationship so critical for outsourced projects?

5. In addition to material mentioned in this chapter, what other means could be undertaken to facilitate a solid long-term relationship with an outsourcer?

6. What can be automated in verifying Section 508 compliance and how can this be accomplished?

7. What are common SOX problems?

8. Which ADP best practices facilitate compliance with SOX?

9. How can ADP facilitate making SOX and perhaps other compliance-approval decisions?

10. Give an example of how ADP can facilitate an implementation of CMMI Level 5 best practices.

CHAPTER 11

CASE STUDY: AUTOMATION AS AN AGENT OF CHANGE

11.1 CASE STUDY: IMPLEMENTING JAVA CODING STANDARDS IN A FINANCIAL APPLICATION[a]

11.1.1 Company Profile

Lehman Brothers is a major financial institution that provides services to corporations, governments and municipalities, institutional clients, and high-net-worth individuals worldwide. In particular, the company maintains market leadership positions in equity and fixed income sales, trading and research, investment banking, private investment management, asset management, and private equity. The company is a member of the S&P 500, with revenue near $12 billion, total capital near $71 billion, and approximately 115,000 common stockholders.

The company's revenues are highly dependent upon their IT systems. For instance, in their commercial paper (fixed income notes within a year of maturity) business, they process approximately $40 billion worth of transactions per day. The transactions must settle by 2:30 P.M. of the current day. Any system downtime can be devastating, considering that 90% of the transactions are performed electronically (70% through an outside trading firm and 20% through the internal sales force; only 10% of transactions are performed in

[a] Printed with permission of Lehman Brothers.

Automated Defect Prevention: Best Practices in Software Management, by Dorota Huizinga and Adam Kolawa
Copyright © 2007 John Wiley & Sons, Inc.

the traditional manner, where clients call in and a trader actually books trades). Even a short, intermittent downtime that prevents the company from sending out data could force them to have to finance $10–$20 million in paper overnight.

The company's U.S. fixed income offering is commonly viewed as its greatest strength. The IT systems that support their Fixed Income division include:

- Money Markets E-trading Services
- Auction Rate Trading System
- Muni Real Time P/L & Risk
- Money Market Back Office Feeds
- Web-Based Money Market sales front end
- MSRB Real Time Regulatory Reporting
- Whole Loan Inventory Management System

The applications that power these systems range in size, but most average approximately 1 million lines of code. These applications are typically multi-platform, multilanguage, and built on a service-oriented architecture. For instance, the Auction Rate Trading System has a .NET front end (written in C#), a J2EE middle tier, and various services that handle pricing, trade processing, and so on.

11.1.2 Problems

The Fixed Income Technologies team, consisting of 30 onsite developers and 27 developers employed by Indian and Canadian outsourcing organizations, was responsible for the critical financial applications listed above.

Two key quality-related problems alerted the management that their software development process needed improvement:

1. Intermittent failures of the Auction Rate Trading System
2. Strained relationships with the outsourcer due to the nonexpandability of the outsourced code

Intermittent Failures of Auction Rate Trading System The Auction Rate Trading System, which is one of the company's critical applications, was experiencing intermittent failures on a weekly basis. The cause of this problem was not known at this point. The application code base contained both locally developed code and outsourced code.

The Fixed Income Technologies team management had previously defined best practices and quality standards for the developers to follow when implementing the business-critical financial applications detailed above. Unfortunately, code reviews, which would normally uncover problems and help maintain such standards, did not occur on a regular basis. Manual inspections required a considerable amount of time and tedious work, and the team had few resources to spare, mainly due to the company's executives expecting team members "to do more with less." With limited resources and difficult tradeoffs to make, the team decided to spend its time meeting expected functionality deadlines rather than performing code reviews. Consequently, code reviews were performed erratically. Soon the accumulated code base grew so large and complex (multiplatform, multilanguage, built-in service-oriented architecture) that with the additional problem of developer turnover, the inspections appeared to be an exercise in futility.

As a result of these complexities, it was unclear whether the intermittent failures resulted from code that did not satisfy the existing quality standards or from an issue that the team had not previously encountered.

The authors of this book concur with Royce [1], who contends that inspections are overestimated as a key part of quality in modern software systems. The high level of complexity of modern software systems with "innumerable components, concurrent execution, distributed resources, and other equally demanding dimensions of difficulty" necessitates the use of automation, leaving only the most critical components to manual inspection.

Strained Relationships with the Outsourcer Due to the Nonexpandability of the Outsourced Code The relationship with the outsourcer was strained when the team manager discovered that the local team could not easily modify and expand the code delivered by the outsourcer.

As software development undergoes multiple iterations, the team is expected to build new functionality onto existing code over a short timeline. Inability to do so could cause missed deadlines and financial hardships. Therefore, the team was in a difficult position. They had already accepted and paid for the outsourcers' code, because it operated satisfactorily. Now they had to discard several application components and spend additional resources to rewrite them. They had turned to outsourcing to reduce costs, but if this trend continued, outsourcing was likely to become a liability.

The team manager decided that in order to make outsourcing a reliable and cost-effective development strategy, the company needed to mandate that outsourced code satisfy a specific set of *objective and measurable* standards. Thus, there was a need for a quality control system that would automatically check and measure the level of compliance of the submitted code with the required standards. It was important that the outsourcers knew exactly what was expected of them, and the company was able to identify noncompliant code during each code delivery.

After evaluating the above problems, the team manager identified the need for a comprehensive approach to enforcing coding standards in order to improve product quality. He realized that "having coding standards has little benefit without a way of enforcing them comprehensively throughout the team." Consequently, he decided to implement the principles and practices of Automated Defect Prevention.

What initially attracted the manager to our methodology was its focus on automation, which would enable him to require that all developers, both local and outsourced, satisfied the required quality standards without slowing down the development process. He knew from experience that manual code inspections required significant team resources, and were commonly neglected when the team had to choose between project-critical tasks and code inspections (a tradeoff that was often required). By automating coding standard enforcement and embedding it into the team's existing infrastructure (which included an Ant automated build process[b] that worked with a source control system), the new quality control could be introduced comprehensively and seamlessly.

11.1.3 Solution

The new practices were initially applied to the Java middle tier[c] of two multilanguage, multiplatform IT systems: the Auction Rate Trading System and the Muni Real Time P/L & Risk System. It was later applied to the Money Market E-trading Service and Money Market Office Feeds.

The *automated defect prevention* principles were applied as follows:

Principle 1: Establishment of Infrastructure The team already had a working source control system and automated build system when the ADP implementation began. An automated testing system and static analysis technologies were integrated into the infrastructure, as was a new automated reporting system. During each automated nightly build, this integrated environment would access the team's most recent code from the source control system, test the code, and then send the results to the reporting system. The reporting system would then organize the results into role-based reports tailored to the specific needs of the manager, architect, and individual developers. Team members could access appropriate reports via a web-based interface.

Principle 2: Application of General Best Practices Even though the system was already deployed, the team manager decided to apply the selected coding standards to both the old and the new code because the intermittent system failures had to be resolved as soon as possible.

The architect suspected that the system's intermittent failures were probably the result of resource leaks (i.e., resources such as network connections, and input and output streams that were allocated but not freed after they were

[b] Apache Ant is a Java-based build tool [2].
[c] In three-tier software architecture, the middle tier is located between the client and server components. It provides process management where business logic and rules are executed.

used), and improperly handled errors (code that does not reroute program control appropriately after an error occurs).

Java's I/O is very powerful and has an overwhelming number of options. The general principle is to open an I/O stream, use it and, then close it. However, if close() is not called to release the I/O stream before the call ends, a resource leak occurs.

Exceptions and error-handling routines are difficult to code because they occur asynchronously to code execution. Thus, regardless of the programming language, developers often struggle with the proper handling of exceptions.

After reviewing the types of defects that various best practices could prevent, the architect selected two practices that he believed would identify the code that caused the intermittent system failures and would prevent subsequent ones.

These two coding standards were:

1. Avoid try, catch, and finally blocks with empty bodies.
2. Close input and output resources in finally blocks.

JAVA'S EXCEPTION HANDLING AND RESOURCE DEALLOCATION

The try Block

The first step in writing an exception handler is to enclose the statements that might throw an exception within a try block. The try block governs the statements enclosed within it and defines the scope of any associated exception handlers (established by subsequent catch blocks).

The catch Block(s)

Next, the exception handlers are associated with a try block by providing one or more catch blocks directly after the try block.

The finally Block

Java's finally block provides a mechanism that allows a method to clean up after itself regardless of what happens within the try block. The finally block should be used to close files and release other system resources.

Enforcing the first coding standard (which is based on the findings of Joshua Bloch [3]) involves identifying try, catch, and/or finally blocks with empty bodies, which indicate unhandled errors. Catch blocks can be used to log information about exceptions that caused the problem. To make code comply with this standard, developers would have to ensure that the application handled every error appropriately (for instance, by logging the problem before continuing program execution).

Enforcing the second coding standard involves identifying code that does not close input and output resources in finally blocks. To make the code comply with this standard, developers would have to structure the code to close and release I/O resources in all cases, even in exception and error conditions.

Principle 3: Customization of Best Practices The manager decided to customize the coding standards best practices. He found that in some cases it was appropriate to have empty catch blocks, and he wanted to ensure two things:

1. That all those instances were well-documented for anyone else who read or worked on this code
2. That they were not reported as errors

As a result, he customized the implementation of the "Avoid try, catch, and finally blocks with empty bodies" coding standard rule. The standard rule reported an error for any empty catch block, whereas the customized rule reported an error only for empty catch blocks that lacked comments.

Principle 4: Measurement and Tracking of Project Status Each night, the automated tool performed static analysis to determine whether the code conformed to coding standards. Additionally, unit testing was conducted and reports were generated to alert team members to violations of standards as well as failed tests. This helped the team identify and correct problems in the existing code base. Once these defects were corrected, the automated scans and tests continued, checking all new and modified code. The data collected measured whether the developers were following the best practices as they were adding and modifying code. This early and frequent checking was essential for preventing additional defects from being introduced into the code base and affecting application reliability.

The generated reports were initially tracking whether the code satisfied a variety of best practices in addition to the few that the team was required to follow. To make it easier to determine if the required best practices were being followed, some reports were customized to show only violations of the required best practices. A customized report with zero violations indicated that the best practices were followed, while any problems reported indicated that the process needed to be improved to ensure best practice compliance.

Principle 5: Automation Enforcement of the new general best practices and their customized versions, which were the coding standards for try, catch, and finally Java statements, was supported by a static analyzer. The static analyzer scanned the source code and flagged an error if the rules were not followed. Both the developers and the architect had the static analyzer installed and appropriately configured.

To further assess and improve the quality of the code base, the architect configured the static analyzer to check whether the code complied with coding standards that have been shown to significantly improve code reliability, security, performance, and maintainability.

Sample rules included:

Reliability Rules:

- Avoid dangling `else` statements.
- Do not assign loop control variables in the body of a `for` loop.

Security Rules:

- Do not compare Class objects by name.
- Do not pass byte arrays to DataOutputStream in the `writeObject()` method.
- Make your `clone()` method final for security.

Performance Rules:

- Prevent potential memory leaks in `ObjectOutputStreams` by calling `reset()`.
- Use `String` instead of `StringBuffer` for constant strings.

Maintainability Rules:

- Provide `Javadoc` comments and descriptions for classes and interfaces.
- Use chain constructors in classes with multiple constructors.
- Declare package-private methods as inaccessible to external interfaces.

While the adherence to nonrequired best practices was also tracked, the architect did not yet require them to avoid overwhelming the team with too many new standards.

The team also decided to use a tool to automate the generation and execution of unit tests and integrate the tool with its existing infrastructure.

Principle 6: Incremental Implementation of ADP's Practices and Policies

Phasing in ADP on a Team-by-Team Basis   The project manager started by implementing defect prevention for his immediate team (including internal, onshore, and offshore developers), with the intention of later implementation across related development teams in the organization.

Phasing in Each Practice Incrementally   It was decided to start the implementation by checking compliance with only one coding standard: "Avoid `try`, `catch`, and `finally` blocks with empty bodies." The automated tool identified all coding standards violations in the code base, and the team members corrected the reported violations. After these violations were corrected, a second coding standard was introduced: "Close input and output resources in `finally` blocks." Once the team corrected all the existing violations of this coding standard, automated unit testing was phased in.

To ensure that the required best practices were being applied to both the new and modified code (an essential task for preventing further application reliability problems), compliance with all of these practices was still checked on a nightly basis.

Implementing a Group Workflow That Guarantees That ADP Practices Are Performed Appropriately   The implemented workflow was as follows:

The architect decided on the configuration of the technology that would automate coding standards verification and unit test execution (what rules would be checked, how test cases would be generated, and so on). He also configured the reporting to be performed automatically during the nightly build.

Since the automated coding standards verification and testing began, developers have been using the reporting system to view results when they arrive at work each morning. They correct the reported problems during the day, and then add the corrected code, as well as new or modified code completed during the day, to the source control system before they leave each evening.

The manager and the architect review the results each morning to ensure that the standards and best practices are being followed and to determine whether the process requires modification (for instance, to phase in additional best practices, modify the test settings, and so on).

11.1.4   Data Collected

The new infrastructure conducted static analysis of the code to verify that it complied with the two coding standards that the architect selected for immediate implementation. It also checked whether code complied with other coding standards, even though the team was not yet required to follow them.

Additionally, the configured infrastructure automatically generated and executed unit test cases for the application.

The data collected included the number of rule violations reported by the static analysis tool, the number of code revisions, and the number of failed tests reported by the dynamic analysis tool. The collected data was stored in a reporting system. The reports allowed developers to quickly identify and

Check-in Code

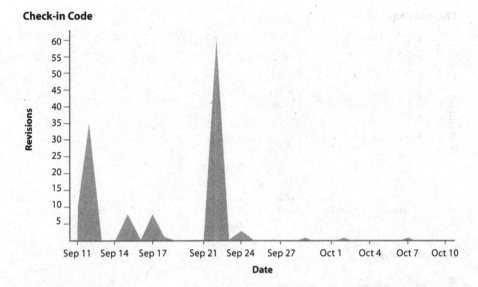

Rules Violations

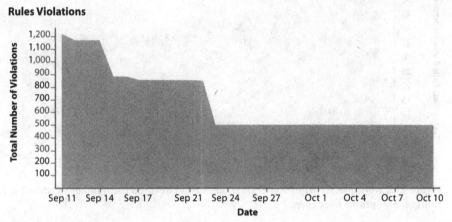

Figure 11.1 Graphs showing how code modifications lowered the number of coding standards violations over time.

locate specific problems in each application and to provide actionable feedback to in-house and outsourcer team members.

The graphs in Figure 11.1 show how the modification of the code affected the number of coding standards violations. The initial number of coding standards violations reported was approximately 1,200. The team corrected all of the violations of the two most critical coding standards (missing closure of resources in `finally` blocks and empty `catch` blocks) required by the architect; later, the team members also corrected many coding standards violations related to other industry-standard Java coding standards that improve code reliability, security, performance, and maintainability. After the initial code

Check-in Code

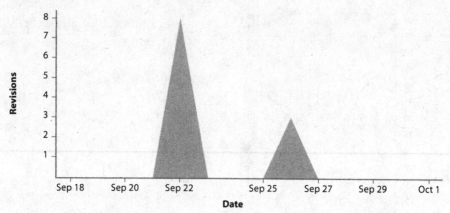

Dynamic Analysis

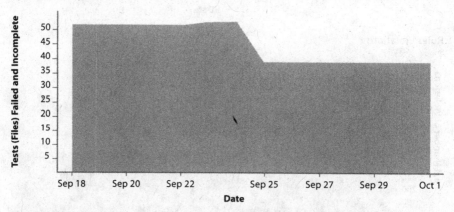

Figure 11.2   Graphs showing how code modification lowered the number of uncaught runtime exceptions over time.

cleanup, the number of coding standards violations was reduced to approximately 500.

The spike in the first graph, followed by a drop in the second graph, indicates that the expected workflow was being followed: developers apparently modified code to correct many of the reported defects and checked in the corrected code (causing the spike in checked-in code), followed by an immediate drop in the number of rule violations.

The graphs in Figure 11.2 show similar results for uncaught runtime exceptions detected during test execution. Initially, over 50 uncaught runtime exceptions were detected in the code base. The team reviewed the reported uncaught runtime exceptions and corrected the ones in the most critical sections of code.

11.1.5 The Bottom Line Results—Facilitating Change

Immediate Benefits The most obvious benefit was improved application reliability. Prior to the initial code cleanup, the system was experiencing intermittent failures and requiring restarts approximately one to two times per week. In this company's business, even a short system failure can be costly: if a trading application fails and trades are not completed by the end of the day, the company must pay a day's interest on the bonds, which can easily be $500 K or higher, based on current rates and volumes.

Since the initial code cleanup, there have been no reported system failures.

Considering that the application has been constantly evolving since the initial ADP implementation in September 2003, and continues to change almost daily, these results indicate that the methodology not only helped the team eliminate the existing defects, but also prevented the introduction of similar defects.

Long-Term Benefits One of the most important long-term benefits of using defect prevention, as evidenced in this case study, is the fact that consistent monitoring of coding standards compliance resulted in the team's *culture change* for both the local and outsourced groups. Developers have learned that code that does not satisfy coding standards will not be accepted, so they now scan the code *before* checking it in. Thus, the group began to focus on building quality into the code and testing new/modified code as soon as it is completed.

This has a positive long-term impact on the maintainability of the Fixed Income applications. Since the code is written in a manner consistent with the organization's standards, the software developers responsible for maintaining and expanding the code can better understand it. This is important because the software developers maintaining the code are often not the original creators of the code.

The company's relationship with the outsourcers dramatically improved. The managers could instantly receive an objective assessment of the code as it was delivered. They knew immediately if code satisfied the quality guidelines; if not, they provided the outsourcer a list of specific problems to fix. When the company requested corrections to the outsourcer's code, the outsourcers realized that it was because the code did not satisfy the guidelines.

Another advantage was an increase in development productivity. Developers now spend less time debugging, and more time creating new functionality. Developer morale has improved because developers are producing higher-quality code and spending more time on creative, interesting tasks rather than rewriting and debugging code. As a result, project predictability has improved.

Moreover, when the manager asked one of his team leaders how implementation of ADP has impacted the team and the project, the team leader replied: "There isn't so much impact because we don't have as many errors now."

This statement highlights the benefits of ADP for this team: the team found a way to reduce the amount of defects without disrupting or diverting resources from their already-hectic schedule. *Positive changes had occurred.*

11.2 ACRONYMS

MSRB	Municipal Securities Rulemaking Board
P/L	Profit and loss

11.3 GLOSSARY

Ant   Apache Ant is a Java-based build tool.

Javadoc   A tool for generating API documentation in HTML format.

middle tier   In a three-tier system architecture, the middle tier is between the user interface (client) and the data management (server) components. This middle tier provides process management where business logic and rules are executed.

11.4 REFERENCES

[1] Royce, W., *Software Project Management: A Unified Framework*. Addison-Wesley, 1998.

[2] The Apache Software Foundation, *Apache Ant*, 2006, http://ant.apache.org/ (Retrieved: February 17, 2006).

[3] Bloch, J., *Effective Java: Programming Language Guide*. Addison-Wesley, 2001.

APPENDIX A

A BRIEF SURVEY OF MODERN SOFTWARE DEVELOPMENT PROCESS MODELS

A.1 INTRODUCTION

This appendix provides a quick survey of the modern software development process models that have evolved from the waterfall model as discussed in Chapter 1.

A.2 RAPID APPLICATION DEVELOPMENT (RAD) AND RAPID PROTOTYPING

Rapid application development (RAD) is an iterative process that relies heavily on user involvement throughout development [1]. This involvement is especially important during an initial design phase. In RAD, the entire team (composed of 10 or fewer developers and users) meets at the beginning of the process to determine requirements and a fundamental project design. It is often difficult to settle on requirements and a design without seeing and using the product, but much time can be wasted developing a product before the requirements and design have been agreed upon. RAD teams break out of this cycle by producing, reviewing, and refining a fundamental prototype during the design phase. Once the project requirements are defined, the

---

Automated Defect Prevention: Best Practices in Software Management, by Dorota Huizinga and Adam Kolawa
Copyright © 2007 John Wiley & Sons, Inc.

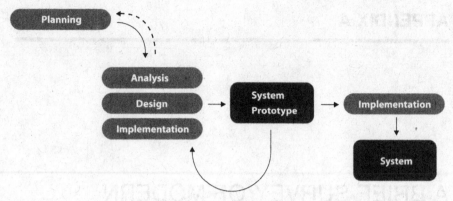

Figure A.1   Prototyping development (adapted from Dennis, Wixom and Roth, 2005 [2]).

developers model the structure and interaction of the objects needed to implement the requirements (Figure A.1).

After the analysis and design is complete, the team implements the design in a series of iterations. Each iteration typically lasts several weeks, and implements the subset of features that the team agreed to implement for that iteration. The features implemented are almost always based on requirements set forth in the design phase; there is some flexibility for refining existing requirements and adding new ones, but only when the modifications will fit within the original design. To ensure that the implementation is indeed rapid, the team uses CASE tools to model and generate the code. After one iteration is completed, the customer can use the product and—if necessary—suggest any necessary refinements. The next iteration will begin, and then the team will continue cycling though iterations until the initial design has been completely implemented. RAD's main advantages stem from its insistence on a design phase. Because developers and customers agree on a design before implementation begins, developers are aware of the "big picture" while they are coding. They know how different units will work together, which in turn allows them to implement the product more elegantly and logically, as well as avoid much of the rewriting.

Having a design phase also helps the team to estimate project deadlines and budgets. With RAD, the team always knows the overall project parameters and milestones that must be met before the project is considered complete. With XP and other processes that lack a design phase, the safest practice is to make short-term estimates at the beginning of each iteration.

RAD is used for a project that is very dynamic or whose scope is difficult to define upfront, problems are likely because RAD is not designed to accommodate substantial change. The original features can be refined during the iterations, but RAD leaves little room for adding new features that do not fit into the original design.

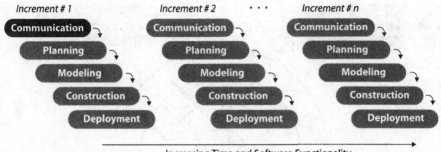

Figure A.2 An incremental development process containing many frequent design/implementation/integration/testing cycles.

A.3 INCREMENTAL DEVELOPMENT

Incremental development involves a series of frequent iterations of the design/implementation/integration/test cycle, as shown in Figure A.2. Each cycle implements *different* features that the customer requests or deems appropriate. New components and functionality are added sequentially. For example, if the software is to control a video game, one would build the control engine for a subset of game rules first, and then add more rules in the next increments until the desired level of functionality is achieved. Thus, the product is designed and constructed as a series of incremental builds, which consists of multiple modules that provide specified capabilities. A typical product consists of 5 to 25 builds [3].

The incremental process is well-suited for situations where there is some general project direction, but the product is continually redefined via the addition of different features. This approach is well-suited to innovative projects because their short iteration times allow the team to quickly show the customer the results of the latest request. This allows for rapid feedback on the success of the most recent iteration and the direction of the next. Such frequent and rapid feedback is not necessary for traditional projects (such as building a standard accounting or database program for internal use), but is critical for more innovative projects (such as the development of Google, Amazon, Yahoo!, or other projects that started with a very loose specification, then evolved in ways never imagined at the project's inception).

A.4 SPIRAL MODEL

The *spiral software development* model proposed by Boehm in 1988 [4] was based mostly on experience from working with large projects using the waterfall approach. This risk analysis–oriented approach is depicted in Figure A.3. The radial dimension of this figure represents cumulative cost incurred in

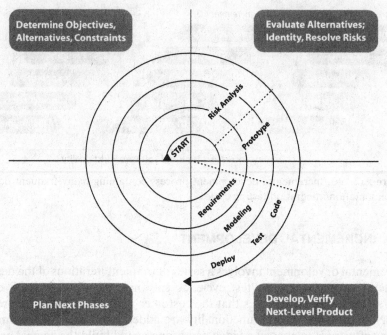

Figure A.3   Spiral development (simplified diagram adapted from Boehm, 1988 [4]).

accomplishing the steps to date; the angular dimension represents the progress made in completing each cycle of the spiral. Each cycle starts with a requirements phase followed by risk analysis and prototyping, then modeling, coding, testing, and finally deployment. Areas of uncertainty that are significant sources of project risk are identified and reevaluated at the beginning of each cycle. Then, a strategy for resolving such risks is proposed based on prototyping, simulation, or benchmarking. These tasks are shared by activities in all phases. Next, phase-specific tasks are accomplished; these tasks include requirements specification and validation, software design and design validation, detailed design, coding, followed by unit, integration, and acceptance testing, and culminating in the product deployment (which Boehm called implementation).

The risk-driven approach in the spiral model accommodates a project-specific mix of software development strategies. The important feature of the spiral model is that each cycle is completed by a user review, whose major objective is to ensure that users are satisfied with the current progress and committed to the next phase.

The plans for the subsequent phases may include partitioning the product into increments for successive development or components to be developed simultaneously by various organizations or teams. This aspect of the spiral approach is similar to the RAD incremental development described above.

The spiral model has been used successfully in large software projects. Its risk-adverse approach, which is its primary advantage, eliminates many potential problems and accommodates the best features of more development-specific methodologies. As reported by Boehm (1988), over 25 projects had at that time used all or portions of the spiral model. All the projects fully using the system had increased their productivity at least 50%.

A.5   OBJECT-ORIENTED UNIFIED PROCESS

By the time that object-oriented methods had gained widespread acceptance in the software engineering community in the early 1990s, there was not a single object-oriented analysis and design standard until Rumbaugh, Booch, and Jacobson defined a Unified Modeling Language (UML) [5]. UML, which is an industry standard today, provides a solid notation for modeling and object-oriented software development. To complement UML, a *unified process* model was developed [6]. (The unified process is sometimes called Rational Unified Process (RUP) after the Rational Corporation, primary builder of the original software tools to support UML and the unified process.) (See Figure A.4.)

The unified process utilizes iterative and incremental development, and it builds on the best features of other models, emphasizing communication with customers and the implementation of *use cases* as the best methods for describing the customer's view of a system. It also takes an "architecture-first" approach, stressing the importance of a high-level system design capable of adapting to future changes and reuse.

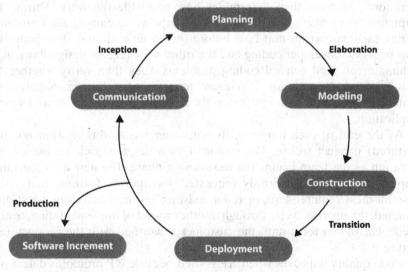

Figure A.4   Object-oriented unified process life cycle model.

Phases of the unified process include inception, elaboration, construction, transition, and production. The *inception* phase encompasses both customer communication and planning activities. The *elaboration* phase consists of planning and modeling. This phase refines the preliminary use cases defined in the inception stage. In the *construction* phase, all the necessary features of the software (or its increment, or release), as defined by the use cases, are implemented. In addition, unit tests, integration tests, and acceptance tests driven by use cases are conducted. The *transition* phase includes *beta testing* by users, which results in user feedback on defects and functionality problems. At the end of this phase, software release takes place. During the phase following the release, referred to as the *production* phase of the unified process, the functioning software is monitored to eliminate possible defects and make requested changes. An important feature of the unified process is that in addition to being iterative and incremental, it employs a high degree of parallel development, with its stages being staggered rather than sequential.

A.6 EXTREME AND AGILE PROGRAMMING

Extreme programming (XP) assumes that product requirements will change, so the application is designed and developed incrementally in a series of brief design-coding-testing iterations [7]. Each iteration begins with a team of 10 or fewer developers and at least one user representative (the "customer") determining what features the upcoming 1- to 2-week iteration will implement. During each iteration's design phase, the user provides a list of "stories" she would like implemented, the developer estimates the time required to implement each story, and then the user decides what to implement in the current iteration. The team then determines how to divide the work. During the implementation phase, the developers might work in pairs (*paired programming*): each pair writes unit tests before they code each unit, then writes the unit with one developer coding and the other watching for design flaws, algorithmic errors, and general coding problems. They then verify whether the unit is correct by running all relevant tests the team has accumulated. On a daily basis, each pair integrates their thoroughly tested code into the application.

At the end of each iteration, the customer has a working (but not full-featured) product to use. The customer provides feedback on the current iteration as the team begins the next design phase. The new iteration might implement features previously requested, incorporate features that satisfy new business requirements, or refine existing features. After this iteration is planned, the process cycles through another round of implementation, testing, feedback, and so forth until the customer is satisfied with the product. (See Figure A.5.)

Code quality improves when XP is used because XP promotes defect prevention in the following ways:

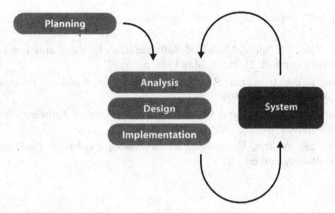

Figure A.5 Extreme programming development stages (adapted from Dennis, Wixom and Roth, 2005 [2]).

- By requiring developers to create unit test cases for each piece of code even before it is written, XP ensures that testing occurs throughout the development process, instead of just at the end. Early testing prevents defects from propagating and becoming deeply embedded in the code.
- By requiring developers to build a large number of test cases and rerun the entire suite rigorously, XP encourages test automation. Test automation reduces the risk of human error. Also, if the testing is automated, defects can be identified and removed quickly.
- By utilizing paired programming, XP prompts developers to engage in perpetual code review, and it encourages developers to follow coding standards that avoid confusing and dangerous coding constructs. When developers follow proven coding guidelines, modifications are much less likely to introduce errors.

Other advantages of XP include:

- It has the ability to accommodate the frequent changes and unexpected requirements common in today's development environments.
- Its insistence on producing correct code and frequently integrating it into the application means that the product can almost always be shown to the customers in a workable state.

A.7 REFERENCES

[1] Martin, J., *Rapid Application Development*. Prentice-Hall, 1991.
[2] Dennis, A., Wixom, B., and Roth, R., *Systems Analysis and Design*. John Wiley & Sons, 3rd ed., 2005.

[3] Schach, S.R., *Object-Oriented and Classical Software Engineering*. McGraw Hill, 2002.

[4] Boehm, B.W., "A Spiral Model of Software Development and Enhancement," *IEEE Computer*, Vol. 21, No. 5, May 1988, pp. 61–72.

[5] Jacobson, I., Booch, G., and Rumbaugh, J., *The Unified Modeling Language User Guide*. Addison-Wesley, 1999.

[6] Jacobson, I., Booch, G., and Rumbaugh, J., *The Unified Software Development Process*. Addison-Wesley, 1999.

[7] Beck, K. and Andres, C., *Extreme Programming Explained: Embrace Change*. Addison-Wesley, 2nd ed., 2004.

APPENDIX B

MARS POLAR LANDER (MPL): LOSS AND LESSONS
BY GORDON HEBERT

The Mars Polar Lander (MPL) could have been a great success. It might have provided precious scientific evidence regarding Martian resources and natural history, including possibly some "evidence of past or present life" [1]. However, MPL has been incommunicado since December 3, 1999 [2]. Rather than dwell on misfortune, we must try to learn from this experience and perhaps contribute to greater future scientific achievements.

B.1 NO DEFINITE ROOT CAUSE

Defect causal analysis is an important aspect of a defect prevention program [3]. In the case of the Mars Polar Lander (MPL), the lack of hard data makes it impossible to be certain of the root cause of its unfortunate outcome. Researchers seem to be in agreement regarding the uncertainty [4]. The various failure possibilities and lack of telemetry contribute to the lack of definitive knowledge of root cause. Product development constraints may have led to increased risk taking. Some of those constraints may have been technical, while others could have been administrative. The undetermined cause of the mission outcome notwithstanding, there are still lessons to be learned regarding future defect prevention. (See Figure B.1.)

Automated Defect Prevention: Best Practices in Software Management, by Dorota Huizinga and Adam Kolawa
Copyright © 2007 John Wiley & Sons, Inc.

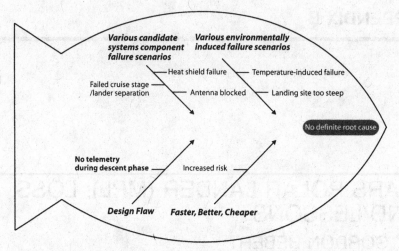

Figure B.1 Fishbone diagram illustrating possible causes of MPL failure.

A Jet Propulsion Laboratory (JPL) Special Review Board (SRB) *Report on the Loss of the Mars Polar Lander and Deep Space 2 Missions* [5] supports the indefinite postmortem, yet still indicates "little doubt about the probable cause":

> [The] probable cause of the loss of MPL has been traced to premature shutdown of the descent engines, resulting from a vulnerability of the software to transient signals.

The JPL SRB report also considers several alternative failure scenarios.

B.2 NO MISSION DATA

Regardless of whether the MPL entry, descent, and landing (EDL) phases were in fact successful, there remains one direct outcome: desired scientific data regarding water or ice on Mars will very likely never be obtained from the MPL mission. That outcome is simply because no signal was received after MPL's initial descent. What happened? What might have prevented it? Could software development process automation have prevented this mission failure? (See Figure B.2.)

While identification of a *single* root cause potentially enables specific process improvements to address the issue, there can be cases of *multiple* or *indefinite* causes. Some defects representing candidate causes may be found during the course of an investigation. The question of whether a product has a defect may still be addressed, regardless of whether a cause of a specific incident is fully understood.

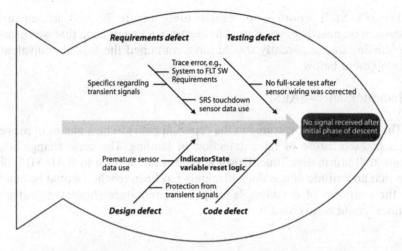

Figure B.2 Fishbone diagram with a focus on the IndicatorState.

There is some evidence of sensor wiring design defects and subsequent system testing defects [6–8]; reports state that "after the wiring was corrected, the test was not repeated."

The JPL SRB report also suggests requirements defects. In that report, "Figure 7-9, MPL System Requirements Mapping to Flight Software Requirements" contains examples that may not be considered acceptable requirements, depending on the process used. Page 488 of *CMMI Guidelines for Process Integration and Process Improvement* [9] discusses "objective criteria for the acceptance of requirements." The book states that requirements must be *complete, uniquely identified*, and *traceable*. While the book referred to was published after the MPL incident, principles mentioned still represent ways to benefit from experience. This assessment relies on the JPL SRB report regarding requirements as represented in Figure 7-9 of that report. That figure surely does not represent all the requirements, but it is all this author has as a basis of requirements-related assessment. It does appear that others [10] have also used the report as a basis of examining requirements-related issues. Not surprisingly, it is also evident from the report itself that other relevant requirements exist. For example, earlier in section 7.7.2 (page 114), the report indicates the need both to prevent turnover of the Lander by insuring timely thrust termination and to prevent premature engine shutdown.

The JPL SRB report clearly and explicitly supports a requirements defect concept. The report identifies a requirements change as follows:

1. The touchdown sensors shall be sampled at 100-Hz rate. The sampling process shall be initiated prior to lander entry to keep processor demand constant. However, the use of touchdown sensor data shall not begin until 12 meters above the surface. [*Note:* The altitude was later changed from 12 meters to 40 meters above the surface.]

The JPL SRB report is not light reading. Figure 7-8 and accompanying discussion on nearby pages is used to illustrate a line of code that was missing. The missing line apparently should have contained the logical equivalent of the statement below:

IndicatorState = FALSE

The code change illustrated in the report appears to be a means of preventing a possible cause of false detection of landing. The code change would ensure that affirmative TouchDown measures taken prior to RADAR indication that an altitude of less than 40 meters has been reached would be ignored for the purposes of detecting landing, and premature shutdown of descent engines would be avoided.

B.3 ROOT CAUSE REVISITED

The JPL SRB report characterizes the probable root cause as a single line of code that was missing from the MPL flight software. Yet the code was apparently missing due to a design defect that was in turn due to a requirements defect. Regression testing that should have been performed did not occur after related sensors were rewired, presumably due to other defects. Requirements defects are explicitly indicated by the JPL SRB report, and in the opinion of this author, requirements management is probably the area where process improvement would be the most beneficial means of preventing recurrence of this problem.

Figure 7-9 of the JPL SRB report includes a list of some System Requirements. The one requirement quoted above is repeated in a different format in Figure B.3.

SYSTEM REQUIREMENTS identification number indicated by JPL SRB report section 7.7.2.	SYSTEM REQUIREMENTS indicated by JPL SRB report section 7.7.2.
1	The touchdown sensors shall be sampled at 100-Hz rate.
	The sampling process shall be initiated prior to lander entry to keep processor demand constant.
	However, the use of the touchdown sensor data shall not begin until 12 meters above the surface. (*Note:* The altitude was later changed from 12 meters to 40 meters above the surface.)

Figure B.3 System requirements for touchdown sensors.

FLIGHT SOFTWARE REQUIREMENTS identification number indicated by JPL SRB report section 7.7.2.	FLIGHT SOFTWARE REQUIREMENTS indicated by JPL SRB report section 7.7.2.
3.7.2.2.4.1.a.	The lander flight software shall cyclically check the state of each of the three touchdown sensors (one per leg) at 100 Hz during EDL.
3.7.2.2.4.1.b.	The lander flight software shall be able to cyclically check the touchdown event state with or without touchdown event generation enabled.

Figure B.4   Software requirements for touchdown sensors.

The table in Figure B.3 uses the number 1 to uniquely identify the starting point in the table where each (in this case, one) System Requirement is defined. The numeric label determination is consistent with the representation in Figure 7-9 of the JPL SRB report. However, this author notes the use of the word *shall* as a countable indicator of a unique, separate requirement, and therefore each *shall* is in a separate row of the table above. In these terms, we have not *uniquely identified* each separate requirement. That makes identification of unique requirements and meaningful requirements tracing difficult. Unique identifiers support complete requirements traceability.

The table in Figure B.4 is also derived from Figure 7-9 of the JPL SRB report. In this case, the Flight Software Requirements are listed along with their unique identifiers.

In contrast with the observation that System Requirements were not uniquely identified, it is interesting to note that the Flight Software Requirements are uniquely identified. Had both System Requirements and Software Requirements been uniquely identified, it may have been possible for some level of automation in tracking, measurement, and change impact area assessment activities.

Why was the last part of System Requirement 7.7.2 not addressed? A requirements trace based on Figure 7-9 of the JPL SRB report, shown in Figure B.5, may help illuminate this. Please note that "Unlabeled System Requirement 1.c" corresponds to the following System Requirement:

However, the use of the touchdown sensor data shall not begin until 12 meters above the surface.

There is no Flight Software Requirement traced to the above System Requirement. The middle column in the table in Figure B.5 has one blank row for the missing Flight Software Requirement at issue. This lack of a trace is a requirements management defect. The "missing line of code" corresponds to

SYSTEM REQUIREMENTS identification number indicated by JPL SRB report section 7.7.2.	FLIGHT SOFTWARE REQUIREMENTS identification number indicated by JPL SRB report section 7.7.2.	Comment
1	3.7.2.2.4.1.a.	
	3.7.2.2.4.1.b.	Unlabeled System Requirement 1.b.
		Unlabeled System Requirement 1.c. Missing Flight Software Requirement

Figure B.5 Unlabeled and missing requirements.

a "missing design" and a "missing test." It also corresponds to "Unlabeled System Requirement 1.c." The System Requirements should be uniquely identified to facilitate accountability and traceability. This is not a novel concept, and there are a variety of commercially available automated tools on the market to provide automated support, measurement, and tracking of requirements development and change management.

B.4   REFERENCES

[1] JPL, *Mars Climate Orbiter/Mars Polar Lander Mission Overview*, 2006, http://mars.jpl.nasa.gov/msp98/mission_overview.html (retrieved: October 10, 2006).

[2] Wikipedia, *Mars Polar Lander*, 2006, http://en.wikipedia.org/wiki/Mars_Polar_Lander (retrieved: October 10, 2006).

[3] Burnstein, I., *Practical Software Testing*. Springer, 2003.

[4] Chaikin, A., *Mars Polar Lander's Demise May Never Be Known, Flight Directory Says*, 2006, http://www.space.com/scienceastronomy/solarsystem/mpl_latest_update.html (retrieved: October 10, 2006).

[5] Jet Propulsion Laboratory (JPL) Special Review Board (SRB) Report, *Report on the Loss of Mars Polar Lander and Deep Space 2 Missions*, 2000, http://www.jpl.nasa.gov/marsreports/mpl_report.pdf. (retrieved: June 17, 2006); also available at http://www.dcs.gla.ac.uk/~johnson/Mars/mpl_report.pdf (retrieved: October 15, 2006).

[6] Bridges, A., *Polar Lander Leg Snafu Discovery a Fluke*, 2006, http://www.space.com/scienceastronomy/solarsystem/lander_leg_000329.html (retrieved: October 10, 2006).

[7] House Science Committee, *Testimony of Thomas Young, Chairman of the Mars Program Independent Assessment Team before the House Science Committee*, 2006, http://www.spaceref.com/news/viewpr.html?pid=1444 (retrieved: October 10, 2006).

[8] Cowing, K., *NASA Reveals Probable Cause of Mars Polar Lander and Deep Space-2 Mission Failures*, 2006, http://www.spaceref.com/news/viewnews. html?id=105 (retrieved: October 10, 2006).

[9] Chrissis, M.B., Konrad, M., and Shrum, S., *CMMI Guidelines for Process Integration and Product Improvement*. Addison-Wesley, 2003.

[10] Easterbrook, S., *Bugs in the Space Program: The Role of Software in System Failures*, 2006, http://www.cs.toronto.edu/~sme/presentations/BugsInTheSpace Program.pdf (retrieved: October 10, 2006).

APPENDIX C

SERVICE-ORIENTED ARCHITECTURE: EXAMPLE OF AN IMPLEMENTATION WITH ADP BEST PRACTICES

C.1 INTRODUCTION

As companies and consumers rely more and more on web services, it becomes increasingly important for web services developers to properly design, develop, deploy, and ultimately maintain such systems.

This appendix summarizes concerns specific to web services development and describes the set of best practices recommended for implementation of a web services–oriented application.

C.2 WEB SERVICE CREATION: INITIAL PLANNING AND REQUIREMENTS

To make our discussion illustrative, we will walk through a sample web service implementation. The example used will be a service for a large realtor with branches across the country. This realtor needs a web services application that supports the following requirements:

- Potential and existing customers submit contact information, desired living location, and desired price range of a home via the web service.

Automated Defect Prevention: Best Practices in Software Management, by Dorota Huizinga and Adam Kolawa
Copyright © 2007 John Wiley & Sons, Inc.

These users shall receive a response from the server that gives them the location of the nearest branch as well as an estimate of the monthly mortgage. This will enable users to contact a real estate agent and begin the process of finding a home.

- Real estate agents from different branches shall submit a request for a list of potential customers who are looking for homes in the local area. This will enable the agents to earn business and establish contacts with interested customers.

C.2.1 Functional Requirements

To build the example web service, we begin with two high-priority target requirements. As the name suggests, these target requirements are landmarks within the development process. These target requirements will help to drive the feature set of our web service and enable us to measure our progress. Both positive and negative use cases are created for each requirement; however, for simplicity we will illustrate only one for each.

Target Requirement 1—Positive Use Case:

- A valid customer request for branches, monthly mortgage, and agents is sent to the web service.
- A SOAP (Simple Object Access Protocol) response is received.
- Verification that the SOAP response contains a list of branches, agents, and monthly mortgage that may be of length zero takes place.

Target Requirement 2—Negative Use Case:

- An invalid agent request for customers is sent to the web service.
- A SOAP response is received.
- Verification that the SOAP response contains a SOAP fault message takes place.

For each target requirement, a conceptual test case is created. These test cases are converted to executable tests during the design phase. These executable tests will originally fail, indicating that the related feature has not yet been implemented.

In this example, we started with the two original target requirements. For a bigger project, we might have 10 target requirements, each one implementing subsequent incremental functionality of the application.

Various technologies can be used to create executable test cases for the requirements. Whatever framework or tools are decided upon, the use cases involve a SOAP client sending a message, waiting for a response, and then verifying the responses.

C.2.2 Nonfunctional Requirements

Whereas the functional requirements drive the features set, the following nonfunctional requirements ensure the robustness of the web service:

- *Normal Use*: The web service must function in the manner in which it was designed. For each operation exposed through the web service, the request and response pair should adhere to the binding and the XML should conform to the message description. In short, the server and client should send and receive what is expected.
- *Abnormal Use*: The web service should function even when an attempt is made for it to be consumed outside of its intended use. An abnormal use would involve sending a value other than those expected or not sending a value at all. For example, one application may send an XML instance document based on an older version of schema, and the receiving application may be using a newer version of schema. In any case, a web service should respond appropriately without any malfunctions.
- *Malicious Use*: The web service should function even when it is deliberately attacked by intruders. For example, intruders may try to gain access to privileged information from a web service transaction without authorization, or they may attempt to undermine the availability of the web service.
- *Use Over Time*: A web service implementation is likely to change over time. For example, a web service might expose an application that is undergoing an iterative development process. Any web service must continue to function properly during its entire lifespan, even as it is evolving.

As seen in Figure C.1, nonfunctional target requirements should be met before moving on to the next target feature.

C.3 WEB SERVICE CREATION: EXTENDED PLANNING AND DESIGN

C.3.1 Initial Architecture

The initial architecture of our web service example will be comprised of the following elements: client, proxy server, server, and database. These elements and their interactions are illustrated in Figure C.2.

- *Client*—the web service client that the customers and agents will use to invoke the web service
- *Proxy server*—allows for security and access management, so that customers and agents have different levels of authority to access available web services

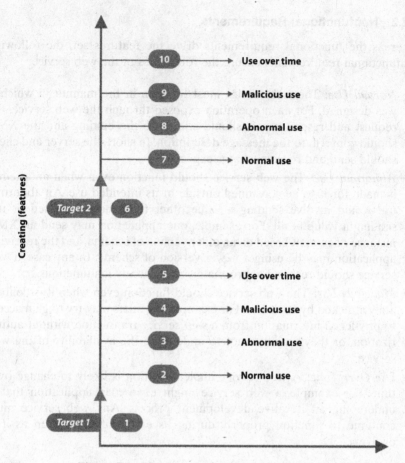

Figure C.1 Target and robustness requirements.

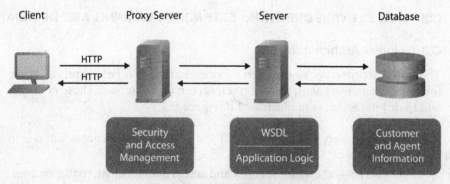

Figure C.2 Initial architecture.

- *Server*—SOAP-enabled HTTP server that handles serialization from XML to application logic objects
  - WSDL (Web Service Description Language) document—a description of the web service
  - Application logic (or business logic)—handles requests from customers and agents, makes necessary connections to the database, and returns responses to customers and agents. For our example, we will use Java for implementation of the application logic. Another option is to use C# for the .NET platform.
- *Database*—stores relevant information about customers and agents. We will use MySQL in our example.

In addition, we will choose HTTP as the transport layer in our example. Also, when reliable messaging is required, SOAP over JMS is a recommended practice.

C.3.2 Extended Infrastructure

The next step is to extend the infrastructure in such way that web services–specific practices can be applied and implemented correctly and consistently throughout the development group. Until this extended infrastructure is in place, the team cannot be expected to follow the defect prevention practices properly and, therefore, effectively develop a web services application.

Figure C.3 illustrates such an extended technology infrastructure. As will be seen, establishing this infrastructure provides the necessary framework for creating reliable web services. There are two key elements of this extended infrastructure: a nightly deployment process and a nightly test process.

Nightly Deployment Process If the nightly build process succeeds, the nightly deployment process should be launched. This process should also be automated via a script that is initiated by a scheduled task. The deployment elements consist of the WSDL document, server, database, client, and proxy server. These elements comprise an *n*-tiered test bed.

First, the WSDL document should be created from the latest source code and exposed to a port on the same machine on which the build process was executed. The WSDL document should reference the most recent versions of the schemas. The application should be then exposed as a web service on the same server. This server should be accessible on the network and should have a reliable connection to the database. The database should be set to its default configuration during this process. The web service client, when applicable, should be created from the latest source code and deployed. The nightly deployment process should also be monitored so that any problems can be detected and fixed immediately.

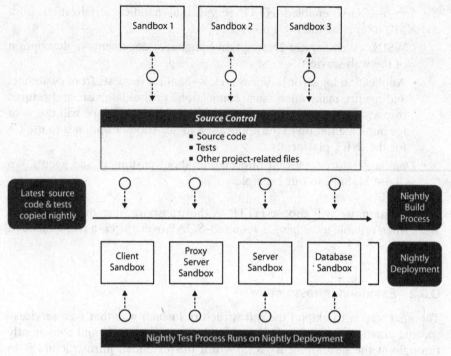

Figure C.3 Extended infrastructure supporting SOA.

Nightly Test Process In this process, the newly built application, WSDL document, web service, and client are automatically tested to verify that they satisfy all of the requirements and that no regressions have occurred in the functionality. All test cases should be shadowed from the source control system before they are executed. Any failures should be reported and monitored the next morning.

C.3.3 Design

Dividing Application Logic into Modules First, we begin by designing the application logic. From a high-level view of initial architectural design, the logic can be divided into modules encapsulating common functionalities. This encapsulation allows for the parallel development of individual modules that will be integrated later. In our example, we identify the following modules:

- *Module 1*: From the customer request, process:
  - Contact information
  - Desired living location
  - Price range

and return:
  • The location of the closest branch, mortgage, and agent information
The following submodules can be identified for Module 1:
  • Submodule A: Submit contact information into the database
  • Submodule B: Calculate mortgage information from the price range
  • Submodule C: Retrieve closest branch(es)/agents from the contact
    information and desired location
  • *Module 2*: From the agent request, process:
  • Agent information
and return:
  • A list of potential customers interested in agent's the area
The following submodules can be identified for Module 1:
  • Submodule A: Verify agent information
  • Submodule B: Based on agent location, query the database for potential
    customers.

Defining Module and Submodule Interfaces and Black Box Test Cases For each module and submodule, interfaces and input and output parameters should be well defined. For instance, we define the following input and output parameters for Submodule B of Module 1:

  • *Inputs*: Cost of home, down payment, estimated interest rate, length of loan in years.
  • *Output*: Monthly payment.
  • *Additional Input Requirements*: The module should identify invalid inputs such as:
    • Cost of home that is less than the down payment
    • Interest rate that is less than 0 or greater than 100%
    • Length of loan that is not one of the following: 10, 15, 20, or 30
  • For valid inputs, return the correct monthly payment rounded to the nearest dollar.

As described below, based on these input and output parameters, submodule interfaces should be implemented and black box test cases created for both valid and invalid inputs.

C.4 WEB SERVICE CREATION: CONSTRUCTION AND TESTING, STAGE 1—MODULE IMPLEMENTATION

In this section, we will describe the progression of implementing individual modules and show examples of coding standards and unit tests created for our application.

C.4.1 Applying Coding Standards

The predefined coding standards will enforce best coding practices among both experienced and new developers on the team. These standards should apply to both application logic and database connections. In particular, we want to ensure that unnecessary database connections that could render the web service unstable are not left open.

The best way to apply coding standards is to enforce them on recently implemented source code. The following example illustrates how using a set of predefined coding standards would change the original code:

```
if (years != 10 || years != 15 || years != 20 ||
years != 30) {...
```

becomes

```
if ((years != 10) || (years != 15) || (years != 20)
|| (years != 30)) {...
```

Similarly:

```
double base = (double)(1 + rate/12);
```
becomes
```
double base = 1 + rate/12
```

due to an unnecessary cast.

C.4.2 Implementing Interfaces and Applying a Test-First Approach for Modules and Submodules

In order to refine the design for Module 1: Submodule B, we begin by sketching the class that encapsulates the input for this module.

```
public class PaymentInfo {
  private double homePrice, downPayment, interestRate;
  private int years;
  public PaymentInfo(double homePrice, double
    downPayment, double interestRate, int years) {
    this.homePrice = homePrice;
    this.downPayment = downPayment;
    this.interestRate = interestRate;
    this.years = years;
  }
  . . . get and set methods. . .
}
```

Next, we write the method that takes PaymentInfo as the input and returns the monthly payment.

```
Public class RealtorServiceImpl {
  . . . other methods . . .
  protected int getMortgageResponse(PaymentInfo
    paymentInfo) {
      // TODO: implement with help of junit test cases
      return 0;
  }
  . . . other methods . . .
}
```

Once the interfaces are defined, the executable black box tests can be created for Submodule B.

C.4.3 Generating White Box JUnit Tests

When writing code, it is tempting to write large blocks. However, by taking many validated small steps, we will have made the equivalent of one large step, except that now we are much more confident about that large step. Our next small step is generating white box JUnit test cases for the getMortgageResponse() method.

Note that this method currently returns 0 for all inputs. We will now create JUnit tests for this method. In this case, the following class with the JUnit test case was generated automatically by a tool to test the getMortgage-Response() method.

```
public class RealtorServiceImplTest extends PackageTestCase {
/**
* Test for method: getMortgageResponse(PaymentInfo)
* @see RealtorServiceImpl#getMortgageResponse(PaymentInfo)
* @author Jtest
* @throws junit.framework.AssertionFailedError
*/
public void testGetMortgageResponse() {
  PaymentInfo t0 = new PaymentInfo(7.0, 7.0, 7.0, 7);
  RealtorServiceImpl THIS = new RealtorServiceImpl();
  // jtest_tested_method
  double RETVAL = THIS.getMortgageResponse(t0);
  assertEquals(0.0, RETVAL, 0.0); //
}
. . . other test cases . . .
}
```

Using the above JUnit test case, we can now write positive test cases. By referencing another source, we know that for a 30-year loan of $100,000 at

6.5%, the monthly payment should be $632, so we now write the JUnit test case that will test for this:

```
public void testGetMortgageResponse() {
  PaymentInfo t0 = new PaymentInfo(100000.0, 0.0, 6.5, 30);
  RealtorServiceImpl THIS = new RealtorServiceImpl();
  // jtest_tested_method
  int RETVAL = THIS.getMortgageResponse(t0);
  assertEquals(632, RETVAL, 632);
}
```

Subsequently, we should add more positive test cases, making sure that we test the second argument of the PaymentInfo object. For instance, here is another test case:

```
public void testGetMortgageResponse2() {
  PaymentInfo t0 = new PaymentInfo(120000.0, 20000.0,
    6.5, 30);
  RealtorServiceImpl THIS = new RealtorServiceImpl();
  // jtest_tested_method
  int RETVAL = THIS.getMortgageResponse(t0);
  assertEquals(632, RETVAL, 632);
}
```

C.4.4 Gradually Implementing the Submodule until All JUnit Tests Pass and Converge with the Original Black Box Tests

Originally, the above JUnit tests will fail. However, when we gradually implement the body of the `getMortgageResponse()` method, the JUnit test cases will start to pass. These white box test will eventually converge with the original submodule black box tests.

```
/*

                    rL(1 + r/12)^(12N)
       P =       ─────────────────────────
                  12((1 + r/12)^(12N) - 1)

where:
       r = interest rate (for 8.25% ==> r = 0.0825)
       L = loan amount
       N = loan time (years)
       P = the monthly payment
*/
protected int getMortgageResponse(PaymentInfo paymentInfo) {
    double amount = paymentInfo.getHomePrice() -
                        paymentInfo.getDownPayment();
    int years = paymentInfo.getYears();
```

```
       double rate = paymentInfo.getInterestRate()/100;
       double base = (double)(1 + rate/12);
       double exponent = (double)(12 * years);
       double result = java.lang.Math.pow(base, exponent);
       double numerator = rate * amount * result;
       double denominator = 12 * (result - 1);
       int monthlyPayment = (int)(numerator / denominator);
       return monthlyPayment;
}
```

Now that our method returns correct monthly payments for valid inputs, we can test how our method handles invalid inputs. For instance, this JUnit test case ensures that a `BadInputException()` is thrown when the down payment is greater than the cost of the house:

```
public void testGetMortgageResponseWithBadInput() {
  BadInputException exception = null;
  try {
      PaymentInfo t0 = new PaymentInfo(0.0, 100001.0,
        6.5, 30);
      RealtorServiceImpl THIS = new RealtorServiceImpl();
      // jtest_tested_method
      int RETVAL = THIS.getMortgageResponse(t0);
   } catch (BadInputException bie) {
      exception = bie;
   }
  assertTrue(exception != null);
  String msg = RealtorServiceImpl.NL_BAD_AMOUNT;
  assertEquals(msg, exception.getMessage());
}
```

After multiple iterations, our modified code looks like this:

```
protected int getMortgageResponse(PaymentInfo paymentInfo)
  throws BadInputException {
  double homePrice = paymentInfo.getHomePrice();
  if (homePrice < 0) {
      throw new BadInputException(NL_BAD_HOME_PRICE);
  }
  double downPayment = paymentInfo.getDownPayment();
  if (downPayment < 0) {
      throw new BadInputException(NL_BAD_DOWN_PAYMENT);
  }
  int years = paymentInfo.getYears();
  if (years != 10 || years != 15 || years != 20 ||
      years != 30) {
    throw new BadInputException(NL_BAD_YEARS);
```

```
    }
    double rate = paymentInfo.getInterestRate()/100;
    if (rate < 0 || rate >= 1) {
        throw new BadInputException(NL_BAD_RATE);
    }
    double amount = paymentInfo.getHomePrice() -
                    paymentInfo.getDownPayment();
    if (amount < 0) {
        throw new BadInputException(NL_BAD_AMOUNT);
    }
    double base = (double)(1 + rate/12);
    double exponent = (double)(12 * years);
    double result = java.lang.Math.pow(base, exponent);
    double numerator = rate * amount * result;
    double denominator = 12 * (result - 1);
    int monthlyPayment = (int)(numerator / denominator);
    return monthlyPayment;
}
```

Notice that the code is now more robust, because the JUnit test cases verify that all of the requirements were met.

C.4.5 Checking Verified Tests into the Source Control System and Running Nightly Regression Tests

Checking Code and JUnit Tests into the Source Control System The source code can now be checked into the source control system. As part of each nightly build process, the new checked-in source code will be compiled with the rest of the application. The JUnit tests are now checked into the source control system as well, and set up so that they are part of the nightly test process.

Once the code meets the first set of requirements, it is "frozen," and construction can move on to the next set of requirements. In order to ensure that the implemented functionality does not regress, the verified tests are checked into the source control system and run as regression tests during the nightly test process. This means that once a test passes on frozen code, it should always pass. There will be times when a change to a seemingly unrelated part of the code causes undesirable behavior in another part of the code. Regression tests will detect these undesirable changes.

The unit tests and coding standards applied in this stage should always pass even as the application logic changes over time. As the functionality becomes increasingly complex, previous tests should continue to pass and tests that test new functionality should be added.

Testing to Verify that the Defects are Detected and Fixed Whenever a defect is detected, it should be fixed, and a test added to verify the new code.

If possible, a coding standard should be created that will catch similar problems in the future.

C.5 WEB SERVICE CREATION: CONSTRUCTION AND TESTING, STAGE 2—THE WSDL DOCUMENT IMPLEMENTATION

It is worth noting that the creation of the WSDL document need not follow the writing of the application code. There are cases in which the WSDL document is created before any code is ever written. This "WSDL-first" approach is effective when dealing with XML in applications and schemas already in place. Various industries are promoting communication via the Internet; the use of XML and common schemas will allow them to work as one global supermarket of products and services. (One example can be seen from the travel industry in which the Open Travel Alliance has created and distributed schemas for business-to-business information exchange).

C.5.1 Creating and Deploying the WSDL Document on the Staging Server as Part of the Nightly Build Process

In our example, the WSDL document should be generated from the code. Tools exist for both the J2EE platform and the .NET platform that facilitate the generation of such documents. The latest WSDL document should be deployed nightly to the staging server environment.

The WSDL can be automatically created from the source code implementation of the following interface:

```
public interface RealtorService {
  CustomerResponse submitRequest(CustomerInfo customer
Info, DesiredLocation desiredLocation, PaymentInfo
  paymentInfo);
  PotentialCustomers queryPotentialCustomers(AgentInfo
agentInfo, DesiredLocation location);
}
```

The WSDL document looks like this:

```
<?xml version="1.0" encoding="UTF-8" ?>
<wsdl:definitions targetNamespace="..."
xmlns="http://schemas.xmlsoap.org/wsdl/"

  xmlns:SOAP-ENC="http://schemas.xmlsoap.org/soap/
    encoding/"
  xmlns:apachesoap="http://xml.apache.org/xml-soap"
  ...other namespaces declared...
  xmlns:xsd="http://www.w3.org/2001/XMLSchema">
<wsdl:types>
```

```
<schema targetNamespace="HTTP://DEFAULTNAMESPACE"
  xmlns="http://www.w3.org/2001/XMLSchema">
<import namespace="http://schemas.xmlsoap.org/soap/
encoding/" />
<complexType name="CustomerInfo">
<sequence>
  <element name="city" nillable="true" type="xsd:
string" />
  <element name="firstName" nillable="true" type="xsd:
string" />
  <element name="lastName" nillable="true" type="xsd:
string" />
  . . . other types defined here . . .
 </schema>
</wsdl:types>
<wsdl:message name="submitRequestRequest">
 <wsdl:part name="in0" type="tns1:CustomerInfo" />
 <wsdl:part name="in1" type="tns1:DesiredLocation" />
 <wsdl:part name="in2" type="tns1:PaymentInfo" />
</wsdl:message>
<wsdl:message name="submitRequestResponse">
 <wsdl:part name="submitRequestReturn" type="tns1:
CustomerResponse" />
</wsdl:message>
<wsdl:portType name="RealtorServiceImpl">
 <wsdl:operation name="submitRequest" parameterOrder="
in0 in1 in2">
 <wsdl:input message="impl:submitRequestRequest" name=
"submitRequestRequest" />
 <wsdl:output message="impl:submitRequestResponse" nam
e="submitRequestResponse" />
 </wsdl:operation>
</wsdl:portType>
<wsdl:binding name="realtorSoapBinding" type="impl:
RealtorServiceImpl">
 <wsdlsoap:binding style="rpc" transport="http://
schemas.xmlsoap.org/soap/http" />
 <wsdl:operation name="submitRequest">
  <wsdlsoap:operation soapAction="" />
  <wsdl:input name="submitRequestRequest">
  <wsdlsoap:body namespace="http://DefaultNamespace"
use="literal" />
  </wsdl:input>
  <wsdl:output name="submitRequestResponse">
   <wsdlsoap:body
```

```
namespace="http://trout.company.com:8080/axis/servlet/
  AxisServlet/realtor" use="literal" />
    </wsdl:output>
  </wsdl:operation>
  </wsdl:binding>
  <wsdl:service name="RealtorServiceImplService">
  <wsdl:port binding="impl:realtorSoapBinding" name=
"realtor">
    <wsdl:soap:address
location="http://trout.company.com:8080/axis/servlet/
AxisServlet/realtor"/>
    </wsdl:port>
  </wsdl:service>
</wsdl:definitions>
```

C.5.2 Avoiding Inline Schemas when XML Validation Is Required

Notice that in the WSDL the `<wsdl:types>` element has a `<schema>` child element. This is called an *inline schema* because the schema is found inside the WSDL. Most SOAP/WSDL toolkits generate WSDLs that have inline schemas. Although this is perfectly legal, it is preferable to have separate files for each schema and to import the schemas using the schema import mechanism. The main reason for this is that during the XML validation of the SOAP request, and the SOAP response, the XML parser may not parse the inline schema. Unless the XML parser is specially configured to parse schemas inside a WSDL, it will not be able to validate elements that are defined in the inline schema.

C.5.3 Avoiding Cyclical Referencing when Using Inline Schemas

When it is not required to validate the SOAP request and the SOAP responses, use of inline schemas is acceptable. However, care should be taken to ensure that the inline schemas do not reference each other. The following example illustrates how two inline schemas reference each other by importing from each other:

```
<types>
<xsd:schema xmlns:xsd="http://www.w3.org/2001/XMLSchema"
targetNamepace="http://soatest.company.com/schemaMath">
    <xsd:import namespace="http://soatest.company.com/
    schemaPhysics">
 . . .
    </xsd:schema>
    <xsd:schema xmlns:xsd="http://www.w3.org/2001/
    XMLSchema"
```

```
        targetNamespace="http://soatest.company.com/schemaPhysics">
    <xsd:import    namespace="http://soatest.company.com/
    schemaMath">
    . . .
  </xsd:schema>
</types>
```

Although the above example is not explicitly forbidden by WSDL or XML schema specifications, cyclical referencing presents a tough problem for most XML schema parsers. In most instances, one of the inline schemas has an unnecessary <import> element, and that element should be removed.

C.5.4 Verifying WSDL Document for XML Validity

The WSDL document should be checked for XML validity nightly. This ensures that the WSDL document conforms to all specifications and that the WSDL parsers will not have trouble parsing it. This check should be incorporated into the nightly test process described earlier.

C.5.5 Avoiding "Encoded" Coding Style by Checking Interoperability

The WSDL document should also be checked for interoperability. This check should also be incorporated into the nightly test process.

Although the WSDL specification allows the "encoded" encoding style, for interoperability reasons, it is wise to avoid the "encoded" style. In fact, WS-I Basic Profile 1.0 says that for web services to be interoperable, a WSDL should use either document-literal or rpc-literal bindings.

C.5.6 Creating Regression Tests for the WSDL Documents and Schemas to Detect Undesired Changes

Just as with the application logic code, the WSDL documents may undergo many implementation iterations. Even after it is published, the WSDL may be modified. After each iteration, the WSDL should be tested for validity and interoperability.

C.6 WEB SERVICE CREATION: SERVER DEPLOYMENT

C.6.1 Deploying the Web Service to a Staging Server as Part of the Nightly Build Process

The application should be deployed as a web service to a staging server environment during the nightly deployment process. This makes the latest version of the web service available for testing. Once deployed, tests can be run that consume the web service under the various use conditions: normal, abnormal, and malicious use.

C.6.2 Executing Web Service Tests That Verify the Functionality of the Web Service

For each operation exposed as a web service, test cases that verify its functionality should be executed. These tests are performed using a "driver" client that can generate various SOAP requests, send them to an endpoint, and then process the SOAP responses.

- *Positive Test Cases Should Return Expected Responses*: Positive test cases should return expected values. For example, a potential customer in Pasadena may want to find a home in Pasadena. If the realtor has an office branch in Pasadena, the customer should receive a response listing the location of this branch. In this instance, a number of different positive test cases should be constructed to flush out any bugs in the web service. The SOAP responses from the web service should be captured and compared with the expected responses. These comparisons should be saved as regression tests.

- *Responses Should be XML Valid and Pass Interoperability Checks*: The captured responses should be verified by an XML validator. They should also be conformant to WS-I Basic Profile 1.0.

- *Web Services Should Gracefully Handle Negative Test Cases that Simulate Abnormal and Malicious Uses*: Negative test cases can be divided into several categories. The first set of negative test cases contains transporlevel errors. The web service should be able to handle various HTTP header errors, such as wrong SOAPAction values (when applicable), wrong Content-Types, and wrong Content-Lengths. In each case, the web service should not fail, but instead return appropriate HTTP-level error messages, or ignore the errors and process the XML request. These return values should be captured and compared against expected results. A negative test case is said to succeed when its comparison succeeds.

  Another set of negative test cases contains XML-level errors. These may involve sending invalid XML or XML with deliberately bad values. In such cases, the expected response is a SOAP fault with a reason for the fault.

- *Feedback from the Test Cases Should be Used to Modify/Fix/Upgrade Elements of the Web Service as Well as the Development Process*: By testing the submitRequest() operation with the tool, we were able to find several problems with our web service. The first problem was that the server could not deserialize the XML request into the appropriate Java objects. As a result, the web service returned a SOAP fault. This often happens when the Java object does not implement all of the methods that a typical *bean* object should—that is, it does not have all the "get" and "set" methods for all of its fields. The obvious fix is to change the Java class that is responsible for the problem. However, a further step should be taken so that this problem can be avoided in the future. This step is to add a coding standard that checks to ensure that the Java classes are properly implemented as a bean.

The second problem resulted directly from the first. The WS-I Analyzer complained about the soap:Fault element in the SOAP response. One reason for this was that the web service had been deployed to a server using Apache Axis version 1.1, which was released before WS-I Basic Profile 1.0 was completed. Because web services standards are rapidly changing, it is important to use the latest stable versions of web services toolkits from the vendors.

- *Both Positive and Negative Test Cases Should be Checked into Source Control and Run As Part of the Nightly Test Process*: As the functionality of the web service grows in complexity, having regression tests will ensure that new functionality is added without breaking the existing functionality. It is very important to build up these test cases and continue their use throughout the development cycle.

C.6.3 Creating Scenario-Based Tests and Incorporating Them into the Nightly Test Process

Finally, the web service should be tested with various scenarios that simulate how real users will actually consume the web service. A typical scenario would involve a call to the web service by a new customer that submits a request, followed by a call to the web service by an agent who should then be able to retrieve the customer's information. Various scenarios should be composed and used to verify that all the operations of the web service work together properly. Again, regression tests should be created from these scenarios, checked into the source control system, and incorporated into the nightly test process.

C.6.4 Database Testing

Database testing can be accomplished in several ways. One way is to add database queries to the positive test cases. For instance, a database query should be made before and after a customer request to verify that the customer contact info is correctly stored in the database.

Another way is through *scenario-based* tests. A proper combination of agent requests and customer requests can be monitored to make sure that the web service is correctly storing into and retrieving from the database.

C.7 WEB SERVICE CREATION: CLIENT DEPLOYMENT

C.7.1 Implementing the Client According to the WSDL Document Specification

A web service client can be created from an existing client application or from scratch. The client should be consistent with the WSDL interface. This guards against the possibility of having client and server implementations that work together, but are not inline with the WSDL.

C.7.2 Using Server Stubs to Test Client Functionality—Deploying the Server Stub as Part of the Nightly Deployment Process

Server stubs should be used to assist in creating and testing the client. Server stubs act as endpoints to which clients can send SOAP requests and from which clients can receive SOAP responses. It is important to test the client not only against the server that is being developed but also against a stub, because otherwise when a problem is encountered, it will not be known whether the problem is due to a defect in the server or due to a defect in the client.

Server stubs should be able to return expected SOAP responses as well as intentionally bad SOAP responses. They should time out at the HTTP level and also refuse connections.

For example, a server stub could simply return a string inside the SOAP body back to the client using a Python script. The script and the server stub can be modified to return various SOAP responses. In this way, the client can be tested against various SOAP responses. Additionally, the server stub can be configured to process the SOAP requests as needed.

C.7.3 Adding Client Tests into the Nightly Test Process

The client tests should be able to be invoked from a command-line script. Scripts can then be written to invoke the client tests against the server stub to test client behavior when it receives expected SOAP responses as well as unexpected SOAP responses. The clients should also be tested to see how they handle connection timeouts and various errors that can happen at the transport level. Finally, the clients should be tested for interoperability against the WS-I Basic Profile 1.0 specifications. All of these tests should be checked into the source control system and run as part of the nightly test process using the latest client implementation built from the latest source code.

C.8 WEB SERVICE CREATION: VERIFYING SECURITY

C.8.1 Determining the Desired Level of Security

Depending on the type of web service being created, an appropriate level of security will need to be implemented. This can range from firewalls, to simple transport-level security such as basic authentication and SSL, to a variety of XML-level security mechanisms such as SAML and XML Digital Signature.

For our example, we do not require any security layer for customer requests. For the agent request operation, we require a username/password token with timestamp per WS-Security specifications. We require that the password digest be sent (with Type = "wsse:PasswordDigest") instead of the plain-text version of the password. As long as the agent's username and actual password are not compromised, our web service will be protected from unauthorized users. We also require that the timestamp be at most five minutes old to account for small differences in time between the client and the server. Beyond that, we do not expect much of a security threat.

C.8.2   Deploying Security-Enabled Web Service on Additional Port of the Staging Server

As part of the nightly deployment process, a security-enabled web service should be deployed. This allows us to begin testing the security layer. Having both a security-enabled web service and a non-security-enabled web service running on the staging server helps us to pinpoint issues with the security layer. For instance, if the security-enabled web service fails for a certain SOAP request, we can try the same SOAP request on the non-security-enabled web service to see whether the problem lies in the security layer or in the general XML processing layer.

C.8.3   Leveraging Existing Tests: Modifying Them to Test for Security and Incorporating Them into the Nightly Test Process

The functional and regression tests that were created to test the web service can be used to test the security layer. All that is needed is to add extra processing steps for security. This processing will be performed by the WS-Security implementations described above. In our case, only the SOAP header should be affected.

First, the web service should be tested with "positive security" test cases. For the agent request operations, this means testing the web service with a good pair of username/password tokens. All of the existing functional and regression tests must pass. This ensures that the server security layer correctly processes the security information in the SOAP request without inadvertently modifying it.

Next, the security layer itself should be tested with a variety of positive and negative test cases. The agent request operation should not return useful data if a valid pair of username/password tokens is not included in the SOAP header. The following is a list of negative conditions to be tested:

- Invalid pair of username/password tokens
- Password not digested (i.e., Type = "wsse:PasswordText")
- No password
- No username
- No SOAP header

C.9 WEB SERVICE CREATION: VERIFYING PERFORMANCE THROUGH CONTINUOUS PERFORMANCE/LOAD TESTING

C.9.1 Starting Load Testing as Early as Possible and Incorporating It into the Nightly Test Process

Load testing is an important task that is frequently underutilized when developing web services. Often, it is left until the end to ensure that the web service continues to work even under unexpected loads. However, load testing is more beneficial if it is done throughout the development process. Before adding the security layer, load testing should be performed and the results saved as a baseline. After adding the security layer, performance testing should be conducted again and the results should be compared to the baseline to see how much the security layer degrades performance. If the performance degradation is too severe, the security layer may need to be modified.

C.9.2 Using Results of Load Tests to Determine Final Deployment Configuration

When choosing the final production environment, such as which application server and which database to use, load testing should be conducted for each combination to find the optimal performance configuration. These results can also be used to select the most appropriate vendor.

APPENDIX D

AJAX BEST PRACTICE: CONTINUOUS TESTING

D.1 WHY AJAX?

AJAX, which stands for *asynchronous JavaScript and XML*, is a popular new development technique used for building highly interactive web applications such as Google Maps and Flicker. The greatest value of AJAX is that it solves the problem that has been troubling developers since the advent of the first web browser: web browsers make great UIs, but they are simply not interactive enough to replace traditional GUIs. With traditional GUIs, a simple mouse click is all that is needed to create the desired GUI change—which can be a small or large-scale change, depending on what is appropriate for the application. Until AJAX, web application GUI changes were always required to be full-page operations. Even a small change in an interface element required the browser to refresh the entire page (interface) or load a new one. AJAX solved this problem by allowing the refreshing of only selected page elements, giving browsers much-needed control and interactivity.

However, before dropping all other methods to develop with AJAX, it is important to recognize that its support for increased interactivity opens the door to a number of new problems, and to plan the development and testing phases accordingly.

Automated Defect Prevention: Best Practices in Software Management, by Dorota Huizinga and Adam Kolawa
Copyright © 2007 John Wiley & Sons, Inc.

D.2 AJAX DEVELOPMENT AND TESTING CHALLENGES

One characteristic that makes AJAX applications difficult to develop correctly is that they use both full-page and partial-page refreshes (traditional web pages only use full-page refreshes). Partial-page refreshes are problematic because what is shown in the web application does not come from a single source (like an HTML page). Rather, it can be the combination of the original HTML page, changes made by JavaScript, and the results of one or more partial-page refreshes initiated by a user (which can result in data being retrieved from a server and inserted into the page using JavaScript).

AJAX application problems may have a number of possible sources. The initial HTML page, along with the included JavaScript and CSS (Cascading Style Sheets) content, may have incorrect data. The data returned when an AJAX component makes a request to the server could be incorrect or the JavaScript could be inserting the data into the page incorrectly. One of the problems of creating AJAX applications is determining the source of the problem. Is the data coming from the server corrupted? Or is the JavaScript operating incorrectly?

The fact that AJAX applications rely so heavily on JavaScript also creates problems. JavaScript is notoriously difficult to write and debug. In addition, browsers support JavaScript differently; what works in one browser often does not work in another. Many of the AJAX frameworks that are being currently developed tout the ability to use AJAX components without having to write JavaScript; the AJAX components are created using tag libraries or other similar methods and the JavaScript is automatically generated by the framework. It is also often claimed that this framework-generated JavaScript is cross-browser compliant, but how well this works in practice is still up for debate.

Another common problem when integrating multiple AJAX code segments into a single page is that they may be incompatible.

Security is another serious concern. AJAX applications move much of the application logic to the client side, thus providing intruders a better view into the web application construction (since they can look at the HTML and JavaScript that is downloaded to the client). Specifically, intruders can see how requests are constructed to retrieve data from the server. Consequently, input validation is more important than ever.

D.3 CONTINUOUS TESTING

In light of the above challenges, defect prevention is critical in the development of AJAX-based applications. Our recommended best practice is a continuous testing process. To accomplish this, the required infrastructure should facilitate testing of the application code as it is built on the server, testing the server on its own (by mimicking client behavior), and testing not only each individual unit on the browser, but also their interactions.

Specific testing practices that should be applied during this comprehensive testing process include:

- *Regression testing* (discussed in Chapter 8) should be used to verify the integrity of the individual services that provide data for the AJAX application. This will aid developers in validating that the services return the correct data, and identify the cause of a possible defect (i.e., whether the defect is in the server data or in the client-side code).
- *Functional regression tests* (discussed in Chapter 8) should be created as soon as new functionality is added to a page in order to validate its new behavior and detect possible conflicts.
- *Functional regression tests* should be run within different browsers to ensure that the application functions correctly across a wide range of browsers.
- *Coding standards* (discussed in Chapter 7) should be applied throughout development, and automatic static analysis should be run on HTML, CSS, and JavaScript code to eliminate common problems in JavaScript that is not compatible across different browsers. This will help to eliminate browser incompatibility and other related issues.
- *Security coding standards* (discussed in Chapter 7) should be applied throughout development. Security test cases (discussed in Chapter 8 and Appendix C) should be executed on the web application for both full-page and partial-page requests. These tests should aim to verify the implementation of the security policy, as discussed in Chapter 6.

To ensure that the testing is performed regularly, correctly, and consistently, these practices should be verified each night as part of an automated build and testing process. Since many of these tests require code deployment to a staging or live server, deployment should also be automated (as described in Chapter 9).

APPENDIX E

SOFTWARE ENGINEERING TOOLS[a]

Given the ever-changing nature of our industry, some of these tools may no longer be available. For more current information, see our website at http://www.solutionbliss.com.

Tool	Development Phase	Open Source or Commercial	Functionality
Accept 360°	All Phases	Commercial	Requirements Management, Defect Tracking, Product Management, Planning
Aegis	All Phases	Freeware	Configuration Management
Aldon Community Manager	All Phases	Commercial	Requirements Management, Defect Tracking
Aldon Lifecycle Manager	All phases	Commercial	Configuration Management
AllChange	All Phases	Commercial	Configuration Management
Atlassian JIRA	All Phases	Commercial	Defect Tracking, Issue Tracking, Project Management
Bazaar-NG	All Phases	Open Source	Source Control
Borland Star Team	All Phases	Commercial	Change Management, Configuration Management
BUGtrack	All Phases	Commercial	Project Management, Problem Tracking

[a] This list of tools is not endorsed by the authors of the book.

Automated Defect Prevention: Best Practices in Software Management, by Dorota Huizinga and Adam Kolawa
Copyright © 2007 John Wiley & Sons, Inc.

Tool	Development Phase	Open Source or Commercial	Functionality
Bugzero	All Phases	Commercial	Defect/Issue Tracking, web based
Bugzilla	All Phases	Open Source	Defect Tracking
BusinessManager Process Modeler	All Phases	Commercial	Process Management
Caliber RM	All Phases	Commercial	Requirements Management
Care 3.2	All Phases	Commercial	Requirements Management
ChangeSynergy	All Phases	Commercial	Change Management, Configuration Management
CodeStriker	All Phases	Open Source	Source Control
CVS	All Phases	Open Source	Source Control System
Debian Bug Tracking System	All Phases	Open Source	Defect Tracking
DocAuthor	All Phases	Commercial	Documentation
DocExpress	All Phases	Commercial	Documentation
DOORS	All Phases	Commercial	Requirements Management
Gemini	All Phases	Commercial	Defect Tracking
Gnats	All Phases	Open Source	Defect Tracking
Mercury Quality Center	All Phases	Commercial	Automated Software Quality Testing and Management
Mercury TestDirector	All Phases	Commercial	Requirements Management, Test Management, Defect Management
Microsoft Sharepoint Services	All Phases	Commercial	Artifact Management
Microsoft Visual Source Safe	All Phases	Commercial	Configuration Management
MKS Portfolio	All Phases	Commercial	Metrics Management
MKS Requirements	All Phases	Commercial	Requirements Management
MKS Source	All Phases	Commercial	Configuration Management
Parasoft GRS	All Phases	Commercial	Development Repository
Perforce	All Phases	Commercial	Software Configuration Management
PVCS	All Phases	Commercial	Source Control
Rational ClearCase			
Rational ClearQuest			
Rational Method Composer	All Phases	Commercial,	Process Management, documentation process improvement
Rational RequisitePro	All Phases	Commercial	Requirements Management
Scarab	All Phases	Open Source	Artifact Management
Serena PVCS Professional	All Phases	Commercial	Issue, Version, Change Management
Serena RTM	All Phases	Commercial	Requirements Management
Serena TeamTrack	All Phases	Commercial	Defect Tracking, Issue Tracking, and Process Management

Tool	Development Phase	Open Source or Commercial	Functionality
SourceSafe	All Phases	Commercial	Source Control
StarTeam	All Phases	Commercial	Software Configuration Management
Subversion	All Phases	Open Source	Source Control
TAU	All Phases	Commercial	Design, Code Generation, Automated Testing
WinCVS	All Phases	Open Source	Source control system
Agitar Management Dashboard	Construction, Testing	Commercial	Testing, management and automation
AntHill Build Server	Construction, Testing	Commercial	Automated Build
Apache Ant	Construction, Testing	Open Source	Automated Build
C++lint	Construction, Testing	Commercial	Source Code Analysis
C++test (for C++). TEST (for C#, VB. NET, MC++) Jtest (for Java)	Construction, Testing	Commercial	Source Code Analysis
Cantata++	Construction, Testing	Commercial	Testing, unit and integration
Coverage	Construction, Testing	Open Source	Code Coverage
Coverity Prevent	Construction, Testing	Commercial	Static Code Analysis
Cruise Control	Construction, Testing	Open Source	Continuous Build Process Framework
Insure ++	Construction, Testing	Commercial	Testing, memory leaks
JCSC	Construction, Testing	Open Source	Coding Standard Enforcement, Style Checker
Jlint (for Java)	Construction, Testing	Freeware	Source Code Analysis
JUnit	Construction, Testing	Open Source	Testing, performance analysis and monitoring
Klocwork K7	Construction, Testing	Commercial	Static Code Analysis
Logiscope	Construction, Testing	Commercial	Testing, QA
Parasoft .Test	Construction, Testing	Commercial	Testing, unit, code compliance
Parasoft CodeWizard	Construction, Testing	Commercial	Coding Standard Enforcement, Style Checker
Parasoft Jtest	Construction, Testing	Commercial	Testing, unit, code compliance
Prexis (for C, C++, Java, JSP, J2EE, STRUTS)	Construction, Testing	Commercial	Source Code Analysis
PyChecker	Construction, Testing	Open Source	Code Checker
PyUnit	Construction, Testing	Open Source	Testing, unit for python
Rational Functional Tester			
Rational Manual Tester	Construction, Testing	Commercial	Testing, manual authoring and execution tool
Rational Performance Tester	Construction, Testing	Commercial	Testing, performance

Tool	Development Phase	Open Source or Commercial	Functionality
Rational Purify Plus	Construction, Testing	Commercial	Testing, runtime analysis
Rational Robot	Construction, Testing	Commercial	Testing
Rational Test Realtime	Construction, Testing	Commercial	Testing components, runtime analysis
Rational TestManager	Construction, Testing	Commercial	Test Management
QA Wizard	Construction, Testing	Commercial	Testing, automated test script generation
QEngine	Construction, Testing	Commercial	Testing, web-based, functional, performance, web services
QJ Pro	Construction, Testing	Open Source	Code Analyzer
QTest	Construction, Testing	Commercial	Testing, load, stress
SOAtest	Construction, Testing	Commercial	Testing, web services, client and server
TeamQuest View	Construction, Testing	Commercial	Testing, performance analysis and monitoring
TestDirector	Construction, Testing	Commercial	Testing Management Solution
TestExplorer	Construction, Testing	Commercial	Testing, manual authoring
TestWise	Construction, Testing	Commercial	Testing and Maintenance
WebKing	Construction, Testing	Commercial	Testing, website risk analysis, security analysis, functional, load, performance testing
Microsoft Visual Studio Team System	Construction, Testing, Deployment	Commercial	Version Control System, Defect Tracking System
Rational Application Developer for Websphere software	Construction, Testing, Deployment	Commercial	Application development tool with automated deployment capability
Visual Build Professional	Construction, Testing, Deployment	Commercial	Automated Build, Deployment
Mercury Deployment Management	Deployment	Commercial	Deployment Management
MKS Deploy	Deployment	Commercial	Deployment Management
AgroUML	Design	Open Source	UML Modeling
BOUML	Design	Open Source	Visual Modeling
Magicdraw	Design	Commercial	UML Modeling, class diagrams, use cases
UModel	Design	Commercial	Visual Modeling

Tool	Development Phase	Open Source or Commercial	Functionality
DBDesigner4	Design, Construction	Freeware	Visual Database Design
Together	Design, Construction	Commercial	Modeling and Code Generation
ARM	Extended Planning	Commercial	Risk Management
COCOMO II	Extended Planning	Freeware	Budget, Effort, Schedule Management
Construx Estimate	Extended Planning	Commercial	Budget, Effort, Schedule Management
Microsoft Project	Extended Planning	Commercial	Budget, Effort, Schedule Management
PQMPlus	Extended Planning	Commercial	Estimation
Case/4/0	Requirements	Commercial	Prototyping
Gorilla eXecution Engine (GXE)	Requirements	Commercial	Prototyping
Rational Software Modeler	Requirements	Commercial	Prototyping
Serena Composer	Requirements	Commercial	Prototyping
RAVE	Requirements, Design, Construction, Testing	Open Source	Modeling, analyzing, and refine system requirements, correct defects

GLOSSARY

abstraction (1) A view of an object that focuses on the information relevant to a particular purpose and ignores the remainder of the information. (2) The process of formulating a view as in (1). (IEEE Std. 610.12-1990, p. 8)*

acceptance testing Testing conducted to determine whether a system satisfies specified acceptance criteria, which is used by the user to determine whether to accept the system. (IEEE Std. 610.12-1990, p. 8)*

adjusted function points A value adjustment factor is multiplied with the number of counted function points to produce an adjusted function point total. (Ch. 5, [11])

agile programming process model A lightweight process model that consists of the following cycle: analysis of the system metaphor, design of the planning game, implementation, and integration.

AJAX A web development technique for creating interactive web applications.

algorithm complexity The number of computational steps required to transform the input data into the result of the computation.

alpha testing Part of the acceptance testing conducted by the developing organization in a laboratory setting.

Ant Apache Ant is a Java-based build tool.

Automated Defect Prevention: Best Practices in Software Management, by Dorota Huizinga and Adam Kolawa
Copyright © 2007 John Wiley & Sons, Inc.

Apache's Jakarta Tomcat Apache Tomcat is the servlet container used in the official Reference Implementation for the Java Servlet and JavaServer Pages technologies. The Java Servlet and JavaServer Pages specifications are developed by Sun under the Java Community Process. It powers numerous large-scale, mission-critical web applications across a diverse range of industries and organizations. (Ch. 5, [4])

architectural design The process of defining a collection of software components and their interfaces to establish the framework for the development of a computer system. (IEEE Std. 610.12-1990, p. 10)*

architecture (1) The organizational structure of a system or component. (2) The structure of components, their interrelationships, and the principles and guidelines governing their design and evolution over time. (IEEE Std. 610.12-1990, p. 10)*

artifact A work item produced during software development. Some examples of software development artifacts are software designs, code, and test cases.

automated build A process for building an application on a periodic basis by automatically executing the required build steps, including compiling and linking of the code at the scheduled time, without any human intervention.

automated reporting system A system that stores information about the project status and generates reports to help in decision making and processes analysis.

automatic code generator A system that converts design artifacts (such as class diagrams) into implementation artifacts such as object-oriented code classes.

beta release The official release of a prerelease version of software that is sent out to a small group of users for testing.

beta testing Part of the acceptance testing conducted both by the customer at the customer's site and by the developing organization.

black box testing A testing strategy that considers a functional design specification to design test cases without regard to the internal program structure. The tested element is treated as a black or opaque box.

block diagram A representation of a system, computer, or device in which the principal parts are represented by suitably annotated geometrical figures to show both the functions of the parts and their functional relationships. (IEEE Std. 610.12-1990, p. 13)*

change request A change request is submitted and evaluated to assess technical merit, potential side effects, overall impact on other configuration objects and system functions, and the projected cost of the change. (Ch. 4, [10])

check-in Placement of a configuration item in the source control system. A check-in occurs when modified local files are copied to the source control system or another shared repository.

checkpoint   A point in a computer program at which program state, status, or results are checked or recorded. (IEEE Std. 610.12-1990, p. 16)*

class   A description of a set of objects that have common properties and behaviors, which typically correspond to real-world items (persons, places, or things) in the business or problem domain.

class diagram   An analysis model that shows a set of system or problem domain classes and their relationships.

client/server protocol   A standardized method for allowing client processes and server processes to communicate. A client process interacts with users, allowing the users to request services from server processes. A server process waits for a request to arrive from the client process and then responds to those requests.

CMMI continuous model   A comprehensive process model that is predicated on a set of system and software engineering capabilities. It defines process areas and levels of capability.

CMMI staged model   A comprehensive process model that is predicated on the staged representation and five levels of maturity. To achieve a specified level of maturity, a set of goals in predefined process areas must be met.

code freeze   A period of time when access to the current code baseline in the version control system is restricted so that only critical changes can be made to the code.

code generator   A software tool that accepts as input the requirements or design for a computer program and produces source code that implements the requirements or design. (IEEE Std. 610.12-1990, p. 17)*

code review   A meeting at which software code is presented to project personnel, managers, users, customers, or other interested parties for comment or approval. (IEEE Std. 610.12-1990, p. 17)*

Commercial off-the-shelf (COTS)   Commercial off-the-shelf (COTS) products are hardware or software solutions that can be purchased ready for use either as a standalone solution or for integration into other applications.

conceptual test case   A high-level natural-language description of a test case. It precedes the code implementation and it is used by developers and testers to generate actual test cases.

confidence factor   A measure that is used to evaluate the product attribute or a set of attributes. It is usually expressed as a percentage with a range of 0–100%.

configuration management system   A broad term for a system that at minimum stores configuration items (units of code, test sets, specifications, test plans, and other documents), facilitates control changes to these items, records and reports change processing and implementation status, and verifies compliance with specified change control process.

copy constructor   The copy constructor is used to copy an object to a newly created object. It is used during initialization, not during ordinary assignment.

correctness   (1) The degree to which a system or component is free from faults in its specification, design, and implementation. (2) The degree to which software, documentation, or other items meet specified requirements. (3) The degree to which software, documentation, or other items meet user needs and expectations, whether specified or not. (IEEE Std. 610.12-1990, p. 22)*

coverage analysis   A set of techniques used to measure how much of the code was exercised with respect to a predefined criterion.

coverage criterion   Test adequacy criterion pertaining to code coverage and used to define test stopping rules. For example, 100% statement coverage requires that 100% of the statements be executed by the tests in question.

CPI   A measure calculated by dividing the budgeted cost of work performed by actual cost of work performed.

critical path   In a graph that shows how tasks in a work plan are related, the longest path from start to finish. This is also the path that does not have any slack, thus the path giving the shortest time in which the project can be completed.

cron   The program that enables UNIX users to execute commands or scripts automatically at a specified time/date.

cyclomatic complexity   Also called McCabe's complexity (Ch. 7, [6]); a measure of code nesting and complexity based on the number of independent program paths.

dangling pointer   A pointer that points to an invalid memory location.

deadlock   A condition when two or more processes or threads are each waiting for another to release a resource or perform an action, creating a circular "wait-for" chain.

defensive programming   The practice of trying to anticipate where errors can occur in programs, and then adding code to identify or work around the issue to avoid program failures or security holes.

deliverable   An artifact that is delivered to a customer or user.

derived class   A derived class inherits from one or more (possibly unrelated) base classes.

design   (1) The process of defining the architecture, components, interfaces, and other characteristics of a system or component. (2) The result of the process in (1). (IEEE Std. 610.12-1990, p. 25)*

design pattern   A documented best practice or core of a solution that has been applied successfully in multiple environments to solve a problem that recurs in a specific set of situations.

Design-by-Contract TM A design technique that focuses on documenting (and agreeing to) the rights and responsibilities of software modules to ensure program correctness. It was developed by Bertrand Meyer for the language Eiffel. (Ch. 7, [9])

efficiency The degree to which a system or component performs its designated functions with minimum consumption of resources. (IEEE Std. 610.12-1990, p. 30)*

encapsulation A software development technique that consists of isolating a system function or a set of data and operations on that data within a module and providing precise specifications for the module. (IEEE Std. 610.12-1990, p. 30)*

entity relationship diagram A diagrammatic technique for illustrating the interrelationships between entities in a database.

equivalence class partitioning A technique for dividing the test input domain into distinct subsets, which are processed similarly by the target software.

estimation by analogy An estimation method involving reasoning by analogy: using experience with one or more completed projects to relate actual cost and development time to the cost and development time of the new project.

EVM A technique that objectively tracks accomplished work.

evolutionary prototype A fully functional prototype created as a skeleton or an initial increment of the final product, which is fleshed out and extended incrementally as requirements become clear and ready for implementation. (Ch. 4, [8])

extensibility The ease with which a system or component can be modified to increase its storage or functional capacity. (IEEE Std. 610.12-1990, p. 32)*

extreme programming An "agile" software development methodology characterized by face-to-face collaboration between developers and an on-site customer representative, limited documentation of requirements in the form of "user stories," and rapid and frequent delivery of small increments of useful functionality. (Ch. 1, [26])

false positive A test result of *yes*, when the correct answer is *no*.

fault An anomaly in the software that may cause it to behave incorrectly, and not according to its specification. A fault or a defect is also called a "bug."

fault density A measure of the number of faults per unit size that can be used to predict remaining faults by comparison with expected fault density in order to determine whether a sufficient amount of testing has been completed, and to establish standard fault densities for comparison and prediction.

feature A functional or quality characteristic of a software element. It is a small block of a system functionality.

FERPA A federal law that protects the privacy of student education records. FERPA gives parents certain rights with respect to their children's education records. These rights transfer to the student when he or she reaches the age of 18 or attends a school beyond the high school level. (Ch. 1, [21])

fourth-generation languages A computer language designed to improve the productivity achieved by high-order (third-generation) languages and, often, to make computing power available to nonprogrammers. (IEEE Std. 610.12-1990, p. 34)*

function point A measure of software size, based on the number and complexity of internal logical files, external interface files, external inputs, outputs, and queries. (Ch. 5, [11])

functional design The process of defining the working relationships among the components of a system. (IEEE Std. 610.12-1990, p. 35)*

functional testing Testing that ignores the internal mechanism of a system or component and focuses solely on the outputs generated in response to selected inputs and execution conditions. (IEEE Std. 610.12-1990, p. 35)*

functioning prototype A working prototype built to determine that the design is within the specifications requirements of the final product.

Gramm-Leach-Bliley Act The Financial Modernization Act of 1999, which includes provisions to protect consumers' personal financial information held by financial institutions. (Ch. 1, [20])

HIPAA An act to amend the Internal Revenue Code of 1986 to improve portability and continuity of health insurance coverage in the group and individual markets, to combat waste, fraud, and abuse in health insurance and health care delivery, to promote the use of medical savings accounts, to improve access to long-term care services and coverage, to simplify the administration of health insurance, and for other purposes. (Ch. 1, [19])

incremental development A software development technique in which requirements definition, design, implementation, and testing occur in an overlapping, iterative (rather then sequential) manner, resulting in incremental completion of the overall software product. (Ch. 1, [23])

information hiding A software development technique in which each module's interfaces reveal as little as possible about the module's inner workings and other modules are prevented from using information about the module that is not in the module's interface specification. (IEEE Std. 610.12-1990, p. 40)*

inheritance A form of software reusability in which programmers create classes that inherit an existing class's data and methods and enhance them with new capabilities.

inspection A static analysis technique that relies on visual examination of development products to detect errors, violations of development standards, and other problems. Types include code inspection; design inspection. (IEEE Std. 610.12-1990)*

Integrated development environment   An integrated development environment (IDE) is a set of integrated tools for software development, which commonly combines a text editor, compiler, linker, debugging tools, profiler, and sometimes version control and dependency maintenance.

integration testing   Testing in which software components, hardware components, or both are combined and tested to evaluate the interaction between them. (IEEE Std. 610.12-1990, p. 41)*

interface   A hardware or software component that connects two or more other components for the purpose of passing information from one to other. (IEEE Std. 610.12-1990, p. 41)*

interoperability   The ability of two or more systems or components to exchange information and to use the information that has been exchanged. (IEEE Std. 610.12-1990, p. 42)*

Ishikawa diagrams   Often called cause-and-effect or fishbone diagrams, are used to display causal relationships by stating a quality characteristic or "effect" at the "head" of the diagram and then listing possible causes along branch arrows. (Ch. 2, [4])

Javadoc   A tool for generating API documentation in HTML format from comments in source code.

library   Also called a software library. A controlled collection of software and related documentation designed to aid in software development, use, or maintenance. Types include master library, production library, software development library, software repository, system library. (IEEE Std. 610.12-1990, p. 68)*

load stress testing   Testing to determine whether the system continues to function properly under extreme loads that cause maximum resource allocations.

maintainability   The ease with which a software system or component can be modified to correct faults, improve performance or other attributes, or adapt to a changed environment. (IEEE Std. 610.12-1990, p. 46)*

make   The utility that keeps a set of executable programs current, based on differences in the modification times of the programs and the source files that each is dependent on.

Makefile   A file that contains a description of the relationships between files, and the commands that must be executed to update the derived files to reflect changes in their prerequisites.

memory management   A technique that involves identifying used and available physical memory units, managing virtual memory mapping onto physical memory, and swapping the virtual memory pages to disk while performing the appropriate address translation.

metric   A quantitative measure of the degree to which a system, component, or process possesses a given attribute. (IEEE Std. 610.12-1990, p. 48)*

middle tier   In a three-tier system architecture, the middle tier is between the user interface (client) and the data management (server) components. This middle tier provides process management where business logic and rules are executed.

mirroring   Direct copying of a data set.

mock-up server   A server that simulates the actual server for the purpose of testing the client.

model-based approach to design   Design based on the idea of identifying high-level models that allow designers to specify and analyze interactive software applications from a semantic-oriented level. MDA provides a set of guidelines for structuring specifications expressed as models.

modularity   The degree to which a system or computer program is composed of discrete components such that a change to one component has minimal impact on other components. (IEEE Std. 610.12-1990, p. 48)*

module   (1) A program unit that is discrete and identifiable with respect to compiling, combining with other units, and loading (e.g., the input to, or output from, an assembler, compiler, linkage editor, or executive routine). (2) A logically separable part of a program. (IEEE Std. 610.12-1990, p. 49)*

multicast   A communication protocol in which data is delivered to all hosts that have expressed interest. This is one-to-many delivery.

object   A specific instance of a class for which a set of data attributes and a list of operations that can be performed on those attributes can be collected.

object-oriented design   A software development technique in which a system or component is expressed in terms of objects and connections between those objects. (IEEE Std. 610.12-1990, p. 51)*

open status   Open indicates the request has been accepted and will be implemented.

Open Web Application Security Project (OWASP)   An organization for developing and supporting open source projects that produce tools, documentation, and standards for application security. (www.owasp.org)

overflow error   An error that occurs when the result of an arithmetic operation exceeds the size of the storage location designated to receive it. (IEEE Std. 610.12-1990, p. 53)*

package   A separately compilable software component consisting of related data types, data objects, and subprograms. (IEEE Std. 610.12-1990, p. 53)*

page fault   An event that occurs when an accessed page is not present in main memory.

paging   A storage allocation technique in which programs or data are divided into fixed-length blocks called pages, main storage is divided into blocks of the same length called page frames, and pages are stored in page frames. (IEEE Std. 610.12-1990, p. 54)*

parallel development   A planning decision that allows multiple developers to work on the same configuration item at the same time.

parametric model   A mathematical representation consisting of formulas that use parameters as the basis of the model's predictive features. The model calculates the dependent variables of cost and duration based on one or more estimated parameters.

Pareto diagram   A graphical representation of defect categories and frequencies that can be helpful to identify the source of chronic problems/common causes in a process. The Pareto principle basically states that a "vital few" of the process characteristics cause most of the quality problems, while a "trivial many" of the process characteristics cause only a small portion of the quality problems. (Ch. 2, [4], pp. 447–448)

path   A sequence of instructions that may be performed in the execution of a computer program. (IEEE Std. 610.12-1990, p. 55)*

pattern-based approach to design   An approach that identifies important and relevant design patterns, so that a complex design can be constructed from these design patterns. (Ch. 5, [10])

pending status   Pending indicates the request has not yet been reviewed.

performance testing   Testing conducted to evaluate the compliance of a system or a component with specified performance requirements. (IEEE Std. 610.12-1990, p. 55)*

piped stream   A communication protocol allowing output from one thread to become input for another thread for communication between programs or to system resources.

portability   The ease with which a system or component can be transferred from one hardware or software environment to another. (IEEE Std. 610.12-1990, p. 56)*

problem tracking system   A repository that is used for tracking of defects, change requests, and ideas.

production server   The server that hosts the deployed application.

protocol   A set of conventions that govern the interaction of processes, devices, and other components within a system. (IEEE Std. 610.12-1990, p. 59)*

prototype   A preliminary type, form, or instance of a system that serves as a model for later stages or for the final, complete version of that system.

rapid prototyping   A type of prototyping in which emphasis is placed on developing prototypes early in the development process to permit early feedback and analysis in support of the development process. (IEEE Std. 610.12-1990)*

RCS   The revision control system (RCS) manages multiple revisions of files. (Ch. 3, [2])

refactoring   A reorganization technique that simplifies the design (or code) of a component without changing its function or behavior. (Ch. 6, [19])

regression testing   Selective retesting of a system or component to verify that modifications have not caused unintended effects and that the system or component still complies with its specified requirements. (IEEE Std. 610.12-1990, p. 61)*

regression testing system   Any tool or combination of tools that can automatically run the core of the existing tests on the entire code base on a regular basis (preferably nightly, as part of the automated build). Its purpose is to help in identifying when code modifications cause previously working functionality to regress, or fail. For example, the regression system may be a script that runs one or more testing or defect prevention technologies in batch mode. (Ch. 3, [7])

rejected status   Rejected indicates that the request was reviewed but will not be implemented. Closed indicates that the request has been implemented.

request for information   A process whereby questions are asked by the contractor and answered by the owner's authorized agent.

request for proposal   The solicitations used in negotiated procurements.

requirement   A statement of a customer need or objective, or of a condition or capability that a product must possess to satisfy such a need or objective. A property that a product must have to provide value to a stakeholder. (Ch. 3, [1])

requirements management system   A system that stores and facilitates tracking requirements status, managing changes to requirements and versions of requirements specifications, and tracing individual requirements to other project phases and work products. (Ch. 3, [1])

requirements stability index   A derived measure defined as a complement of requirements change rate. When the requirements change rate approaches zero, the requirements stability index approaches 100%.

reusability   The degree to which a software module or other work product can be used in more than one computer program or software system. (IEEE Std. 610.12-1990, p. 64)*

risk management   An approach to problem analysis that relies on identifying the risks, assessing their probabilities of occurrence and their impact to give a more accurate understanding of potential losses, and creating a plan for avoiding and mitigating them.

runtime exception   An exception thrown when incompatibility is detected at runtime.

sandbox   A subset copy of the project's files.

Sarbanes-Oxley Act of 2002   An act to protect investors by improving the accuracy and reliability of corporate disclosures made pursuant to the securities laws, and for other purposes. (Ch. 1, [18])

scalability   The ability of a program to gracefully adapt to growing demands on the system resources.

SCAMPI   Standard CMMI Appraisal Method for Process Improvement.

scenario   A description of a specific interaction between a user and a system to accomplish some goal. An instance of usage of the system. A specific path through a use case. Often presented in the form of a story. (IEEE Std. 610.12-1990)*

script   A sequence of computer commands written in batch language.

Section 508   An amendment to the Rehabilitation Act of 1973 that requires that any technology produced by or for federal agencies be accessible to people with disabilities. It covers the full range of electronic and information technologies in the federal sector. (Ch. 1, [17])

security   The establishment and application of safeguards to protect data, software, and computer hardware from accidental or malicious modification, destruction, or disclosure. (Ch. 6, [8])

service-oriented architecture   A conceptual business architecture where business functionality, or application logic, is made available to SOA users, or consumers, as shared, reusable services on an IT network. Services in an SOA are modules of business or application functionality with exposed interfaces, and invoked by messages. (Ch. 2, [20])

Simple Object Access Protocol   A protocol for exchanging XML-based messages over a computer network.

SLIM   A commercial estimation and tracking software tool.

software development model   A model of the software development process. The process by which user needs are translated into a software product. The process involves translating user needs into software requirements, transforming the software requirements into design, implementing the design in code, testing the code, and sometimes installing and checking out the software for operational use. (IEEE Std. 610.12-1990)*

software development plan   A plan for a software development project. (IEEE Std. 610.12-1990)*

software life cycle   The period of time that begins when a software product is conceived and ends when the software is no longer available for use. The software life cycle typically includes a concept phase, requirements phase, design phase, implementation phase, test phase, installation and checkout phase, operation and maintenance phase, and sometimes a retirement phase. (IEEE Std. 610.12-1990, p. 68)*

software project management   The process of planning, organizing, staffing, monitoring, controlling, and leading a software project. (IEEE Std. 1058.1-1987, p. 10)*

software project management plan   The controlling document for managing a software project. A software project management plan defines the technical and managerial project functions, activities, and tasks necessary to satisfy the requirements of a software project, as defined in the project agreement. (IEEE Std. 1058.1-1987)*

quality assurance group   A group that audits the process and products. The process is audited to ensure that it is properly followed and the product is audited to ensure that it satisfies standards and requirements.

software requirements specification (SRS)   A complete description of expected functionality and behavior of the system. The SRS document should contain a complete list of requirements, their categories, and priorities, and it should reference corresponding use cases.

source control system   A database where source code is stored. Its purpose is to provide a central place where the team members can store and access the entire source code base. We use this as a generic term for both version control systems and configuration management systems. The code is organized, versioned, and accessible to all team members. Conflicts due to parallel updates are automatically detected and rollback features are supported. Examples include SVN, CVS, RCS, Visual SourceSafe, and ClearCase.

SPI   A measure calculated by dividing the budgeted cost of work performed by the budgeted cost of work scheduled.

spiral model   A model of the software development process in which the constituent activities, typically requirements analysis, preliminary and detailed design, coding, integration, and testing, are performed iteratively until the software is complete. (IEEE Std. 610.12-1990, p. 69)*

SQL injection   A technique to inject crafted SQL into user input fields that are part of web forms. It can also be used to login to or even to take over a web site.

stack trace   A back trace of stack activities during the program execution.

staging server   A server that is a mirror of the live application server. New content is deployed to the staging server, tested, and then published to the live server.

staging system   A staging system is an environment that mirrors the target application environment. New content is moved to the staging system and tested before it is deployed to the production area.

stakeholders   People who benefit in a direct or indirect way from the system that is being developed; they can be customers, partners, team members, and management.

statement of work   A document that establishes the contractual foundation of the project. It provides the project team with a clear vision of the scope and objectives of what they are to achieve. (Ch. 10, [11], p. 1)

static web page   A web page that is completely created in advance, with all text and images in place, and housed on a web server, ready for use.

stub   (1) A skeletal or special-purpose implementation of a software element, used to develop or test a unit that calls or is otherwise dependent on it. (2) A computer program statement substituting for the body of a software element that is or will be defined elsewhere. (IEEE Std. 610.12-1990, p. 72)*

style checker A static analysis tool that verifies conformance to style and format rules in code.

Subversion A type of version control system.

synchronization point A point where two or more parallel activities can be brought together.

system testing Testing conducted on a complete, integrated system to evaluate the system's compliance with its specified requirements. (IEEE Std. 610.12-1990, p. 74)*

tar file A single archive file containing many other files.

test case A set of test inputs, execution conditions, and expected results developed for a particular objective, such as to exercise a particular program path or to verify compliance with a specific requirement. (IEEE Std. 610.12-1990, p. 74)*

test-driven development A programming practice that instructs developers to write tests of the code before the code is implemented.

test harness The auxiliary code supporting execution of test cases. It consists of drivers that call the tested code and stubs that represent called elements. (Ch. 8, [10]).

throwaway prototype A prototype that is created with the express intent of discarding it after it has served its purpose of clarifying and validating requirements and design alternatives. (Ch. 4, [8])

trap doors Unprotected entries to the system.

Trojan horse A disguised, malicious code embedded within a legitimate program.

unified process Also known as Rational Unified Process; a software development approach that is iterative, architecture-centric, and use case driven. (Ch. 1, [25])

unit A unit is a logically separable part of a computer program. (IEEE Std. 610.12-1990, p. 79)*

unit test Testing of individual hardware or software units or groups of related units. (IEEE Std. 610.12-1990, p. 79)*

usability The ease with which a user can learn to operate, prepare inputs for, and interpret outputs of a system or component. (IEEE Std. 610.12-1990, p. 80)*

use case A use case describes a sequence of actions that are performed by an actor (e.g., a person, a machine, another system) as the actor interacts with the software. An actor is a role that people or devices play as they interact with the software. Use cases help to identify the scope of the project and provide a basis for project planning. (Ch. 1, [25])

user testing Testing that requires users to perform required system functionalities. (Ch. 8, [4] p. 55)

version control system A system that keeps track of multiple versions of the source code files and other project artifacts. It is common, but inadvisable, to use the terms "configuration management" and "version control" indiscriminately. A company should decide as to which meaning it will attach to "version control" and define the term relative to the meaning of "configuration management."

vertical prototype A partial implementation of a software system that slices through all layers of the architecture. It is used to evaluate technical feasibility and performance. It is also called a structural prototype or proof of concept. (Ch. 5, [5])

Vision and Scope document The document that presents the business requirement for a new system. This document covers the statement of the vision of the project, which is what the project will accomplish in the long term. The project scope description defines what parts of the vision will be implemented in the short term. (Ch. 3, [1])

waterfall model A model of the software development process in which the constituent activities, typically a concept phase, requirements phase, design phase, implementation phase, test phase, and installation and checkout phase, are performed in that order, possibly with overlap but with little or no iteration. (IEEE Std. 610.12-1990, p. 81)

web accessibility initiative WAI develops strategies, guidelines, and resources to help make the Web accessible to people with disabilities. (Ch. 10, [16])

white box testing A testing strategy that requires knowledge of the internal structure of a program to design test cases. The testing element is treated as a white or glass box.

Wideband Delphi method A consensus-based method for estimating originated by the Rand Corporation. Multiple team members participate in estimating each other's task efforts until they reach a consensus.

work breakdown structure An outline that organizes the tasks and activities necessary to achieve the project objective.

WSDL An XML format that describes how to communicate using web services, including the protocol bindings and message formats required to interact with the web services.

XML A markup language for documents containing structured information. (Ch. 6, [18]).

INDEX

80/20 rule 6
Acceptance plan 126
Acceptance testing 126, 270–271
Accessibility, Web 322–323
Actions, in user interface 195–196
Adjusted function points (AFP) 143
Adoption obstacles 77–78
ADP *See* Automated Defect Prevention (ADP)
AEP *See* Automated Error Prevention (AEP)
AFP *See* adjusted function points (AFP)
Agile programming process 12, 13, 358–359
AJAX *See* Asynchronous JavaScript and XML
Algorithmic and processing defects 208
Alpha testing 270–271
Analyzing
  cost 301
  defects 299–301
  schedule 301
  source code growth 294–296
  test results 296–299

Application logic
  defining 185
  dividing into modules 374–375
  Web services 373
Architect, role in ADP 59–61, 76
Architectural and detailed design
  best practices 168
  critical attributes 168
  defining policies for 172
  managing changes 188
  modules 178
Architectural attributes
  correctness 169
  efficiency and scalability 170
  interoperability 171
  maintainability and extensibility 171
  modularity 169
  portability 171
  reusability 170
  security 172
Architectural design 125
Architecture-first model 12
Ariane 5 41–42
Assertions 213–214

Automated Defect Prevention: Best Practices in Software Management, by Dorota Huizinga and Adam Kolawa
Copyright © 2007 John Wiley & Sons, Inc.